UNDERSTANDING INTELLECTUAL & DEVELOPMENTAL DISABILITIES

Written by psychologists engaged in research, teaching, and practice, *Understanding Intellectual and Developmental Disabilities* encourages a nuanced, contextually informed understanding of the development of individuals with developmental disabilities. This accessible book contextualizes developmental disability across the lifespan and within social systems. It will help you understand the complex interaction between genetics, environments, and experiences, in relation to specific conditions such as ADHD, autism, foetal alcohol spectrum conditions, and Down syndrome. It also introduces you to the wide range of real-world applications of developmental disabilities research and to some of the current ethical issues around genetic screening and behavioural intervention.

Key learning features include:

- Learning objectives
- Focus boxes that deliver additional helpful context
- Chapter summaries
- Reflective exercises and questions, to test what you've learned
- Recommended videos

This book is ideal for students studying atypical development, developmental neuropsychology, and related subjects.

Grace Iarocci is Professor of Psychology and the Director of the Autism and Developmental Disabilities Research Lab at Simon Fraser University. She is also a practising psychologist in British Columbia, Canada.

Jacob A. (Jake) Burack is Professor of Educational and Counselling Psychology at McGill University in Montreal, Canada. He is the Director of the McGill Youth Study Team and Scientific Director of the Summit Centre for Education, Research, and Training.

Dermot M. Bowler is Professor of Psychology and founder member of the Autism Research Group at City, University of London.

UNDERSTANDING INTELLECTUAL & DEVELOPMENTAL DISABILITIES

GRACE IAROCCI
JACOB A. BURACK
DERMOT M. BOWLER

1 Oliver's Yard
55 City Road
London EC1Y 1SP

2455 Teller Road
Thousand Oaks, California 91320

Unit No 323-333, Third Floor, F-Block
International Trade Tower Nehru Place
New Delhi – 110 019

8 Marina View Suite 43-053
Asia Square Tower 1
Singapore 018960

Editor: Charlotte Bush and Amy Maher
Editorial Assistant: Emma Yuan
Production Editor: Gourav Kumar
Copyeditor: Martin Noble
Proofreader: Sarah Cooke
Indexer: KnowledgeWorks Global Ltd
Marketing Manager: Camille Richmond
Cover Design: Wendy Scott
Typeset by KnowledgeWorks Global Ltd
Printed in the UK

Chapters 1, 2, 3, 5, 7, 8, 10, 11 and 13 © Grace Iarocci, Jacob A. Burack and Dermot M. Bowler 2024
Chapters 4, 6, 9 and 12 © Deborah J. Fidler 2024

Apart from any fair dealing for the purposes of research, private study, or criticism or review, as permitted under the Copyright, Designs and Patents Act, 1988, this publication may not be reproduced, stored or transmitted in any form, or by any means, without the prior permission in writing of the publisher, or in the case of reprographic reproduction, in accordance with the terms of licences issued by the Copyright Licensing Agency. Enquiries concerning reproduction outside those terms should be sent to the publisher.

Library of Congress Control Number: 2023946197

British Library Cataloguing in Publication data

A catalogue record for this book is available from the British Library

ISBN 978-1-4462-8761-3
ISBN 978-1-4462-9646-2 (pbk)

CONTENTS

Authors' Positionality and Context of Work	vii
About the Authors	ix
Preface	x
Pedagogical Features	xii
Acknowledgements	xiv

Part I: Foundations   **1**

1. Introduction: The Basics of a Developmental Approach   3
2. Gene–Environment Interactions and Intellectual Disability   23
3. Screening, Assessment, and Diagnosis of Intellectual and Developmental Disabilities   59

Part II: Intellectual Disabilities   **81**

4. Down Syndrome   83
5. Foetal Alcohol Spectrum Disorders   105
6. Neurogenetic Syndromes and Rare Disorders Associated with Intellectual Disability   125

Part III: Developmental Disabilities   **143**

7. Autism Spectrum Disorder (or Difference): Features, Identification and Screening   145
8. Autism Spectrum Disorder: Psychological Theories and Explanations   175
9. Language and Communication   221

| 10 | Specific Learning Disorder | 239 |
| 11 | Attention Deficit/Hyperactivity Disorder | 259 |

Part IV: Developmental Disability in Context — 285

| 12 | Intellectual Disability in the Family Context | 287 |
| 13 | Broadening Perspectives on Developmental Disability | 307 |

Index — 313

AUTHORS' POSITIONALITY AND CONTEXT OF WORK

People with developmental disability are diverse, with distinct cognitive, language, social and emotional profiles, yet they share many commonalities: particularly, a shared experience of being neurodivergent and different from the majority. In many ways, they represent a subculture that has been marginalized, excluded, and mistreated by the dominant culture. Although developmental disability is not an illness or disease, it has frequently been viewed from a Western medical model of health. In this model, challenges experienced by people with developmental disabilities have been seen as abnormalities, deficits, and impairments rooted solely within individuals. Research studies have largely been conducted on rather than with them and their issues are often misrepresented, resulting in research that is poorly aligned with their own needs and perspectives.

The authors of this textbook align themselves with a broader model of disability, which emphasizes the need for accommodation, support, and amelioration of issues that threaten the individual's health and quality of life. We do not believe that developmental disabilities should be prevented, normalized, or cured. However, at least one of the authors is a practising psychologist, specializing in supporting individuals with neurodevelopmental conditions and their families. She works within a clinical context that necessitates the use of the Diagnostic and Statistical Manual of Mental Disorder (DSM). Despite the requirements to use medical labels to help individuals gain access to government funds and services, her conceptualization of developmental disability remains one that aligns with the neurodiversity perspective, that people with developmental disability are a valuable expression of human diversity in neurocognitive development.

Within the developmental disability communities, preferences differ on the use of person-first (i.e., person with) vs disability-first or identity-first language (e.g., autistic person). Thus, we use both terms in the text. We use the DSM diagnostic terms sparingly and only when referring to information from specific sources. Most often the term disability or difference(s) rather than disorder(s) is employed to avoid pathologizing developmental disabilities.

The authors of this textbook are white cisgender women and men of mostly European ancestry. We have not been diagnosed with, or identify as having, a developmental disability. We recognize that this limits our understanding of the lived experience of developmental disability. However, we consider ourselves to be allies of developmental disability communities and we have all had the opportunity to work in partnership with members of the developmental disability communities on various research projects, responding to community research needs and government policy initiatives. Our writing of this textbook has been informed by our professional, and at times, personal, experiences with members of the developmental disability communities from whom we have had the privilege to learn. We look forward to many more years of collaboration.

ABOUT THE AUTHORS

Grace Iarocci is Professor of Psychology and the Director of the Autism and Developmental Disabilities Research Lab at Simon Fraser University. She is also a practising psychologist in British Columbia, Canada.

Jacob A. (Jake) Burack is Professor of Educational and Counselling Psychology at McGill University in Montreal, Canada. He is the Director of the McGill Youth Study Team and Scientific Director of the Summit Centre for Education, Research, and Training.

Dermot M. Bowler is Professor of Psychology and founder member of the Autism Research Group at City, University of London.

We share a common theoretical framework on development and developmental disability and are actively involved in teaching and research in the area. As well, we share a vision to promote an understanding of developmental disability that considers the whole child and from a lifespan perspective. We hope to inspire students and instructors alike to gain a deeper understanding of developmental disabilities as not merely residing within individuals but rather, a complex dynamic interaction between genetics, environments, and experiences. We are leading experts and active researchers in the area of developmental disabilities and represent the countries (UK, US, and Canada) that are leading contributors to this field. Thus, the book is inclusive of issues pertinent to an international context.

PREFACE

Developmental disability is an essential area of study for students interested in the development of children generally as well as those interested in promoting the growth and well-being of children with developmental disabilities. The unifying theme in this book is that the study of development and that of its myriad disabilities are mutually beneficial. For example, understanding the phenomena of hurricanes and tornadoes would be challenging, to say the least, without having a proper understanding of the principles of atmospheric forces, balances, and weather systems. Similarly, our understanding of the ways development follows a different pathway in the case of developmental disabilities is best grounded in the substantial body of knowledge that we possess about the typical course of development. However, what we learn about developmental disabilities is also critical to providing the necessary detail and refinement to what we already know about typical development.

The introduction of the developmental approach to understanding intellectual disability, and the subsequent delineation of the two-group approach to studying individuals with cognitive disabilities, have led to remarkable advances in the study of developmental disability. We now know that a singular category such as intellectual disability or autism, or performance measures such as IQ, are insufficient. Rather, research into behavioural phenotypes is necessary to understand the specific profiles of strength and challenges across many domains of development among children with different types of developmental disabilities. Paradoxically, such a framework both narrows and broadens the scope of research in the field. The narrowing entails a more fine-tuned approach to diagnosis, a more precise delineation of skill in relation to specific causal mechanisms and developmental level, and fine-tuned matching strategies that involve comparisons that are based on specific aspects of functioning. The broadening of the scope involves consideration of the 'whole child' in terms of personality, social, and emotional development within the context of families, communities, and societies. This far-reaching developmental perspective has revolutionized the study of intellectual disability with its theoretical, methodological, and interpretive innovations, while the more precise approach to the study of persons with intellectual disabilities has in turn served to transform developmental theory by challenging, extending, and reconceptualizing well-established developmental principles.

The topic of developmental disabilities covers exciting debates about the role of genes and environments in typical and atypical development, the role of peer and parent–child relationships in shaping development, social attitudes, and policies with regard to diversity and ethical issues surrounding genetic screening and behavioural intervention.

As you read through the chapters of this book, we hope you will be inspired to think about the mutuality of development and developmental disability. We encourage you to pose both the question, 'how does considering development help me understand a particular developmental disability such as Down syndrome?', as well as 'how can what I have learned about Down syndrome help me to understand development better?'

PEDAGOGICAL FEATURES

The main pedagogical goal of the book is to encourage a deeper, contextualized understanding of the development of individuals with developmental disabilities across the lifespan. In order to achieve this goal, we provide an historical perspective on the developmental approach to research into developmental disability that highlights key milestones and achievements in the field.

A deeper understanding of the link between theory and research

We achieve this by engaging the reader with demonstrations of the wide range of real-world applications of research on developmental disabilities. We include text boxes containing recent examples of research to highlight the topic under discussion as well as practical applications of the research in question. YouTube videos are also linked into the text so that students can view actual examples of research methods used to investigate specific theoretical questions. Using examples from actual research labs will resonate more personally with the experiences of the students and encourage excitement in the research process, enhance the learning experience, and improve students' retention and understanding of the material.

An understanding of the concept of behavioural phenotype

We define the construct and revisit the term in several chapters to solidify the learning as well as provide visual aids through the use of short videos. Each of the videos captures the essence of the phenotypic profile for each of the disabilities discussed. This provides a real-life illustration of what the phenotypic profile represents as well as a point of comparison across disabilities.

An understanding of the whole person with disability throughout the lifespan

We contextualize discussions about disability and present a holistic account of development. In each of the chapters that pertain to specific disabilities we discuss the course of development.

The ability to contextualize developmental disability within social systems

We link ideas and concepts across chapters and focus specifically on developmental disability in context. We provide direct reference to real-world events and practices with case examples and videos to illustrate concepts.

The book takes a developmental perspective on developmental disability with an emphasis on the 'whole person' within the context of families, communities, and society. The narrative weaves together discussions about commonalities across developmental disabilities with those that are unique to specific phenotypic profiles all the while referencing up-to-date research literatures. We will begin with Part I: Foundations: this section includes foundational chapters that cut across various disability types. For example, Chapters 1–3 provide the background in developmental psychopathology theory, key practices and challenges in the field, gene–environment interactions and diagnosis and assessment. These chapters will set the stage for many of the subsequent chapters on specific disabilities (i.e. 4–11). These chapters are also a source of reference for more specific issues related to the particular disability type in each of the chapters 4–11.

Part II: Intellectual Disabilities: this section will include Chapters 4 through 6 and will address each of the most common intellectual disabilities covered in most undergraduate courses internationally (i.e. Down syndrome, foetal alcohol spectrum disorder, and other rare disabilities). In addition to an overview of the known genetic/environmental causes of the specific disability, each of these chapters will cover phenotypic profiles, that is, the behavioural patterns of strengths and challenges across different domains of development that make the disability unique such as memory, attention, cognition, language, social and emotional functioning.

Part III: Developmental Disabilities: this section will include Chapters 7 through 11 and will address each of the most common developmental disabilities (that do not necessarily lead to intellectual disability) such as autism spectrum disorder, language disabilities, learning and reading disabilities, and attention deficit disorder. Each of these chapters will cover phenotypic profiles, that is, the behavioural patterns of strengths and challenges across different domains of development such as memory, attention, cognition, language, social and emotional functioning that make each particular disability unique.

Part IV: Developmental Disability in Context: In Chapters 12 and 13 and within each of the other chapters we focus on the whole person with disability within context. From a developmental framework, children are embedded within various socio-cultural systems that interact to either support or hinder their development. These dynamic systems are conceptualized as different spheres of influence and include those that have a distal (i.e. indirect) effect and those that have a proximal (i.e. direct) effect on the individual. Direct influences include the child's interaction with significant persons or events in their lives such as parents and other family members, and community resources. Indirect influences are thought to emanate from various formal and informal social structures in the child's environment such as government policies on education and health. This helps students appreciate the forces that shape the various aspects of development presented in the text. The concluding chapter will be an integrative chapter that will bring together themes from across the chapters together with a discussion of future directions in the field.

ACKNOWLEDGEMENTS

With thanks to Reyhan Bakhtiari for her work on Chapter 10: Specific Learning Disorder. We thank Kristi Atkinson, Maya Ahia, and Ajeetpall Singh for their work on Chapter 5: Foetal Alcohol Syndrome Disorders.

PART I
FOUNDATIONS

1
INTRODUCTION: THE BASICS OF A DEVELOPMENTAL APPROACH

> **Learning Objectives**
>
> After reading this chapter, you should be able to:
>
> - Review essential developmental theory
> - Link the orthogenetic principle and other developmental theories to real-world life
> - Promote the notion of a universal inclusive developmental approach (versus pathologizing, segregating deficit approaches) in the study of persons with intellectual and developmental conditions
> - Introduce the notion of a 'whole person' when studying or working with persons with intellectual and developmental conditions

In this textbook, we use a developmental approach to examine the knowledge about children with intellectual and developmental disabilities. We note that the very term developmental disabilities correctly implies the importance of developmental factors in the lives of persons with these disabilities, but also that developmental theory and its implications are unfortunately often ignored in the research and applied work with these populations. Accordingly, we use this chapter to introduce developmental approaches that should guide the study of persons with intellectual disability and other developmental disabilities. We briefly highlight the vast contributions of the developmental approach, while also noting its inherent limitations, in the work with the persons who are the focus of this volume.

As an introduction to the developmental approach, please search for two people online, Shaun Johnson and Yao Ming. You'll find that they both participated in the 2008 Olympics. Now tell yourself, your roommate, a friend, your partner, or a parent about these two people. When asked to do this task, most people will start by pointing to the obvious differences between these two athletes, starting with their sex, ethnicity, and height (one of the reasons that this comparison is so compelling is that at 7 ft 6 inch Yao is exactly 50% taller than the 5 ft 0 inch Johnson). Some will also remark on the obvious differences in abilities with Johnson's phenomenal abilities to tumble, flip, and catapault herself through space and land on her feet, while Yao's abilities to shoot baskets and prevent others from doing so were exceptional. Only a very few people will start by pointing to what is common to both, such as that they are exceptional athletes and both appeared at the Olympic Games. And, only a very, very few will point to the most obvious similarity between them – that they are both human. In this book, the focus is on groups of people who differ in many ways from each other and/or from the general population and, as a result, are too often only discussed with regard to these differences. Yet, to the extent that we can, we invoke a developmental approach with the starting point of a universal humanity that binds us all together.

The primary disciplines, including special education, abnormal psychology or psychopathology), and psychiatry, that involve the study of people with developmental disabilities often invoke what we call a 'splitter' framework in which differences between persons or groups of persons are highlighted, and ostensible defects or other aspects of pathology are central to the narrative. And, as is seen by looking through the Contents, this text is similarly largely organized around different groups of persons based on their specific developmental disabilities – and for good reason. Over decades and even centuries of research and intervention, scientists, educators, and clinicians have successfully identified many genetic, physiological, behavioural, cognitive, social, experiential, and emotional characteristics of the various conditions. Even given the inevitable diversity across the individuals who share any disability, the more we understand about common group characteristics and the extent to which they are shared within or across groups, the better able we are to fine-tune our educational, clinical, and other intervention programmes for each specific group as well as for each individual.

Despite the importance of recognizing and highlighting the unique characteristics of each group, we advocate for an overarching conceptual framework that is more universal and for which the commonality of humanity is the essence. Throughout the text, we will emphasize the physiological (genotypic) and behavioural (phenotypic) characteristics of each group along with the many differences between groups in order to familiarize you, the reader, with the unique characteristics of each of these groups. However, we begin by reminding you that the essence for all this work is the humanity of each individual. In doing so, we emphasize a developmental approach, in which the focus is on understanding patterns of development, or growth, over time. Whereas traditional approaches in special education might be considered *deconstructionist* as they are primarily focused only on the aspects of the specific person or groups of persons that are different or deficient from others, the developmental approach is considered *constructivist* in that it is focused on the 'whole person' including all aspects of their functioning and of the environments in which they live. The constructivist approach also involves the construction of theories about how all the various aspects of an individual's functioning can be understood in some meaningful and unifying, or universal, way. It is particularly evident in theories of child development, such as those of the noted Swiss psychologist Jean Piaget who argued that development is the product of children's own construction, through their interaction with their environments, of the cognitive rules that allow them to understand the world in which they live.

In introducing the developmental approach to persons with developmental conditions, we begin by citing another European theorist, the Austrian-born and trained psychologist, Heinz Werner, who emigrated to the United States in the 1930s in order to escape the Nazis. In describing the developmental process, Werner H. (1957) wrote that, 'wherever there is life there is growth and development, that is, formation in systematic, orderly sequence'. You will note the essential universal aspects of Werner's statement. One, development is integrally related to growth in all aspects of life in every single living organism. Two, development is systematic and orderly, indicating that it happens in some way that is meaningfully sequential – i.e., the order of development must follow a specific progression.

In order to illustrate Werner's point, please take a look at Figure 1.1. You will recognize this as the human foetus at different points of its development in the mother's womb. Here, the progression is clearly immutable, or unchangeable. You cannot imagine the depiction of the foetus at six months preceding that at three months, or any other change in order. Clearly, each point in development of the foetus reflects growth from that, or those, which preceded it. In this case, the trajectory of development is clearly systematic and orderly. Notice something else universal about the foetus. You would have immediately recognized it as a human foetus. And regardless of the ethnicity, colour, sex, or size of the foetus or the person who eventually develops from it, the foetus is intrinsically recognizable by any of us, and its various parts are also readily identifiable. Its overall integrity, or health, could generally be determined by a doctor anywhere in the world based on a broad understanding of the universal progression of the foetus. Of course, human foetuses all differ from one another in uncountable ways, including size, sex, rate of development, and even period of gestation, but that does not change or affect the inherent and inevitable universal sequence of development that is seen across all of them.

This innate and necessary ordering of development in a specific sequence is a fundamental aspect of all developmental theories. In the study of children, this is best highlighted in Piaget's theory of cognitive development and genetic epistemology, or the origins of knowledge over time. His extensive study of how children come to make sense of the world around them was largely based on his observation of his own children as well as of the performance of other children on various experimental tasks. On these tasks, the children were presented information that was inconsistent with the rules that they thought governed the physical world around them and, therefore, they had to engage in the process of developing new rules of understanding. Through these direct observations, Piaget identified a series of four inherently distinct and

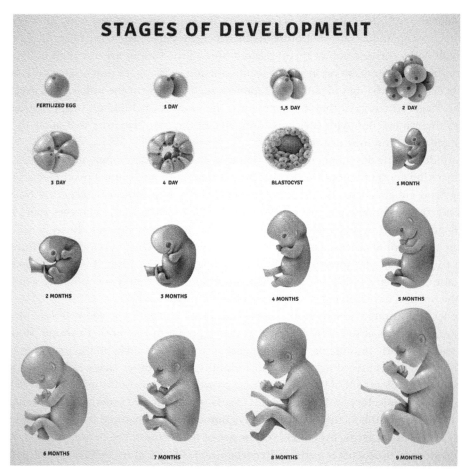

Figure 1.1 The development of the human foetus
Source: Macrovector/Shutterstock: 684146356.

sequential stages of cognitive development that roughly corresponded with certain age ranges through the first 18 years or so of life – sensorimotor from birth to two years, pre-operational from two to seven years, concrete operational from seven to 11 years, and formal operational from 11 years through till the end of adolescence, although for all practical purposes this last stage is evident through the rest of the lifespan except when dementia sets in Piaget J. (1970).

The sensorimotor stage is characterized by the infants' sensory curiosity and basic motor exploration of the world. Infants interact with the environment around them through basic actions such as sucking, grasping, looking and listening while starting both to problem-solve through trial and error and to grasp the concept of object permanence: that things continue to exist even when they cannot be seen. During the preoperational stage, children learn to think symbolically as they begin to use words and images as language symbols to represent objects and ideas, although they remain egocentric and their logic is still largely intuitive and subjective, rather than rational or objective. During the concrete operational stage, children exhibit logical and rational thinking, problem solving, and reasoning that are restricted to concrete or physical objects and situations rather that hypothetical scenarios or concepts. During the formal operational stage, adolescents use logic, problem solving, and reasoning to think about abstract and hypothetical concepts and ideas that include both concrete and hypothetical situations. This ultimate stage of Piagetian development is noteworthy due to the emergence of abstract concepts, which are defined as ideas that involve the consideration of prospective theories and hypotheses in addition to previous knowledge, experience, and concrete information that were the sources of earlier thinking. This description of the primary four stages represents a very basic or simplistic representation of Piaget's conceptualization of cognitive development in which the development of each of the essential stages involves several substages, which are also thought to occur in an invariant order across all children. According to Piaget, these stages and substages reflected the child's increasing conceptual abilities to interact with the physical environment around them and to construct ways of thinking about, or understanding, that world. Although all of these stages are associated with approximate age ranges, those ranges are incidental to the process and the order of that process – development can occur faster or slower but the stages, the transitions among them, and their ordering are all universal.

According to Piaget, development is an active process in which an entrenched schema, or understanding of the world, is challenged when children are confronted with information that is inconsistent with it. A new stage is attained when the children are forced to rethink their understanding of the way that the world works. The successful accommodation of this new information involves a revised schema in which a new understanding predominates. Thus, the accommodation process sets the stage for the subsequent assimilation of information and ideas into the new schema. This point in the process is referred to as equilibration and reflects a period of relative calm or stability in the ways of thinking, or schema, according to which the child governs their understanding of the world until the arrival of the next challenge that is so potent that it necessitates a reorganization of the system. These various periods or ways of thinking are the stages that are so central to Piaget's theory. They reflect qualitative differences in ways of thinking across development and the unique and meaningful ordering of the developmental process.

Universal sequences of stages are also essential to other prominent developmental theories, such as Freud's psychosexual and Erikson's psychosocial theories. Best known as the father of psychoanalysis, Sigmund Freud was a Viennese psychiatrist, who, like Werner, left Vienna to escape the Nazis; however he only emigrated at the end of his career and of his life, and he moved to the United Kingdom rather than to the United States. Although psychoanalysis is a psychotherapeutic approach primarily used with adults, it is essentially based in the child-focused developmental theory referred to by Freud as that of psychosexual development. Like Piaget's theory, Freud's involves primary stages that individuals traverse in a clear sequence from birth through adolescence with approximate age periods for each – the oral stage during the first year, the anal stage from age one to three years, the phallic stage from three to six years, the latent stage from six to 12 years, and the genital stage from 12 to 18 years.

In outlining these stages, which lie at the intersection of conscious thought and unconscious desire, Freud both described his theory of the developmental progression of psychosexual development and laid down a foundation of the sources of later psychiatric conditions or concerns. During the oral stage, infants seek pleasure and nutrition from their mothers and the failure to attain these can lead to all sorts of deleterious developmental outcomes, such as feelings of greed that arise due to the development of a lack of trust of both self and others. Later in one's development, this might lead to feelings of mistrust, the rejection of others, and difficulties in establishing intimate relationships. During the anal stage, which includes the seminal developmental milestone of toilet training, the child begins to display autonomy, self-control, and identifying and expressing anger. During the phallic stage, unconscious conflicts relating to the libido emerge in the context of sexual desires toward the opposite sex parent and feelings of rivalry toward the same sex parent. During the latency stage, these posited sexual desires become dormant as the child becomes increasingly social within the realms of school, friendships, and sports. The genital stage begins with puberty and involves considerable sexual energy that is expressed through various social activities and ultimately in seeking out a romantic partner. As in Piagetian theory, the order of Freud's theoretical developmental stages is invariant, even if the specific ages at which they are salient can differ somewhat and if level of mastery of the specific developmental stage can vary considerably Freud S. (1905).

A third developmental theory that is based in the notion of stages is Erik Erikson's Theory of Psychological Development in which stages 1–4 occur during childhood, stage 5 throughout adolescence, and stages 6–8 during adulthood. Each of the stages is marked by essential social milestones that are associated with salient contrasting feelings of social relevance and meaning for approximate age ranges. (Please remember that again the age ranges provided for the developmental stages are intended as rough indicators rather than as precise boundaries.) The first putative stage is referred to as the 'infancy period' and spans from birth to 18 months during which time infants are highly dependent on their caregiver to fulfil their needs and therefore begin to develop understandings of trust and mistrust. The second stage, the 'early childhood period', spans from 18 months to three years of age, during which time children become increasingly independent, as evident in successful toilet training and the hypothesized prominence of feelings of autonomy and shame. The third stage, known as the 'Play Age Period', spans from three to five years old and is highlighted by the caregivers' encouragement of the children's personal interests and the children's feelings of initiative and guilt. During the fourth stage, the 'School Age Period' that spans from five to 12 years of age, expectations and accomplishments are central as are feelings of initiative and inferiority. In the fifth stage, the adolescence period which spans from 12 to 18 years old, individuals seek to find themselves, contrasting past experiences with societal expectations, as identity and identity confusion feelings are become salient. Stage 6, the Young Adult Period, spans from 18 to 40 years, during which time longer-term relationships and friendships are central and associated with intimacy and isolation. Stage 7, the Adulthood Period, which spans the ages from 40 to 65 years, is largely characterized by interactions with children and younger colleagues or friends and for which the contrast of generativity and self-absorption is significant. Stage 8, the old-age period, spans from 65 years old until death, during which time reflections on life's accomplishments and the imparting of wisdom are associated with integrity and despair.

Although the various developmental theories differ so much with regard to the domains that are their focus as well as to certain specifics about ages and relevant psychological constructs, they share several essential characteristics. They are all characterized by stages that are qualitatively different from those before and/or after and they are intended to depict development that unfolds in a universally sequential way such that the order of stages is always the same.

The idea of a stage is a complex one that is the source of considerable discussion and debate. In developmental terms, it seen as a complete reorganization of the relevant developmental understanding such that each stage stands separate from the others. The extent of the differences across stages was often echoed in the description of the transition across Piaget's stages as involving an 'a-ha' experience – as in, 'a-ha, now I understand'. And, especially for Piaget's theory, once a stage has been passed and a later one attained, there is no going back. As an example, try to imagine to yourself that you are in an earlier stage of development when you couldn't read. It's impossible. If we write the letters r – e – d, any of us automatically read it as red, the colour. We can't imagine that we can't read those letters as the word red, we can't act as if those letters don't have some intrinsic meaning when they are presented in that specific order. The same is true for arithmetic – we can't imagine not knowing that 2 + 2 = 4. And, yet, of course, there was a time in all of our lives when we couldn't read 'red' nor add '2 + 2'. However, those stages are no longer accessible to us, nor were they accessible even shortly after those abilities were attained – a qualitative change has occurred and cannot be reversed (at least not without some catastrophic event in an individual's life).

As we conclude our discussion of stage theories of development, one essential point or caveat about them – they are just ideas and not reality. Although the theories are compelling in many ways, we must keep in mind that developmental stage theories, like all theories, are just ideas imposed by scholars to provide meaning to their observations of the world around them. So, they both are constructed by the theorists based on their own knowledge and understanding of the real world by their own world views and are limited by the very same factors – the theorists' knowledge, understanding, and world views. Therefore, we need to ask some essential questions.

1. Do the proposed stages reflect the reality of development?
2. Are stages the best way to think about functioning and the transitions across development?
3. Is the order of development really universal, or invariant, or do we see some variability across individuals and groups?

These questions are particularly compelling when considering the populations covered in this textbook for whom development is often considered and labelled as atypical or even by some as pathological. We will return to some of these ideas later in this chapter as well as in some of the other chapters throughout this volume.

In addition to the notion of stages, two other key issues across developmental theories are that the transition from one stage to another is driven by the individuals' encounters with events in the world in which they live. In Piagetian theory, the developing children can be seen as 'little scientists' trying to make sense of the world around them. In doing so, they actively engage and manipulate the physical world as they try to understand the rules that govern them. Using developmental terminology, children actively 'construct' their understanding of the world.

The same active construction is true for Freudian theory as children are active participants in the relevant aspects of the world, which for Freud was the world of socialization and sexuality in some general sense. In Freud's theory, development is driven by the individual's ongoing struggles and tension between the basic biological sexual and aggressive impulses of the id and the moderating effects of the ego that functions according to a so-called 'reality principle' of the superego that attempts to impose cultural values on the id. These struggles evolve as the ego and superego emerge in development in relation to the people and events in the child's life and lead to real-life tensions as depicted by Freud in his notions of the Oedipal and Electra Complexes. Similarly, we can readily see that the social developmental dichotomies described by Erikson have much to do with a person's ongoing struggles, challenges, and triumphs as they navigate through the social issues that are especially salient at each of the key different age periods across the lifespan. Although these essential developmental theories are quite disparate in their foci, several common themes emerge. One, we are actively involved in the construction of our understanding of the world as we strive to comprehend it. Two, we traverse through stages of understanding that facilitate our functioning in the world. Three, we encounter new information that forces us to re-evaluate the understanding at specific stages and compels us to rethink and interact with our world in such a way that we will eventually engage with it in a meaningfully different way. Four, that transition to a new way of thinking reflects arrival at a new stage. In this way, we are all inherently involved participants in our own development as we propel ourselves through the various stages of development.

As an aside, these notions of one's participation in their own development were all antithetical to the behaviourist beliefs that changes in persons are due to events or occurrences in the environment. Traditional behaviourist processes such as stimulus–response, reinforcement, and punishment were all cited as potential causes of changes in behaviour. In the behaviourist context, the individual is largely a passive bystander as external factors are thought to impel change, rather than the internal ones that propel development in developmental theories. Thus, behaviourist theories cannot be considered developmental as changes are not constructed by the individual, nor do they inherently or necessarily occur in a systematic orderly way – changes occur as functions of the environment, which, of course, can be different for any given individual. For developmental theorists the agent of change is the individual rather than the environment; for behaviourist theorists the environment propels change.

THE ORTHOGENETIC PRINCIPLE AND THE COMPLEXITY OF DEVELOPMENTAL PROGRESSION

Even if we accept the basic tenets of universal, orderly, and sequential change as central to development in both theory and reality, we still haven't explained the process of the progression. Our first instinct in thinking about the development from one stage to another might be to characterize that change as simply linear, with transitions from one stage to another, until all the stages in the theory or particular domain of functioning (e.g., language development) had been traversed. In this kind of framework, in which one stage leads to another, the stages could be seen as equivalent, much the way the stairs leading up a stairwell in a building might all be the same but lead from one to another until a given height is attained. However, this analogy fails across all developmental theories, as the stages are quite different from one another. They are not simply one step after another or one layer after another. Rather, like development itself, the stages become increasingly complex.

In order to get a better sense of the process, we turn again to Werner, who provides us with a guide to the nature of the process of developmental change in what he coined as the 'orthogenetic principle'. According to the orthogenetic principle, 'wherever development occurs it proceeds from a state of relative globality and lack of differentiation to a state of increasing differentiation, articulation, and hierarchic integration' Werner, H. (1957). And, again, we can use the foetus as a model to best understand Werner's point. Early on, you can see that the foetus is unformed – a tiny 'blob' or 'dust ball' with no distinguishable features. Over time, this changes – the human form slowly emerges beginning with the early stages of a head and then face, along with the limbs, and then fingers and toes. You will note that in this process, the human form develops, in Werner's terms, from a state of 'relative globality' (the blob or dust ball stage) to 'increasing differentiation or articulation' (as the various parts of the body begin to emerge). But, simple differentiation is not the end-state. Rather, the end-state is the integration of these increasingly differentiated, or distinct, parts in such a way that they work in some coordinated manner. In this case, it's not just that, for example, the hands and fingers emerge, but that they do so in ways that are increasingly 'hierarchically integrated', able to work together with the rest of the body in volitional, meaningful and interconnected ways. That is development – the process of the integration of emerging parts into a cohesive and coherent system.

In keeping with our original Werner quote, the process described in the orthogenetic principle occurs 'wherever there is life'. And we see the same neonatal type of developmental process everywhere in the animal world – development in a specified, universal way that is essentially immutable in the progression to birth. But to Werner, life also included thought, so we can see evidence of the orthogenetic principle in how we understand the world. As a simple example, imagine someone watches an ice hockey game for the first time in their lives. Their experience would be a blur of 16 people – six wearing one colour uniform, six wearing a different colour uniform, and four wearing black and white striped shirts – skating up and down the sheet of ice while holding a wooden stick with a blade at the bottom that is swung at a black disk that is directed toward goals at either end of the ice. The neophyte hockey observer might realize during that first game that the two groups wearing the different colours are competing against each other, while those in the black and white shirts are tasked with maintaining order in the game. When watching their second or third game, the viewer might comprehend that the two teams are trying to shoot the puck with their sticks into the goal at one end while preventing the other team from doing so at the goal in the other end. The next step in their understanding might be to realize that the different players on the ice have different responsibilities, or positions. However, to fully understand the role of each of the six different positions, our new hockey fan needs to understand how the different positions each fit within the functioning of the team. In Werner's terms, the team concept represents the hierarchic integration of the differentiated parts, or in this case, the positions.

Now, let's take a look at how we can apply the orthogenetic principle to human development. Figure 1.2 is a photo of the daughter of one of the authors. In this photo, she is clearly in her first few weeks of life, and in terms of her repertoire of behaviour might be described as a blob. As a baby, she can't do much, she can't even turn over, much less crawl, walk, or run. She's pretty much stuck where she is now, for at least a few more weeks. But, then a few weeks later, as seen in Figure 1.3, development has progressed considerably as she is able to hold herself up and pose for the photo. She's no longer a blob, as she has some ability to propel herself, displays a greater repertoire of behaviours and facial expression. And, as depicted in Figure 1.4,

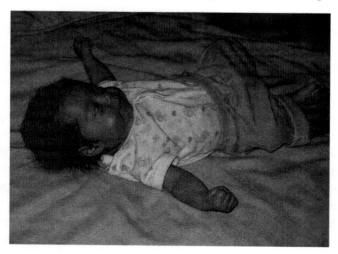

Figure 1.2 Newly born infant
© Jacob A. Burack

Figure 1.3 Changes in the developing infant
© Jacob A. Burack

Figure 1.4 Chessmaster at 18 months
© Marc Tannenbaum

by the age of 18 months, she's able to play chess with a family friend – well, not really, but she is able to gain someone's attention and to engage meaningfully in social interactions. You will note the contrast in physical movement and social activity with her one-month-old brother, who is in the early blob stage in which we originally found his older sister.

The development of communication provides us another opportunity to observe the orthogenetic principle unfold before us. You'll see in Figure 1.5 that the author's daughter was not always a happy-go-lucky kid and had her moments! So ask yourself: why was she crying? At the risk of attempting to undertake the impossible task of entering the mind of an infant, we can speculate any number of reasons that an infant might have been crying… She might have been

14 • UNDERSTANDING INTELLECTUAL AND DEVELOPMENTAL DISABILITIES

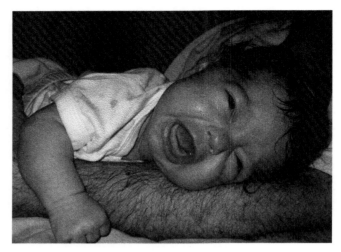

Figure 1.5 Crying as communication
© Jacob A. Burack

hungry or thirsty, feeling uncomfortable in a dirty diaper, experiencing pain, feeling excessively tired, in need of some social companionship. Any of these options seems a reasonable hypothesis for the crying, but note that same response (crying) is used for all of these different experiences and emotions. In this way, the crying is a form of language, a way of social interaction, and an expression of emotion. In Werner's terms, an undifferentiated response. Now look several years later in Figure 1.6. She has managed to verbally negotiate with her parents to get that package of Twizzlers as a reward for participating in the photo session, about which she had resisted joining. You can see in this picture that even her expression and posture convey information and are sources of communication in addition to the words and tone of voice that were part of the discussion with her parents. Only a few years after that period in which a single way was used to communicate a multitude of emotions and/or social needs or desires, in the later picture, we observe the ability to communicate a single emotion or need in many different ways – clearly the ways of communicating are becoming more differentiated, but also integrated – as evidenced by the ability to capitalize on the situation to attain a favorite snack food. This developmental journey from crying as an undifferentiated response, to the point of considerable sophistication in her communications, social interaction, and emotion, is yet another clear example of the orthogenetic principle.

Our two essential quotes from Werner along with the developmental theories of Piaget, Freud, and Erikson provide insight into the essential concepts and paradoxes of classic developmental theory. One, development occurs in a prescribed order; implying that all change is part of a process towards an end-goal. Two, development involves qualitative changes, often referred to as stages, which reflect very distinct ways of being from the previous stage or stages. This stage process might best be framed within the metaphor of a caterpillar morphing into a

Figure 1.6 The growing child and increased sophistication in communication
© Jacob A. Burack

butterfly. The integrity of the individual remains intact – the individual is the same individual throughout the process – but the ways of being and interrelating with the world are so different among the different stages as to almost be unrecognizable from each other. Three, development is inherently complex, and increasingly so over time, but still organized in meaningful ways. In the example of the foetus, the blob that we saw in those early phases evolves through the later stages into a considerably more complex entity as the different body parts emerge and form physically while being transformed into integrated functioning parts and mechanisms.

We have also seen that the developmental transformations that we observe physically are largely mirrored at the conceptual level with different aspects of functioning becoming more integrated and sophisticated throughout childhood and adolescence. Both Werner and Piaget highlight specific trajectories of developmental thinking. For example, we saw with Piaget that early development in the sensorimotor stage is physical, as children need to interact by touching and manipulating the objects in the world around them. Over time, thinking is determined less by physical interaction and more by thought processes. Thus, cognitive development has been described as following a trajectory from action to thought. Cognitive trajectories have also been characterized by Werner and Piaget and others as developing from reflexive or automatic to reflective, again indicating a movement from action to thought. As an example, imagine a soccer ball rolling from the family backyard onto a street – a young child will likely chase after the ball, whereas that child's parents would immediately begin considering where the ball, their child, and any oncoming traffic all might be in relation to each other, and they might even consider lessons potentially learned from their reactions and instructions to their child. That action to thought process can also be seen in the emotional reactions of younger children, such as we saw when the author's daughter was crying. Her crying was a physical and usually immediate reaction to any number of situations. In contrast, we as adults would be able to consider the situation and think through an appropriate response for each different situation. Clearly as we develop through childhood into adolescence and eventually into adulthood, the thought processes become more sophisticated and (in Werner's terms) differentiated as we are able to choose the appropriate responses in relation to the particular situations and contexts that we face. To a large extent, the same could be said of Freud's or Erikson's stages – that as more mature processes of development guide us, we are better able to thoughtfully select more adaptive opportunities.

As another example, part of that increasing complexity of thinking is that ideas go from concrete to abstract. Again, the author's daughter provided an example of this – in this case as she was learning her colours. At the time, she very much enjoyed watching Sesame Street. So, at the beginning she labelled, or called, everything red 'Elmo' and everything yellow was called 'Big Bird'. This reflects clearly concrete levels of language usage and of thinking. She needed to attach the concept to something that was tangible. Over time, her language and thinking about colours became increasingly abstract and she began to apply the labels of red and yellow – the use of labels rather than tangible objects is an indicator of more abstract thinking, as was her ability to consider the different shades and variations of both colours. This process from concrete to abstract is reminiscent of Plato's theory of forms, in which the essential nature of things is conveyed by ideas about it rather than by the physical form. Plato famously used the chair in his description of ideal and forms, with the notion that the idea of a chair is more essential and true than an actual chair, which is tangible but only a single representation of the concept of chair. The same is true for our example of the transition in understanding colours. The labelling of Elmo and Big Bird were concrete examples of red and yellow for the author's daughter, but the real understanding of the colours was attained when she was able to use the label to abstractly think about the colours and all the variations independent of any specific physical entity.

As we conclude our brief introduction to general developmental theories, we again remind you that these are just that – 'theories' – which are used to organize observations and our ways of thinking about the phenomena of changes that are observed among persons from birth though childhood, adolescence, and even adulthood. They are largely based on observations of all kinds – including anecdotal, clinical, experimental, and empirical – and cannot be considered as reality, but rather as tools to help us understand and eventually to test reality.

We leave you with two thoughts about these theories. One, all of these theories were necessarily developed from the external perspective of adults observing, watching, inferring, or otherwise collecting data from children and adolescents. This data is retrospective in nature – looking back at where or how the individual is functioning now and then understanding the process of getting there. For example, how did the author's daughter attain the skills to use language to communicate her social wishes? What were the steps or what was the process? However, real development is a prospective journey. The individual enters and negotiates the world from an entirely different perspective, only able to act with issues, objects, or events that are attainable and salient at the specific developmental level at which they find themselves. And, they are unable to say that 'once I pass this stage I'll eventually be able to function at the next stages' – infants seek to master the Piagetian sensorimotor level because that is what they can understand and act upon at the specific moment and not because they have some inkling that they can eventually get to the formal operations stage. That child trying to make sense of the letters r-e-d is doing so because that is the level of task at which they have arrived and not because they have a vision that one day they will be a Shakespearean scholar. Development framed this way is a proactive journey – but a journey that, according to the theorists, is one that is shared, at least to some extent, universally.

Our second caveat has to do with the assumption of universality. With increasing awareness of the vast differences among people, their physiologies, behaviours, experiences, and environment, the notion of a universal development seems overly simplistic. Further, critics have argued that these and most other psychological theories (including other developmental theories that we will discuss) are too Western-centric as they have been developed in Western countries and focused on people from Western countries. Although cultural and related differences among individuals are seminal and the focus of some of our own work, we invoke this universality as a starting point for a narrative that is inclusive of all people regardless of their developmental conditions and is focused on the humanity of each individual rather than on the defining features of the conditions or locale within which they live.

CONSIDERING THE ENVIRONMENT

With the emphasis of the classic developmental theories (like those of Piaget, Werner, Freud, and Erikson) on the individual, we need to ask about the impact of the environment on development. Some of the most basic questions include (1) is the environment simply a backdrop against which development unfolds or does it play a role in development?, (2) if so, what is that role?, and (3) is that role the same for all aspects of the environment? These questions were addressed by Urie Bronfenbrenner, a Russian-born American-raised developmental psychologist who spent most of his career at Cornell University and is best known for his role as one of the members of the committee struck by American President Lyndon Johnson to found the Head Start programme that was developed to prepare children living in poverty for elementary school. The idea was that by providing opportunities for the children and their mothers that were not typically available in their environments, Head Start could facilitate these children's opportunities for academic success and subsequent stages throughout the lifespan.

In his bio-ecological or Ecological Systems theory, Bronfenbrenner emphasized the essential role in development of the transactions, or ongoing and evolving relationships, between individuals and the environments in which they live. According to his theory, the environment is complex and multi-layered. Bronfenbrenner articulated four levels, which are commonly pictorially displayed as concentric circles, that he labelled from the most proximal to the most distal as the microsystem, mesosystem, exosystem, and macrosystem. Each of these levels involves physical components, such as home, school, or workplace, and the social relationships with which the areas are each associated, such as family, friends, and colleagues, respectively. The aspects of the environment at each level directly or indirectly influence development in unique ways that differ at different points across the lifespan.

Level 1 is known as the 'microsystem' and refers to the individual's most proximal and immediate environment that includes the family and their home, daycare or school, and the local neighbourhood. At this level, relationships are generally limited to the children, their families or other caregivers, and a few playmates. Consistent with the developmental notion that earlier development is less complex and differentiated than later development, the microsystem is where early development is almost entirely situated. The Mesosystem involves the interaction among various microsystems that include home, playmate settings, and school, each of which can impact any of the others, such as the home environment can influence the school environment. The Exosystem influences children's development distally and impacts through the microsystem and mesosystem systems. One example is that accomplishments or demands of the parents at their workplace can positively or deleteriously impact their relationships (microsystem) with their children. The Macrosystem is the outermost level, or the one that is the farthest from the child, but still influences the child's attitudes and behaviours. Governmental or societal policies can indirectly impact the children by impacting the child's environment with regard to economic, educational, health, and other factors.

In highlighting contributions of Brofenbrenner's Ecological Systems Theory, we note two essential considerations. One: even in our framework of development through a lens of universal humanity, we emphasize the vast differences across the environments in which children grow up even within the same communities, not to mention around the globe. In this context, Bronfenbrenner provides a universal framework to organize our thinking about the different influences that can affect growth throughout the lifespan. Two: the various levels are not discrete, but rather influence each other, typically with the distal (outside) ones influencing the more proximal (close) to a greater extent than the reverse, even as the proximal ones have a more direct and stronger influence on an individual's development.

FUNDAMENTALS OF A DEVELOPMENTAL APPROACH TO INTELLECTUAL AND DEVELOPMENTAL DISABILITIES

The beginnings of a formal developmental approach to the study of persons with intellectual and developmental conditions is often dated to a series of articles about persons with intellectual disability by Edward Zigler (1967, 1969), an American psychologist at Yale University who, along with Bronfenbrenner, was one of the two psychologists who founded the Head Start programme. Zigler, who had originally studied as a clinical psychologist with behaviourist training, was largely influenced by Werner's developmental theories as he sought to understand the life experiences of persons with intellectual disability. Borrowing concepts from Werner and Piaget, Zigler argued that understanding the developmental process was just as important for persons with intellectual disability as for any other person. As with Werner and Piaget, the key aspect of development was the process of development, rather than the speed of development. Clearly, the rate, or speed of development, is slower among persons with intellectual disability – that is the de facto definition of the condition – but tells us little about the developmental process per se.

As described in considerable detail in Chapter 3, persons with intellectual disability are those who score in the lowest 2–3% of the entire population on standardized tests of intelligence and social adaptation. Zigler raised concerns about what he labelled as 'the defect' approach that was prevalent at the time and was generally centred around identifying some common deficit that causes all intellectual disability. Zigler argued that this way of thinking obscured the basic humanity of persons with intellectual disability and led to inherently flawed and essentially distorted understandings of persons with intellectual disability. Within a developmental framework, Zigler and his colleagues emphasized four essential, and somewhat overlapping, points that are at the essence of this volume.

One: persons with intellectual disability are remarkably diverse with regard to aetiology, or the cause of the intellectual disability, as well as to the phenotype, or the way that the intellectual disability is expressed across groups and individuals. As examples, we point to the chapters on Down syndrome and organic syndromes for discussions of different etiologies and specific patterns of development that are associated with each group.

Two: universal developmental patterns can be identified in all groups, such as the sequence in which specific abilities are attained, but unique patterns of developmental strengths and weaknesses can still be found in specific groups. The strengths and weaknesses of the specific groups included in this volume are at the heart of the individual chapters.

Three: the identification of weaknesses, and strengths, are only meaningful if they are addressed in relation the individuals' general level of developmental functioning or mental age (rather than chronological age). For example, the finding that a specific area of functioning is not as advanced in a child with intellectual disability as compared to a typically developing child is uninteresting as, by definition, the former would always be expected to display lower levels of functioning than the latter. A more informative finding is the identification of a weakness, or strength, when the groups are equated on level of developmental functioning (e.g. they both function as six years-olds). However, keep in mind that if a group of persons with intellectual disability functions at the same level of cognitive functioning with a group of TD persons then they will, again by definition, be considerably older chronologically).

Four: the performance of persons with intellectual disability on an experimental task or on behaviours in real life is essentially impacted by their life experiences and self-perceptions. When Zigler was writing, many persons with intellectual disability lived much of their, if not their entire, lives in institutions; almost exclusively attended special schools or classrooms; were generally segregated from the rest of the community; and rarely experienced success.

These generally deleterious life histories were thought to negatively affect the way that persons with intellectual disability thought of themselves that in turn led to personality-motivational styles, including lowered levels of expectancy of success and the search for clues from others as how to act and avoid failure.

Consistent with our universal notion of development, Zigler highlighted that these patterns of behaviour are not unique to persons with ID, but rather would be displayed by anyone who faced consistent failure in their lives. For example, Zigler argued that the same behaviours could be found among children who lived in poverty or were from marginalized communities. Conversely, if these same groups could be afforded opportunities for success, they would not be expected to display these styles (for a discussion, see Burack et al. 2021). The importance of these personality-motivation traits is highlighted by findings that success in the realms of employment, relationships, and other such areas among persons with developmental conditions is related more to personality characteristics than to IQ per se (Zigler & Hodapp 1986).

One of the authors of this volume often tells an anecdote about the impact of life experiences on personality and behaviour among people with developmental conditions. 'When I was in college, I worked summers in a camp for children, adolescents, and adults with intellectual disability and/or autism. As it turned out, one of the campers lived only a few blocks from my parents, so when I would come home for holidays, my mom would invite him over for a holiday meal. He was a really capable guy. He was about my age (early twenties at the time) and one of the most able campers – he used to read the newspapers every day and was very knowledgeable about world events – and lived semi-independently in an apartment.

'Once before my friend came over, my mother pointed out that she had noticed that he would never start eating until he checked out what I did, which utensil I picked up, etc. I'll point out here that I grew up in a very informal household, so the table wasn't really set and utensils were just put on the table in a pile in the middle and everyone just took what they needed. When we served the soup that evening, I waited to see what my friend would do and didn't pick up any utensil. Sure enough he didn't make a move and continued to watch me. After a minute or so, I did a kind of mean thing and picked up my fork to see what he would do – he looked at me quizzically, didn't say anything, but still sat there, looking unsure of himself. Finally, I picked up my spoon and so did he…'

The point of the story is that the friend clearly knew what to do – use a spoon to eat his soup. But, he didn't want to make a mistake and didn't trust his own judgement, so he looked outside himself for some cues as to how to act. This story captures two of the essential characteristics that Zigler identified among persons with intellectual disability: an expectancy of failure rather than success, and outerdirectedness, a dependence on others for guidance about how to act. Yet this anecdote provides an example of the beauty of a universal approach. Outerdirectness is not at all a type of behaviour evidenced only by persons with intellectual disability or other marginalized youth who often experience failure, but is used by all of us in certain circumstances when we find we are faced with novel or complex tasks or situations. For example, imagine that the King of England invited you for dinner (it hasn't happened to me yet) and had his staff prepare a beautiful meal for you with elaborate settings of multiple plates, several bowls, numerous glasses, and many utensils. It would be awesome but overwhelming. When the first course or first drinks were served, you'd probably hesitate a few seconds before digging in to look around to observe the other invitees to make sure which glass/plate/bowl/utensil should be used. The difference between this case and that of the author's friend is that most of us only resort to outerdirected strategies in the case of considerable complexity, novelty, or uncertainty about how to proceed, whereas the friend resorted to outerdirectedness even on a task (i.e. choosing a spoon rather than a fork to consume the soup) for which he has considerable experience. So, we learn the important developmental lesson that behaviours and style of interacting are universal rather than unique to a specific group, although they may be utilized differently in relation to the context. Accordingly, we also note that if children with developmental conditions could be provided opportunities to succeed, they would not be expected to display these styles (for a discussion, see Burack et al. 2021). This finding takes on even more significance in light of research highlighting that success in the realms of employment, relationships, and other such areas is related more to personality characteristics than to IQ per se among persons with intellectual disability (Zigler & Hodapp 1986).

Zigler's lessons resonate until today among persons with intellectual disability as well as all other developmental conditions. Although many of the issues that Zigler raised might seem obvious today, they challenged longstanding and prevailing world views of segregation and prejudice, while emphasizing the notion of universal humanity. We hope that these developmental lessons will provide a helpful and meaningful framework as you read through this volume and, more importantly, as you encounter and engage with persons with intellectual and developmental conditions.

Reflective Questions

1. What are the essential components of a developmental approach?
2. What are the advantages of a developmental approach to the study of persons with developmental and intellectual disabilities?
3. What are some challenges in implementing a developmental approach?
4. What are some real-world implications of a developmental approach?

REFERENCES

Burack, J. A., Evans, D. W., Russo, N., Napoleon, J.-S., Goldman, K. J., & Iarocci, G. (2021). Developmental perspectives on the study of persons with intellectual disability. *Annual Review of Clinical Psychology, 17*(1), 339–363. https://doi.org/10.1146/annurev-clinpsy-081219-090532.

Freud, S. (1905). Three Essays on the Theory of Sexuality (Trans. James Strachey). New York Basic Books.

Piaget, J. (1970). Piaget's theory. In P. H. Mussen & W. Kessen (Eds.), Handbook of child psychology: Vol. 1, History, theory, and methods. New York: Wiley.

Werner, H. (1957). The concept of development from a comparative and organismic point of view. In D. Harris (Ed.), The concept of development. Minneapolis: University of Minnesota Press.

Zigler, E. (1967). Familial mental retardation: A continuing dilemma: A controversy exists between the general developmental and defect approaches to the problem of etiology. *Science, 155*(3760), 292–298. https://doi.org/10.1126/science.155.3760.292.

Zigler, E. (1969). Developmental versus difference theories of mental retardation and the problem of motivation. *American Journal of Mental Deficiency, 73*(4), 536–556.

Zigler, E., & Hodapp, R. M. (1986). *Understanding Mental Retardation*. Cambridge University Press.

2
GENE-ENVIRONMENT INTERACTIONS AND INTELLECTUAL DISABILITY

> ### Learning Objectives
>
> After reading this chapter, you should be able to:
> - Understand genotype and phenotype and the intermediary processes that lead to particular developmental outcomes
> - Differentiate between organic and familial influences on cognitive development and in particular intellectual disability
> - Understand the interaction between genotype and environment
> - Consider the policy implications of genetic research
> - Understand prenatal genetic screening and diagnosis of intellectual disability

Imagine for the moment that you had been born in a different part of the world, with a different language, cultural and social upbringing. Would you still be you? Although we could not ethically put this question to empirical study, we can explore this idea with what we know about research on behavioural genetics – the study of how genes and environments interact.

If your biological parents remain the same, your *genotype*, the particular set of genes that a person inherits from their parents, would remain the same. This means that inside the nucleus of each of your body cells you would have the same unique set of 46 chromosomes, 23 inherited from your mother and 23 inherited from your father. However, the *environment* within which you would be developing would be quite different. As a result, your *phenotype*, the behavioural product of the interaction of a person's **genotype** with the environment (e.g. how you think, what you feel, how you communicate and interact with others), would likely be quite different. How do we know this?

Researchers have discovered that genes and environments work synergistically, meaning that genes respond to environmental demands/pressures (e.g. language exposure) and environments mould to genetic proclivities (e.g. a child's temperament). For example, researchers have found **Genotype-Environment Correlations,** that is, parents give their biological offspring both their genes and a home environment, but both are a function of the parents' own genes, providing a built-in correlation between the individual's genotype (inherited characteristics) and their early home environment. There are different ways that this synergy plays out:

1. **Reactive Interaction:** Different persons (e.g. siblings) exposed to the same environment experience it, interpret it, and react to it differently. One sibling may interpret a parent's directive as controlling whereas the other may feel security in being guided by someone they trust.
2. **Evocative Interaction:** Each individual's personality evokes distinctive responses from others. A child with an exuberant temperament may evoke delight, in a parent who appreciates the unexpected, and anxiety in a parent who has difficulty tolerating the unexpected.
3. **Proactive Interaction:** Different individuals select and construct different environments. For example, a child who is interested in, and excels at, physical activities may begin to select peers who are similarly inclined. As the child develops, they begin to select and construct environments of their own, the effect of the built-in genotype-environment correlation diminishes, and the influence of proactive interaction increases. However, reactive and evocative interactions remain important throughout life.

When we consider the hypothetical situation of being raised in a new environment, your inherited genotype and your family environment would mostly influence your phenotype early on in development but over time you would increasingly select and construct your own environment as a function of a **bidirectional** influence between your inherited proclivities and the available environmental opportunities. Imagine again that you were raised in the remote and rural South Pacific Island of Vanuatu, would you find yourself studying a course in Psychology? Not likely, but your interest in humans may be expressed through other means, such as practising healing or teaching in your village. With this illustration you can see how characteristics persist over time, and yet there is flexibility in phenotype as one adapts to their surroundings. Keep this in mind as we begin the discussion of gene-environment interactions in intellectual and developmental disability. The same principle of **bidirectional** influence applies even in cases of chromosomal or genetic differences.

BRIEF HISTORY OF THE GENETIC STUDY OF INTELLIGENCE

The quest to understand the role of genetics in the development of intelligence may be traced back to the work of Francis Galton (1869, 1883, 1889). Galton was a geneticist concerned with the study of the inheritance of genius. He believed that identifiable behavioural differences among individuals, such as social class or influence, reflected underlying genetic endowment. Galton further proposed that the distribution of people in the various social classes was Gaussian and symmetrical: that is, a bell curve. Thus, he estimated that there would be an equal number of 'eminent' men and 'imbeciles',[1] suggesting that intelligence was normally distributed in the general population. Galton's work on quantifying the variation in human intelligence was pioneering, in particular; his ideas about the distribution of intelligence in the general population would later lead other researchers to the discovery that people with intellectual disability were over-represented on the **Normal distribution** (Lewis 1933).

With the development of standardized tests of intelligence, his successors were able to show that, contrary to the theoretical predictions from the bell curve on which IQ scores are based, the distribution of intelligence obtained in large-scale epidemiological studies consistently revealed an excess of individuals in the lowest range of intellectual functioning (IQ < 50) that was not matched by the number of cases in the opposite tail at the highest range of intellectual functioning (IQ > 150) (Pearson & Jaederholm 1914; Roberts, Norman & Griffiths 1938; Penrose 1954, 1963; Tarjan 1959). Conversely, the remainder of people with IQs in the range of intellectual disability, most with IQs above 50, as predicted by the bell curve, blended into the lower end of the normal distribution of intelligence.

To explain these findings, two distributions of intelligence were proposed (Dingman & Tarjan 1960). One group was thought to comprise persons with mild intellectual disability whose genetic endowment was not pathological, but nevertheless put them on the lower end of the symmetrical, bell-shaped distribution of IQ (Lewis 1933; Penrose 1963; Zigler 1967). The other group consisted of persons with more pronounced intellectual disabilities that were associated with processes considered to be pathological (e.g. abnormal genetic variant, organic insult) interfering with cognitive development (Burack 1990).

Leading developmental theorists, such as Zigler (1967), used the knowledge and principles of typical development to inform the study of persons with intellectual disability. Werner and Strauss emphasized the difference between 'endogenous' (factors from within) and 'exogenous' (factors from without) intellectual disability. The former referred to intellectual disability that was associated with a family history of intellectual disability, no organic damage, and positive response to modifications in the **environment**. The latter was commonly associated with pathological damage, no family history of intellectual disability, and little benefits from environmental changes (Strauss & Kepart 1940) (see Table 2.1).

---

[1] The term 'imbecile' was used to refer to people with intellectual disability. Terminology of the time does not reflect the nuanced understanding that we have now and, therefore, the word is seen as quite pejorative and inappropriate today.

Table 2.1 The definition, diagnosis, causes, and characteristics of organic and familial mental retardation[2]

	Organic	Familial
Definition	Individual shows a clear organic cause of intellectual disability	Individual shows no obvious cause of intellectual disability. Family member may have intellectual disability
Diagnosis	Typically at birth or infancy	School-age
	Frequent co-occurring disabilities	No co-occurring disabilities
	No change in ID status	Likely, upon leaving school
Causes	Prenatal (genetic disorders, accidents *in utero*)	Polygenic (i.e. parents of low IQ)
	Perinatal (prematurity, anoxia)	Environmentally deprived
	Postnatal (head trauma, meningitis)	Undetected organic conditions
Characteristics	More prevalent in moderate, severe, and profound intellectual disability	More prevalent in mild intellectual disability
	Equal or near-equal rates across all ethnic and SES levels	Higher rates within minority groups and low SES groups
	More often associated with other physical disabilities (e.g. epilepsy, cerebral palsy)	Few associated physical disabilities
	Often accompanied by severe health problems	Health within normal range
	IQ most often below 50	IQ rarely below 50
	Siblings usually of average intelligence	Siblings often exhibit unusually low IQ scores
	Unusual dysmorphologies in physical appearance often present	Normal appearance
	Mortality rate higher (more likely to die at a younger age than the general population)	Normal mortality rate
	Often dependent on care of others throughout life	With some support and accommodations can lead an independent existence as adults
	Unlikely to mate and often infertile	Likely to marry; children may also have relatively low IQ scores
	Unlikely to experience neglect in home	More likely to experience neglect in their homes

Source: Adapted from Zigler, Balla, & Hodapp 1984; Hodapp & Dykens 1996; MacMillan, Siperstein, & Gresham 1996.

---

[2] Mental retardation was a term used at the time but is no longer considered accurate or appropriate. We now use the term intellectual disability.

In the 1960s and early 70s, Zigler and his colleagues extended this work by providing a developmental rationale for the need to differentiate between aetiologies of intellectual disability and a series of impressive studies that supported the notion that the organic/familial subgroups of persons with intellectual disability had different developmental trajectories (Zigler & Hodapp 1986). They reported that a majority, approximately 50% of people diagnosed with mild intellectual disability on the basis of low IQ scores and poor social adaptiveness, did not have an identifiable organic pathology known to cause intellectual disability (Zigler & Hodapp 1986). Furthermore, these individuals showed no physical or health abnormalities and their mortality rate was normal. Individuals considered to have a familial type of intellectual disability were more likely to come from families with low socio-economic status (SES), to have at least one biological parent with mild intellectual disability without an organic basis, and to have siblings with below average IQs (Zigler, Balla, & Hodapp 1984). Moreover, although the rate of cognitive development was slower among persons with familial intellectual disability, they followed the same sequences of development and showed similar patterns of cognitive development across domains when compared to typically developing peers of the same mental age (MA) (Weisz & Yeates 1981; Zigler 1986). Thus, developmental theory and empirical data had begun to help researchers make sense of the initial clinical and behavioural observations of persons with intellectual disability and this would later lead to refinements in the conceptualization of intellectual disability as consisting of many underlying causes with one common outcome: a below average IQ.

ORGANIC AND FAMILIAL FACTORS IN INTELLECTUAL DISABILITY

When a child is born with a chromosomal or genetic anomaly, the cause of the intellectual disability is referred to as organic (as in relating to the organism). To date, researchers have identified over 1000 known organic causes of intellectual disability (Winnepenninckx, Rooms, & Kooy 2003) that account for intellectual disability in two-thirds of the individuals in the moderate to profound range of intellectual disability (Stromme & Hagberg 2000). In some cases (e.g. Fragile X, Down syndrome), the different genetic processes have been well established (e.g. Zechner et al. 2001). However, genetic aetiology is still unknown in the majority of cases wherein intellectual disability is mild (IQ from 50 to 70), even though persons in this IQ range constitute approximately 75% of all cases of intellectual disability (Zigler & Hodapp, 1986; Raynham, Gibbons, Flint, & Higgs 1996). Over 50% of individuals diagnosed with mild intellectual disability show no known pre-, peri-, or **postnatal** cause for their low IQ and, although delayed, cognitive development is as orderly and organized as that of their typically developing (TD) peers (Hodapp & Zigler 1990, 1995). Intellectual disability in these cases may be familial and non-pathological, constituting the lower end of the bell curve of IQ in the general population (Zigler 1967, 1969).

POLYGENIC INHERITANCE AND FAMILIAL INTELLECTUAL DISABILITY

General cognitive ability (as indexed by IQ) is consistently shown to be highly familial and heritable. For example, in over 30 **twin studies** involving approximately 10,000 pairs of twins, the average identical and fraternal twin correlations for IQ scores were 0.86 and 0.60, respectively (Bouchard & McGue 1981). This pattern of twin correlations suggests that half of the variance in IQ scores is due to the genetic transmission of multiple genes and that approximately one-third of the variance is due to environmental factors shared by family members (Plomin 1997, 1999a, 2002; Plomin & Petrill 1997). The **heritability** of IQ increases throughout the lifespan beginning at 25% in infancy (Spinath, Ronald, Harlaar, Price, Plomin 2003) and increasing to 40% in childhood and 60% in adulthood (McGue, Bouchard, Iacono, & Lyken 1993; McClearn et al. 1997). One explanation for this developmental change is that relatively small genetic effects early in life have non-specific but cumulative effects on cognitive development. Plomin (2002) argues that genetic factors contribute to continuity over time, whereas environmental factors are largely responsible for change, citing evidence from adoption studies that correlations between biological parents and their adopted-away offspring increased from 0.1 in infancy to 0.3 in adolescence. Heritability appears to be substantial at all ages, while **shared environmental** influence is negligible after four years; however, to the extent that they have an effect, shared familial environmental influences (e.g. SES) appear to be of a global nature with a relatively constant influence (Bishop et al. 2003).

In addition to developmental outcome, **behavioural geneticists** have begun to focus their efforts on exploring the process by which genes and environments interact over time. The evidence suggests that as children mature, genetic factors influence the ways in which they select, interpret, modify, and create experiences (Plomin 2002). The behavioural expression of the genotype will vary with the potential range of environmental conditions; this interplay between the genotype and environment determines the **phenotype**. Therefore, the genetic influences on cognitive development are potentially modifiable by environmental input throughout development; however, the environmental influences on development are integrally associated with the genes or structures to which the genes have contributed (Neisser et al. 1996). The practical implications are that environmental influences on cognitive development whether positive (intervention) or negative (psychosocial adversity), need to be examined in relation to the intensity and duration of exposure, and motivational factors (Zigler & Hodapp 1986).

Polygenic or multiple gene systems determine a child's potential range of cognitive ability and account for familial resemblance and consistency in IQ scores. According to the **polygenic inheritance** model, IQ, much like other quantitative traits such as height or weight, follows a Gaussian distribution or bell curve. Gottesman (1963a) illustrated the bell curve of IQ scores using a hypothetical five-gene model (see Figure 2.1). He reasoned that if two genes influenced IQ and each gene has two **alleles** (one of maternal and the other of paternal origin), an offspring may inherit IQ-enhancing alleles A+ B+ or IQ-non-enhancing alleles A- B- from each parent. Thus, 16 permutations of alleles are possible and, if expressed completely, five categories of genotype for IQ would be produced. The distribution of IQ would be roughly symmetrical as one offspring inherits all IQ-non-enhancing alleles (A- A- B- B-) four offspring inherit mostly non-enhancing alleles (A+ A- B- B-), six offspring inherit an equal share of IQ-enhancing and non-enhancing alleles (A+ A+ B- B-), four offspring inherit mostly enhancing alleles (A+ A+ B+ B-) and one offspring inherits all IQ-enhancing alleles (A+ A+ B+ B+) (Gottesman 1963b).

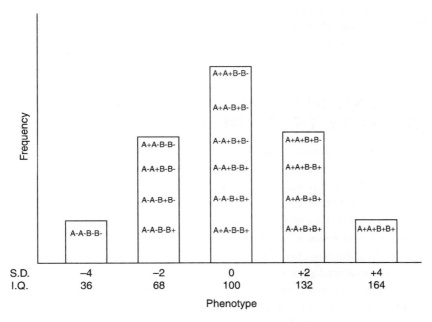

Figure 2.1 Gottesman's five gene model of the Normal Distribution of IQ. The hypothetical case of two genes contributing to IQ, each including a maternal and a paternal allele that is either enhancing or non-enhancing with regard to IQ.

Source: From Gottesman (1963b).

Behavioural geneticists contend that the heritability of familial intellectual disability may be due to maternal and paternal polygenic influences that derive from multiple genes, each contributing a small effect that additively combine to produce diversity in general cognitive ability in the population (Plomin 2002). Thus, familial intellectual disability, with no apparent pathological cause for the low IQ, may represent the low end of the distribution in cognitive ability that is quantitatively but not qualitatively different from the rest of the distribution.

Polygenic inheritance of intelligence applies to all offspring including those who are afflicted by a chromosomal or other genetic anomaly. Despite the similar organic effect caused by a genetic mutation (e.g. trisomy 21), considerable variation in cognitive ability is evident among aetiologically homogenous groups (e.g. children with Down syndrome) (Carr 2000). This variation in IQ may, in part, be accounted for by the children's cognitive endowment. Thus, **polygenes** co-exist but are distinguished from non-additive single-gene mutations that have specific effects on the organism and are associated with qualitatively distinct phenotypes (e.g. Down syndrome). Polygenic influences additively affect phenotype (e.g. IQ) and produce familial resemblance (correlation between parent and child IQ), whereas, non-additive genetic influences are not shared by first-degree relatives (parents, offspring, siblings) (Plomin 1994). Quantitative genetic methodologies are designed to explore familial resemblance with regard to a specific behavioural phenotype, such as IQ, in order to determine the relative contributions of genetics and environments (Plomin 1994).

ENVIRONMENTAL INFLUENCES ON INTELLECTUAL DISABILITY: THE EXAMPLE OF DOWN SYNDROME

The search for a genetic basis for familial intellectual disability, in many ways, parallels the quest for social and environmental influences on the development of children with genetic conditions such as Down syndrome. In the latter case, however, the challenges are reversed. The chromosomal differences that cause Down syndrome are well known and the genetic processes responsible for the intellectual disability and associated physical effects continue to be a significant focus of research. Similarly, the developmental profile of children with Down syndrome, including the sequences, stages, and rate of development across domains of functioning, have been explored extensively (Dykens, Hodapp, & Evans 2006). In contrast, there is a paucity of research on environmental and social influences on the development of children with DS. Aside from the occasional hand waving from developmental researchers interested in parent/family influences (Hodapp 2007; Cicchetti & Beeghly 2009), the field has largely ignored the role of contextual factors.

Down Syndrome is the most common non-inherited 'organic' cause of intellectual disability and occurs in approximately one in every 792 live births (de Graaf et al. 2015). Down syndrome is a well-defined genetic anomaly; the additional **chromosome** 21 was identified, is small in size, and is the second-most heavily mapped human chromosome (Leshin 2003). During **meiosis**, each pair of the 23 chromosomes typically separates and each goes to different spots in the dividing cell; this event is called 'disjunction'. Down syndrome is the result of the presence of all or a portion of an extra copy of chromosome 21. Complete trisomy 21, an extra 21st chromosome in all cells of the body, accounts for over 95% of all full-term cases (Simonoff et al. 1998). In three to four per cent of cases translocation occurs, whereby the 21st chromosome breaks off and attaches to other chromosomes (usually the 14th). In this case, genetic material is rearranged so that some of chromosome 14 is replaced by extra chromosome 21. One to two per cent of cases are due to post-conception non-disjunction that produces three copies of chromosome 21 in some but not all cells (i.e. mosaicism) (Cooley & Graham 1991).

The 21st chromosome contains the smallest number of genes (200–250 genes) and an even smaller percentage of those may be involved in producing the features of Down syndrome. The over-expression of the 200–250 genes, the associated proteins and processes involved in causing this form of intellectual disability are widely studied (Patterson 1995; Lesch 2004). However, the identification of genes and the products of their expression may only provide part of the explanation for Down syndrome. There is wide variability in physical features, intellectual disability, and cognitive profile among people with Down syndrome and little research to account for the potential environmental sources (e.g. **prenatal**, **perinatal** and postnatal factors) of the developmental variation in outcome. Questions remain regarding the intervening processes that operate between genes and the diverse developmental outcomes observed among children with Down syndrome. Thus, in the case of Down syndrome, knowledge about genetic processes is more readily available and at the forefront of the quest for understanding developmental outcomes of intellectual disability. Environmental factors that may be involved may be more difficult to identify and study.

We know that the genetic differences of Down syndrome have powerful and specific influences on the development of the child, but it also inadvertently affects significant people (i.e. parents, siblings, teachers, friends) in the child's life. The unique profile of disabilities associated with Down syndrome that includes medical, motor, social, affective, and cognitive features may interact with contextual factors associated with the child's family, peer group, school, community, and culture to determine variability in development. Thus, understanding the context within which children with Down syndrome live will provide important insights into the variability in developmental outcome as well as the constraints posed by the genetic differences.

Brief History of the Study of Environment and Context on Intelligence

The most notable example of the role of environment on intelligence is found in Lev Vygotsky's (1978) theory, the Zone of Proximal Development, which proposed that the development of foundational processes that comprise intelligence occur as a result of constructive interactions with significant adults in the child's life such as parents and teachers. The related notion that adults were integral to scaffold learning in developing children implied that knowledge was neither within nor external to the child, but rather emerged within the context of social interactions between the child and significant others in their lives. Vygotsky's ideas foreshadowed later developmental psychopathology notions of risk and resilience and the ability of children with disabilities to thrive in society despite their many challenges (Burack, Hodapp & Zigler 1998). Bell (1968) introduced the role of interactional styles and specifically emphasized the bidirectional view that both parents and children mutually influence the other's behaviour. Sameroff and Chandler's (1975) seminal paper on the transactional model of development underscored the power of the parental caretaking environment to buffer the effects of adversity. Cicchetti and colleagues (Cicchetti 1984) built on these dynamic and transactional views of development and incorporated postulates from Bertanlanffy's general systems theory (e.g. multifinality) to understand the complexity of typical and atypical development. Urie Bronfenbrenner contributed a more nuanced perspective on the various facets of the environments that children both rely on and are shaped by. Bronfenbrenner's (1977, 1979) ecological model of human development proposed that the child's development occurs within various contexts and is supported by many interdependent and interacting socio-cultural systems. Bronfenbrenner's model attempted to refine conceptualizations of the environment by identifying different spheres of influence, each nested or contained within the other. These levels include those that have a distal (i.e. indirect) effect and those that have a proximal (i.e. direct) effect on the individual (Cicchetti & Toth 1997). Indirect influences are thought to emanate from macrosystems, which encompass the patterns, beliefs, and values of the culture in which the child exists, and the exosystems, which contain the various formal and informal social structures in the child's environment, including the neighbourhood, communication, and transport facilities, and government policies on education and health (Bronfenbrenner 1977, 1979; Cicchetti & Toth 1997).

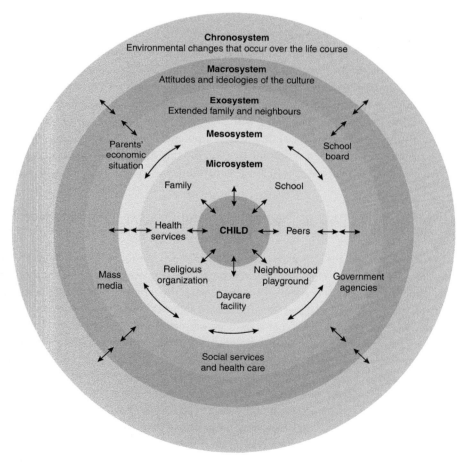

Figure 2.2 Bronfenbrenner's ecological systems theory

Source: Rhodes, *Theories of Child Development*, 2013.

CONCEPTUALIZING THE INTERPLAY BETWEEN GENES AND ENVIRONMENT

Reaction range is a developmental concept that bridges the genetic and contextualist studies of intelligence. Behaviour geneticist, Iriving Gottesman (1963), first introduced the term **reaction range** as referring to the idea that a human's genotype establishes a range of possible developmental outcomes (Gottesman 1963a). He stated that 'a genotype determines an indefinite but circumscribed assortment of phenotypes, each of which corresponds to one of the possible environments to which the genotype may be exposed' (p. 254). Within these boundaries it is environmental factors that largely determine how the person develops over time. One way to think about it is the analogy of the rubber band. The rubber band can only stretch so far as it has constraints on its upper and lower limits, but it is flexible nonetheless and therefore pliable to environmental pressures. See Figure 2.3 for a hypothetical illustration of the reaction range for four different genotypes: a group of children with Down syndrome (A), a group of children with other unknown form of intllectual disability (B) a group of typically developing children (C) and a group of gifted children (D), under restricted, natural and enriched environments. Note that genotype A has the smallest reaction range. Can you explain why?

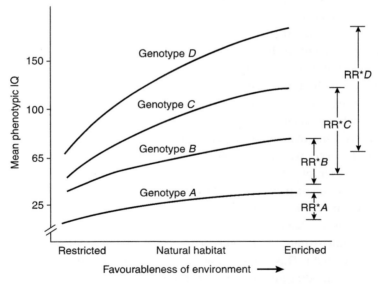

Figure 2.3 Illustration of the reaction range concept for four hypothetical genotypes

Source: From Gottesman, 1963a.

IQ test performance may vary by as much as 20 or 25 points, depending on the type of environment in which a child develops. When the child's environment is enriched, the child moves closer to the upper end of his reaction range. When the environment becomes impoverished, they fall towards the lower end. However, there is also the child's genotype to consider.

In the case of Genotye A, the chromosomal differences of Down syndrome create particular constraints on the organism that may be more difficult to overcome with simply providing an enriched environment. Thus, the reaction range for Genotype A remains small compared with the range observed in children with other genotypes. When considering the outcome of intellectual disability (whether stemming from organic or familial causes), it is important to conceptualize the implicated genes and environmental factors as working in tandem (setting upper and lower limits) to create a range of phenotype possibilities.

Although the concept of reaction range emphasizes the interplay between genes and environment, might it portray an overly deterministic view of development whereby environmental factors can only act within a restricted set of parameters that are established at conception by the inherited genotype (Perrett et al 1992; Gottlieb 1995)? Gottesman would argue that is not the case if we consider that the form and function of genes are not fixed and the expression of any one gene occurs within a biological system influenced by numerous other genetic and environmental pressures (Gottesman & Hanson 2005). Moreover, the phenotypic ranges depicted in the curve in Figure 2.3 apply to the specified environments as indicated on the x axis (i.e. restricted, natural, and enriched) however those are defined. The phenotypic outcomes outside the current reaction range may result with other environments that may be encountered or with focused and targeted interventions.

Gottlieb (1992), a developmental psychobiologist, argued that the interplay between genes and environment is bidirectional and involves a causal relationship termed '*co-action*' of genes and environment in the outcome of a child's development. As such development is characterized as probabilistic as the dynamic interplay between genes and environment would be active throughout the course of development. This implies that the dynamic influences would be reciprocal; environments could influence gene function (e.g. diet, stress turning genes on or off) and genes could influence environments (e.g. temperament and choice of peers). Moreover, the dynamic interplay would not be confined to genes and environments but may also occur within genes, at the level of neural activity, behaviour, and within environments. For example, there are genes that may suppress or trigger other genes at various points in development (Lettice et al. 2002). Similarly, poor sibling relationships in the home setting may influence peer relations in the school context and vice versa. Gottlieb (2003) believed that a behavioural genetics approach that has the goal of understanding individual development must study potential as well as actual differences in phenotypes (Griffiths & Tabery 2008). This would entail using experimental methods such as targeted interventions or the modification of genes at the molecular level by unmethylating genes which were methylated as a result of earlier life experience (Weaver et al. 2004) to extend the genetic and environmental parameters to values that would not be expected in nature (Griffiths & Tabery 2008). Another strategy may be the 'experiment in nature': studying a genetic difference such as William's syndrome and its **co-occurring** 'extreme' phenotype of hypersociability to begin to uncover the relations between genetic and phenotypic differences (Iarocci, Elfers, & Yager 2007).

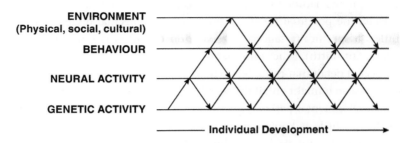

Figure 2.4 'Co-action' of genes and environment
Source: From Gottlieb 1992, 186 with permission of Taylor and Francis.

Horowitz and Haritos (1998) emphasize the need to consider the match between the individual's genotype and their experience when studying the impact of intervention or disability on developmental outcome. For example, purposely engineered opportunities for learning or tailored and targeted interventions may be more important for those with atypical intellectual endowment such as children with intellectual disability and gifted children than those who have a typical intellectual endowment. This may be because the full 'potential' in the former case can only be expressed when the individual's propensities are effectively matched with specific instructional and learning opportunities. Individual differences are relevant here as one considers how the same method of instruction or learning opportunity (e.g. highly visually stimulating) may be enriching for one child and distracting to another (Horowitz & Haritos 1998). Drawing a parallel between intellectually disabled and gifted children highlights the importance of considering atypicality (in all its forms) as a unique circumstance requiring special attention. It also illustrates that genetic endowment (whether deemed favourable or unfavourable by society) is not expressed phenotypically in a prescribed fashion but rather is embedded with an environmental context that can be quite varied (Horowitz & Haritos 1998).

It is now well recognized that the relation between genes and environments is collaborative; environments cannot be viewed as merely triggering factors in development, but rather, as essential components of development. Similarly, genes may be responsible for protein regulation, but the expression of their products is inextricably linked to the structured developmental systems that they serve (Flint 1999). Thus, the genotype–phenotype connection may be characterized as both deterministic and probabilistic. The interesting questions for developmental researchers are: *How* does this dynamic process unfold over time?; *What* aspects are more or less flexible (or elastic in keeping with the rubber band analogy)?; and *When* is the best time to intervene? For example, the intellectual disability that results from phenylketonuria (PKU) – a genetic mutation that leads to a lack of, or deficiency of, the enzyme that is needed to process an amino acid called phenylalanine – may be largely prevented but only when the intervention (i.e. phenylalanine free diet) is introduced early after the child's birth (Elhawary et al. 2022). Here, the potential for the expression of intellectual disability is high (genetic mutation) unless a specifically tailored intervention (i.e. diet) is introduced at a particular time in development (birth). Exact information of this kind is rarely available; however, it is precisely this level of detail that is needed to make behavioural genetic research useful to practitioners. Future research might entail the search for cognitive and behavioural mediators and moderators of developmental pathways between genes and environments and the outcome of low IQ. Although little is known about the intervening processes that operate between genes and the outcome of intellectual disability, the empirical evidence suggests that genetic influences on IQ are relatively non-specific and operate throughout development. Atypical gene processes are influenced by interactions with other genes in age specific ways and affect several different pathways, which in turn, lead to outcomes that interact downstream (Plomin 1999b; Lickliter & Honeycutt 2003). Genes determine the tissue-specific regulation of proteins involved in controlling the phenotype, but the expression of genes is routinely affected and/or modified by the local cellular and extracellular environments as well as by other genes (Lickliter & Honeycutt 2003).

We now turn to a discussion on epigenetics, a compelling example of the interplay between genes and environment, specifically how genes may be regulated by external input from the environment.

EPIGENETICS: ENVIRONMENTAL INPUT ON GENE REGULATION

Epigenetics refers to *externally (to genes)* elicited modifications that turn genes 'on' or 'off'. Although modifications do not change the DNA sequence within genes, they affect how cells 'read' genes, thus, changing or regulating gene function via the amount of protein that is produced by a person's cells. For example, the strands of chromatin that contain genetic information can unwind or coil more tightly and interact with other proteins to turn specific genes on and off. There are three well-known epigenetic mechanisms:

1 DNA methylation – the addition of a methyl group, or a 'chemical cap,' to part of the DNA molecule, which prevents certain genes from being expressed.
2 histone modification – histones are proteins that DNA wraps around. Without histones, DNA would be too long to fit inside cells. Thus, with fewer histones the DNA may become too long and thus, cannot be 'read' by the cell. However, modifications that relax the histones can make the DNA accessible to proteins that 'read' genes and, therefore, these genes would be more likely to be expressed.

3 small interfering RNA – a process that can suppress the activity of specific genes, causing changes in gene transcription and translation. This mechanism may be involved in gene expression in **Fragile X syndrome**, Down syndrome, and Tuberous Sclerosis. These epigenetic modifications occur, in part, because of certain environmental conditions or changes in the environment. Thus, epigenetic mechanisms provide a clear example of the role of environment modulating gene expression.

Many neurodevelopmental disabilities are associated with an increase in prenatal, perinatal, and postnatal environmental risk. Thus, it is important to consider the possible epigenetic mechanisms involved in these disabilities so that we can better understand the nature of the risks and take steps to prevent or intervene early. There is now research linking atypical epigenetic processes to several developmental disabilities including Prader Willi syndrome, Angelman's syndrome, Fragile X syndrome, and autism spectrum disorder (Gropman & Batshaw 2010; Hall & Kelly 2014). Genomic imprinting is a natural epigenetic mechanism in which the activity of the gene is modified depending on the sex of the transmitting parent. Typically, we inherit two complete sets of chromosomes (alleles), one from the mother and the other from the father. Most genes (except those on the sex chromosomes) are expressed in

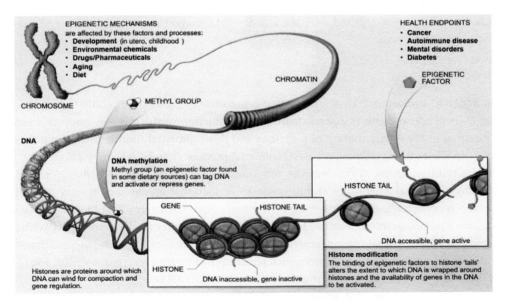

Figure 2.5 The location of epigenetic changes within chromosomes, depicting direct methylation of DNA or the histones that bind to the DNA sequence.

Source: National Institute of Health / Public domain

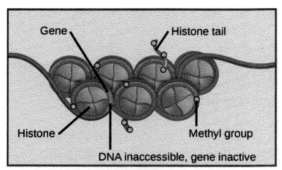
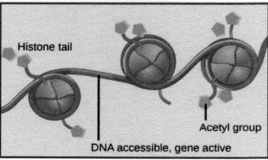

Figure 2.6 Methylation (top) and acetylation (bottom) of histones cause the packing and unpacking of DNA strands.

Source: CNX OpenStax / CC-BY 4.0

both maternal and paternal alleles. Imprinted genes show expression from only one allele (the other is silenced), and this is determined during production of the **gamete**. Imprinted genes are essential in the differentiation of functions and developmental timing, thus, if expression from both alleles is not maintained, developmental processes can be adversely affected.

Prader-Willi syndrome (PWS) was the first human imprinting condition discovered. It is caused by a paternal deletion in chromosome 15 or maternal uniparental disomy (UPD) (in which both chromosome 15s come from the mother). Approximately 75% of individuals with PWS have a particular microdeletion, 15q11.2–q13. One per cent of individuals with PWS have a detectable chromosomal rearrangement resulting in a deletion of 15q11.2-q13. Less than 1% of individuals have a balanced chromosomal rearrangement with breakpoints within 15q11.2-q13. Less than 5% have an imprinting defect, and 20% have UPD.

Angelman's syndrome (AS) involves a microdeletion of chromosome 15q11.2-q13 that affects the UBE3A gene, which encodes ubiquitin protein ligase E3A. This enzyme is involved in targeting proteins for degradation within cells. Both copies of the UBE3A gene are active in most of the body's tissues, but in the brain only the maternal copy is normally active. If this copy is mutated or missing, it affects many developmental processes. Most cases of AS occur when part of the maternal copy is missing or damaged. In a few cases, AS is caused when two paternal copies of the gene are inherited, instead of one from each parent.

Fragile X is the most common inherited cause of intellectual disability. Nearly all cases of Fragile X are caused by a mutation in which a DNA segment is unusually long (i.e. the number of cytosine-guanine-guanine (CGG) triplet repeats) within the FMR1 gene (fragile X intellectual disability protein gene). Inheritance of the instability in CGG regions leads to expansion from the normal number of repeats (6–40) to a premutation state (50–200) or from a premutation state to full mutation (>200 repeats). The full mutation state, in people with Fragile X, results in hypermethylation of the promoter region of the FMR1 gene. This has the effect of turning off (silencing – prevents transcription and translation) the *FMR1* gene, effectively preventing the gene from producing Fragile X Mental Retardation Protein (FMRP). The loss or shortage of this protein disrupts nervous system functions and leads to the signs and symptoms of Fragile X syndrome. The increasing likelihood of CGG expansion from one generation to another is a phenomenon referred to as anticipation.

The known genetic causes of autism (e.g. autism in PWS, AS, and Fragile X) only account for 10–20% of cases. However, the majority of autism cases are likely polygenic and involve multiple genes that interact with environmental factors. There is growing evidence that epigenetic processes may be involved in the expression of autism and that the interplay between genes and environment may better capture the complex reality of autism (Hall & Kelley 2014; Tordjman et al. 2014). There are two compelling examples of epigenetic processes in the **aetiology** of autism. Both of these involve foetal exposure to **teratogens** during the prenatal period. For example, mothers who used valproate (an anticonvulsant drug used in seizures, bipolar disorder, or migraine headaches) (Newschaffer et al. 2007; Bromley et al. 2013), or thalidomide (Stromland, Nordin, Miller, Akerstrom, & Gillberg 1994) during pregnancy were more likely to have an autistic child as compared to mothers who did not use these substances. Valproate is known to affect histone modification and DNA de-methylation. Perinatal complications such as hypoxia and low birth weight and postnatal factors such as maternal depression, severe social deprivation, and severe sensory deprivation (visually or hearing impaired) are also associated with an increased likelihood of autism. However, no pre-, peri, or postnatal factor on its own has been consistently shown to confer increased likelihood of autism. Thus, it is likely that autism emerges due to an interactive effect that involves a combination of genetic and environmental factors.

There are several environmental factors (e.g. drugs, stress, social and sensory deprivation) implicated in epigenetic modifications (Grafodatskaya et al. 2010; Dominguez-Sala et al. 2014) and the epigenetic effects may be passed down to the next generation if they occur in the germline (see YouTube for a demonstration: https://www.youtube.com/watch?v=kp1bZEUgqVI) (Chong & Whitelaw 2004; Kaati, Bygren, Pembrey, & Sjostrom 2007). Although epigenetic mechanisms were originally considered irreversible, recent studies suggest that they are dynamic and can be reversed even in fully differentiated cells such as neurons (Graff et al. 2012). Thus, the study of epigenetic mechanisms involved in developmental disabilities holds great promise for identifying ways to prevent or reduce the risk of poor developmental outcomes.

POLICY IMPLICATIONS OF GENE-ENVIRONMENT INTERACTIONS

The nature–nurture controversy and the related contentious debate over whether to allocate more resources to bio-medical research or educational, social, and rehabilitation efforts (Doris 1970) have been particularly lively in the field of developmental disability. However, rather than create a false dichotomy between genetics and behavioural research, a shared focus of research should be how genetic and environmental influences maintain or support developmental trajectories. Plomin (1999a) considers behavioural genetics research on cognitive abilities as extending the discourse beyond issues of simple heritability to questions about development, about multivariate relations among specific cognitive abilities, and about the interplay between nature and nurture.

This extends to the relative influences of genetic factors and shared and **non-shared environments** that can vary throughout the lifespan. Genetic factors are clearly important for IQ throughout the lifespan, but the role of environment changes: the effects of shared environment are weak in childhood and decline to negligible levels in adulthood, and non-shared environmental effects increase with age (Plomin 2000). However, the notion of age-to-age continuity among persons with familial intellectual disability needs to be explored. More specifically, research on siblings' experiences is needed to assess the extent to which certain aspects of the environment are shared and others are not. Research on more dynamic aspects of non-shared environment revealed that siblings growing up in the same family perceive their parents' treatment of them quite differently, although parents report that they treat their children similarly (Dunn & Plomin 1990). The children's perspective appears to be supported by observational data (Plomin 1994). A question that may be particularly pertinent for children with intellectual disability concerns the extent to which parental skills and expectations are shared by siblings with and without intellectual disability in the same family.

As children with intellectual disability enter school and as they move towards adolescence, non-shared experiences outside the family may be even more influential. Siblings do not experience the same peers, social support, or life events and these diverse experiences along with genetic makeup contribute to different developmental paths (Plomin 1994). Thus, small differences in experience, over time, may have widespread and cumulative effects that can lead to large differences in long-term outcome (Plomin 1999a, 1999b). Although genetic factors are known to contribute to measures of family environment, their association with intellectual disability and the functional relations between child specific familial and nonfamilial (e.g. peers) sources of variation in experiences need to be identified. A better integration of genetic and environmental levels of understanding of cognitive development is needed in order to exploit genetic discoveries associated with low IQ and developmental disability (Flint 1999).

PRENATAL GENETIC SCREENING AND DIAGNOSIS IN INTELLECTUAL DISABILITY

Genetic screening for developmental disability is a controversial issue in the field of genetics and intellectual disability, with ethical, political, social, and personal ramifications. With the growing public access to genetic information, and the technological advances that now make it possible to reliably screen for developmental disabilities such as Fragile X and Down syndrome, ethical considerations abound (Raymond 2003). Of potential concern is that prenatal screening and diagnostic testing may more frequently lead to a decision to terminate the pregnancy when an abnormality is detected (Benn & Chapman 2010). However, the choice to have prenatal screening or diagnosis is different for every caregiver and may not necessarily result in the termination of the pregnancy (Acharya 2011) but may be an important factor in decision-making for those considering their options.

Technological advances in genetic screening have spurred controversy in the areas of ethical and policy decision making. Critiques of the genetic screening for developmental disabilities are centred around the issue of informed consent. Currently, screening for certain conditions such as DS are freely available and conducted almost routinely for women over 40 years of age. A prevailing concern among disability advocates is that routinizing the process of screening renders the individual's right to informed consent tenuous because the future parent(s) does not have the opportunity to reflect on whether they should have the screening in the first place and, if so, what to do once the screening results are provided to them. Disability advocates argue that there are persuasive pressures on choice through the very offer of screening tests. There are difficulties of opting out of the process. For example, the future parent(s) may not know that they can say no to screening when it is offered as part of a routine ultrasound. During the screening procedures medical professionals lack the time to properly discuss options with the future parent(s) and this leads to decisions being made with limited information. There is also the recognition that societal attitudes toward disability may be negatively skewed: that is, many aspects of disability are socially constructed and currently, in industrialized societies the focus is on the negative aspects of having a developmental disability, negative aspects which are often caused or exacerbated by inaccessibility, inadequate supports, and discrimination. Rarely is the future parent(s) provided with information about a particular disability that is nuanced and fully captures the risks but also the potential resilience of persons with disabilities. Advocates have suggested that perhaps a new kind of genetic counsellor is needed with a dual focus on the functional aspects of genetic conditions and family life with genetic disabilities.

Who should be involved in policy decisions regarding genetic screening? In a democratic society, only the biological parents (most often the biological mother) have the right and the burden of making decisions about genetic screening and termination of the pregnancy. However, advocates have called for a broad representation of stakeholders to be involved in social decisions about prenatal tests, because the potential impact of policy concerning prenatal testing is significant for many but also has broader implications on society. For example, we are often faced with decisions wherein we must balance individual rights and social benefit and, therefore, we must stipulate explicitly under which conditions screening would be prohibited bearing in mind the longer-term consequences for our society/species (e.g. for selecting the sex of the offspring) (Shakespeare 1999).

Considering the values of a democratic society such as the rights of women and parental right and autonomy, the pertinent question may not be whether to, but rather how to, provide genetic information to potential caregivers. One important consideration would be on what basis we make a decision to screen. The response may vary depending on whom we ask (Williams, Alderson, & Farsides 2002). From a medical practitioner's perspective, it may not be helpful to screen for a condition that cannot be treated or prevented. Parents may be more concerned with avoiding physical and emotional pain and suffering for their future child. Social values may dictate that there be freedom of choice or that the rights of the child be protected. Research evidence may be used to help us determine the prevalence, severity, and accuracy of screening techniques to aid in decision making (Williams, Alderson, & Farsides 2002). However, the decision to screen or not to screen ultimately depends on how helpful the information provided will be to the decisions that the future caregivers will have to make. Will they opt for prenatal screening in order to help inform on the termination of pregnancy or psychological preparation for an affected child, or forgo the genetic screening and accept the care of the child regardless of the outcome (Raymond 2003)?

Prenatal screening tests are not usually confirmatory, and even when they are conclusive, they cannot inform on the severity of the condition, so fully informing potential caregivers of this limitation is essential (Raymond 2003). In addition, there is often confusion between prenatal screening and diagnosis; the risks associated with each and the potential information that each will contribute to decision making.

The inclusion of persons with disabilities in debates has been largely overlooked, yet is seen as essential in matters that concern screening for specific disabilities: 'disabled people, not doctors, are the real experts on disability, because of their personal experience of living with impairments' (Shakespeare 1999: 685). As members of society and persons with personal experience on the disability they have a unique vantage point on issues that are particularly relevant to the genetic screening process. It is also critical that we consider the effects that prenatal screening policies and decisions have on disabled people, such as: reducing the availability of targeted supports; increasing societal stigma; removing their opportunity to be part of a community of like-minded people; and internalizing the view that you are unworthy of existence.

Advocates have argued that genetic counsellors need to take a more nuanced approach to discussions about positive screening results. For example, 'a wider discussion which includes what are available options, treatment, what the outlook is, where one can make predictions about that for an individual condition, that presents the family with a range of options that aren't focused solely on avoidance of the genetic disease' (Shakespeare 1999).

Screening and Diagnosis

Screening is typically used to identify anyone at risk for a particular condition from a group of individuals who are healthy or asymptomatic. When screening mothers at greater risk for having a child with a developmental disability such as Down syndrome, usually the group is a subset of women who are over the age of 40 years and at greater likelihood of having a child with DS. Here, the goal is to identify those mothers who have indicators that their fetus may have DS. The Triple Screen test is one type of screening for DS conducted during the second trimester between 15 and 20 weeks. The Triple Screen measures the levels of three important substances in the placenta: alpha-fetoprotein (AFP), human chorionic gonadotropin (HCG), and estriol. The former is a protein produced by the foetus and the latter two are pregnancy-produced hormones in the mother's blood. During the second trimester, the levels of AFP and estriol increase and the amount of HCG decreases. Thus, when the Triple Screen is positive for DS, the results tend to show decreased levels of AFP and estriol and increased levels of HCG.

Detection Rate

The detection rate of a test is also called the test's sensitivity. It is the chance of screening positive (increased risk) when the baby is truly affected with a condition. Thus, it reflects the ability of the screening tool to accurately detect the pregnancies that are affected with the condition. For example, 100 people are affected with a condition, and a screening test correctly identifies 95 of them as having the condition, then the test would have a 95% detection rate.

False Positive

A false positive is a false alarm. The false positive rate is the number of women who screen positive (increased risk) when they are actually carrying unaffected babies. If you have 100 people who are unaffected, and 30 of these people incorrectly screen as having the condition when in fact they are unaffected, then the test would have a 30% false positive rate.

Positive Predictive Value

The positive predictive value (PPV) is a measure of the reliability of a screen positive result.

It is the chance that a positive screen is correct; of all the women who screen positive, it is the number of women who actually have an affected pregnancy. For example, a screening test with a PPV of $1/2$ (50%) is better than a screening test with a PPV of $1/4$ (25%). With a PPV of $1/2$ (50%), half of the individuals screening at increased risk on a screening test will truly be affected with the condition. Whereas with a PPV of $1/4$ (25%), only one-quarter of individuals screening at increased risk will truly be affected with the condition. A higher PPV means that fewer individuals will be caused unnecessary worry from falsely labelled at risk for the condition.

Thus, the ideal screening tool would have the following properties:

- high sensitivity
- low false positive rate
- high positive predictive value

The results of the screening guide the doctor in determining whether or not to ask for a diagnostic test to confirm or rule out a condition. A positive screening test indicates the possibility that the foetus may have the suspected condition, and this can then be confirmed by a diagnostic test such as an amniocentesis. Amniocentesis is an example of a diagnostic test. It is typically performed at 15–20 weeks gestation. The amniotic fluid contains foetal skin cells that can be used to perform a karyotype of the foetus' chromosomal array. Once the chromosomes are visualized the doctor can detect whether there is an additional chromosome 21 as in DS.

Accurate and well-balanced information is critical for informed decision making. Wertz (2000) suggested that genetic counselors may be more effective if they had a dual focus that included a discussion on the functional aspects of the genetic condition but also on what family life with the developmental disability would be like. However, the timing of this discussion is also critical and needs to be considered with regard to the particular family's situation and preference. Further, the inclusion of disabled voices provides the essential perspective from those with lived experience for a more balanced approach to the relaying genetic screening/diagnostic information to potential caregivers.

With increasing technological advances, genetic screening will be more sophisticated, readily accessible and less costly. However, other ethical, political, social, and personal challenges will remain. What is becoming clear is that we will need to consider how best to disseminate genetic information to potential stakeholders in a way that is balanced and respectful, considering the many perspectives. In addition, professionals will need to be well informed and carefully relay the caveat that screeners and diagnostic tests are just tools (with associated risks and limitations) and provide the family with the comprehensive information needed to make an informed decision for their future.

SUMMARY

A person's genotype is fixed in terms of the genes that one inherits from each biological parent, but, malleable in terms of the function of those genes. The function is determined by environmental factors that regulate genes through epigenetic processes that either increase or restrict gene function and timing. The interaction between genotype and environment is *bidirectional*. Developmental outcomes such as intelligence are not predetermined but, rather, have a *reaction range,* meaning that the interaction between one's genotype and potential environments establishes a range of possible developmental outcomes (e.g. intellectual disability). In the case of an organic anomaly (e.g. Down syndrome's extra chromosome 21) the individual's genotype sets substantial constraints on development, however, specialized and targeted interventions tailored to the individual's needs may have widespread and cumulative effects over time that can lead to large positive differences in long-term outcome. As genetic screening becomes more sophisticated, readily accessible and less costly in the future, we must consider how best to disseminate genetic information to potential stakeholders in a way that is balanced and respectful of the many perspectives. For families, understanding the distinction between screeners and diagnostic tests, as well as their associated risks and limitations, will help them make an informed decision.

Reflective Exercises

1. Discuss genotype-environment correlations and give an example of reactive, evocative and proactive interaction from your childhood.
2. Describe Gottesman's concept of 'reaction range' and Horowitz and Haritos' 'purposely engineered opportunities for learning' and discuss how they may be related.
3. Explain the parallel between intellectually disabled and gifted individuals.
4. How does the study of epigenetics help us identify ways to prevent or reduce the risk of poor developmental outcomes?
5. Discuss how genetic screening poses challenges for ethical, political, social and personal decision making.
6. Discuss the difference between screening and diagnostic tests and how you might present this information to potential parents.
7. If you were considering genetic screening for your foetus, what information would you need to know and why?

Recommended Videos

See this video on Epigenetics:

https://www.youtube.com/watch?v=kp1bZEUgqVI

See this video on Prader Willi and imprinting genes:

https://www.youtube.com/watch?v=8CKN6idlE80

See this TED talk on DS and medical professionals:

https://www.youtube.com/watch?v=x16wGajCHIw

REFERENCES

Acharya, K. (2011) Prenatal testing for intellectual disability: Misperceptions and reality with lessons from down syndrome, *Developmental Disabilities Research Reviews, 17*(1), 27–31.

Akesson, H. O. (1984). Intelligence and polygenic inheritance. A dogma to re-examine. *Acta Paediatr Scand, 73*(1), 13–17.

Akesson, H. O. (1986). The biological origin of mild intellectual disability. A critical review. *Acta Psychiatr Scand, 74*(1), 3–7.

Ball, D., Hill, L., Eley, T. C., Chorney, M. J., Chorney, K., Thompson, L. A., Detterman, D. K., Benbow, C., Lubinski, D., Owen, M., McGuffin, P., & Plomin, R. (1998). Dopamine markers and general cognitive ability. *Neuroreport, 9*(2), 347–349.

Bell, R. Q. (1968). A reinterpretation of the direction of effects in studies of socialization. *Psychological Review, 75*(2), 81–95. https://doi.org/10.1037/h0025583

Benn, P. A., & Chapman, A. R. (2010). Ethical challenges in providing noninvasive prenatal diagnosis. *Current Opinion in Obstetrics and Gynecology, 22*(2), 128–134.

Bishop, E. G., Cherny, S. S., Corley, R., Plomin, R., DeFries, J. C., & Hewitt, J. K. (2003). Development genetic analysis of general cognitive ability from 1 to 12 years in a sample of adoptees, biological siblings, and twins. *Intelligence, 31*(1), 31–49.

Bouchard, T. J., Jr., & McGue, M. (1981). Familial studies of intelligence: a review. *Science, 212*(4498), 1055–1059.

Broman, S., Nichols, P. L., Shaughnessy, P., & Kennedy, W. (1987). *Retardation in Young Children: A Developmental Study of Cognitive Deficit.* Hillsdale, NJ: Erlbaum.

Bromley R. L. et al. (2013). The prevalence of neurodevelopmental disorders in children prenatally exposed to antiepileptic drugs. *J Neurol Neurosurg Psychiatry, 84*(6), 637–643.

Bronfenbrenner, U. (1979). Contexts of child rearing: Problems and prospects. *American Psychologist, 34*(10), 844–850. https://doi.org/10.1037/0003-066X.34.10.844

Brown, R. I. (2000). Quality of life: Challenges and confrontation. In K. D. Keith & R. L. Schalock (ed)., *Cross-cultural Perspectives on Quality of Life* (pp. 347–361). Washington, DC, US: American Association on Intellectual Disability.

Burack, J. A. (1990). Differentiating intellectual disability: The two group approach and beyond. In J. A. Burack, R. M. Hodapp, & E. Zigler (ed.), *Issues in the Developmental Approach to Intellectual Disability* (pp. 27–48). New York: Cambridge University Press.

Burack, J. A. (1997). The study of atypical and typical populations in developmental psychopathology: The quest for a common science. In S. Luthar, J.A. Burack, D. Cicchetti and J.R. Weisz (ed.), *Developmental Psychopathology: Perspectives on adjustment, risk and disorder* (pp. 139–165). New York: Cambridge University Press.

Burack, J. A., Hodapp, R. M., & Zigler, E. (1988). Issues in the classification of intellectual disability: differentiating among organic etiologies. *J Child Psychol Psychiatry, 29*(6), 765–779.

Burack, J. A., Hodapp, R. M., & Zigler, E. (1990). Technical note: Toward a more precise understanding of intellectual disability. *Journal of Child Psychology and Psychiatry, 31*, 471–475.

Burack, J. A., Hodapp, R. M., & Zigler, E. (1998). *Handbook of Intellectual Disability and Development.* New York: Cambridge University Press.

Carr, J. (2000). Intellectual and daily living skills of 30-year-olds with Down's syndrome: Continuation of a longitudinal study. *Journal of Applied Research in Intellectual Disabilities, 13*(1), 1–16.

Cherny, S. S., Fulker, D. W., & Hewitt, J. K. (1997). Cognitive development from infancy to middle childhood. In R. J. Sternberg & E. L. Grigorenko (eds), *Intelligence: Heredity and Environment.* Cambridge: Cambridge University Press.

Chong, S., & Whitelaw, E. (2004). Epigenetic germline inheritance. *Current Opinion in Genetics & Development, 14,* 692–696.

Chorney, M. J., Chorney, K., Seese, N., & et al. (1998). A quantitative trait locus (QTL) associated wtih cognitive ability in children. *Psychological Science, 9,* 1–8.

Cicchetti, D., & Toth, S. L. (1997). Transactional ecological systems in developmental psychopathology. In S. S. Luthar, J. A. Burack, D. Cicchetti, & J. R. Weisz (Eds.), *Developmental psychopathology: Perspectives on adjustment, risk, and disorder* (pp. 317–349). Cambridge University Press.

Cicchetti, D., & M. Beeghly (eds) (1990). *Children with Down Syndrome: A Developmental Perspective.* New York: Cambridge University Press.

Cicchetti, D. (1984). The emergence of developmental psychopathology. *Child Development, 55*(1), 1–7. https://doi.org/10.2307/1129830

Cicchetti, D., Pogge-Hesse, P. (1982). Possible contributions of organically retarded persons to developmental theory. In E. Zigler & D. Balla (ed.), *Intellectual Disability: The Developmental-Difference Controversy.* Hillsdale, NJ: Erlbaum Associates.

Cicchetti, D., & Sroufe, L. A. (1976). The relationship between affective and cognitive development in Down's Syndrome infants. *Child Dev, 47*(4), 920–929.

Clarke et al. (2015). Common polygenic risk for autism spectrum disorder (ASD) is associated with cognitive ability in the general population, *Molecular Psychiatry, 21,* 419–425.

Cooley, W. C., & Graham, J. M., Jr (1991). Down syndrome--an update and review for the primary pediatrician. *Clinical pediatrics, 30*(4), 233–253. https://doi.org/10.1177/000992289103000407

Corder, E. H., Saunders, A. M., Strittmatter, W. J., Schmechel, D. E., Gaskell, P. C., Small, G. W., Roses, A. D., Haines, J. L., & Pericak-Vance, M. A. (1993). Gene dose of apolipoprotein E type 4 allele and the risk of Alzheimer's disease in late onset families. *Science, 261,* 921–923.

de Graaf, G., Buckley, F., & Skotko, B. G. (2015). Estimates of the live births, natural losses, and elective terminations with Down syndrome in the United States. *American Journal of Medical Genetics. Part A, 167A*(4), 756–767. doi:10.1002/ajmg.a.37001

Detterman, D. K., Thompson, L. A., & Plomin, R. (1990). Differences in heritability across groups differing in ability. *Behaviour Genetics, 20,* 369–384.

Dingman, H. F., & Tarjan, G. (1960). Mental retardation and the normal distribution curve. *American Journal of Mental Deficiency, 64,* 991–994.

Dominguez-Salas et al. (2014). Maternal nutrition at conception modulates DNA methylation of human metastable epialleles, *Nat Commun, 5,* 3746.

Doris, J. (1970). Science, action, and values in familial retardation. *Journal of Special Education, 4*(2), 161–170.

Dunn, J., & Plomin, R. (1990). *Separate Lives: Why Siblings Are So Different.* New York: Basic Books.

Dykens E. M, Hodapp R. M, & Evans D. W (2006). Profiles and development of adaptive behavior in children with Down syndrome. *Down Syndrome Research and Practice. 9*(3), 45–50.

Dykens, E. M., Hodapp, R. M., & Finucane, B. (2000). *Genetics and Intellectual Disability Syndromes: A New Look at Behavior and Intervention.* Baltimore: Brookes.

Elhawary, N.A., AlJahdali, I.A., Abumansour, I.S., et al. (2022). Genetic etiology and clinical challenges of phenylketonuria. *Hum Genomics*, 16(22). https://doi.org/10.1186/s40246-022-00398-9.

Fenson, L., Dale, P. S., Reznick, J. S., Bates, E., Thal, D. J., & Pethick, S. J. (1994). Variability in early communicative development. *Monographs of the Society for Research in Child Development*, 59(5), 1–173.

Fischer, K. W., & Bullock, D. (1984). Cognitive development in school-age children: Conclusions and new directions. In *Development during Middle Childhood* (pp. 70–146). Washington, DC: National Academy Press.

Fischer, K. W., Bullock, D. H., Rotenberg, E. J., & Raya, P., (1993). The dynamics of competence: How context contributes directly to skill. Development in Context (93-117). Hillsdale, NJ: Erlbaum.

Fisher, R. A. *The Genetical Theory of Natural selection*. Oxford: Oxford University Press, 1930.

Flint, J., Corley, R., DeFries, J. C., Fulker, D. W., Gray, J. A., Miller, S., & Collins, A. C. (1995). A simple genetic basis for a complex psychological trait in laboratory mice. *Science*, 269(5229), 1432–1435.

Flint, J., Mott, R. Finding the molecular basis of quatitative traits: successes and pitfalls . *Nat Rev Genet*, 2, 437–445 (2001). https://doi.org/10.1038/35076585

Galton, F. (1889). Co-relations and their measurement, chiefly from anthropometric data. *Proc. Roy. Soc. London*, 45, 135–145.

Galton, F. (1883). Inquiries into human faculty and its development. MacMillan Co. https://doi.org/10.1037/14178-000.

Galton, F. (1869). *Hereditary genius: An inquiry into its laws and consequences*. Macmillan and Co. https://doi.org/10.1037/13474-000

Goodman, J. F. (1990). Problems in etiological classifications of intellectual disability. *J Child Psychol Psychiatry*, 31(3), 465–469.

Gostason, R. (1985). Psychiatric illness among the mentally retarded. A Swedish population study. *Acta Psychiatr Scand Suppl*, 318, 1–117.

Gottesman, I.I. (1963a). Genetic aspects of intelligent behavior. In N. R. Ellis (ed.), *Handbook of Mental Deficiency* (pp. 253–296). New York: McGraw-Hill Book Company, Inc.

Gottesman, I.I. (1963b). Heritability of personality: a demonstration. *Psychol Monogr*, 77(9), 1–21.

Gottesman, I. I., & Hanson, D. R. (2005). Human Development: Biological and Genetic Processes. *Annual Review of Psychology*, 56, 263–286. https://doi.org/10.1146/annurev.psych.56.091103.070208

Gottlieb, G. (1992). *Individual Development and Evolution*. Oxford, NY: Oxford University Press.

Gottlieb, G. (1995). Some conceptual deficiencies in "developmental" behavior genetics. *Human Development*, 38(3), 131–141. https://doi.org/10.1159/000278306

Gottlieb, G. (2003). On making behavioral genetics truly developmental. *Human Development*, 46(6), 337–355. https://doi.org/10.1159/000073306

Grados-Johnson, J., & Russo-Garcia, K. A. (1999). Comparison of the Kaufman Brief Intelligence Test and the Wechsler Intelligence Scale for Children-Third Edition in economically disadvantaged African American youth. *Journal of Clinical Psychology*, 55(9), 1063–1071.

Graff et al. (2012). An epigenetic blockade of cognitive functions in the neurodegenerating brain, *Nature, 483*(7388), 222–226.

Grafodatskaya, D., Chung, B., Szatmari, P., & Weksberg, R. (2010). Autism spectrum disorders and epigenetics. *Journal of the American Academy of Child and Adolescent Psychiatry, 49*(8), 794–809.

Griffiths, P. E., & Tabery, J. (2008). Behavioral genetics and development: historical and conceptual causes of controversy. *New Ideas in Psychology, 26*, 332–352.

Gropman, A., & Batshaw, M. (2010). Epigenetics, copy number variation, and other molecular mechanisms underlying neurodevelopmental disabilities: New insights and diagnostic approaches. *Journal of Developmental and Behavioral Pediatrics, 31*(1). https://hsrc.himmelfarb.gwu.edu/smhs_neuro_facpubs/794

Gusella, J. F., Wexler, N. S., Conneally, P. M., Naylor, S. L., Anderson, M. A., Tanzi, R. E., Watkins, P. C., Ottina, K., Wallace, M. R., Sakaguchi, A. Y., et al. (1983). A polymorphic DNA marker genetically linked to Huntington's disease. *Nature, 306*(5940), 234–238.

Hagberg, B., Hagberg, G., Lewerth, A., & Lindberg, U. (1981a). Mild intellectual disability in Swedish school children. I. Prevalence. *Acta Paediatr Scand, 70*(4), 441–444.

Hagberg, B., Hagberg, G., Lewerth, A., & Lindberg, U. (1981b). Mild intellectual disability in Swedish school children. II. Etiologic and pathogenetic aspects. *Acta Paediatr Scand, 70*(4), 445–452.

Hall, L., & Kelley, E. (2014). The contribution of epigenetics to understanding genetic factors in autism. *Autism, 18*(8), 872–881. https://doi.org/10.1177/1362361313503501

Hill, L., Chorney, M. J., Lubinski, D., Thompson, L. A., & Plomin, R. (2002). A quantitative trait locus not associated with cognitive ability in children: a failure to replicate. *Psychol Sci, 13*(6), 561–562.

Hodapp, R., & Zigler, E. (1997). New issues in the developmental approach to intellectual disability. In W. E. MacLean (ed.), *Ellis' Handbook of Mental Deficiency, Psychological Theory and Research, 3rd Edition*. New Jersey: Lawrence Earlbaum Associates, Inc.

Hodapp, R. M., & Dyckens, E. M. (1996). Intellectual disability. In E. J. Mash & R. A. Barkley (eds), *Child Psychopathology* (pp. 362–389). New York: Guildford.

Hodapp, R. M., & Zigler, E. (1990). Applying the developmental perspective to individuals with Down Syndrome. In D. Cicchetti & M. Beeghly (eds), *Children with Down Syndrome: A Developmental Perspective* (pp. 1–28). New York: Cambridge University Press.

Hodapp R. M. (2007). Families of persons with Down syndrome: New perspectives, findings, and research and service needs *Intellectual disability and Developmental Disabilities Research Reviews, 13*(3), 279–287.

Horowitz, F. D., & Haritos, C. (1998). The organism and the environment: Implications for understanding mental retardation. In J. A. Burack, R. M. Hodapp, & E. Zigler (Eds.), *Handbook of mental retardation and development* (pp. 20–40). New York: Cambridge University Press.

Iarocci, G., & Burack, J.A. (1998). Understanding the development of persons with intellectual disability: Challenging the myths. In J. A. Burack, R.M. Hodapp, & E. Zigler (ed.), *Handbook of Intellectual Disability and Development* (pp. 349–381). New York: Cambridge University Press.

Iarocci, G., Yager, J., & Elfers, T. (2007). What gene-environment interactions can tell us about social competence in typical and atypical populations. *Brain and Cognition*, *65*(1), 112–127. https://doi.org/10.1016/j.bandc.2007.01.008

Ireland, W. W. (1877). *On Idiocy and Imbecility*. London: J&A Churchill.

Kaati, G., Bygren, L.O., Pembrey, M., & Sjostrom, J. (2007). Transgenerational response to nutrition, early life circumstances and longevity. *European Journal of Human Genetics*, *15*, 784–790.

King, B. H., State, M. W., Shah, B., Davanzo, P., & Dykens, E., (1997). Intellectual disability: A review of the past 10 years. *Child and Adolescent Psychiatry*, 36(Part I), 1656–1663.

Knight, S. J., Regan, R., Nicod, A., Horsley, S. W., Kearney, L., Homfray, T., Winter, R. M., Bolton, P., & Flint, J. (1999). Subtle chromosomal rearrangements in children with unexplained intellectual disability. *Lancet*, *354*(9191), 1676–1681.

Lesch, K. P. (2004). Gene-environment interaction and the genetics of depression. *Journal of Psychiatry & Neuroscience*, *29*(3), 174–184.

Lettice, L. A., Horikoshi, T., Heaney, S. J. H., van Baren, M. J., van der Linde, H. C., Breedveld, G. J., et al. (2002). Disruption of a long-range cis-acting regulator for Shh causes preaxial polydactyly. *Proceedings of the National Academy of Sciences*, *99*(11), 7548–7553.

Lickliter, R., & Honeycutt, H. (2003). Developmental Dynamics: Toward a Biologically Plausible Evolutionary Psychology. *Psychological Bulletin*, *129*(6), 819–835. https://doi.org/10.1037/0033-2909.129.6.819

Lewis, A. (1934) Inheritance of mental disorders. In: Blacker, CP (ed.) *The Chances of Morbid Inheritance*. London: Lewis, 86–133.

Lickliter, R., & Honeycutt, H. (2003). Developmental Dynamics: Toward a Biologically Plausible Evolutionary Psychology. *Psychological Bulletin*, *129*(6), 819–835. https://doi.org/10.1037/0033-2909.129.6.819

MacMillan, D. L., Siperstein, G. N., & Gresham, F. M. (1996). A Challenge to the Viability of Mild Mental Retardation as a Diagnostic Category. *Exceptional Children*, *62*(4), 356–371. https://doi.org/10.1177/001440299606200405

McClearn, G. E., Johansson, B., Berg, S., Pedersen, N. L., Ahern, F., Petrill, S. A., & Plomin, R. (1997). Substantial genetic influence on cognitive abilities in twins 80 or more years old. *Science*, *276*(5318), 1560–1563.

McGue, M. (1997). The democracy of the genes. *Nature*, *388*(6641), 417–418.

McGue, M., Bouchard, T. J., Iacono, W. G., & Lykken, D. T. (1993). Behavioural genetics of cognitive ability: A life span perspective. In R. Plomin & G. E. McClearn (eds), *Nature, Nurture and Psychology* (pp. 59–76). Washington, DC: American Psychological Association.

Mervis, C. B. (1990). Early conceptual development of children with Down syndrome. In D. Cicchetti & M. Beeghly (Eds.), *Children with Down Syndrome: A Developmental Perspective* (pp. 252–301). chapter, Cambridge: Cambridge University Press.

Nadeau, J. H., & Frankel, W. N. (2000). The roads from phenotypic variation to gene discovery: mutagenesis versus QTLs. *Nat Genet*, *25*(4), 381–384.

Neisser, U., Boodoo, G., Bouchard, T. J., Jr., Boykin, A. W., Brody, N., Ceci, S. J., Halpern, D. F., Loehlin, J. C., Perloff, R., Sternberg, R. J., & Urbina, S. (1996). Intelligence: Knowns and unknowns. *American Psychologist*, *51*(2), 77–101. https://doi.org/10.1037/0003-066X.51.2.77

Newschaffer, C. J., Croen, L. A., Daniels, J., Giarelli, E., Grether, J. K., Levy, S. E., Mandell, D. S., Miller, L. A., Pinto-Martin, J., Reaven, J., Reynolds, A. M., Rice, C. E., Schendel, D., & Windham, G. C. (2007). The epidemiology of autism spectrum disorders. *Annual review of public health*, *28*, 235–258. https://doi.org/10.1146/annurev.publhealth.28.021406.144007

Nichols, P. L. (1984). Familial intellectual disability. *Behav Genet*, *14*(3), 161–170.

Patterson, G. R. (1995). Coercion as a basis for early age of onset for arrest. In J. McCord (Ed.), *Coercion and punishment in long-term perspectives* (pp. 81–105). Cambridge University Press. https://doi.org/10.1017/CBO9780511527906.005

Pearson, K., & Jaederholm, G. A. (1914). *On the Continuity of Mental Defect*. London: Dalau & Co.

Penrose, L. S. (1954). Distance, size and shape. *Ann. Eugen. 18*: 337–343.

Penrose, L. S. (1963). Measurements of likeness in relatives of trisomics. *Annals of Human Genetics*, *27*(2), 183–187.

Penrose, L. S. (1970). Measurement in mental deficiency. *British Journal of Psychiatry*, *116*(533), 369–375.

Perrett, D. I., Hietanen, J. K., Oram, M. W., & Benson, P. J. (1992). Organization and functions of cells responsive to faces in the temporal cortex. *Philosophical transactions of the royal society of London. Series B: Biological sciences*, *335*(1273), 23–30.

Petrill, S. A., Ball, D. M., Eley, T. C., et al. (1998). Failure to replicate a QTL association between a DNA marker identified by EST00083 and IQ. *Intelligence*, *25*, 179–184.

Petrill, S. A., Johansson, B., Pedersen, N. L., Berg, S., Plomin, R., Ahern, F., & McClearn, G. E. (2001). Low cognitive functioning in nondemented 80+ year old twins is not heritable. *Intelligence*, *29*, 31–43.

Petrill, S. A., Saudino, K., Cherny, S. S., Emde, R. N., Hewitt, J. K., Fulker, D. W., & Plomin, R. (1997). Exploring the genetic etiology of low general cognitive ability from 14 to 36 months. *Dev Psychol*, *33*(3), 544–548.

Plomin, R. (1993). Nature and nurture: Perspective and prospective. In R. Plomin & G. E. McClearn (eds), *Nature, Nurture, and Psychology* (pp. 457–483). Washington, DC: American Psychological Association.

Plomin, R., (1994). Genetic research and identification of environmental influences. *Journal of Child Psychology and Psychiatry*, *35*, 817–834.

Plomin, R. (1999a). Genetic research on general cognitive ability as a model for mild intellectual disability. *Int Rev Psychiatr*, *11*, 34–36.

Plomin, R. (1999b). Genetics and general cognitive ability. *Nature*, *402*(6761 Suppl), C25–29.

Plomin, R. (2000). Quantitative trait loci (QTLs) and general cognitive ability ('g'). In J. Benjamin, R. Ebstein, & R. H. Belmaker (eds), *Molecular Genetics of Human Personality*. Washington, D.C.: American Psychiatric Publishing, Inc.

Plomin, R. (2002). Quantitative trait loci and general cognitive ability. In J. Benjamin, R. Ebstein, & R. H. Belmaker (eds), *Molecular Genetics and the Human Personality*. Washington, DC: American Psychiatric Publishing, Inc.

Plomin, R., & Craig, I. (1997). Human behavioural genetics of cognitive abilities and disabilities. *Bioessays*, *19*(12), 1117–1124.

Plomin, R., DeFries, R., McClearn, J. C., et al. (2001). *Behavioral Genetics*. New York: Worth Publishers.

Plomin, R., McClearn, G. E., Smith, D. L., et al. (1995). Allelic associations between 100 DNA markers and high versus low IQ. *Intelligence, 21*, 31–48.

Plomin, R., McClearn, G. E., Smith, D. L., Vignetti, S., Chorney, M. J., Chorney, K., Venditti, C. P., Kasarda, S., Thompson, L. A., Detterman, D. K., et al. (1994). DNA markers associated with high versus low IQ: the IQ Quantitative Trait Loci (QTL) Project. *Behav Genet, 24*(2), 107–118.

Plomin, R., & Neiderhiser, J. M. (1991). Quantitative genetics, molecular genetics and intelligence. *Intelligence, 15*, 39–387.

Plomin, R., & Petrill, S. A. (1997). Genetics and intelligence: What's new? *Intelligence, 24*(1), 53–77. https://doi.org/10.1016/S0160-2896(97)90013-1

Plomin, R., & Rutter, M. (1998). Child development, molecular genetics, and what to do with genes once they are found. *Child Dev, 69*(4), 1223–1242.

Plomin, R. (2000). Behavioural genetics in the 21st century. *International Journal of Behavioral Development, 24*(1), 30–34. https://doi.org/10.1080/016502500383449

Rao, J. M. (1996). A population-based study of mild mental handicap in children. Preliminary analysis of bostetric associations. *Journal of Mental Deficiency Research, 34*, 59–65.

Raymond, F. (2003). Genetic services for people with disabilities and their families. *Journal of intellectual disability research: JIDR. 47.* 509–14. 10.1046/j.1365-2788.2003.00529.x.

Raynham, H., Gibbons, R., Flint, J., & Higgs, D. (1996). The genetic basis for intellectual disability. *Qjm, 89*(3), 169–175.

Reed, E. W., & Reed, S. C. (1965). *Intellectual Disability: A Family Study*. Philadelphia: Saunders.

Rhodes, S. (2013). Theories of Child development [Powerpoint]. Retrieved from https://slideplayer.com/slide/11143669/

Richardson, S. A., & Koller, H. (1996). *Twenty-Two Years: Causes and Consequences of Intellectual Disability*. Cambridge: Harvard University Press.

Richardson, S. A., Koller, H., & Katz, M. (1985). Relationship of upbringing to later behavior disturbance of mildly mentally retarded young people. *American Journal of Mental Deficiency, 90*(1), 1–8.

Risch, N., & Merikangas, K. (1996). The future of genetic studies of complex human diseases. *Science, 273*, 1516–1517.

Roberts, J. A., Norman, R. M., & Griffiths, R. (1938). Studies on a child population. IV. The form of the lower end of the frequency distribution of Stanford-Binet intelligence quotients with advancing age. *Ann. Eugen. (London), 8*, 319.

Roubertoux, P. L., & Le Roy-Duflos, I. (2001). Quantitative trait locus mapping: fishing strategy or replicable results? *Behavior Genetics, 31*(1), 141–148.

Rutter, M., Simonoff, E., & Plomin, R. (1996). Genetic influences on mild intellectual disability: concepts, findings and research implications. *J Biosoc Sci, 28*(4), 509–526.

Sameroff, A., (1990). Neo-environmental perspectives on developmental theory. *Issues in the Developmental Approach to Intellectual Disability* (pp. 93–113). New York: Cambridge University Press.

Sameroff, A. J., & Chandler, M. J. (1975). Reproductive risk and the continuum of caretaking casualty. *Review of child development research, 4*(1), 187–244.

Saudino, K. J., Plomin, R., Pedersen, N. L., & Mcclearn, G. E. (1993). The etiology of high and low cognitive-ability in later life. *Behavior Genetics*, 23(6), 564–564.

Scarr, S., & Weingberg, R. A. (1978). The influence of 'family background' on intellectual attainment. *American Sociological Review*, 43, 674–692.

Shakespeare, T. (1999). 'Losing the plot'? Medical and activist discourses of contemporary genetics and disability. *Sociology of Health & Illness*, 21(5), 669–688.

Simonoff, E., Bolton, P., & Rutter, M. (1996). Intellectual disability: genetic findings, clinical implications and research agenda. *Journal of Child Psychology and Psychiatry*, 37(3), 259–280.

Simonoff, E., Pickles, A., Hervas, A., Silberg, J. L., Rutter, M., & Eaves, L. (1998). Genetic influences on childhood hyperactivity: Contrast effects imply parental rating bias, not sibling interaction. *Psychological Medicine*, 28(4), 825–837. https://doi.org/10.1017/S0033291798006886

Skuder, P., Plomin, R., & McClearn, G. E. (1995). A polymorphism in mitochondrial DNA associated with IQ? *Intelligence*, 21(1), 1–11.

Sliwinski, M., Lipton, R. B., Buschke, H., & Stewart, W. (1996). The effects of preclinical dementia on estimates of normal cognitive functioning in aging. *J Gerontol B Psychol Sci Soc Sci*, 51(4), P217–225.

Spinath, F. M., Ronald, A., Harlaar, N., Price, T. S., & Plomin, R. (2003). Phenotypic g early in life: On the etiology of general cognitive ability in a large population sample of twin children aged 2-4 years. *Intelligence*, 31(2), 195–210. https://doi.org/10.1016/S0160-2896(02)00110-1

State, M. W., King, B. H., & Dykens, E. (1997). Intellectual disability: a review of the past 10 years. Part II. *Journal of the American Academy of Child Adolescent Psychiatry*, 36, 1664–1671.

Strømme, P., & Hagberg, G. (2000). Aetiology in severe and mild mental retardation: a population-based study of Norwegian children. *Developmental medicine and child neurology*, 42(2), 76–86.

Strauss, A. A., & Kephart, N. C. (1940). Behavior differences in mentally retarded children measured by a new behavior rating scale. *American Journal of Psychiatry*, 96(5), 1117–1126

Stromland, K, Nordin, V., Miller, M., Akerström, B., & Gillberg, C (1994). Autism in thalidomide embryopathy: a population study. *Dev Med Child Neuro*, 36(4): 351–356.

Tarjan, G. (1959). Prevention, a program goal in mental deficiency. *American journal of mental deficiency*, 64(1), 4–11.

Thapar, A., Gottesman, I. I., Owen, M. J., O'Donovan, M. C., & McGuffin, P. (1994). The genetics of intellectual disability. *British Journal of Psychiatry*, 164, 747–758.

Thelen, E., & Smith, L. B. (1998). Dynamic systems theories. *Handbook of Child Psychology* (5th edn, Vol. 1, pp. 563–633). New York: Wiley.

Tordjman, S., Somogyi, E., Coulon, N., Kermarrec, S., Cohen, D., Bronsard, G., Bonnot, O., Weismann-Arcache, C., Botbol, M., Lauth, B., Ginchat, V., Roubertoux, P., Barburoth, M., Kovess, V., Geoffray, M. M., & Xavier, J. (2014). Gene × environment interactions in autism spectrum disorders: Role of epigenetic mechanisms. *Frontiers in Psychiatry*, 5(AUG), Article 53. https://doi.org/10.3389/fpsyt.2014.00053

Vygotsky, L. S. (1978). *Mind in Society: Development of Higher Psychological Processes* (M. Cole, V. Jolm-Steiner, S. Scribner, & E. Souberman, Eds.). Harvard University Press. https://doi.org/10.2307/j.ctvjf9vz4

Weaver, I., Cervoni, N., Champagne, F. et al. (2004) Epigenetic programming by maternal behavior. *Nat Neurosci*, 7, 847–854. https://doi.org/10.1038/nn1276

Weiss, B., Weisz, J. R., & Bromfield, R. (1986). Performance of retarded and nonretarded persons on information-processing tasks: further tests of the similar structure hypothesis. *Psychol Bull*, 100(2), 157–175.

Weisz, J. R., & Yeates, K. O. (1981). Cognitive development in retarded and nonretarded persons: Piagetian tests of the similar structure hypothesis. *Psychol Bull*, 90(1), 153–178.

Wertz, D. C. (1999). Ethics and Genetics in International Perspective: Results of a Survey. In: Nippert, I., Neitzel, H., Wolff, G. (eds) *The New Genetics: From Research into Health Care*. Springer, Berlin, Heidelberg. https://doi.org/10.1007/978-3-642-58486-2_9

Wickelgren, I. (1998). Tracking insulin to the mind. *Science*, 280, 517–519.

Williams, C., Alderson, P., & Farsides, B. (2002). Is nondirectiveness possible within the context of antenatal screening and testing? *Social science & medicine*, 54(3), 339–47.

Winnepenninckx, B., Rooms, L., & Kooy, R. F. (2003). Intellectual disability: A review of the genetic causes. *British Journal of Developmental Disabilities*, 49(96), 29–44.

Zechner, U., Wilda, M., Kehrer-Sawatzki, H., Vogel, W., Fundele, R., & Hameister, H. (2001). A high density of X-linked genes for general cognitive ability: a run-away process shaping human evolution? *Trends in genetics: TIG*, 17(12), 697–701. https://doi.org/10.1016/s0168-9525(01)02446-5

Zetlin, A. G., & Morrison, G. M. (1998). Adaptation through the life span. In J. A. Burack & R. M. Hodapp (eds), *Handbook of Intellectual Disability and Development* (pp. 481–503).

Zigler, E. (1967). Familial intellectual disability: A continuing dilemma. *Science*, 155, 292–298.

Zigler, E. (1969). Developmental versus difference theories of intellectual disability and the problem of motivation. *Am J Ment Defic*, 73(4), 536–556.

Zigler, E., Balla, D., & Hodapp, R. (1984). On the definition and classification of intellectual disability. *Am J Ment Defic*, 89(3), 215–230.

Zigler, E., & Hodapp, R. M. (1986). *Understanding Intellectual Disability*. New York: Cambridge University Press.

GLOSSARY

Aetiology: The study of the causes of disabilities and conditions. With respect to childhood disabilities, aetiology considers how biological, psychological, and environmental processes interact.

Allele: One member of a pair or series of genes that occupy a specific position on a specific chromosome.

Allelic association = association = linkage disequilibrium: Refers to covariation between allelic variation in a marker and phenotypic variation in the population. Occurs when the RFLP is located very close to the trait gene and is therefore almost never separated during meiotic crossing over of chromosomes. The advantages of association are that it is equally appropriate for a continuous dimension and a dichotomous condition/disability and it allows the use of large samples of unrelated individuals, which can be used to provide sufficient power to detect associations that account for a small amount of variance. It can also be thought of as the presence of specific alleles at marker loci contiguous to QTLs at higher frequencies than expected by chance. Considered this way, it is clear that the power of association to detect a QTL depends not only on the magnitude of the effect of the QTL on the trait but also on the magnitude of linkage disequilibrium between the QTL and a marker. Research suggesting that levels of linkage disequilibrium differ in different populations (e.g. different ethnic populations) complicates this matter.

Behavioural genetics: A branch of genetics that investigates possible connections between a genetic predisposition and observed behaviour. Research in behavioural genetics examines the effects of genotype and environment on a range of phenotypic traits such as anxiety, intelligence, sexual orientation, and antisocial behaviour.

Central nervous system (CNS) malformation: Abnormal or anomalous formation or structure, of the portion of the vertebrate nervous system consisting of the brain and spinal cord.

Cerebral palsy: A disorder usually caused by brain damage occurring at or before birth and marked by muscular impairment. Often accompanied by poor coordination, it sometimes involves speech and learning difficulties.

Chromosome: A threadlike body in the cell nucleus that carries the genes in a linear order.

Co-occurring: The overlapping of two or more conditions/disabilities at a rate that is greater than would be expected by chance alone.

Concordance rate: The presence of a rate of a given trait in both members of a pair of twins.

Congenital: Of or relating to a condition that is present at birth, as a result of either heredity or environmental influences: *a congenital heart defect; congenital syphilis.*

Cretinism: A congenital condition caused by a deficiency of thyroid hormone during prenatal development and characterized in childhood by dwarfed stature, intellectual disability, dystrophy of the bones, and a low basal metabolism. Also called congenital myxedema.

DF extremes analysis: Uses quantitative data for continuous traits rather than artificially dichotomizing the traits. It measures differential regression to the mean, and thereby yields 'group' statistics that address the aetiology of the average difference on a quantitative trait between the selected group and the rest of the population. It assumes that if a particular condition/disability, such as intellectual disability, is linked genetically with a measured quantitative trait, such as IQ, then the probands will be more similar for identical than for fraternal twins (there will be less regression to the mean).

Deoxyribonucleic acid (DNA): A nucleic acid that carries the genetic information in the cell and is capable of self-replication and synthesis of RNA. DNA consists of two long chains of nucleotides twisted into a double helix and joined by hydrogen bonds between the complementary bases adenine and thymine or cytosine and guanine. The sequence of nucleotides determines individual hereditary characteristics.

Dizygotic (DZ) twins: Non-identical or DZ twins, like other siblings, share, on average, 50% of their genes.

DNA pooling: Pools DNA from cases and controls and compares the two pooled results for DNA markers. It is conceptually similar to genotyping two individuals (one pooled group of cases and one pooled group of controls) for each DNA marker rather than genotyping each individual (although individual genotyping can be used to confirm the results of DNA pooling).

Dysmorphic syndrome: Related to dysmorphism, abnormality of shape.

Eclampsic: Related to eclampsia, coma and convulsions during or immediately after pregnancy, characterized by oedema, hypertension, and proteinuria.

Environment: An individual's environment is to be understood very broadly. It includes everything that influences an individual's phenotype, apart from his or her genotype. Environmental factors include where a person lives and how many siblings he or she has, but also biological factors such as to which chemicals a person might have been exposed to before and after birth.

Family pedigree: An individual's ancestors used in human genetics to analyse Mendelian inheritance of certain traits, especially of familial diseases.

Family studies: Studies of genetically related individuals in order to explore familial aggregation and inherited risk of a disease or disorder.

Fragile X syndrome: An inherited disability caused by a gene on the X-chromosome that causes intellectual disability, enlarged testes, and facial abnormalities in males and mild or no effects in heterozygous females. It is the most common inherited cause of intellectual disability.

Gamete: A mature sexual reproductive cell also referred to as sex cells. Female **gametes** are called ova or egg cells, and male **gametes** are called sperm. **Gametes** are haploid cells, and each cell carries only one copy of each chromosome.

Gestational: Of or relating to gestation. Gestation: the period of development in the uterus from conception until birth; pregnancy.

Genotype: The genetic makeup, as distinguished from the physical appearance, of an organism or a group of organisms. The combination of alleles located on homologous chromosomes that determines a specific characteristic or trait.

Group heritability (GH): The extent to which the mean difference between the extreme group and the unselected population is due to heritable factors.

Group common environment (GCE): The extent to which the mean difference between the extreme group and the unselected population is due to shared family environmental factors. GF, GH, and GCE are all elements of DF analysis.

Group familiarity (GF): The regression to the mean of the quantitative trait score of the sibling on a proband selected for an extreme quantitative trait score. The more that the siblings regress to the population mean the lower the familiarity. When Monozygotic twins > Dizygotic twin group familiarity implies group heritability.

Heritability: Describes the proportion of the variance of a trait is attributable to genetic influences in the population.

Hippocampus: A complex neural structure (shaped like a sea horse) consisting of grey matter and located on the floor of each lateral ventricle; intimately involved in motivation and emotion as part of the limbic system; has a central role in the formation of memories.

Hydrocephalic: Related to hydrocephalus, a usually congenital condition in which an abnormal accumulation of fluid in the cerebral ventricles causes enlargement of the skull and compression of the brain, destroying much of the neural tissue.

Hypothyroidism: Insufficient production of thyroid hormones. A pathological condition resulting from severe thyroid insufficiency, which may lead to cretinism or myxedema.

Linkage analysis: Attempts to determine whether a DNA marker and a trait gene are within millions of nucleotide base pairs on the same chromosome. Detects deviations from independent assortment for a marker and a disease locus within families. Linkage is not powerful in detecting QTLs of small effect size; however, it is possible to scan the entire genome with just a few hundred markers. Sib-pair QTL linkage is more powerful than traditional linkage because it assumes a quantitative distribution but it cannot detect QTLs that account for less than 10% of the variance.

Macrocephaly: Abnormal largeness of the head. Also called megacephaly, megalocephaly.

Marker genes: Genes with a known function related to the trait being investigated (e.g. intelligence). Targeted in allelic association.

Meiosis: The process of cell division in sexually reproducing organisms that reduces the number of chromosomes in reproductive cells from diploid to haploid, leading to the production of gametes in animals and spores in plants.

Microcephaly: Abnormal smallness of the head.

Micro-deletions: Extremely small loss, as through mutation, of one or more nucleotides from a chromosome.

Mitochondrial: Related to mitochondrion, a spherical or elongated organelle in the cytoplasm of nearly all eukaryotic cells, containing genetic material and many enzymes important for cell metabolism, including those responsible for the conversion of food to usable energy. Also called chondriosome.

Molecular genetics: The branch of genetics that deals with the expression of genes by studying the DNA sequences of chromosomes.

Monozygotic (MZ) twins: MZ twins come from the same fertilized egg and are genetically identical, that is, they have 100% of their genes in common.

Morphology: The branch of biology that deals with the form and structure of organisms without consideration of function.

Neurotransmitter: A chemical substance, such as acetylcholine or dopamine, that transmits nerve impulses across a synapse.

Nomenclature: The procedure of assigning names to the kinds and groups of organisms listed in a taxonomic classification: *the rules of nomenclature in botany.*

Nonadditive genetic variance: Genetic factors which contribute to variance in a non-additive way. Important because they do not contribute much to resemblance between relatives, except in the case of identical twins. Implied when the phenotypic correlation for first-degree relatives is less than half the correlation for identical twins. E.g. in the case of dominance and epistasis.

Non-shared environment: Environmental influences not shared by children growing up in the same family (e.g. peer relationship).

Normal distribution: A theoretical frequency distribution for a set of variable data, usually represented by a bell-shaped curve symmetrical about the mean. Also called Gaussian distribution.

Nucleotide: Any of various compounds consisting of a nucleoside combined with a phosphate group and forming the basic constituent of DNA and RNA.

Perinatal: Of, relating to, or being the period around childbirth, especially the five months before and one month after birth: *perinatal mortality; perinatal care.*

Phenotype: The constitution of an organism as determined by the interaction of its genetic constitution and the environment. An individual's phenotype consists of all his or her measurable or observable properties and characteristics aside from his or her genes. These could include characteristics such as hair colour, height, and IQ score. Researchers in behavioural genetics often include such diverse traits as marital status, taste in music, and religious beliefs as part of the phenotype.

Polygenes: Any of a group of nonallelic genes, each having a small quantitative effect, that together produce a wide range of phenotypic variation. Also called multiple factor, quantitative gene.

Polygenic inheritance: The sum of characteristics genetically transmitted through ploygenes from parents to offspring.

Postnatal: Of or occurring after birth, especially during the period immediately after birth.

Prenatal: Existing or occurring before birth.

Reaction range: the phenotype or behavioural expression of the genotype will vary with the potential range of environmental conditions. Environments that are favourable for a particular trait will broaden the potential range of outcomes whereas unfavourable conditions will narrow the range.

Shared environment: Environmental influences shared by children growing up in the same family (e.g. socio-economic status).

Teratogen: An agent, such as a virus, a drug, or radiation, that causes malformation of an embryo or foetus.

Twin studies: Studies of MZ and DZ twins allow researchers to examine what proportion of the total phenotypic variance is explained by genetic factors, shared environmental factors non-shared environmental factors. Greater similarity or correlation between MZ twins than DZ twins indicates a genetic influence.

3
SCREENING, ASSESSMENT, AND DIAGNOSIS OF INTELLECTUAL AND DEVELOPMENTAL DISABILITIES

> **Learning Objectives**
>
> After reading this chapter, you should be able to:
> - Contrast the definition of intelligence and intellectual disability
> - Become familiar with the diagnostic criteria for intellectual disability in the DSM/ICD
> - Understand developmental screening goals and properties of tools used,
> - Differentiate between screening and diagnosis
> - Understand the main components of a comprehensive assessment of ID/DD

DEFINITION OF INTELLECTUAL DISABILITY

With the rapid pace of progress in modern society, human intelligence will be key to the long-term survival of our species. We are now faced with solving complex problems (mostly of our own doing) that threaten our very existence (e.g. global warming, pandemics, and terrorism).

Although modern-day problems seem insurmountable, it wasn't all that long ago that humans solved equally complex problems that led to the discovery of fire, the invention of the wheel, and organized agriculture. In retrospect these discoveries may seem unimpressive to us but imagine how challenging the problems were for our ancestors at the time. Intelligence plays an important role in problem solving big and little problems. In our day-to-day life it is thought to be essential to our ability to function effectively with tasks that are familiar and to adapt to new situations as they arise.

How do we know intelligence when we see it? Describing the products of intelligent behavior is easier than conceptualizing intelligence. Despite many attempts to define the construct of intelligence, no one definition seems to fully capture all of the facets of this complex construct. A few examples of definitions of intelligence are provided below:

- 'individuals' abilities to understand complex ideas, to adapt effectively to the environment, to learn from experience, to engage in various forms of reasoning, to overcome obstacles by careful thought' (Neisser et al. 1996).
- '[intelligence is] a psychobiological potential to solve problems or to fashion products that are valued in at least one cultural context' (Gardner 1998).
- 'mental activity directed toward purposive adaptation to, selection and shaping of, real-world environments relevant to one's life' (Sternberg 1985: 45).

The notion of intelligence as the ability to learn from and readily adapt to one's changing environment figures prominently in many definitions (Neisser et al. 1996). Theorists have also maintained that abilities must be evaluated within a particular cultural context (Gardner 1998).

Intelligence is particularly difficult to conceptualize and define in persons with developmental disabilities who frequently have uneven cognitive abilities and atypical experiences. For example, a large proportion of people with autism spectrum disorder (ASD) interact intensely with objects or topics of interest and a minority of these individuals have what is referred to as savant skills or islets of abilities. In this case, intelligence may take some unusual forms such as exceptional abilities that exceed norms even for same age peers (e.g. drawing, perfect pitch, mathematical calculations) within the context of impaired functioning in other areas (e.g. fluid reasoning, working memory). Savants are an example of individuals who have overall low IQ, typically in the intellectually disabled range, while also holding exceptional skills in a specialized area. Typically savants have extraordinary skill in either music, art, calendar calculations, or mathematics (Treffert 2009). Approximately 10–30% of autistic people are savants.

Although intelligence is considered complex and multi-facetted, the concept of intellectual disability is relatively clearly defined and quantified by medical classification systems. For example, the International Statistical Classification of Diseases and Related Health Problems by the World Health Organization (now in its 11th version – ICD 11 and the Diagnostic and Statistical Manual of Mental Disorders (now in its 5th version – DSM 5) by the American Psychiatric Association are widely used for the purposes of rendering clinical diagnoses. These classification systems are not based on a specific theory of intelligence, however, they do reflect research on persons with intellectual disability and social and policy concerns with regard to how best to provide appropriate supports to persons whose intelligence and social competence are so low that they cannot function independently in society.

It is important to make a distinction between the terms, intellectual disability/disorder (IDD) and developmental disability (DD), commonly used in the research literature and in clinical contexts. The former, intellectual disability, generally refers to individuals who have cognitive or intellectual delay or impairment and the latter, developmental disability, includes those with IDD but also refers to those who may have developmental delays and deficits but do not necessarily have an intellectual disability. One example is persons with autism spectrum disorder (ASD) who have specific challenges in social-communication and repetitive behaviours and restricted interests yet, in the majority of cases, have average or above average cognitive ability as indexed by their performance on standardized tests of intelligence. The term developmental disability encompasses those with IDD but not all persons with DD have an intellectual disability.

INTELLECTUAL DISABILITY DEFINED AS A DIAGNOSTIC CATEGORY

Many professionals in the field of developmental disabilities use the Diagnostic and Statistical Manual of Mental Disorders (DSM), now in its 5th revision or The International Statistical Classification of Diseases and Related Health Problems, commonly referred to as ICD, now in its 11th revision, to diagnose intellectual disability. The ICD is the international diagnosis classification set that translates the healthcare provider's qualitative assessment into a quantitative value for reporting purposes. The DSM includes only mental disorders, however, the ICD includes conditions and diseases related to all other body systems.

In the latest 5th revision of the DSM, persons with intellectual disability are categorized under the diagnosis of Intellectual Developmental Disorder (IDD). According to the DSM-5, three criteria must be met for the diagnosis of IDD (APA, 2013). One DSM 5 criterion is that there is the presence of *deficits in intellectual abilities such as reasoning, problem solving, abstract thinking, judgement, and learning.* These must be confirmed using clinical observations and assessments as well as standardized tests such as the Stanford Binet Intelligence Scales or the Wechsler Scales of Intelligence. These IQ tests typically measure verbal and spatial abilities, processing speed, and memory. To assess these cognitive abilities we rely on standardized measures of intelligence that provide an Intellectual Quotient (IQ) score. After standardizing the IQ scores, a cutoff score which is associated with a statistical calculation – usually two standard deviations below the mean for the general population (e.g. IQ 70) – is determined. IQ scores at and below this cutoff indicate that the individual's IQ score falls at approximately the bottom 3% of the population. However, standardized tests of intelligence include a margin for measurement error (+5 points). This means that on tests that have a mean standard score of 100 and a standard deviation of 15, a score of 70 ± 5 would be interpreted as an estimated score of 65–75. This allows the clinician to use their training and judgement to interpret the test results along with other relevant information collected during the assessment, e.g. information pertaining to the individual's behaviour during the testing, how much intervention the individual has had, and their socio-economic status. Each of these pieces of information helps the clinician paint a picture of the different factors that contribute to the individual's current functioning. The clinician must then determine how much weight to give each piece of information, consider whether there is consistency across data collected from different sources of information, and synthesize the information in a way that provides a satisfactory account of the weight of evidence in the determination of the diagnosis of ID.

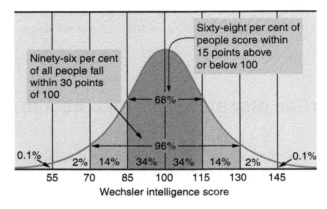

Figure 3.1 The Normal curve showing IQ scores and their distribution

Source: Dmcq, CC BY-SA 3.0.

One reason for designating 70 and below as the cutoff is because the designation provides a rough estimate of the numbers of persons who are eligible for some combination of additional funding, resources, services, and supports. However, IQ score is derived using a statistical formula and does not necessarily reflect the individual's actual day-to-day functioning. For example, two people with the same IQ of 65 may be impacted differently; in the one case, the individual may be quite socially adept and able to function relatively independently, in the other, the individual may not be able to accomplish basic daily living tasks. Whereas standardized IQ test scores provide a convenient cutoff score for determining eligibility for a specific social programme or service, they do not provide any information on the type of intellectual disability (there are more than 1000 possible aetiologies) or about the profiles of relative strengths and weaknesses across a range of cognitive (e.g. attention, executive function) and social processes (e.g. inferencing, emotion regulation) thought to impact an individual's intelligence.

Despite the limitations of the IQ score, it is an essential component of the diagnosis of persons with intellectual disability and those who may be at developmental risk. This is because IQ scores in childhood are seen as reliable indexes of a child's current rate of intellectual development and of future levels of functioning in relation to that of their same-aged peers (Shulman et al. 2011). Although IQ scores are used as estimates of a child's intellectual abilities in relation to those of other children of the same age, they are essentially indicators of the rate of development of intellectual abilities that is associated with relative level of functioning in adulthood. To estimate a child's developmental progress, one can divide their mental age (MA), the level of cognitive development attained by the individual, by chronological age (CA) and then multiply that number by a constant (usually 100) (for discussions, see Zigler & Hodapp 1986; Hodapp, Burack, & Zigler 1990; Shulman et al. 2011). For IQ, the numerator is MA, the developmental distance 'travelled' by the individual in their attainment of cognitive abilities and the denominator is CA, the length of time which the individual has lived. In this case, a greater numerator, or more distance travelled, in relation to a smaller denominator, less time passed, indicates faster developmental growth. A child who attains the types of skills common to a six year old in six years, and therefore has an IQ of 100 according to our developmental formula, is developing faster than a child for whom it takes eight years and who has an IQ of 75, but slower than one for whom it took only five years, and who has an IQ of 120.

The second DSM 5 criterion for a designation of IDD requires *deficits in adaptive functioning that result in the failure to meet developmental, socio-cultural, and domain specific expectations of personal independence and responsibility*. Deficits in adaptive functioning are a key criterion of the diagnosis of IDD. Although an IQ score provides a quantitative estimate of cognitive impairment, it does not necessarily reflect how an individual performs or functions in their everyday life. However, poor communication, social participation, independent living across school, home, and community contexts, more clearly indicate adaptive limitations that require support. To assess adaptive deficits a thorough assessment including a standardized interview of adaptive behaviour in areas such as communication, socialization, and daily living skills is recommended. Thus, a person must show IQ two standard deviations below the population mean and adaptive behaviour concurrently to qualify for a diagnosis of IDD (see American Association on Intellectual and Developmental Disabilities (AAIDD) 2010).

The third criterion for the DSM diagnosis of IDD is that the onset of intellectual and adaptive deficits must have occurred within the *developmental period*. Although the term 'developmental period' does not provide a definitive age, it is meant to refer to the developmental period of childhood and adolescence, which in most districts is thought to end when a child reaches, approximately, 18 years of age. In the DSM 5, IDD is categorized as a neurodevelopmental disorder and is distinct from neurocognitive disorders that are associated with a loss of cognitive functioning (e.g. dementia, Alzheimer's disease). Brain injuries or other acute medical conditions (e.g. brain tumour) that may cause an individual to have cognitive impairment are also theoretically distinct as any associated intellectual disability is as a result of the injury or disease and was not likely present prior to the injury or disease.

The cognitive impairment that results from a brain injury is also different in its manifestation since, for the most part, these individuals have specific cognitive impairments and intact abilities in many other areas of functioning. Also, individuals who have had a brain injury typically had average or above premorbid (prior to their injury) cognitive functioning and generally had typical lives and experiences prior to their injury, whereas those with a developmental disability from birth have had atypical experiences throughout their lives. Neurocognitive disorders may co-occur with intellectual disability. For example, an individual with Down syndrome may develop Alzheimer's disease or may incur a head injury. In either case, the individual would be diagnosed with IDD and the neurocognitive disorder. However, for the purposes of diagnosis and access to services, an acquired insult to the organism *during the developmental period* would also be classified as intellectual disability, if all other criteria are also met.

For children showing developmental delays under the age of five years, where IQ assessments are not reliable or feasible, the diagnosis of *Global Developmental Delay* may be given. This diagnosis applies to children who are failing to meet expected developmental milestones in several areas that affect cognitive functioning including speech, motor, social-emotional, and reasoning skills. In certain children global developmental delay is suspected soon after birth due to a chromosomal difference (e.g. Down syndrome) or gene mutation (Williams syndrome) and associated difficulties in feeding or poor muscle-tone. In others it is suspected later when milestones are not reached at the expected time (e.g. phrase speech by two or three years of age). Regular screening and monitoring is essential to detect global developmental delay and later re-assessment to determine a more precise diagnosis, if possible.

For children over the age of five years who are not able to be assessed with standardized assessment procedures because of severe sensory or physical impairments or behaviour difficulties, the diagnosis *Unspecified Intellectual Disability/Developmental Disorder* is given. In this case, re-assessment after a period of time is required to determine a more precise diagnosis, if possible.

In addition to the diagnosis of IDD, specifiers are used to provide more descriptive and relevant clinical information such as the age of onset, clinical course and severity of the condition (i.e. mild, moderate, severe and profound) with regard to adaptive function in academic, social, and practical domains. The assessor may also specify the associated medical (e.g. epilepsy) or genetic condition (e.g. Down syndrome) or environmental factors (low birth weight, foetal alcohol exposure) that play a role in the aetiology and course of the condition. This information may help professionals determine appropriate supports and interventions as well as provide the family with referrals to specific resources available in their community. This is a welcome improvement from the previous DSM–IV version.

THE APPLICATION OF THE DIAGNOSTIC CRITERIA

Influential groups representing people with intellectual disabilities such as the American Association on Intellectual and Developmental Disabilities (AAIDD; formerly the AAMR) (Schalock et al. 2011) raised concerns about the DSM 5 diagnostic criteria with regard to its potential influence on public policy. The DSM or ICD are frequently used to designate eligibility criteria for government funding and services for individuals with intellectual and developmental disabilities. In the current DSM 5, 'All symptoms must have an onset during the developmental period' (DSM 5, 2013), leaves the age at which the developmental period ends open to interpretation. The AAIDD suggests that this will cause confusion and result in inconsistent use of developmental periods across jurisdictions. Similarly, the AAIDD voiced their concerns with regard to the use of the terms adaptive behaviour and adaptive functioning as potentially confusing. According to the AAIDD, 'adaptive behaviours' are the conceptual, social, and practical skills a person may have, whereas 'adaptive functioning' is how well or independently the person is able to use those skills to handle common demands in life.

These definitional critiques are not trivial because how the diagnostic criteria are interpreted will impact who receives funding/services and who does not. The application of diagnostic criteria also has important implications for educational designations with regard to who will receive accommodations or modifications to the regular educational curriculum. Those children designated as having an intellectual disability usually require modifications to their curriculum and, thus, are less likely to meet the standard high school graduation requirements. Historically, the American Association of Mental Deficiency (AAMD) (later the AAIDD) had concerns regarding the narrow focus of, and potential cultural bias of, intelligence tests and their exclusive use in defining intellectual disability because disproportionate numbers of minority children were being diagnosed with mild intellectual disability. These advocacy groups argued that intelligence tests underestimated the abilities of minority children (Hays 2001; Valencia and Suzuki 2001) and, therefore, low scores on adaptive behaviour should be considered, along with low IQ scores, in the DSM's criteria for a diagnosis of intellectual disability (Borthwick-Duffy, 2007).

SCREENING, DIAGNOSIS AND ASSESSMENT OF INTELLECTUAL AND DEVELOPMENTAL DISABILITIES

Screening for Developmental Delay

Early screening and diagnosis are critical to identify children showing signs of developmental delay who may benefit from early intervention. The purpose of developmental screening is to detect risk factors or 'red flags' in children who may be at risk for a developmental disability among a large population of healthy children. A diagnostic assessment is usually administered after a positive screening test to establish a definitive diagnosis of IDD/DD.

Delays in identification and intervention often have a negative impact on the child's ability to communicate and learn adaptive skills (Chadwick et al.) and may heighten the child's risk for behaviour problems and aggression. Related to this is increased caregiver stress and strain, particularly when a child has behavioural challenges and the diagnostic status of the child is unknown. Elevated stress may contribute to negative outcomes in a variety of aspects of parent functioning when caring for children with ID/DD, particularly, in families where the child may have autism spectrum disorder (ASD). Caregivers of children with ASD are at high risk for depression and anxiety, marital problems, family functioning difficulties, and lower parental physical health, even when compared to other caregivers of children with DD (Ingersoll & Hambrick 2011; Johnson, Frenn, Feetham, & Simpson 2011; Karst & van Hecke 2012; Foody, James, & Leader 2014; Reed, Howse, Ho, & Osborne 2016). Both from the perspective of the child and caregiver it is important to mitigate negative outcomes by identifying developmental delays and deficits early.

Whereas population-wide screening for autism is potentially quite costly, targeted screening among children referred to infant development programmes may be more feasible and economical. These children are referred because they are showing signs of delay, yet the cause of the delay is frequently unknown. A screening tool with adequate psychometric properties including standardization, reliability, validity, with acceptable sensitivity (i.e. 70–80%) and specificity (i.e. 80%), should reduce the costs of false negatives and false positives (Charman et al. 2007). See Table 3.1 for ideal properties of a screening tool. In addition to the accuracy of the tool, ethical considerations surrounding early screening and identification are necessary. For example, if children are screened for a developmental disability then adequate resources need to be available to further assess the children who screen positive. The screening tool will only indicate risk; a diagnostic assessment is needed to confirm a diagnosis (see Chapter 2 for more information on the difference between screening and diagnosis). A screening tool that results in too many false positives may result in overly long waitlists for diagnostic assessments, delaying services for children who need it. False positives may also unduly stress families about the developmental status of their child when particular milestones, although slower to achieve, may still be within the normal range.

Although screening tools are primarily used to identify children at risk, they can also highlight potential targets for early intervention. For example, the *Screening Tool for Autism in Toddlers & Young Children (STAT)* is ideally suited for screening toddlers as young as two years who may be showing signs of ASD (Stone et al., 2004). This screening tool can be used by a wide range of community professionals to increase the rates of early detection in children referred for developmental delays, but also, to enhance professional and caregiver awareness of the early signs of ASD. It is an interactive screening tool designed as an observational measure of the core autism deficits within a play context. As an interactive measure, observations of children's behaviour during the screening can be used to develop individualized intervention goals and activities for the child. For those children who are referred for further assessment and possible diagnosis, caregivers would be taught intervention strategies that they can implement immediately and while they wait for their child to be assessed. This proactive screening strategy achieves multiple goals; (1) it identifies delays and deficits in child's development early; (2) it uses valuable time to educate parents that would otherwise be lost to those who wait for diagnostic assessments; and (3) it encourages parent self-efficacy as the parents learn strategies to better engage their child in play interactions.

Screening tools have also been used to educate parents about the child's abilities and challenges as the parents wait for a formal diagnosis. For example, researchers have begun to explore models of service delivery that incorporate screening and intervention in at risk toddlers (e.g. siblings of children with ASD). This entails providing parent coaching to those parents whose toddlers screen at high risk for ASD. Using principles derived from evidence based Naturalistic Developmental Behavioural Interventions (NDBI) have been shown to improve play interactions and daily activities in children diagnosed with ASD. There are several versions of NDBI parent coaching models but the underlying principles are similar and their effectiveness ratings are comparable (APA, 1995). For example, parent coaching models such as Improving Parents as Communication Teachers (ImPACT) (Ingersoll & Wainer, 2013) and the Early Start Denver Model (ESDM) (Rogers et al., 2012) are manualized early interventions for young children with ASD. A common component of these parent coaching approaches is training parents to follow the child's lead and to encourage the child to imitate them. Imitation, voluntarily matching the behaviours of others, is a foundational skill that is critical to young children's social learning-acquiring knowledge from people and the world around them (Jones 2009). Imitation is a pivotal skill because the child learns *how* to learn, and this enhances the rate of learning of other social-communicative behaviours (Stone & Yoder 2001; Toth, Munson, Meltzoff, & Dawson 2006). The Reciprocal Imitation Training (RIT) was developed based on the ImPACT curriculum but specifically focuses on improving spontaneous imitation and gestures in young children with ASD (e.g. imitating gestures and actions) during play interactions and daily activities (Ingersoll & Schreibman 2006). It helps parents optimize the play environment, observe and better understand their child, heighten their affect, simplify their language, teach object imitation, describe and comment on their child's play and expand their child's play skills.

Imitation, voluntarily matching the behaviours of others, is a foundational skill that is critical to young children's social learning-acquiring knowledge from people and the world around them. The foundational skill acquisition that this approach affords facilitates 'increased receptivity' so the child can benefit from more advanced learning opportunities in the future (Whalen, Schreibman, & Ingersoll 2006). It may be that at this early stage, prior to a formal diagnosis, providing parent coaching may help practitioners effectively tackle common developmental needs that all young children with developmental delays present with. Focusing on the precursors of social and language development may provide the quickest effects across a wide variety of skill areas. In addition, the parent coaching approach allows families to use their own resilience to overcome challenges, improving child outcomes as well as family quality of life.

In many jurisdictions, children under three years who are at risk of having developmental delays may be eligible for early intervention services even if the child has not received a formal diagnosis. Intervention for particular symptoms, such as speech therapy for language delays, may be provided to the child prior to a formal diagnosis through infant development programmes. However, these services frequently cease once the child is three years of age.

Table 3.1 Psychometric properties of a good screening tool

Standardization	The screening tool should be standardized against a large population of children from different geographical areas, socioeconomic and ethnic backgrounds, age, and gender. This sets the 'normative' base for a screening tool. Ideally, the screening tool should be standardized for each target population that the screen claims to identify.
Reliability	A screening tool should give similar results for an individual each time it is administered irrespective of time intervals or who is administering or scoring the test.
Validity	This ensures that the screening tool is measuring what it is set out to measure. There are a number of different forms of validity including: • Face validity, i.e. the extent to which the screening tool looks like it is measuring what it sets out to measure; • Discriminative validity, i.e. the extent to which a tool can correctly predict which group a person belongs to; • Concurrent validity, i.e. the degree to which the scores of a screening test agree with the scores of an established intellectual assessment or an adaptive behaviour assessment.
Sensitivity	This is the probability that a true positive (in this case a child with an intellectual disability) will be correctly identified as such by the screening tool. It is found by dividing the number of true positives by the number of true positives added to the number of false negatives [$Sn = TP / (TP + FN)$].
Specificity	This is the probability that a true negative (in this case a child who does not have an intellectual disability) will be correctly identified as such. It is found by dividing the number of true negatives by the number of true negatives added to the number of false positives [$Sp = TN / (TN + FP)$].
Positive predictive value	This identifies the proportion of those who are identified as positive by the test in question (in this case as having an intellectual disability) who are correctly identified as such. This is given by the number of true positives divided by the total number of positives (both tine and false positives) given by the test [$PW=TP/(TP+FP)$].
Negative predictive value	This identifies the proportion of those who are identified as negative by the test in question (in this case as not having an intellectual disability) who are correctly identified as such. This is given by the number of true negatives divided by the total number of negatives (both true and false negatives) given by the test [$NPP=TN/(TN+FN)$].

Source: McKenzie, K. & Megson, P. (2011) Screening for intellectual disability in children: a review of the literature. *Journal of Applied Research in Intellectual Disabilities*, 25(1), 80–87. DOI:10.1111/j.1468-3148.2011.00650.x

Diagnostic Assessment

Once a child is screened and deemed to be at risk for intellectual or other developmental disability, they are typically referred for a comprehensive, multi-disciplinary diagnostic assessment. The goal of a diagnostic assessment is to confirm or rule out a particular developmental disability. For example, the child who has specific learning disorder is distinguished from children who have learning difficulties associated with intellectual disability. In the former case, children have learning difficulties in the presence of average or above intellectual functioning whereas in the latter, learning difficulties are expected given the general developmental delays associated with intellectual disability. However, specific learning disorder could also be diagnosed in children with intellectual disability when a specific area of learning is affected beyond what is expected for their mental age. Generally, the core elements of a diagnostic assessment for intellectual or other developmental disabilities consist of a thorough health/medical evaluation, developmental history, cognitive ability (IQ), and adaptive behaviour assessments. For certain developmental disabilities such as ASD, other specialized assessments speech–language–communication, physical or occupational, neurological, or psychiatric assessments may be needed. Assessment by different disciplines provides a comprehensive picture of the child's developmental and symptom profile as well as level of functional skills.

The diagnosis and assessment of a child suspected of having an intellectual or developmental disability has a number of specific goals. First, genetic or other medical tests are needed to identify potential aetiologies as well as to investigate whether specific pre- or post-natal exposure to environmental toxins such as lead, mercury, or radiation may be associated with the ID in the children. For example, a recognizable medical or genetic disorder is found in up to 25% of cases of children showing some atypicality on physical examination. Assessment by different disciplines provides for a comprehensive picture of the individual child's functional skills. Within an interdisciplinary social developmental framework, the evaluation of a child with a potential intellectual disability emphasizes early diagnosis, identification of the specific support needs, and the provision of the necessary individual and family services. The resulting service plan needs to facilitate communication among the various professionals and with the parents about the child's on-going support needs, particularly during major developmental transitions (e.g. preschool to formal schooling).

Health/Medical Evaluation

A paediatrician or specialized developmental paediatrician will usually see a child showing signs of developmental delay in order to perform a medical exam. The examination entails various standard procedures including measurements of head circumference and reflexes, review of growth charts, and interviewing parents to update environmental, medical, family, and social history for additional risk factors. Medical evaluations are essential to rule out physical or genetic differences that may be causing the developmental delays and atypical behaviour. Hearing and vision tests are often good starting points to rule out any physical cause for speech or motor delays. When warranted, special genetic tests are requisitioned by the doctor to investigate the presence of uncommon genetic conditions such as fragile X or Rett syndrome. Fragile X is the most common inherited condition causing global developmental delay. Rett syndrome is a leading cause of global developmental delay in girls. Girls with Rett syndrome appear to develop normally until six to 18 months and, shortly thereafter, begin to regress in their functioning.

Metabolic tests are blood and urine tests needed to identify disorders of the body's chemistry, particularly if there is a family history of developmental delay. For example, infants with phenylketonuria (PKU) are lacking an enzyme needed to metabolize phenylalanine-an amino acid found in protein. A blood test can uncover the level of phenylalanine in the baby's blood to determine if it is in a normal range.

Environmental causes for developmental delay should also be ruled out. For example, lead is the most common toxic substance in the environment known to harm the nervous system. Very high lead levels have been linked to developmental delays and deficits. Since children have a tendency to explore toys and other objects with their mouths, a blood test for lead screening would reveal if the child has had too much lead exposure. Thyroid blood tests are done to check if the thyroid gland is producing sufficient hormone. Thyroid dysfunction may result in abnormal growth and development, as well as developmental delay.

A neurological exam may be needed if the child is showing signs of unusual neural activity such as fits, fainting spells, or seizures. An electroencephalogram (EEG) records the electrical activity of the brain and will confirm if the child has epilepsy, however, an EEG does not determine the cause of the developmental delays. Neuroimaging, techniques such as Magnetic Resonance Imaging tests (MRI) or Computed Tomography scan (CT) are used to take pictures of the brain. These brain imaging techniques can help with detecting any damage to tissues in the central nervous system that may be associated with global developmental delay.

Identification of a medical cause may help professionals and parents better understand their child's disability and prognosis. This information may also be used in various aspects of treatment planning, including genetic counselling around recurrence risk and family planning, specific medical treatments for improved health and function of the child, and intervention and educational programming. However, it is important to note that the cause of intellectual or developmental disabilities is not known in the majority of cases.

Developmental History

There is extensive evidence that parental concerns about communication, development and behaviour are highly sensitive and specific and should always receive serious consideration (Glascoe 2000). For children suspected of having ASD, a thorough developmental interview is recommended using a standardized parent interview. For example, the Autism Diagnostic Interview – Revised (ADI-R) – is a standardized investigator based interview with over 90 questions about the child's development that relates specifically to the symptoms of autism. Traditional methods of examining cognitive and adaptive abilities with standardized instruments are often supplemented with a thorough developmental and family history. Developmental histories have several components: (1) prenatal histories including any complications during pregnancy, exposure to alcohol or other substances, infections and diagnoses (i.e. Down syndrome); (2) perinatal history (during the birth process) including any complications during the birth such as hypoxia (lack of oxygen), seizures, infections and baby health status scores (i.e. APGAR); (3) medical history of child since birth including the use of antibiotics, frequent ear infections that could affect hearing; (4) behaviour of child indicating any regressions, delays, or deficits; (5) family history including genetic conditions that are familial, syndromes or other family members who had developmental delays; and (6) social history including any possible trauma, abuse, or neglect experienced by the child that may have a negative impact on the child's development.

A comprehensive understanding of the child's developmental status is obtained with parent and teacher interviews (when available) and evaluations of medical and school records.

In addition to developmental histories, environmental assessments are also informative as specific factors in the child's social environment and everyday routines may facilitate or hinder development (e.g. sleep hygiene). Understanding the circumstances of the child's home, school, and community environment is important to determine if any factors may be contributing to the child's behavioural challenges.

Assessing Cognitive Ability

No one single instrument will assess the full range of cognitive skills and deficits that are thought to impact the child's overall cognitive functioning. However, it is important to consider the child's developmental level, language skills, and attention span when selecting an appropriate IQ test. The test must be appropriate to the mental and chronological age of the child; provide an appropriate range of standard scores based on current norms; provide measures of verbal and nonverbal abilities along with an overall index of ability; consider the child's ability to remember, solve problems, and develop concepts and measure motor and visual-motor skills.

The most commonly used standardized measures of intellectual ability are: The Wechsler Scales of Intelligence (6–16:11 years) (Wechsler, 2016) and the Stanford Binet Intelligence Scale (2–85+ years); for young children (Roid, 2003), the Bayley Scales of Infant and Toddler Development (1–42 months) (Bayley, 2006) and the Mullen Scales of Early Learning (birth to 68 months) (Mullen 1995) and for non-verbal children, the Leiter International Performance Scale (revised norms) (Roid & Miller, 1997). These measures are interactive and involve the assessor engaging with the individual in a clearly prescribed manner indicated in the test manual procedure.

The assessment of individuals with intellectual or developmental disabilities (especially younger children) using standardized procedures may pose a particular challenge for the assessor. At times, procedures must be adapted to address difficulties children commonly encounter with testing. This includes limited language and associated problems in understanding verbal instructions, limited attention span, distractibility, unusual responses to social reinforcement, and limited frustration tolerance. Providing more frequent breaks, tangible rewards and visual schedules may facilitate assessment.

The assessor's behavioural observations are an essential aspect of the cognitive assessment and provide the opportunity for the assessor to clearly document any behaviours that are interfering with the accurate assessment of the individual or that are particularly reflective of a strength or challenge that the individual demonstrates. For example, if the individual is especially distracted, fatigued, or restless it may be noted later in the report as a potential factor(s) that limits the accuracy of the results and may underestimate the cognitive ability assessed. It is also important to consider the effect of the individual's behaviour and how it may impact their learning or functioning in different contexts. For example, the assessment situation typically involves one-to-one contact, in a context that is highly structured, minimally distracting, paced, and has relatively low social demands. If an individual has difficulty performing effectively in this context, it would be fair to say that they are likely to struggle in formal learning or work contexts that are generally less structured, often distracting, and fast-paced and socially demanding. Thus, behavioural observations during the assessment provide valuable information about a person's actual functioning within a particular context. This information complements test scores that typically reflect an individual's abilities or potential. For example, 'testing the limits' is a common technique that assessors use to determine whether, and under what conditions, the individual is able to achieve the correct answer to an item on a standardized test after they have failed the item. By scaffolding the assessor may break down the item or provide a cue(s) based on hypotheses they might have about why the individual struggles with a particular test item(s). If the individual is able to achieve the correct answer with support, this indicates that he/she may have partial understanding of the concept but requires scaffolding to achieve an optimal level of performance. The individual who does not achieve the correct answer with support may need additional help to learn the concept before they can apply it in a task (with or without scaffolding).

Assessing Adaptive Behaviour

IQ assessment results alone can be misleading or incomplete when the goal is to determine a diagnosis of intellectual disability and the needed supports for the individual. The American Association of Mental Deficiency (AAMD), now the AAIDD, has, since the 1950s, emphasized the importance of adaptive behaviour as well as cognitive functioning in its definition of intellectual disability (Borthwick-Duffy 2007). Adaptive behaviour, defined as the application of intelligence to the practical skills of everyday life, provides the necessary complementary information for the assessor to determine the type and quantity of support services needed for the individual. Adaptive behaviour is assessed in three main domains of functioning:

1. Conceptual skills such as communication and literacy; money, time, and number concepts; and self-initiative;
2. Social skills including interpersonal skills, social responsibility, social understanding and problem solving, and the ability to follow rules/obey laws and to avoid being victimized; and
3. Practical skills, the activities of daily living (personal care), occupational skills, healthcare, travel/transportation, schedules/routines, safety, use of the telephone.

An assessment of adaptive functioning can be made using standardized norm-referenced instruments such as the Vineland Adaptive Behavior Scales; the Scales of Independent Behavior – Revised (Sparrow, Cicchetti & Saulnier, 2016), or Adaptive Behavior Assessment System (ABAS-II) (Harrison & Oakland, 2003). Each of these measures requires information from an informant, such as a parent or caregiver, who lives with the individual and has had the opportunity to observe the individual in their daily routines for an extended period of time. The measures can either be in interview or questionnaire format. However, it is important to clearly explain to the informant that they must respond to each item by clearly differentiating what skill the individual is able to do independently, with support, or not at all. For example, the Vineland Adaptive Behavior Scales Daily Living Skills question: 'Bathes or showers and dries self' will receive a full score of '2' if the individual bathes or showers on their own, a score of '1' if the individual needs some help with adjusting the water temperature or rinsing themselves, and a score of '0' if they do not bathe or shower on their own or unless reminded. These distinctions are important because they reflect the level of support needed by the individual to accomplish specific tasks.

It is important to establish that limitations in adaptive skills occur within a context of environments that are typical of the child's same-age peers. Environments are specific settings in which the person lives, learns, plays, works, socializes, and interacts. Positive environments are settings that are typical of their age peers and appropriate for the individuals' cultural background. Characteristics of a desirable environment include opportunities for fulfilling one's needs, foster well-being in physical, social, material, and cognitive life, and promote a sense of stability, predictability, and control in a child's life. Adaptive limitations often coexist with strengths in other adaptive skills or personal capabilities and therefore it is advisable to explore all aspects, including strengths and challenges in adaptive behaviour, to fully understand a child's capacity. Strengths may be useful in motivating change in areas that are more challenging and effortful for the individual.

Additional Considerations

Testing behaviour changes and results become more reliable with time. For example, IQ assessments are much more reliable after age five years, when testing conditions (e.g. attention span, ability to follow instructions) improve with formal schooling. This is especially evident in children with developmental disabilities and thus assessment results prior to age five years may not fully reflect the child's potential due to extraneous variables (i.e. test taking behaviors) that interfere with accurate evaluations.

It is important to consider that a diagnostic label and associated testing results may be misinterpreted or lead to unrealistic expectations or overly negative views of the child's aptitude by professionals and parents. Therefore, professionals need to be aware of the potential effects of labels and clearly articulate that intellectual/developmental disability is only one aspect of an individual. In addition, discussions about the results of assessments need to include their limitations and assessors need to be clear about what they imply about a child's long-term outcomes as well as the limits of those predictions. Related to this, it is critical that the intervention team understand that assessments must be conducted on a regular basis (preferably every two years) to monitor progress and document any changes in the child's developmental profile.

In a subgroup of children with developmental disabilities cognitive profiles are uneven and can change quite markedly with intervention. It is also expected that early intervention will improve cognitive development and thus, these changes are important to chart to show evidence of the continued benefit of interventions or modified if improvements are not found. However, even when children with developmental disabilities receive intensive intervention, their IQ score is not likely to change much, yet the impact of intellectual limitations on their functioning may change quite significantly. This means that the intervention will mostly improve their adaptive functioning and practical knowledge. This is because with appropriate supports over a sustained period, the day-to-day functioning of persons with ID will generally improve. As such, the person with intellectual limitations may move in and out of the constraints of the definition of intellectual disability. For example, if their IQ remains sub-average yet their adaptive behaviour improves to an extent that they no longer need supports to function adequately, they may no longer meet the criteria for intellectual disability. The same applies to individuals with ASD. If they received a diagnosis of ASD as a child and through intensive intervention and appropriate supports they were able to achieve adequate functioning and social adaptation in adolescence or adulthood they may no longer meet the criteria for ASD. It is important to note that a diagnosis of intellectual or developmental disability, as with many other diagnostic categories in the DSM, is only warranted when the symptoms interfere with the individual's life in some way. This means that the symptoms cause impairment in social, occupational, or other important areas of functioning. Every person with ID/DD will differ in the nature, extent, and severity of functional limitations depending on demands/constraints of their environment (e.g. farming community vs big city). If the individual has a low IQ but they are functionally independent and their low IQ does not negatively affect their social, occupational, or other important areas of functioning then they would no longer meet the criteria for a diagnosis of intellectual disability.

A LIFESPAN PERSPECTIVE

Comprehensive assessment involves life-long monitoring because most individuals with ID/DD will require on-going support throughout the lifespan. However, there will be differences in what is assessed at different ages. For example, for many adolescents transitioning to high school, assessments are focused on providing information necessary for decisions about educational placements, yet for young adults, assessments will be needed to determine the best option for vocational placements. Mental health needs to be assessed and continually monitored since the rates of psychiatric problems in people with ID/DD are markedly higher than that of typically developing individuals. Quality of life for the individual and their family is of utmost concern and should not be taken for granted. Questionnaire measures such as the Multifaceted Lifestyle Satisfaction Scale (MLSS; Harner & Heal 1993) and the Beach Center Family Quality of Life Scale (FQOL; Hoffman, Marquis, Poston, Summers, & Turnbull 2006) are available to assess quality of life yet it can also be ascertained by simply asking family members or the individual how satisfied they are with various aspects of their lives (e.g. social, emotional, financial, service supports). Because people with ID/DD often have communication and cognitive impairments, the onus is on professionals and service providers to find the means to understand how they want to live and, to the extent possible, direct their own services and supports. A disability, no matter how severe, should never prevent an individual from leading a happy, healthy and meaningful life.

SUMMARY

Intelligence is a complex construct and is especially difficult to capture in individuals with intellectual and developmental disabilities who frequently have uneven cognitive abilities and atypical experiences. In contrast, the concept of intellectual disability is relatively clearly defined and quantified by medical classification systems such as the DSM 5 and ICD 11. Standardized intelligence tests operationalize the concept of intelligence. These tests are used to establish an intellectual quotient (IQ), an estimate of intellectual functioning. The diagnosis of intellectual developmental disorder (IDD) is assigned when three criteria are met: (1) an individual's IQ is 70 or at least 2 standard deviations below the mean for the general population; (2) there are deficits in adaptive functioning that result in the failure to meet developmental, socio-cultural, and domain specific expectations of personal independence and responsibility; and (3) the intellectual disability was present during the developmental period, meaning prior to 18 years of age.

Early screening and diagnosis is critical to identify children showing signs of developmental delay who may benefit from early intervention. The purpose of developmental screening is to detect delays and differences in children who may be at risk for a developmental disability among a large population of typically developing children. A diagnostic test is usually administered after a positive screening test to establish a definitive diagnosis.

Although screening tools are primarily used to identify children at risk, they can also highlight potential targets for early intervention. Interactive screening tools, such as the *Screening Tool for Autism in Toddlers & Young Children (STAT)*, provide observations of children's behaviour during the screening that can be used to develop individualized intervention goals and activities for the child. Researchers have begun to explore models of service delivery that incorporate screening and intervention in at risk toddlers (e.g. siblings of children with ASD).

Once a child is screened and deemed to be at risk for intellectual or other developmental disability, they are referred for a comprehensive, multi-disciplinary diagnostic assessment. The goal of a diagnostic assessment is to confirm or rule out a particular developmental disability. The core elements of a diagnostic assessment for intellectual or other developmental disabilities consist of a thorough health/medical evaluation, developmental history, cognitive ability (IQ), and adaptive behaviour assessments. Other tests (e.g. neurological) are provided when needed.

Comprehensive assessment involves life-long monitoring because most individuals with ID/DD require on-going support throughout the lifespan. Transition planning is required at different developmental stages as well as mental health and quality of life monitoring. The individual's perspective as well as that of their caregivers is important to ensure that they are living a happy, healthy, and meaningful life.

Reflective Questions

1. What is the difference between developmental screening and a diagnostic assessment?
2. How can developmental screenings be useful for caregivers and professionals?
3. How do we define intellectual disability according to the DSM 5?
4. What are the main components of a comprehensive diagnostic assessment when a child is suspected of having an intellectual or developmental disorder?
5. Why are regular re-assessments important for children with intellectual or developmental disorder?

Recommended Videos

See these videos on savants:

https://www.youtube.com/watch?time_continue=7&v=ckqDX2XpdyY

https://www.youtube.com/watch?time_continue=3&v=3oZaCrkCxu8

https://www.youtube.com/watch?v=OR36jrx_L44

REFERENCES

American Academy of Pediatrics, Committee on Children with Disabilities (2001). Technical report: the pediatrician's role in the diagnosis and management of autistic spectrum disorder in children. *Pediatrics, 107*(5). Available at: www.pediatrics.org/cgi/content/full/107/5/e85

American Association on Intellectual and Developmental Disabilities (AAIDD) (2010). *Intellectual Disability: Definition, Classification, and Systems of Supports*. Washington, DC: AAIDD.

American Psychological Association. (1995). Task force on promotion and dissemination of psychological procedures, division of clinical psychology, training in and dissemination of empirically-validated psychological treatments: Report and recommendations. *The Clinical Psychologist, 48*, 3–23.

American Psychiatric Association. (2013). *Diagnostic and Statistical Manual of Mental Disorders* (5th edn). Arlington, VA: American Psychiatric Publishing.

Bayley, N. (2006). Bayley scales of infant and toddler development.

Borthwick-Duffy, S.A. (2007). Adaptive behavior. In J.W. Jacobson, J.A. Mulick, & J. Rojahn (eds), *Handbook of Intellectual and Developmental Disabilities* (pp. 279–293). New York: Springer.

Chadwick, P., Hember, M., Mead, S., Lilley, B., & Dagnan, D. (2005). Responding mindfully to unpleasant thoughts and images: Reliability and validity of the mindfulness questionnaire. *Assessment, 11*. 206–216.

Charman, T., Baird, G., Simonoff, E., Loucas, T., Chandler, S., Meldrum, D., & Pickles, A. (2007) Efficacy of three screening instruments in the identification of autism spectrum disorder. *British Journal of Psychiatry, 191* (6) 554–559.

Foody, C., James, J., & Leader, G. (2014). Parenting stress, salivary biomarkers, and ambulatory blood pressure in mothers of children with autism spectrum disorders. *The Journal of Autism Research, 8*, 99–110.

Gardner, H. (1999). *Intelligence reframed: Multiple intelligences for the 21st century.* Basic Books.

Glascoe, FP (2000) Evidence-based approach to developmental and behavioural surveillance using parents' concerns. *Child: Care, Health and Development, 26*: 137–149.

Harner C. J. & Heal L. W. (1993) The Multifaceted Lifestyle Satisfaction Scale (MLSS): psychometric properties of an interview schedule for assessing personal satisfaction of adults with limited intelligence. *Research in Developmental Disabilities, 14*, 221–236.

Harrison, P.L., & Oakland, T. (2003). Adaptive Behavior Assessment – Second Edition Manual (ABASII). San Antonio, TX: Harcourt Assessment.

Hays, P. A. (2001). Putting culture to the test: Considerations with standardized testing. In P.A. Hays (eds), *Addressing Cultural Complexities in Practice: A Framework for Clinicians and Counsellors* (pp. 11–127). Washington, DC: American Psychological Association.

Hodapp, R. M., & Burack, J. A. (1990). What mental retardation teaches us about typical development: The examples of sequences, rates, and cross-domain relations. *Development and Psychopathology, 2*, 213–225.

Hodapp, R. M., Burack, J. A., & Zigler, E. F. (1990). The developmental perspective in the field of mental retardation.

Hoffman, L., Marquis, J., Poston, D., Summers, J. A., & Turnbull, A. (2006). Assessing family outcomes: Psychometric evaluation of the Beach Center Family Quality of Life Scale. *Journal of Marriage and Family, 68*, 1069–1083.

Ingersoll, B., & Hambrick, D. Z. (2011). The relationship between the broader autism phenotype, child severity, and stress and depression in parents of children with autism spectrum disorders. *Research in Autism Spectrum Disorders, 5*, 337–344.

Ingersoll, B., & Schreibman, L. (2006). Teaching reciprocal imitation skills to young children with autism using a naturalistic behavioral approach: Effects on language, pretend play, and joint attention. *Journal of Autism and Developmental Disorders, 36*(4), 487–505.

Ingersoll, B., & Wainer, A. (2013). Initial efficacy of Project ImPACT: A parent-mediated social communication intervention for young children with ASD. *Journal of autism and developmental disorders, 43*, 2943–2952.

Johnson, N., Frenn, M., Feetham, S., & Simpson, P. (2011). Autism spectrum disorder: Parenting stress, family functioning and health-related quality of life. *Families, Systems, & Health, 29*, 232–252.

Jones, S. S. (2009). The development of imitation in infancy. *Philosophical Transactions of the Royal Society of London B: Biological Sciences, 364*(1528), 2325–2335.

Karst, J. S., & Van Hecke, A. V. (2012). Parent and family impact of Autism Spectrum Disorders: A review and proposed model for intervention evaluation. *Clinical Child and Family Psychology Review, 15*, 247–277.

McKenzie, K., & Megson, P. (2012). Screening for intellectual disability in children: A review of the literature. *Journal of Applied Research in Intellectual Disabilities, 25*(1), 80–87.

Mullen, E. M. (1995). *Mullen scales of early learning* (pp. 58-64). Circle Pines, MN: AGS.

Neisser, U., Boodoo, G., Bouchard, T. J., Jr., Boykin, A. W., Brody, N., Ceci, S. J., Halpern, D. F., Loehlin, J. C., Perloff, R., Sternberg, R. J., & Urbina, S. (1996). Intelligence: Knowns and unknowns. *American Psychologist, 51*(2), 77–101. https://doi.org/10.1037/0003-066X.51.2.77

Reed, P., Howse, J., Ho, B., & Osborne, L. A. (2016). Relationship between perceived limit-setting abilities, autism spectrum disorder severity, behaviour problems and parenting stress in mothers of children with autism spectrum disorder. *Autism*. doi: 10.1177/1362361316658775.

Roid, G. H. (2003). Stanford-Binet intelligence scales, fifth edition (SB:V). Riverside Publishing.

Roid, G. H., & Miller, L. J. (1997). Leiter international performance scale-revised (Leiter-R). *Wood Dale, IL: Stoelting, 10*.

Rogers, S. J., Estes, A., Lord, C., Vismara, L., Winter, J., Fitzpatrick, A., ... & Dawson, G. (2012). Effects of a brief Early Start Denver Model (ESDM)–based parent intervention on toddlers at risk for autism spectrum disorders: A randomized controlled trial. *Journal of the American Academy of Child & Adolescent Psychiatry, 51*(10), 1052–1065.

Schalock, R. L., Borthwick-Duffy, S. A., Bradley, V. J., Buntinx, W. H., Coulter, D. L., Craig, E. M., ... & Yeager, M. H. (2010). *Intellectual Disability: Definition, Classification, and Systems of Supports* (Vol. 26). Washington, DC: American Association on Intellectual and Developmental Disabilities.

Schalock, R. L., Verdugo, M. A., & Gomez, L. E. (2011). Evidence-based practices in the field of intellectual and developmental disabilities: An international consensus approach. *Evaluation and program planning, 34*(3), 273–282.

Shulman, C., Flores, H., Iarocci, G., & Burack, J. (2011). Intellectual disability: Concepts, definitions, and assessment. In P. Howlin, T. Charman, & M. Ghaziuddin (eds), *The SAGE Handbook of Developmental Disorders* (pp. 365–385). London: SAGE Publications Ltd.

Sparrow, S. S., Cicchetti, D. V., & Saulnier, C. A. (2016). *Vineland adaptive behavior scales* (3rd ed.). Pearson.

Sternberg, R. J. (1985). *Beyond IQ: A triarchic theory of human intelligence*. Cambridge University Press.

Stone, W. L., & Yoder, P. J. (2001). Predicting spoken language level in children with autism spectrum disorders. *Autism, 5*(4), 341–361.

Stone, W. L., Coonrod, E. E., Turner, L. M., & Pozdol, S. L. (2004). Psychometric properties of the STAT for early autism screening. *Journal of autism and developmental disorders, 34*(6), 691–701.

Toth, K., Munson, J., Meltzoff, A. N., & Dawson, G. (2006). Early predictors of communication development in young children with autism spectrum disorder: Joint attention, imitation, and toy play. *Journal of Autism and Developmental Disorders, 36*(8), 993–1005.

Treffert D. A. (2009). The savant syndrome: an extraordinary condition. A synopsis: past, present, future. *Philos Trans R Soc Lond, B, Biol Sci., 364*(1522), 1351–1357. doi:10.1098/rstb.2008.0326.

Treffert, D. A. (2009). The savant syndrome: an extraordinary condition. A synopsis: past, present, future. *Philosophical transactions of the Royal Society of London. Series B, Biological sciences, 364*(1522), 1351–1357. https://doi.org/10.1098/rstb.2008.0326

Valencia, R. R., & Suzuki, L. A. (2001). *Intelligence Testing and Minority Students: Foundations, Performance Factors and Assessment Issues.* Thousand Oaks, CA: Sage.

Wechsler, D. (2016). *Wechsler Intelligence Scale for Children* (5th ed.). NCS Pearson, Incorporated.

Whalen, C., Schreibman, L., & Ingersoll, B. (2006). The collateral effects of joint attention training on social initiations, positive affect, imitation, and spontaneous speech for young children with autism. *Journal of Autism and Developmental Disorders, 36*(5), 655–664.

Zigler, E., & Hodapp, R. (1986). *Understanding Mental Retardation.* New York, NY: Cambridge University Press.

PART II
INTELLECTUAL DISABILITIES

4
DOWN SYNDROME

> **Learning Objectives**
>
> After reading this chapter, you should be able to:
>
> - Understand the genetic causes of Down syndrome and the environmental factors that impact outcomes
> - Become familiar with the range of biomedical, developmental, and behavioural outcomes associated with Down syndrome
> - Understand how people with Down syndrome grow and change throughout the lifespan
> - Understand the educational and intervention needs of people with Down syndrome

WHAT IS DOWN SYNDROME?

Unlike many other conditions associated with ID, Down syndrome (DS) is familiar to many, and is often represented in popular culture and media. In contemporary Western culture, people with DS can be found on television, starring in movies, and featured in popular viral videos online. Most notably, the testimony of Frank Stephens to the United States Congress in 2017 became a viral video sensation, with his heartfelt declaration that, 'I am a man with Down syndrome, and my life is worth living.' With millions of views, Mr Stephens' testimony has given a voice to the lived experience of people with Down syndrome all over the world. He, and other self-advocates like him, have contributed to the change in our contemporary representations of people with DS to emphasize the appreciation of an individual's gifts and their potential contributions to their communities, even when faced with obstacles.

Down syndrome is a neurogenetic syndrome (see Chapter 6 for a definition) that impacts development from its earliest stages prenatally through infancy, childhood, adolescence, and adulthood. Down syndrome is 'multi-system' in nature, which means that it impacts not only behavioural and cognitive development, but also the development of various organ systems with important implications for health, a topic that will be discussed in subsequent sections of this chapter. Outcomes that are linked to Down syndrome, often described as *phenotypic outcomes* associated with this genetic condition, emerge during early childhood, and manifest themselves in changing ways throughout the lifespan. Understanding the dynamic nature of the developmental presentation in this population, which will be explored later in this chapter, is critical for supporting healthy outcomes and promoting well-being for people with the most common chromosomal cause of intellectual disability.

Down syndrome is caused by the presence of additional copies of the genes found on chromosome 21. Approximately 95% of cases of DS are caused by trisomy 21, which refers to the presence of three copies of chromosome 21, instead of two. The trisomy can either be complete (an extra copy of *all* of chromosome 21) or, in rare cases, partial (an extra copy of *part* of chromosome 21). Approximately 5% of the time, DS is caused by a translocation, which occurs when some or all of an extra chromosome 21 is attached to a different chromosome, often chromosome 14, and in some cases, the translocation can take place on another chromosome 21. DS can also be caused by mosaicism, which happens when cell division after conception leads to an extra chromosome 21 found in some cells in the body, but not others.

Rates of DS

DS occurs in approximately 1 in every 792 live births (de Graaf et al. 2015). There is evidence of elevated likelihood of DS when certain factors are present, including aspects of maternal folate metabolism (Coppedè 2016) and maternal exposure to certain types of chemical solvents in work environments (Keen et al. 2020). However, the most common factor associated with DS is maternal age. For some causes of DS, like mosaicism, approximately 67% of diagnoses are thought to be related to advanced maternal age (Morris 2012). In fact, one of the earliest scientific discoveries in the study of DS was made by Penrose (1933, 1934), who reported a maternal, but not paternal, age effect in a cohort of 150 families of children with Down syndrome. Other candidate factors at that time, such as birth order, were found not to have an influence on the presence of a Down syndrome diagnosis.

This early insight regarding the role of maternal age in DS has now been well-researched, and we now know that approximately 90% of cases of trisomy 21 are caused by *maternal non-disjunction* (Sherman et al. 1994), a process that is susceptible to the effects of environmental exposures over time (Coppedè 2016). Non-disjunction occurs during cell division in the ovaries or testes when homologous chromosomes in germ cells do not segregate from one another, and the result is a gamete (sperm or ovum) that contains an additional copy of chromosome 21. In maternal nondisjunction cases, this takes place during oogenesis, or the cell division process that produces the ovum (Allen et al. 2009). The remaining cases of nondisjunction are either paternal in origin, taking place during spermatogenesis (8%), or originate during cell division after conception (5%; Antonarakis et al. 2020).

In North America, Europe, and other Western societies, Down syndrome is often diagnosed prenatally, though many newborns receive a diagnosis at birth (Carlson & Vora 2017). Prenatal screening has become increasingly more accurate over the past decade; however, many infants with DS are not diagnosed prenatally, even with current technology. In one study, approximately 39% of new parents whose infants were diagnosed at birth reported that they had received a negative prenatal screen result (Nelson Goff et al. 2013). Certain physical factors at birth may lead medical providers to seek testing for the presence of DS, including specific facial features and low muscle tone overall (Groot-van der Mooren et al. 2014). For some families, then, the birth of a child, which is already a major life event that involves a great deal of transition, may be accompanied by the adjustment to the news of a DS diagnosis.

Consequently, there is an important ongoing discussion regarding the most appropriate ways to deliver the news of a DS diagnosis, both prenatally and postnatally (Crombag et al. 2020). In one study, some parents reported that their diagnosis confirmation was respectful and helpful, while other parents described that they were provided with little information, and the delivery of the diagnosis was accompanied by an emphasis on biomedical challenges. Clinicians and researchers continue to discuss how best to provide information in ways that support parent preferences (Crombag et al. 2020). According to one set of recommendations, the delivery of a diagnosis of DS at birth should include: delivery of the diagnosis in person by a health care provider who has familiarity with the contemporary scientific knowledge base regarding DS (there is an interesting TED talk on this: https://www.youtube.com/watch?v=vjRlFCgQ1e8); congratulations should be given to the family members on the birth of their newborn; the infant with DS should be present; health care providers should refer to the infant with DS by their name; the diagnosis should be delivered with sensitivity and compassion with careful attention paid to language; medical providers should present a balanced description of the positive and challenging aspects of living with DS; and referrals to additional providers should be offered (Groot-van der Mooren et al. 2014). These and other identified best practices, such as the opportunity to speak to community voices like family members, can provide important supports to families during a time of transition, and can promote the well-being of both the newborn and their caregivers during their earliest moments together.

Considering DS in time and place

From birth, DS is associated with increased likelihood of demonstrating a range of co-occurring biomedical conditions and a distinct pattern of developmental strengths and challenges. The nuances of these predispositions will be discussed throughout this chapter. However, one critical factor that often goes unnoticed, but is essential for understanding outcomes associated with Down syndrome, is socio-historical context.

Until approximately 20 years ago, the lifespan of individuals with DS was considerably shorter than it is today. In 1950, a person born with DS was expected to live until about age

12 years on average (Bittles & Glasson 2004). These days, the average lifespan of individuals with DS is estimated to be in the mid-forties and many individuals with DS live into their 60s and 70s (Presson et al. 2013). This change in average life expectancy is attributed to the improved medical care that is now available to people with DS (Leonard et al. 2000), who may require treatments for cardiac, digestive, immunological, and respiratory conditions. It is for this reason that any description of outcomes associated with DS must be understood within a specific historical era and social context. The assumption of 'fixed genetic factors' in a condition like DS must be reconsidered when taking these influences into account. In fact, the scientific basis for the section on adult development and aging in DS (below) has only been made possible in the past several decades, as health and well-being in this population has improved enough for outcomes to unfold over time.

The importance of the interaction between genetic condition and outcome, therefore, is influenced by social and historical context. Nevertheless, there are aspects of development in individuals with DS that are observed cross-culturally, and that are rooted in the genetic influences associated with the over-expression of genes on chromosome 21. The complex coaction of genetic and environmental influences is not new to the study of behaviour and development (see Chapter 2), and in this case, takes on the extra importance of the potential of malleability in outcome. To the extent that outcomes are influenced by context, they may also respond to personalized interventions that promote well-being and increased quality of life.

HEALTH

Genetic Influences

How does the presence of extra copies of the genes on chromosome 21 lead to the range of biomedical and behavioural outcomes associated with DS? There are two main longstanding hypotheses. One hypothesis focuses on what are called 'gene-dosage effects' (Pritchard & Kolaa 1999). When trisomy 21 occurs, some or all of the genes on chromosome are overexpressed, leading to the production of too many proteins, which may lead to direct outcomes or may impact the expression of other genes. The second hypothesis of how trisomy 21 leads to a range of outcomes is related to 'developmental instability' (Shapiro 1983). Within this perspective, the presence of extra copies of the genes on chromosome 21 leads to broader alterations in developmental processes and dysregulation in many biological systems, which causes a range of biomedical and behavioural outcomes. Though researchers continue to debate these hypothetical frameworks, the mechanisms and pathway from gene to outcome in DS have not yet, for the most part, been elucidated. Researchers acknowledge that establishing the link between genetic factors and specific outcomes associated with DS is, and will continue to be, a complex scientific challenge.

Congenital Heart Defects

DS is associated with ID, but it is also described as a 'multi-system' disorder that impacts many developing systems in addition to the nervous system (Capone et al., 2018). Approximately 40–50% of infants born with Down syndrome are also born with a congenital heart defect (CHD), which often requires early surgical intervention. The presence of CHD may place children with DS at additional risk for delays in skill acquisition, though these results have not been shown consistently across studies. It may be the case that extended recuperation time following surgery during infancy may have an indirect impact on early interactions with environment. From this perspective, time spent in physical recovery during infancy means that some infants with DS have fewer opportunities to engage with their early physical and social environments, and therefore may have an altered set of early experiences.

Sensory Impairments

Many individuals with DS have sensory loss, especially hearing loss (Kinnear et al. 2018). Approximately 33% of children with DS have 'conductive hearing loss', which refers to the phenomenon where sounds cannot travel from the outer ear to the inner ear (Nightengale et al. 2017). Another 30% of children with DS have sensorineural hearing loss (Nightengale et al. 2017), which involves complications in the inner ear or the nerves that connect the ear to the brain. DS is also associated with increased risk for multiple co-occurring hearing loss conditions at the same time (Nightengale et al. 2017). These and other hearing-related conditions not only have treatment planning implications, but they also place an individual at risk for additional language delays that may impact social interactions, which have implications for overall well-being.

Children with DS are also at elevated risk for ocular conditions, such as nystagmus, which makes it difficult to hold a steady eye gaze and causes repetitive unsteady eye movements (Weiss et al. 2016). Many children with DS also experience inflammation of the eyelids (blepharitis) and difficulty aligning their eyes (strabismus; Makateb et al. 2020). These conditions impact many aspects of adaptation that require visual processing, and adequate screening for both visual and hearing conditions is essential to promote well-being in individuals with DS as they grow and develop.

Other Medical Conditions

Individuals with DS are at higher risk for certain auto-immune conditions, such as alopecia and thyroid disease (Whooten et al. 2018; Rachubinski et al. 2019). Sleep disorders, such as obstructive sleep apnea, are common in DS as well, with prevalence estimates at 66% (Maris et al. 2016a), but with some estimates as high as 97% (Skotko et al. 2017). As in the general population, sleep apnea impacts the development of cognitive and communication skills during childhood in children with DS (Breslin et al. 2014; Maris et al. 2016b). In addition, DS is associated with increased risk for preterm birth, with one recent population-based study estimating that 21% of infants born with DS were born prematurely (Bergström et al. 2016). Prematurity has been linked to infant cognition during early development in DS, and may have specific implications for the development of early attention skills (Fidler et al. 2019b).

Elevated risk for these health conditions is important to consider when aiming to understand the developmental and educational needs of an individual with DS. Cognitive, social, language, and emotional development, which will be discussed below, are each influenced by many factors. Daily experiences with chronic conditions, life-threatening medical factors, and sensory processing difficulties can impact the physical and emotional resources with which an individual is able to face their day-to-day activities in home, educational, community, and employment settings. When considering lifespan development in an individual with Down syndrome, it is important to recognize that emotional development may take place in the context of recovery from a surgery, and social development may take place in the context of hearing loss. These and other co-occurring conditions contribute to the larger picture of overall well-being in individuals with Down syndrome.

Co-occurring Neurodevelopmental Conditions and Maladaptive Behaviour

Along with other biomedical concerns, individuals with DS are also at elevated likelihood of certain co-occurring neurodevelopmental conditions. Compared to the general population, where the prevalence of autism spectrum disorder (ASD) is estimated to be approximately 2% (Baio et al. 2018), individuals with DS are diagnosed with ASD at much higher rates (15-20%; DiGuiseppi et al. 2010; Richards et al. 2015). Early surveillance for ASD is essential during childhood in DS in order to provide access to empirically based interventions that promote more adaptive outcomes in children with ASD. However, accurately diagnosing ASD in DS introduces an additional level of complexity to the current recommended practices in ASD surveillance. In ASD surveillance in the general population, key markers observed during infancy include slower visual disengagement, lower levels of motoric exploration, low activity level, limited response to name, and perceptual hyper-responsivity. ASD in DS emerges during early childhood in the context of an already impacted neurodevelopmental landscape and is, therefore, more challenging to detect. Additional discovery is necessary to identify those factors that signal the emergence of ASD features specifically in children with DS.

Individuals with DS are also at higher likelihood of demonstrating symptoms of Attention Deficit and Hyperactivity Disorder (ADHD), with rates of co-occurring diagnoses ranging from 34% to 43.9% (Ekstein et al. 2011; Oxelgren et al. 2017). It is unclear what factors place some individuals with DS at increased risk for ADHD symptoms at this time. The degree of ID might be hypothesized as a plausible factor, however, no association between ADHD symptoms and degree of ID has been found (Ekstein et al. 2011). There is still a great deal that is unknown about how and why individuals with DS may demonstrate co-occurring neurodevelopmental conditions. Addressing these questions has become an important part of the scientific research agenda of funding agencies, including the US National Institutes of Health. Indeed, understanding sources of within-group variability in these outcomes may hold the key to increased well-being for a larger percentage of people with DS throughout their lives.

Behavioural Outcomes Associated with Down Syndrome

Early in the study of behavioural and developmental outcomes in DS, researchers tended to consider DS as a condition that involved overall developmental delay, with little nuance or specificity from one domain to another. For this reason, individuals with DS were often included as a control group in studies of other conditions to represent the presence of ID. Decades of research has now taught us that phenotypic outcomes associated with DS are complex, involving cognitive, social-emotional, communication/language, motoric, and self-regulation dimensions. We also know that there is a pronounced degree of within-group variability in outcome, and that many differences in presentation among individuals with DS may be attributable to the presence of additional co-occurring conditions, such as ASD or ADHD. Nevertheless, there is mounting evidence that individuals with DS have a higher likelihood of demonstrating certain patterns of developmental strength and challenge when compared to those without DS, and this phenotypic profile is of great importance for effective educational and service-related planning.

Cognition

Individuals with DS, on average, demonstrate moderate-to-severe degrees of intellectual disability. Those with mosaicism are more likely to have IQs in the mild and borderline range than those with trisomy 21. Beyond this wide range of outcomes, however, a complex landscape of cognitive performance can be observed in this population. Some aspects of information processing, such as auditory processing, are more likely to be observed as areas of challenge than others, like visual processing (Lanfranchi et al. 2004; Brock & Jarrold 2005). In addition, certain aspects of cognition are vulnerable to even more pronounced delays than would be expected based on overall developmental functioning. Key aspects of cognition, including executive functioning and memory skills, tend to be areas of particular difficulty for many individuals with DS. Understanding areas of potential vulnerability for people with DS makes it possible to plan and support mastery and independence in skill acquisition and activities of daily living.

Executive function

Individuals with DS are likely to have difficulties in the area of executive function, or the thinking skills required for purposeful, goal-oriented behaviour. These skills include the temporary storage of information while completing a task (working memory), resisting distraction and impulsive responses (inhibitory control), the ability to flexibly adjust from one schema to another (shifting), and the ability to sequence behaviours in goal-directed ways (planning; see Daunhauer & Fidler 2013 for a review). Teacher and parent ratings of executive function suggest that school-age children with DS are 5–9 times more likely to have clinically elevated levels of difficulty with various aspects of EF when compared to younger typically developed children who are at similar developmental levels (Daunhauer et al. 2014). On laboratory tasks, children with DS tend to show the most pronounced difficulties in the areas of working memory, inhibition, and planning (Daunhauer et al. 2017).

While challenges with the development of EF are of great significance for later outcomes in DS, differences in the degree of organized, goal-directed action can be detected already among infants with DS (Fidler et al. 2019b). In one study, two distinct profiles were observed among a group of infants with DS when presented with an engaging object (an unconventionally shaped red teether). Some infants coordinated the use of eye gaze, manual exploration, and mouthing the object to learn more about its properties across a one-minute segment. Other infants were also interested in the object, but primarily used their eyes for exploration, without organizing and coordination with their hands and mouths. This study offers a hint that some infants with DS plan and organize their behaviour in purposeful ways from the earliest stages, while others are in need of more direct, targeted support to develop these critical, foundational skills. Similarly, another study of infants with DS demonstrates that the early ability to flexibly shift visual attention from one object to another is correlated with overall cognitive skill acquisition, even when accounting for the effects of chronological age (Fidler et al. 2018). With early links between cognitive skill development and this type of early cognitive control, and detectable differences among infants readily observed, it is possible that executive function will be an important early skill to monitor and target with empirically supported intervention (Fidler et al. 2011).

Measuring Early Planning in Infants with Down Syndrome (excerpted from Fidler et al. 2019)

> All infants participated in a one-minute object exploration trial. Prior to the beginning of the trial, infants were seated on the lap of their caregiver at a table with their hands level with the table. Caregivers supported the infant's posture, if necessary, by holding their arms around the infant's torso. Some infants were also supported by a pillow, when necessary, to ensure proper postural support and arm positioning. Once adequate positioning was established, the examiner presented the infant with an unconventionally shaped teether at eye level, in the infant's line of vision. The examiner waited until the infant visually oriented to the teether, and then placed the teether on the table top at midline for one minute to allow the infant to explore further visually, manually, and/or orally. In instances when the teether fell out of reach, the examiner quickly placed the teether within reach at the infant's midline. Video was captured using one camera, positioned in front of the infant, in order to capture eye gaze, hand movement, and mouthing behaviour.
>
> (Fidler et al. 2019)

Two profiles were observed among the infants: a more active exploration profile and a more passive exploration profile. The more active exploration profile involved more time spent exploring the object manually and orally, while the passive profile involved mostly visual exploration. The active exploration profile was associated with more advanced cognitive performance overall, and is likely an indicator of more advanced planning through the coordination of multimodal exploration.

Memory

Memory is another important feature of cognition in individuals with DS that plays a critical role in skill development and functional outcomes. In adulthood, DS is associated with an increased risk for co-occurring Alzheimer's Disease, which involves declines in the ability to formulate new memories and retrieve them. However, outcomes related to memory in DS are far more complex than an increased risk for loss of memory function in adulthood.

Memory is comprised of different components, many of which appear to be impacted by the presence of DS. 'Retrospective memory', or the ability to remember information that has already been learned, has a unique presentation in many people with DS. In particular, one aspect of retrospective memory called 'implicit memory', or the ability to remember information without awareness, appears to be in line with overall developmental status in DS (Vicari et al. 2000). In other words, for people with Down syndrome, the ability to remember how to do previously learned activities, such as brushing teeth or getting dressed, is comparable with the abilities of others at similar overall developmental levels.

Explicit Memory: A type of long-term memory that involves recalling information 'on purpose', with an awareness that one possesses that information and conscious effort to access that information.

Implicit Memory: A type of long-term memory that involves recalling information without conscious awareness that the information is being accessed.

However, a different aspect of retrospective memory, called 'explicit memory', appears to be an area of distinct difficulty for many people with DS, even when overall levels of developmental delay have been accounted for. Explicit memory refers to the ability to remember information that was learned intentionally, such as words or numbers, or information acquired consciously, such as personal information and life experiences. While performing similarly to their developmentally equated counterparts without DS on implicit memory tasks, individuals with DS show greater difficulty on tasks that involve the recall of newly acquired information about pictures and words (Vicari et al. 2000).

Another aspect of memory that has an important impact on daily functioning is 'working memory', or the temporary storage and manipulation of information while completing tasks. If you have been reading this chapter closely, you will recall that working memory is considered to be a component of executive function. Working memory is critical for executive function because it helps us keep track of progress on task completion, brainstorm alternative ways of completing a task, and hold on to several pieces of information at the same time to organize our thoughts. Many individuals with DS, however, have extra challenges in the area of working memory, and in particular, verbal working memory. Having difficulty processing and manipulating incoming verbal information (e.g. the spoken language of others) makes it challenging to hold on to information like instructions for how to play a game. In fact, working memory skills are associated with employment outcomes in adults with DS (Tomaszewski et al. 2018), and are also connected to learning outcomes in school age children with DS in combination with other aspects of cognition (Will et al. 2016).

Difficulties with remembering information about words, numbers, and life experiences (explicit memory), and additional challenges related to updating and manipulating incoming information (working memory) together place a burden on many individuals with DS. These memory skills impact adaptation and functioning in a range of home, school, and community settings. Researchers and professionals seeking to support outcomes in this area can have a profound impact on quality of life. There is a pressing need to both support the development of stronger memory foundations, and to accommodate the needs of people with DS who may benefit from additional scaffolds and supports to address memory-related challenges.

Language

People with DS have a high likelihood of difficulty with speech, language, and communication skills. However, within this broader domain, there are areas of relative competence and areas that are more vulnerable. Understanding the nuances of this profile can be helpful for supporting skill development and planning interventions. Clinicians and interventionists who monitor particularly vulnerable areas more closely, from an informed perspective, are able to provide interventions in an anticipatory way. They may be able to support early areas of vulnerability as they present themselves in their earliest manifestations during infancy. This type of approach capitalizes on an important window of opportunity during the infant and toddler years, wherein environmental influences may have a sizable impact on neurodevelopment.

Which areas are particularly vulnerable in the development of speech, language, and communication in DS? Overall, many individuals with DS have greater difficulty with expressive language when compared to receptive language (Miller 1999). This suggests that an individual with DS is likely to understand much more language than they may produce during a social interaction. Difficulties with expressive language (usually in the form of speech) are evident during the earliest stages of development, as infants with DS produce prelinguistic vocalizations, like babbling, later than typically developing infants and continue to babble for longer (Roberts, Price, & Malkin 2007). Approximately 12% of one-year-olds with DS have uttered their first spoken words, and there is a lot of variability in the timing of this milestone during the first few years of development (Berglund et al. 2001). Roughly 90% of young children with

DS have spoken their first words by the time they turn four years old (Berglund et al. 2001). Beyond building a vocabulary, the development of more complex aspects of language is also challenged in many people with DS, particularly in the development of morpho-syntactic skills, or the development of grammar (Chapman et al. 1998; Abbeduto et al. 2003).

During childhood and into adolescence in DS, most studies show that receptive vocabulary grows with greater competence and is generally on par with overall developmental status (Abbeduto et al. 2003). The focus on challenges with expressive language relative to receptive language, however, can be reframed with the understanding that many people with DS can understand much more language than they are able to spontaneously produce. With this change in framing, it is possible to appreciate that many people with DS have a more advanced understanding of their language and communication environment than they present to others. This has important implications for educators, interventionists, and others working to support the acquisition of developmental skills in this population. A useful recommendation for many professionals working with people with DS is to teach to a person's level of language understanding, not their level of language production. If the only factor considered is a child's language production skills, it may result in an underestimation of their abilities.

Social-emotional Development

Social relatedness has been an important area of research in DS, as initial conceptualizations of DS were often presented in unidimensionally positive ways describing a social, engaging persona. We now know that there is a wide range of social-emotional outcomes associated with DS, and that approximately 15–20% of people with DS meet criteria for a diagnosis of autism.

Though autism does occur at higher rates in people with DS when compared to the general population, people with DS who do not have ASD are predisposed to certain social-emotional developmental features. The majority of young children with DS develop early nonverbal social communication skills with competence. Certain critical skills tend to develop with strength, such as the development of *joint attention*, or the use of eye gaze, gesture, and vocalizing for the purposes of social sharing (Fidler et al. 2005; Hahn et al. 2019; see Chapter 9 for more on early social communication). The use of early nonverbal communication skills as a means to interact with others and share experiences may serve as a compensatory set of skills, even as expressive language may develop more slowly.

Motor Development

Gross motor skills, or the movement of the trunk and body, are an area of pronounced delay for many individuals with Down syndrome. During early development, the onset of key milestones like sitting independently, crawling, standing, and walking takes place later, with delays that range from three months to 20 months slower than the onset norms for the general population of children (Tudella et al. 2011; Winders et al. 2019). Sitting independently is usually observable between nine and 15 months, and quadruped crawling usually emerges during the second year (14–29 months; Winders et al. 2019). There is a great degree of variability in the onset of independent walking, with some young children with DS demonstrating this skill during the middle of their second year (19 months) and some demonstrating an onset closer to three years (Winders et al. 2019). Fine motor skills are similarly delayed, the ability to move an object from one hand to the other generally occurs between 12 and 18 months and a pincer grasp usually emerges between 22 and 66 months (Frank & Esbensen 2015).

Though often we think of development in silos – motor skills develop on one path and cognitive skills on another – in reality, these areas of development influence one another greatly. Pronounced delays in motor skill acquisition in early development in DS may have a cascading impact on the development of cognitive skills. That is because infants learn about their early environments through exploration (Gibson, 1988; Fidler et al. 2019a). Early ideas about objects and how to use them in purposeful ways are dependent upon the ability to move in the direction of an object, reach for it, successfully grasp it, and then manipulate it. With delays in the onset of sitting, crawling, transferring objects, and other hand use skills, young children with DS may experience reduced opportunities for the formative, continuous interactions that typical infants have with their environments. Effectively targeting early motor development via early intervention may have an important impact on the development of early cognitive skills, like understanding cause-and-effect, strategizing, and organizing behaviour in purposeful ways (Fidler et al. 2019a).

Down Syndrome throughout the Lifespan: Infancy and Early Childhood

Though developmental and behavioural features are often studied in older children, adolescents, and adults with DS, there is growing evidence that early manifestations of phenotypic outcomes can be observed even during infancy. When compared to TD infants, many infants with DS already show delays in the development of certain precursors of executive function, including attention regulation and early planning (Schworer et al. 2020). As noted above, early cognitive skill development in DS is related to early aspects of attention control, which may shed light on potential sources of cognitive delays that become pronounced during the early childhood years (Fidler et al. 2019a).

Learning more about the early developmental presentation of infants with DS is important because it allows educators and interventionists to capitalize on neuroplasticity. 'Neuroplasticity' refers to the developing brain's ability to adapt and change its connections, and the infant and early childhood years are a period when this type of adaptive connection is at its peak. In the many Western countries, children with DS participate in early intervention services in their local communities. Intervention approaches that are informed by early phenotypic profiles are better able to target potential areas of vulnerability, and capitalize on this window of neurodevelopmental opportunity.

Middle Childhood

During the school-age years, children with DS demonstrate a range of performances in academic, home, and community environments. Certain phenotypic features associated with DS can influence participation and achievement during this period. As described earlier, executive function skills, including working memory and inhibitory control, have been shown to predict math and reading performance in children with DS (Will et al. 2016). In addition, the presence of challenging behaviours influences how well a student with DS adapts to their school environment (Will et al. 2016). Strategizing to reduce the incidence of challenging behaviours and to support the development of self-regulation during childhood may promote a greater sense of well-being and achievement during this critical phase of the lifespan.

Adolescence

The teenage years are filled with complex physical and psychological changes in the general population, and the same is true for teens with DS. Oftentimes, adolescents with DS show fewer outward behaviour challenges, but they may show an increase in more internal mood and thought-related difficulties (Dykens & Kasari 1997; Dykens et al. 2002). One study found that more than half of adolescents with DS demonstrated some type of social withdrawal (Dykens et al. 2002). Other studies report that adolescence in DS is associated with a more sedentary lifestyle, which may have health-related implications (Baumer & Davidson 2014).

Adolescence is also associated with increased risk for developmental regression, or the loss of skills that had been acquired previously, in people with DS, with some clinical researchers identifying cases of 'Down Syndrome Disintegrative Disorder' (Worley et al. 2015). One DS clinic identified 11 children and adolescents with DS (average age of 11 years) who either showed a new onset or a distinctive increase in autistic behaviours and cognitive decline (Worley et al. 2015), but no apparent onset of any other diagnosis. Interestingly, when these individuals were re-examined during late adolescence/early adulthood (average age of 20 years), approximately 70% of them had reductions in their autistic and cognitive changes. However, all of the adolescents in the study continued to demonstrate more autism symptoms and reduced cognitive skills than they had prior (Worley et al. 2015). Thus, adolescence is a time of potential vulnerability to the onset of additional co-occurring conditions for individuals with DS.

Adulthood

Because of the increased life expectancy of individuals with DS in the past 50 years, we are newly able to characterize and describe the adult development phase of the lifespan. Along with these life expectancy advances, there have also been innovations related to participation of adults with DS in their communities and within society in general. Many adults with DS are employed, and increased access to inclusive higher education means that many adults with DS are continuing with their education and training after they graduate from high school. We are only beginning to understand which skills set the stage for these positive adult outcomes in DS, but understanding aspects of the phenotypic outcomes associated with DS offers some important clues. For example, just as more advanced working memory skills support stronger educational achievement in children with DS, this same construct can predict whether or not an adult with DS is employed for ten hours per week or more (Tomaszewski et al. 2018).

Despite these optimistic outcomes, adulthood in DS also brings increased risks for additional difficulties. The neuropathological features of Alzheimer's Disease are found almost universally in adults with DS as they age (Mann & Esri 1989), and dementia is considered a leading cause of death in adults with DS (Englund et al. 2013). Approximately 80% of adults with DS over the age of 65 will be diagnosed with Alzheimer's Disease, which is a much higher rate than observed in the general population (McCarron et al. 2014). Adults with DS who are diagnosed with Alzheimer's Disease will tend to demonstrate increased difficulties with aspects of episodic memory, or the memory skills that help us track what happens to us on a day-to-day basis. They may also, however, demonstrate the onset of behavioural and psychiatric symptoms, including irritability, self-injury, social withdrawal and increased lethargy (Prasher et al. 1998; Urv et al. 2008).

Why Are People with DS at Increased Risk of Alzheimer's Disease?

The increased risk of Alzheimer's Disease has been attributed to the location of several Alzheimer's Disease-related genes on chromosome 21 (Zis & Strydom 2018). One hypothesis is that the presence of an extra gene that encodes for Amyloid Precursor Protein (APP) leads to over-expression of this protein, and increased APP expression is associated with early-onset Alzheimer's in the general population (Zis & Strydom 2018). In fact, when only a partial trisomy of chromosome 21 is present with no extra copy of the gene that encodes for APP, the early-onset of Alzheimer's Disease is not observed (Doran et al. 2017). As a result of this intersection between DS and Alzheimer's Disease risk, researchers have become interested in understanding the special case of these co-occurring conditions, as this dually diagnosed population may bring about a more advanced understanding of this pathology and treatment for people with Down syndrome, and for people with Alzheimer's Disease in the general population.

TREATMENT FOR DS: PROMISE AND CHALLENGES

As the neurocognitive and the neuroanatomical phenotype associated with DS has been increasingly well-understood, there has been a call for new pharmaceutical treatments to support outcomes in this population throughout the lifespan (Hart et al. 2017). To date, several potential treatments have been tested in clinical trials to address cognition and information processing difficulties for adults with DS, with few notable findings to date (Hart et al. 2017).

One important factor that researchers have begun to consider is that many of the structural neurodevelopmental differences that lead to cognitive outcomes in DS unfold during prenatal and early development. Treatments that are designed to support early neurodevelopment may set the stage for greater skill acquisition for individuals with DS throughout the lifespan (Bianchi et al. 2010).

Researchers in this area argue that, with early diagnosis, there is the possibility to intervene to support neurodevelopment and to reduce the effects of the overexpression of genes on chromosome 21 (Guedj et al. 2014). An intriguing new area within DS treatment science has considered the potential for prenatal treatment of cognitive and developmental features associated with DS. This work is still in its early stages, and much work lies ahead to demonstrate the effects and the safety of such an approach. Should these advances move forward, an important discussion regarding the ethics of treatments for conditions like DS will be necessary in the coming years. Biomedical and behavioural science in DS have yielded powerful changes in terms of lifespan and quality of life for people with DS, but this new frontier may yet add another chapter that involves critical questions regarding ability, disability, and ethical treatment approaches.

Phenotype-informed Intervention

While biomedical intervention are underway, developmental and behavioural treatments in DS continue to advance as well. There is an ongoing call to translate syndrome-related information regarding phenotypic profiles into targeted, anticipatory treatments (Fidler et al. 2007). Work of this nature has been championed by pioneers in the field of DS research for decades (Buckley 2000), and has continued to gain momentum in recent years. Within this approach, researchers work to identify areas of known vulnerability during childhood, adolescence, and adulthood in DS, and use that information to inform early developmental interventions that target precursor or foundational skillsets. Though the promise of this approach has not yet been fully realized to date, there are some important examples of DS-informed interventions that have made a positive impact. DS-informed reading interventions (Lemons et al. 2018), motor interventions (Ulrich et al. 2008), and physical exercise interventions (Ptomey et al. 2018) have begun to demonstrate the utility of such a model. With time, it may be possible for interventionists to monitor early development in informed ways, and provide anticipatory enrichments that promote more positive, adaptive cascades for cognition, language, and other critical skill areas.

Inclusion and Well-being in DS

We began this chapter citing the remarkable testimonial from Frank Stephens in front of the US Congress. He, and so many others with DS, are exemplars of the impact that people with ID can have on our society. The list of achievements that may have been deemed out of reach for people with DS one generation ago are now becoming more common: people with DS starring in television shows and movies, presenting awards at the Oscars, attending universities, starting businesses, and living long, fulfilling lives. And as scientific research continues to uncover new knowledge about DS, this work underscores that the constellation of biomedical and developmental outcomes associated with DS are just parts of a whole person, and not nearly the most important parts. With investments in social supports, educational resources, and biomedical technology in the not too distant future, we will likely see people with DS elevating themselves to even greater and greater heights.

Reflective Questions

1. What are some ways that knowledge about Down syndrome can influence your future professional practices?
2. How should an educator or intervention best use developmental information about Down syndrome?
3. What are some ways to support families of young children with Down syndrome after receiving a diagnosis and throughout childhood?
4. What are some ways to support individuals with Down syndrome and their families during adolescence and adulthood?
5. What are the next steps in terms of research about Down syndrome that you believe will have the greatest impact?

Recommended Videos

Watch Frank Stephens' opening statement to the United States Congress

https://www.c-span.org/video/?c4687834/frank-stephens-opening-statement-syndrome

Watch this TEDTalk from Tamara Taggart, an Anchor for CTV news and mother to Beckett, who has DS.

https://www.youtube.com/watch?v=vjRlFCgQ1e8&feature=emb_logo

REFERENCES

Abbeduto, L., Murphy, M. M., Cawthon, S. W., Richmond, E. K., Weissman, M. D., Karadottir, S., & O'Brien, A. (2003). Receptive language skills of adolescents and young adults with Down syndrome or fragile X syndrome. *American Journal on Mental Retardation, 108*(3), 149–160. doi:10.1352/0895-8017(2003)108<0149:RLSOAA>2.0.CO;2

Allen, E. G., Freeman, S. B., Druschel, C., Hobbs, C. A., O'Leary, L. A., Romitti, P. A., ... Sherman, S. L. (2009). Maternal age and risk for trisomy 21 assessed by the origin of chromosome nondisjunction: a report from the Atlanta and National Down Syndrome Projects. *Human genetics, 125*(1), 41–52. doi:10.1007/s00439-008-0603-8

Antonarakis, S. E., Skotko, B. G., Rafii, M. S., Strydom, A., Pape, S. E., Bianchi, D. W., ... Reeves, R. H. (2020). Down syndrome. *Nature Reviews. Disease Primers, 6*(1), 9. doi:10.1038/s41572-019-0143-7

Baio, J., Wiggins, L., Christensen, D. L., Maenner, M. J., Daniels, J., Warren, Z., ... Dowling, N. F. (2018). Prevalence of Autism Spectrum Disorder among children aged 8 years – autism and developmental disabilities monitoring network, 11 Sites, United States, 2014. *Morbidity and Mortality Weekly Report. Surveillance Summaries (Washington, DC: 2002), 67*(6), 1–23. doi:10.15585/mmwr.ss6706a1

Baumer, N., & Davidson, E. J. (2014). Supporting a happy, healthy adolescence for young people with Down syndrome and other intellectual disabilities: recommendations for clinicians. *Current Opinion in Pediatrics, 26*(4), 428–434. doi:10.1097/MOP.0000000000000122

Berglund, E., Eriksson, M., & Johansson, I. (2001). Parental reports of spoken language skills in children with Down syndrome. *Journal of Speech, Language, and Hearing Research, 44*(1), 179–191. doi:10.1044/1092-4388(2001/016)

Bergström, S., Carr, H., Petersson, G., Stephansson, O., Bonamy, A.-K. E., Dahlström, A., ... Johansson, S. (2016). Trends in congenital heart defects in infants with Down Syndrome. *Pediatrics, 138*(1). doi:10.1542/peds.2016-0123

Bianchi, P., Ciani, E., Guidi, S., Trazzi, S., Felice, D., Grossi, G., ... Bartesaghi, R. (2010). Early pharmacotherapy restores neurogenesis and cognitive performance in the Ts65Dn mouse model for Down syndrome. *The Journal of Neuroscience, 30*(26), 8769–8779. doi:10.1523/JNEUROSCI.0534-10.2010

Bittles, A. H., & Glasson, E. J. (2004). Clinical, social, and ethical implications of changing life expectancy in Down syndrome. *Developmental Medicine & Child Neurology, 46*(4), 282–286. doi:10.1017/S0012162204000441

Breslin, J., Spanò, G., Bootzin, R., Anand, P., Nadel, L., & Edgin, J. (2014). Obstructive sleep apnea syndrome and cognition in Down syndrome. *Developmental Medicine & Child Neurology, 56*(7), 657–664. doi:10.1111/dmcn.12376

Brock, J., & Jarrold, C. (2005). Serial order reconstruction in Down syndrome: Evidence for a selective deficit in verbal short-term memory. *Journal of Child Psychology and Psychiatry, 46*(3), 304–316. doi:10.1111/j.1469-7610.2004.00352.x

Buckley, S. (2000). *Living with Down syndrome*: Down Syndrome Educational Trust.

Capone, G. T., Chicoine, B., Bulova, P., Stephens, M., Hart, S., Crissman, B., ... Smith, D. (2018). Co-occurring medical conditions in adults with Down syndrome: A systematic review toward the development of health care guidelines. *American Journal of Medical Genetics. Part A, 176*(1), 116–133. doi:10.1002/ajmg.a.38512

Carlson, L. M., & Vora, N. L. (2017). Prenatal diagnosis: screening and diagnostic tools. *Obstetrics and Gynecology Clinics of North America, 44*(2), 245–256. doi:10.1016/j.ogc.2017.02.004

Chapman, R. S., Seung, H.-K., Schwartz, S. E., & Bird, E. K.-R. (1998). Language skills of children and adolescents with Down syndrome: II Production deficits. *Journal of Speech, Language, and Hearing Research, 41*(4), 861–873. doi:10.1044/jslhr.4104.861

Coppedè, F. (2016). Risk factors for Down syndrome. *Archives of Toxicology, 90*(12), 2917–2929. Retrieved from https://ezproxy2.library.colostate.edu/login?url=http://search.ebscohost.com/login.aspx?direct=true&AuthType=cookie,ip,url,cpid&custid=s4640792&db=cmedm&AN=27600794&site=ehost-live

Crombag, N. M., Page-Christiaens, G. C., Skotko, B. G., & de Graaf, G. (2020). Receiving the news of Down syndrome in the era of prenatal testing. *American Journal of Medical Genetics. Part A, 182*(2), 374–385. doi:10.1002/ajmg.a.61438

Daunhauer, L. A., & Fidler, D. J. (2013). Executive functioning in individuals with Down syndrome. In K. C. Barrett, N. A. Fox, G. A. Morgan, D. J. Fidler, & L. A. Daunhauer (Eds.), *Handbook of Self-regulatory Processes in Development: New Directions and International Perspectives.* (pp. 453–472). New York, NY: Psychology Press.

Daunhauer, L. A., Fidler, D. J., Hahn, L., Will, E., Lee, N. R., & Hepburn, S. (2014). Profiles of everyday executive functioning in young children with Down syndrome. *American Journal on Intellectual and Developmental Disabilities, 119*(4), 303–318.

Daunhauer, L. A., Gerlach-McDonald, B., Will, E., & Fidler, D. J. (2017). Performance and ratings based measures of executive function in school-aged children with Down syndrome. *Developmental Neuropsychology, 42*(6), 351–368. doi:10.1080/87565641.2017.1360303

de Graaf, G., Buckley, F., & Skotko, B. G. (2015). Estimates of the live births, natural losses, and elective terminations with Down syndrome in the United States. *American Journal of Medical Genetics. Part A, 167A*(4), 756–767. doi:10.1002/ajmg.a.37001

DiGuiseppi, C., Hepburn, S., Davis, J. M., Fidler, D. J., Hartway, S., Lee, N. R., ... Robinson, C. (2010). Screening for autism spectrum disorders in children with Down syndrome: Population prevalence and screening test characteristics. *Journal of Developmental and Behavioral Pediatrics, 31*(3), 181–191. doi:10.1097/DBP.0b013e3181d5aa6d

Doran, E., Keator, D., Head, E., Phelan, M. J., Kim, R., Totoiu, M., ... Lott, I. T. (2017). Down syndrome, partial trisomy 21, and absence of Alzheimer's disease: The role of APP. *Journal of Alzheimer's Disease, 56*(2), 459–470. doi:10.3233/JAD-160836

Dykens, E. M., & Kasari, C. (1997). Maladaptive behavior in children with Prader-Willi syndrome, Down syndrome, and nonspecific mental retardation. *American Journal of Mental Retardation: AJMR, 102*(3), 228–237. Retrieved from https://ezproxy2.library.colostate.edu/login?url=http://search.ebscohost.com/login.aspx?direct=true&AuthType=cookie,ip,url,cpid&custid=s4640792&db=cmedm&AN=9394132&site=ehost-live

Dykens, E. M., Shah, B., Sagun, J., Beck, T., & King, B. H. (2002). Maladaptive behaviour in children and adolescents with Down's syndrome. *Journal of Intellectual Disability Research, 46*(6), 484–492. doi:10.1046/j.1365-2788.2002.00431.x

Ekstein, S., Glick, B., Weill, M., Kay, B., & Berger, I. (2011). Down syndrome and attention-deficit/hyperactivity disorder (ADHD). *Journal of Child Neurology, 26*(10), 1290–1295. doi:10.1177/0883073811405201

Englund, A., Jonsson, B., Zander, C. S., Gustafsson, J., & Annerén, G. (2013). Changes in mortality and causes of death in the Swedish Down syndrome population. *American Journal of Medical Genetics. Part A, 161A*(4), 642–649. doi:10.1002/ajmg.a.35706

Fidler, D.J., Philofsky, A., Hepburn, S., & Rogers, S. (2005). Nonverbal requesting and problem solving in toddlers with Down syndrome. *American Journal on Mental Retardation, 110*, 312–322.

Fidler, D. J., Philofsky, A., & Hepburn, S. L. (2007). Language phenotypes and intervention planning: bridging research and practice. *Mental Retardation and Developmental Disabilities Research Reviews, 13*(1), 47–57. Retrieved from https://ezproxy2.library.colostate.edu/login?url=https://search.ebscohost.com/login.aspx?direct=true&AuthType=cookie,ip,url,cpid&custid=s4640792&db=cmedm&AN=17326117&site=ehost-live

Fidler, D. J., Hepburn, S., Osaki, D., Rondal, J., & Perera, J. (2011). Goal-directedness as a target for early intervention in Down syndrome. *Neurocognitive Rehabilitation of Down syndrome: Early years*, 191–204.

Fidler, D. J., Needham, A. W., & Schworer, E. (2019a). Chapter Two – Infant foundations in Down syndrome: early constraints on cognitive skill acquisition. In S. Lanfranchi (ed.), *International Review of Research in Developmental Disabilities* (Vol. 56, pp. 41–65): Academic Press.

Fidler, D. J., Schworer, E., Prince, M. A., Will, E. A., Needham, A. W., & Daunhauer, L. A. (2019b). Exploratory behavior and developmental skill acquisition in infants with down syndrome. *Infant Behavior and Development, 54*, 140–150.

Fidler, D.J., Schworer, E., Will, E., Patel, L., & Daunhauer, L. (2018). Correlates of early cognition in infants with Down syndrome. *Journal of Intellectual Disability Research, 63*, 205–214.

Frank, K., & Esbensen, A. J. (2015). Fine motor and self-care milestones for individuals with down syndrome using a retrospective chart review. *Journal of Intellectual Disability Research, 59*(8), 719–729. doi:10.1111/jir.12176

Gibson, E. J. (1988). Exploratory behavior in the development of perceiving, acting, and the acquiring of knowledge. *Annual Review of Psychology, 39*(1), 1–42.

Groot-van der Mooren, M. D., Gemke, R. J. B. J., Cornel, M. C., & Weijerman, M. E. (2014). Neonatal diagnosis of Down syndrome in the Netherlands: Suspicion and communication with parents. *Journal of Intellectual Disability Research, 58*(10), 953–961. doi:10.1111/jir.12125

Guedj, F., Bianchi, D. W., & Delabar, J.-M. (2014). Prenatal treatment of Down syndrome: a reality? *Current Opinion in Obstetrics & Gynecology, 26*(2), 92–103. doi:10.1097/GCO.0000000000000056

Hahn, L. J., Brady, N. C., & Versaci, T. (2019). Communicative use of triadic eye gaze in children with down syndrome, autism spectrum disorder, and other intellectual and developmental disabilities. *American Journal of Speech-Language Pathology, 28*(4), 1509–1522. doi:10.1044/2019_AJSLP-18-0155

Hart, S. J., Visootsak, J., Tamburri, P., Phuong, P., Baumer, N., Hernandez, M.-C., … Spiridigliozzi, G. A. (2017). Pharmacological interventions to improve cognition and adaptive functioning in Down syndrome: Strides to date. *American Journal Of Medical Genetics. Part A, 173*(11), 3029–3041. doi:10.1002/ajmg.a.38465

Keen, C., Hunter, J. E., Allen, E. G., Rocheleau, C., Waters, M., & Sherman, S. L. (2020). The association between maternal occupation and down syndrome: A report from the National

Down Syndrome Project. *International Journal of Hygiene and Environmental Health, 223*(1), 207–213. doi:10.1016/j.ijheh.2019.09.001

Kinnear, D., Morrison, J., Allan, L., Henderson, A., Smiley, E., & Cooper, S.A. (2018). Multi-morbidity in a cohort of adults with intellectual disabilities, with and without Down syndrome. *BMJ Open.*

Lanfranchi, S., Cornoldi, C., & Vianello, R. (2004). Verbal and visuospatial working memory deficits in children with Down syndrome. *American Journal on Mental Retardation, 109*(6), 456–466. doi:10.1352/0895-8017(2004)109<456:VAVWMD>2.0.CO;2

Lemons, C. J., King, S. A., Davidson, K. A., Puranik, C. S., Al Otaiba, S., & Fidler, D. J. (2018). Personalized reading intervention for children with Down syndrome. *Journal of School Psychology, 66*, 67–84. doi:10.1016/j.jsp.2017.07.006

Leonard, S., Bower, C., Petterson, B., & Leonard, H. (2000). Survival of infants born with Down's syndrome: 1980–1996. *Paediatric and Perinatal Epidemiology, 14*(2), 163–171. Retrieved from https://ezproxy2.library.colostate.edu/login?url=http://search.ebscohost.com/login.aspx?direct=true&AuthType=cookie,ip,url,cpid&custid=s4640792&db=cmedm&AN=10791661&site=ehost-live

Makateb, A., Hashemi, H., Farahi, A., Mehravaran, S., Khabazkhoob, M., & Asgari, S. (2020). Ocular alignment, media, and eyelid disorders in Down syndrome. *Strabismus, 28*(1), 42–48. doi:10.1080/09273972.2019.1699582

Mann, D. M., & Esiri, M. M. (1989). The pattern of acquisition of plaques and tangles in the brains of patients under 50 years of age with Down's syndrome. *Journal of the Neurological Sciences, 89*(2–3), 169–179. https://doi.org/10.1016/0022-510x(89)90019-1

Maris, M., Verhulst, S., Wojciechowski, M., Van de Heyning, P., & Boudewyns, A. (2016a). Prevalence of obstructive sleep apnea in children with Down syndrome. *Sleep, 39*(3), 699–704. doi:10.5665/sleep.5554

Maris, M., Verhulst, S., Wojciechowski, M., Van de Heyning, P., & Boudewyns, A. (2016b). Sleep problems and obstructive sleep apnea in children with Down syndrome, an overview. *International Journal of Pediatric Otorhinolaryngology, 82*, 12–15.

McCarron, M., McCallion, P., Reilly, E., & Mulryan, N. (2014). A prospective 14-year longitudinal follow-up of dementia in persons with Down syndrome. *Journal of Intellectual Disability Research, 58*(1), 61–70. doi:10.1111/jir.12074

Miller, J. F. (1999). Profiles of language development in children with Down syndrome. In J. Miller, M. Leddy, & L. A. Leavitt (eds), *Improving the communication of people with Down syndrome* (pp. 11–40). Brookes.

Morris, J. K. (2012). Trisomy 21 mosaicism and maternal age. *American Journal of Medical Genetics. Part A, 158A*(10), 2482–2484. doi:10.1002/ajmg.a.35571

Nelson Goff, B. S., Springer, N., Foote, L. C., Frantz, C., Peak, M., Tracy, C., … Cross, K. A. (2013). Receiving the initial Down syndrome diagnosis: a comparison of prenatal and postnatal parent group experiences. *Intellectual and Developmental Disabilities, 51*(6), 446–457. doi:10.1352/1934-9556-51.6.446

Nightengale, E., Yoon, P., Wolter-Warmerdam, K., Daniels, D., & Hickey, F. (2017). Understanding hearing and hearing loss in children with Down syndrome. *American Journal of Audiology, 26*(3), 301–308. doi:10.1044/2017_AJA-17-0010

Oxelgren, U. W., Myrelid, Å., Annerén, G., Ekstam, B., Göransson, C., Holmbom, A., ... Fernell, E. (2017). Prevalence of autism and attention-deficit–hyperactivity disorder in Down syndrome: A population-based study. *Developmental Medicine & Child Neurology, 59*(3), 276–283. doi:10.1111/dmcn.13217

Penrose, L. (1933). The relative effects of paternal and maternal age in mongolism. *Journal of genetics, 27*, 219–224.

Penrose, L. (1934). The relative aetiological importance of birth order and maternal age in mongolism. *Proceedings of the Royal Society (Biology)*, 431–450.

Prasher, V. P., Chung, M. C., & Haque, M. S. (1998). Longitudinal changes in adaptive behavior in adults with Down syndrome: Interim findings from a longitudinal study. *American Journal on Mental Retardation, 103*(1), 40–46. doi:10.1352/0895-8017(1998)103<0040:LCIABI>2.0.CO;2

Presson, A. P., Partyka, G., Jensen, K. M., Devine, O. J., Rasmussen, S. A., McCabe, L. L., & McCabe, E. R. B. (2013). Current estimate of Down syndrome population prevalence in the United States. *The Journal of Pediatrics, 163*(4), 1163–1168. doi:10.1016/j.jpeds.2013.06.013

Pritchard, M. A., & Kola, I. (1999). The 'gene dosage effect' hypothesis versus the 'amplified developmental instability' hypothesis in Down syndrome. *Journal of neural transmission. Supplementum, 57*, 293–303. Retrieved from https://ezproxy2.library.colostate.edu/login?url=http://search.ebscohost.com/login.aspx?direct=true&AuthType=cookie,ip,url,cpid&custid=s4640792&db=cmedm&AN=10666684&site=ehost-live

Ptomey, L. T., Szabo, A. N., Willis, E. A., Gorczyca, A. M., Greene, J. L., Danon, J. C., & Donnelly, J. E. (2018). Changes in cognitive function after a 12-week exercise intervention in adults with Down syndrome. *Disability and Health Journal, 11*(3), 486–490. doi:10.1016/j.dhjo.2018.02.003

Rachubinski, A. L., Estrada, B. E., Norris, D., Dunnick, C. A., Boldrick, J. C., & Espinosa, J. M. (2019). Janus kinase inhibition in Down syndrome: 2 cases of therapeutic benefit for alopecia areata. *JAAD case reports, 5*(4), 365.

Richards, C., Jones, C., Groves, L., Moss, J., & Oliver, C. (2015). Prevalence of autism spectrum disorder phenomenology in genetic disorders: A systematic review and meta-analysis. *The Lancet Psychiatry, 2*(10), 909–916. doi:10.1016/S2215-0366(15)00376-4

Roberts, J. E., Price, J., & Malkin, C. (2007). Language and communication development in Down syndrome. *Mental retardation and developmental disabilities research reviews, 13*(1), 26–35.

Schworer, E., Fidler, D., & Daunhauer, L. (2020). *Foundations of executive function in infants with Down syndrome*. Manuscript Submitted for Publication. Human Development and Family Studies. Colorado State University.

Shapiro, B. L. (1983). Down syndrome – a disruption of homeostasis. *American Journal of Medical Genetics, 14*(2), 241–269. Retrieved from https://ezproxy2.library.colostate.edu/login?url=http://search.ebscohost.com/login.aspx?direct=true&AuthType=cookie,ip,url,cpid&custid=s4640792&db=cmedm&AN=6220605&site=ehost-live

Sherman, S. L., Petersen, M. B., Freeman, S. B., Hersey, J., Pettay, D., Taft, L., ... Hassold, T. J. (1994). Non-disjunction of chromosome 21 in maternal meiosis I: evidence for a maternal age-dependent mechanism involving reduced recombination. *Human molecular genetics,*

3(9), 1529–1535. Retrieved from https://ezproxy2.library.colostate.edu/login?url=http://search.ebscohost.com/login.aspx?direct=true&AuthType=cookie,ip,url,cpid&custid=s4640792&db=cmedm&AN=7833907&site=ehost-live

Skotko, B. G., Macklin, E. A., Muselli, M., Voelz, L., McDonough, M. E., Davidson, E., … Rosen, D. (2017). A predictive model for obstructive sleep apnea and Down syndrome. *American Journal of Medical Genetics. Part A, 173*(4), 889–896. doi:10.1002/ajmg.a.38137

Tomaszewski, B., Fidler, D. J., Talapatra, D., & Riley, K. (2018). Adaptive behaviour, executive function and employment in adults with down syndrome. *Journal of Intellectual Disability Research, 62*(1), 41–52. doi:10.1111/jir.12450

Tudella, E., Pereira, K., Basso, R. P., & Savelsbergh, G. J. P. (2011). Description of the motor development of 3–12 month old infants with down syndrome: The influence of the postural body position. *Research in Developmental Disabilities, 32*(5), 1514–1520. doi:10.1016/j.ridd.2011.01.046

Ulrich, D. A., Lloyd, M. C., Tiernan, C. W., Looper, J. E., & Angulo-Barroso, R. M. (2008). Effects of intensity of treadmill training on developmental outcomes and stepping in infants with Down syndrome: a randomized trial. *Physical therapy, 88*(1), 114–122. Retrieved from https://ezproxy2.library.colostate.edu/login?url=https://search.ebscohost.com/login.aspx?direct=true&AuthType=cookie,ip,url,cpid&custid=s4640792&db=cmedm&AN=17940103&site=ehost-live

Urv, T. K., Zigman, W. B., & Silverman, W. (2008). Maladaptive behaviors related to dementia status in adults with Down syndrome. *American Journal on Mental Retardation, 113*(2), 73–86. doi:10.1352/0895-8017(2008)113[73:MBRTDS]2.0.CO;2

Vicari, S., Bellucci, S., & Carlesimo, G. A. (2000). Implicit and explicit memory: A functional dissociation in persons with Down syndrome. *Neuropsychologia, 38*(3), 240–251. doi:10.1016/S0028-3932(99)00081-0

Weiss, A. H., Kelly, J. P., & Phillips, J. O. (2016). Infantile nystagmus and abnormalities of conjugate eye movements in Down syndrome. *Investigative ophthalmology & visual science, 57*(3), 1301–1309. doi:10.1167/iovs.15-18532

Whooten, R., Schmitt, J., & Schwartz, A. (2018). Endocrine manifestations of Down syndrome. *Current opinion in endocrinology, diabetes, and obesity, 25*(1), 61–66. doi:10.1097/MED.0000000000000382

Will, E. A., Gerlach-McDonald, B., Fidler, D. J., & Daunhauer, L. A. (2016). Impact of maladaptive behavior on school function in Down syndrome. *Research in Developmental Disabilities, 59*, 328–337. doi:10.1016/j.ridd.2016.08.018

Winders, P., Wolter-Warmerdam, K., & Hickey, F. (2019). A schedule of gross motor development for children with Down syndrome. *Journal of Intellectual Disability Research, 63*(4), 346–356. doi:10.1111/jir.12580

Worley, G., Crissman, B. G., Cadogan, E., Milleson, C., Adkins, D. W., & Kishnani, P. S. (2015). Down syndrome disintegrative disorder: New-onset autistic regression, dementia, and insomnia in older children and adolescents with Down syndrome. *Journal of Child Neurology, 30*(9), 1147–1152. doi:10.1177/0883073814554654

Zis, P., & Strydom, A. (2018). Clinical aspects and biomarkers of Alzheimer's disease in Down syndrome. *Free Radical Biology & Medicine, 114*, 3–9. doi:10.1016/j.freeradbiomed.2017.08.024

5
FOETAL ALCOHOL SPECTRUM DISORDERS

> **Learning Objectives**
>
> After reading this chapter, you should be able to:
> - Understand the diagnosis and causes of Foetal Alcohol Spectrum Disorder
> - Understand the diagnostic process of Foetal Alcohol Spectrum Disorder
> - Review the cognitive, neurobehavioural, and social impact of Foetal Alcohol Spectrum Disorder

INTRODUCTION

We made the point in Chapter 1 that the development of all children, including those with neurodevelopmental conditions, is impacted by the many different aspects of the environment in which children live. However, the situation of children with foetal alcohol spectrum disorders (FASD) is entirely unique among all the other populations discussed in this book and all those that are classified with a developmental disability. The aetiology, or cause, of the FASDs is entirely contingent on an action undertaken by someone in the environment – in this case, drinking by the biological mother during pregnancy. Thus, FASD is different than the other disabilities in that it is not present in the child's genetics, nor is it part of the child's physiology or biological makeup at conception, and therefore it is entirely preventable. In addition, the social consequences of having a mother who drinks during pregnancy can be associated with any number of risk factors of everyday life. While certainly not all mothers of children with FASD drink excessively, at least some do and their ability to provide nurturing environments is thereby compromised, especially considering some of the difficulties associated with FASD that we will discuss. In some cases, these challenges may be so pervasive that the biological mother is unable to care for their child on a consistent basis, and the child will need to be fostered or adopted (Badry & Harding 2020).

The reason that drinking during pregnancy is so problematic is that alcohol is a teratogen, an agent that disrupts the growth and development of the foetus. In the case of alcohol, the teratogenic effects are pervasive, as they extend to the physical, cognitive, and social aspects of development. The impact is so widespread because the alcohol that is drunk by the mother enters her bloodstream and then crosses the placenta into both the bloodstream and amniotic fluid of the infant. The alcohol permeates every part of the foetus through its bloodstream and by its drinking of the amniotic fluid. As the foetus' ability to metabolize and remove the alcohol is not yet well developed, the alcohol can remain in its system for a relatively long time. Since alcohol is easily able to cross the blood–brain barrier and affects developing foetuses in a variety of ways, both increased exposure of the foetus to alcohol and sustained alcohol intake during any trimester of pregnancy are associated with increased likelihood of developing FASD (Uban et al. 2010). However, the extent of the impact is not entirely determined by the drinking behaviour. Rather, certain environmental factors can either exacerbate or diminish these effects. For example, specific genetic influences, low socioeconomic status, maternal smoking, older maternal age at pregnancy, poor maternal diet, and paternal chronic alcohol use have all been cited as increasing the risk of developing FASD after alcohol exposure (Gupta et al. 2016).

WHAT ARE FOETAL ALCOHOL SPECTRUM DISORDERS?

The clinical term foetal alcohol spectrum disorders (FASD) refers to a group of conditions that occur as a result of the prenatal exposure to alcohol (PAE) discussed above. Each of these conditions is characterized by specific symptom clusters and the severity of impairment (Centers for Disease Control and Prevention [CDC] 2021). They include foetal alcohol syndrome (FAS), alcohol-related neurodevelopmental disorder (ARND), alcohol-related birth defects (ARBD), and neurodevelopmental disorder associated with prenatal alcohol exposure (ND-PAE). As a group, they loosely share a few general physical, cognitive, and social characteristics and challenges, although as we will see, they are each unique in their own ways. The common physical symptoms include low body weight, vision and hearing difficulties, shorter-than-average height, small head size, and abnormal facial features such as displaying a smooth ridge between the nose and upper lip (a region called the philtrum). The general cognitive signs of the FASDs include restricted motor coordination, hyperactive behaviour, memory challenges, difficulties in school and with learning, poor reasoning, and in some cases, intellectual disability (CDC 2021). Socially, children with FASDs often exhibit a range of social challenges that can be exacerbated by their higher risk of experiencing environmental adversity due to the early caregiver instability that may even lead to removal from their home. Later in the chapter, we will provide a more detailed description of some of these aspects of development in relation to the different FASDs.

As the symptoms of the FASDs vary considerably in their impact, the FASDs are referred to as a spectrum. Yet, the spectrum should not be thought of as simply linear one extending from mild to severe. But rather one that is multidimensional since the signs and symptoms of FASDs are heterogeneous, or mixed, in their presentation across the various associated conditions. Within the umbrella of the FASDs, individuals may receive a range of diagnoses and treatments that are based on their unique pattern of symptoms and difficulties.

Understanding the Course of FASDs

The study of FASDs is still in its beginning stages. For example, the extent of the negative effects of maternal drinking during pregnancy on child well-being only became apparent in the 1970s when alcohol was recognized as a teratogen that can disrupt and negatively affect both prenatal and postnatal development (Jones & Smith 1973; Jones et al. 1973). Even a half-century later, we only know basic information about the link between drinking and the negative outcomes of the FAS-related conditions. Although we do know that any amount of alcohol during gestation can potentially negatively affect a foetus' central nervous system, we still do not know essential information, including precise details about how either the quantity or the timing of the alcohol exposure impacts the development of the foetus. Researchers suspect that the sensitive periods of development in which alcohol exposure occurs would be among the most essential determining factors of the extent of the damage to the developing foetus (Guerri et al. 2009; Jones 2011). During critical brain development periods, which occur early in pregnancy, foetuses would be the most vulnerable to the effects of prenatal alcohol exposure (Maier & West 2001).

Despite the severity of the impact of alcohol on development, prenatal alcohol exposure is quite common in the first weeks following conception as mothers often are not yet even aware that they are pregnant. Continued drinking during pregnancy, and subsequently the rates of FASD-related conditions, vary considerably by country, culture, and other demographic factors. The highest cited rates of FASD have been reported in South Africa (Adebiyi & Mukumbang 2021) with estimates of 29 to 290 children per 1,000 across different provinces (Olivier, Curfs & Viljoen 2016). In contrast, in the United States, the Center for Disease Control and Prevention (CDC) reports rates of .2% to 1.5% infants with FAS out of every 1,000 live births, as well as 6–9/1,000 school-aged children. This is consistent with estimates from the United States and Western European countries that 1% to 5% of the population may have a FASD-related condition (May et al. 2009, 2014, 2018).

Diagnosis of Foetal Alcohol Spectrum Disorder

As with the other developmental disabilities, the FASDs are included in the Diagnostic and Statistical Manual 5th edition (DSM-5). They are presented in Section 3, Conditions for further study, as 'neurodevelopmental disorder-prenatal alcohol exposure'. The diagnostic criteria included in DSM-5 are exposure to alcohol, impaired neurocognitive function (cognitive challenges), impaired self-regulation (behaviour problems), and adaptive functioning problems in two areas that should be present in childhood and lead to significant interference in life functions. However, the varied outcomes and developmental trajectories of prenatal alcohol exposure make the diagnosis of FASD difficult. The diagnostic process can be quite lengthy as it involves a medical evaluation and neurodevelopmental assessment by a multidisciplinary team (Cook et al. 2016), including physicians, psychologists, occupational therapists, speech-language pathologists, and others.

To illustrate the extensive process involved in diagnosis we highlight the published comprehensive guidelines for FASD diagnosis published in 2005 by Public Health Canada's National Advisory Committee on FASD. The guidelines include the following categories of recommendations.

Screening and Referral

The screening component of these recommendations is based on the idea that all pregnant and post-partum women should be screened for alcohol use with validated tools. This would allow doctors to keep track of which infants may have an elevated likelihood for FASDs. In turn, these infants may be referred for a possible FASD diagnosis if they have three characteristic facial features, including one or more characteristic facial features that are generally associated with growth deficits.

Physical Examination and Differential Diagnosis

General physical and neurologic examinations are required in order to exclude other genetic or disorders that present with features that are similar to those found among children with FASD. In addition, growth and facial features should be monitored at all ages, as they are considered clear indicators of FASD.

Neurobehavioural Assessment

A diagnosis of FASD is dependent on the identification of impairment in at least three neurobehavioural domains – neurologic signs (ex. sensorimotor), brain structure (ex. occipito-frontal circumference, MRI, etc.), cognition (typically assessed through IQ), receptive and expressive communication, academic achievement, memory, executive functioning and abstract reasoning, attention deficit and hyperactivity, and adaptive behaviour, including social skills and communication. Although, as discussed earlier in this book, development is an integrated process with all of its components interrelated in meaningful ways, the assessment process is considerably less integrated. The child's functioning on each of these domains is assessed as if it were independent from the others. In these types of tests, we consider a domain to be impaired if the scores are two or more standard deviations below the mean, which is a statistical term indicating that the scores would fall in approximately in the bottom 3% of the relevant population for children of the same age. However, we need to keep in mind that, as is the case for all psychological tests, any cutoff must be seen as entirely arbitrary – there is no score that can be seen as a 'magical' or a meaningful divide between functioning that might be considered impaired or not (Burack et al. 2016, 2021). And, as the designations are arbitrary, they can vary significantly between places and/or over time (Burack et al. 2021; Russo et al. 2021).

Treatment and Follow Up

In keeping with our theme of the first chapter on the need for understanding the whole child, all diagnostic teams should prioritize the education of the families of children with FASD about the effects of FASD. This broadened approach is more integrative as it entails communication with the family about the referral and treatment plans for the child with FASD. In this way, treatments are seen as a life-long collaborative processes that extend beyond the child to include the family and others in the community.

Maternal Alcohol Use in Pregnancy

Aside from FASD, the diagnosis of all disorders included within the FASD umbrella require confirmation of prenatal exposure to alcohol (PAE). Evidence based on hearsay, assumptions based on lifestyle, other drug use, or history of alcohol consumption in previous pregnancies are not considered sufficiently informative of alcohol consumption patterns during the pregnancy. Thus, the importance of screening is highlighted.

Diagnostic Criterion by Disorder

As discussed previously, the more fine-tuned we can be in our diagnoses of children with neurodevelopmental conditions, the better our understanding of their development and, ultimately, the better our abilities to provide effective programmes for them. This is reflected in the work on children with FASD as the differentiation among the various FASDs, based on the specific symptom clusters and the severity of impairments they cause (CDC 2021), is considered an essential step to personalizing and optimizing educational and other intervention efforts. In this section, we briefly review key characteristics of each of the FASDs. In the following section, we will highlight some essential cognitive and social aspects of development in relation to the ways that they are manifested generally across all FASDs as well as in specific FASDs.

Foetal Alcohol Syndrome (FAS) is clinically considered to be on the pronounced end of the FASD spectrum due to the breadth of disability and impairment (CDC 2021). It is characterized by central nervous system (CNS) impairments, dysmorphic features, and abnormal growth (CDC 2021). Individuals with FAS often exhibit a mix of pronounced forms of cognitive, physical, intellectual, learning, and behavioural challenges. Signs of FAS include memory problems, difficulty paying attention, communication difficulties, as well as visual and auditory loss (CDC 2021). Together, these symptoms and the responses (or lack thereof) of others to them lead to difficulties both in school and with peer relationships (CDC 2021). The average age of diagnosis for FAS is about 48 months; however, this timeline is often extended as children with FAS are often misdiagnosed or diagnosed later if there is no admission of the mother's prenatal drinking or if the child's presenting symptoms are more subtle in their presentation. The necessity of the mother's contribution to the diagnosis are highlighted by Denny et al. (2017) who note that, 'This documentation also includes a measure of alcohol consumption as levels reported by the gestational carrier three months before pregnancy recognition or at the time of a positive pregnancy test. This information must be obtained by the mother or through another reliable source, such as family member, social service agency, or via medical records.' The finding that later diagnoses have been associated with worse prognoses is thought to be further evidence of the need for early intervention and, conversely, the deleterious outcome of delays in providing the appropriate care and programmes.

Partial Foetal Alcohol Syndrome (pFAS)

A diagnosis of Partial FAS (pFAS) is given to children who do not meet the full diagnostic criteria for FAS. This may occur when a child has a history of prenatal alcohol exposure, two or more facial abnormalities, as well as potential impairments in three or more of the CNS domains listed in the FAS criteria above (American Academy of Pediatrics 2018).

Alcohol-Related Neurodevelopmental Disorders (ARNDs)

The diagnosis of ARNDs is based on evidence of neurocognitive and neurobehavioural impairment, intellectual disability, as well as other learning and behavioural problems (Denny et al. 2017). Children with ARND exhibit impairments in memory, attention, judgement, and impulse control, all of which are associated with poor performance in school and on various indicators of developmental functioning. As children with ARND do not show the facial dysmorphology characteristic of FAS, the documentation of prenatal exposure to alcohol (American Academy of Pediatrics 2018), along with either some other defining characteristics of FAS or test scores that reflect impairments in at least two of the neurobehavioural domains mentioned above, are often required to confirm this diagnosis.

Alcohol-Related Birth Defects (ARBD)

In contrast to the other FASDs, the diagnosis of ARBDs is based on physical symptoms, including defects and dysfunction of the organs, rather than on indicators of CNS difficulties or dysregulation. Any diagnosis of ARBD must include evidence both of prenatal alcohol exposure and of significant problems in at least one of the following – the heart, the kidneys, the bones (often the spine), visual system (visual impairments), or auditory system (hearing impairments) (American Academy of Pediatrics 2018).

Neurodevelopmental Disorder Associated with Prenatal Alcohol Exposure (ND-PAE)

A diagnosis of ND-PAE must include documentation of prenatal alcohol exposure and significant difficulties across multiple domains. In particular, impairments are often evident on neurocognitive and neurobehavioural tasks with regard to adaptive functioning, and in the regulation of a range of aspects of functioning including attention, thinking, mood, and behaviour. Yet, despite this rather extensive list of challenges across many different areas of functioning, the diagnosis of ND-PAE cannot be attributed to CNS (central nervous system) dysfunction (American Academy of Pediatrics 2018).

OUTCOMES OF THE FASDs

Among the children affected with FASD, around half will display marked developmental delays before the age of three years. Others will not show signs of disability until they are in preschool or elementary school age. In this section, we focus on the cognitive and social phenotypes associated with the FASDs.

Cognitive

Intellectual Functioning

Diminished intellectual functioning has been established as a key cognitive outcome of PAE, although the variability in IQ scores among those with FASD is quite large. In a study of 473 individuals with PAE, Streissguth et al. (1996) found that IQs among those with FAS ranged from 29 to 120 (with a mean 79), whereas among those with pFAS and ARND they ranged from 42 to 142 (mean: 90). These findings indicate that intellectual functioning is generally diminished as a consequence of PAE, but that a majority of children with FASD still do not meet the criteria for ID. This variability in intellectual functioning may be partially associated with the extent of a foetus' alcohol exposure. Regardless of whether a child displays the physical characteristics of FAS, IQ has been shown to decrease with greater PAE. Still, the children with FAS show the greatest impairments in intellectual functioning (Streissguth et al. 1989). These findings highlight both a clear and consistent pattern of diminished intellectual functioning among children with FASDs, and that, as is the case with other heterogenous populations (e.g. persons with intellectual disability), is @ a more fine-tuned differentiation among subgroups of persons which may lead to more nuanced and specific patterns of functioning (Burack et al. 2016; Burack et al. 2021).

Attention

Attention problems are commonly associated with FASD, and attention deficit/hyperactivity disorder (ADHD) has been identified as the most common comorbid disorder among individuals with PAE (Streissguth et al. 1996). Children with FASD and ADHD show similarities on parent-reported measures of attention. However, children with these conditions differ on various cognitive outcomes. As compared to children with 'pure' ADHD, children with FASD show greater difficulty with shifting attention and encoding, and show deficits in their verbal learning abilities because of said encoding difficulties (Coles et al. 1997). Moreover, the psychostimulants typically prescribed to children with ADHD reduce the hyperactivity and impulsivity of children with FASD, but do not affect their encoding abilities or inattention (Coles et al. 1997). These differences point to a qualitative difference in the origins of the attentional problems among these two populations, the importance of inquiring about maternal alcohol use when suspecting ADHD in a child, and the need for the development of a testing model that allows for differential diagnoses.

The attention processing among children with FASD can best be described as extremely variable, suggesting that the deficits are not global. Children with prominent PAE have been observed to display slower performance and greater difficulty in establishing, organizing, and sustaining their attention (Nanson & Hiscock 1990). In the few studies of auditory attention, deficits were either not apparent or were, at least, considerably diminished relative to visual attention (Coles et al. 2002; Mattson et al. 2006). Therefore, like other cognitive domains discussed in this section, attention is not uniformly impaired across children with FASD.

Although this section was focused on reports of attentional problems among children with FASDs, we conclude it with an essential developmental consideration forwarded by Lane et al. (2014) that may necessitate a rethinking of the accepted narrative of an attention deficit. In their paper, Lane et al. hypothesized that since children with FASD typically display below average levels of cognitive functioning, their attentional processing, which is considered to be an essential part of cognition, should be expected to be commensurate with mental age rather than their chronological age. Sure enough, this was the case in their study in which children with FASD were administered a clinical test of attention. The children's performance on this test was only weaker in relation to chronological age expectations, but not when mental age was considered. Thus, the reports of attention problems among children with FASD by parents, educators, and clinicians may simply reflect an overall delayed pattern of development rather than a specific deficit. If reframed within a developmental framework, no deficits would be cited.

As discussed in Chapter 1, recasting our understanding of problem areas within a developmental framework is an essential step toward taking a holistic approach and considering how a child's life, ways and styles of being, and aspects of functioning all impact each other. With regard to attention, this is consistent with the imperative that the questions about attentional processing among children with neurodevelopmental conditions should not necessarily be about how well someone attends, but rather about the styles, biases, and motivational factors that affect how they attend (Burack et al. 2016). Thus, we remind educators, psychologists, doctors, therapists, and all professionals that an understanding of the entire developmental picture is a necessary pre-condition to any intervention.

Executive Functions

Unlike the two previously discussed cognitive domains, executive functions appear to be universally impaired across persons with FASD. For example, in a study of 419 adolescents and adults across the foetal alcohol spectrum, Connor et al. (2000) found a similar degree of executive problems along the spectrum. Substantial difficulties in goal executive function, emotional and non-emotional set-shifting, verbal fluency, flexible thinking, working memory, planning, and problem-solving have been reported. The pervasive and universal nature of executive dysfunction suggests that assessment of neurocognitive impairment is essential to the accurate diagnosis of FASD (Davies et al. 2013), although again a developmental framework might be particularly helpful in detailing the extent to which the reported difficulties simply reflect overall developmental delays rather than specific areas of impairment.

Language

A range of language problems, including those in both receptive and expressive skills and grammatical ability, have been reported (Mattson et al. 2019). These deficits appear to be global in childhood, with difficulties becoming more specific to syntax with age (Carney & Chermak 1991). Children with PAE have been found to make grammatical errors at a higher rate than others. This has been shown to be a more accurate indicator of FASD than have measures of productivity and grammatical complexity, suggesting that language skills may be particularly useful in understanding both the developmental course of FASD, and the changes associated with diagnostic processes (Thorne 2017).

Learning and Memory

Children with FASD show impairments in both learning and memory, processes that are dependent on each other and on brain plasticity. Prolonged PAE has been thought to reduce brain plasticity by impairing the cortical neurons' ability to reorganize themselves and their connections (Larroque & Kaminski 1998). Both verbal memory and learning have been repeatedly demonstrated to be impaired in this population (Mattson et al. 2019). These impairments remain even when controlling for IQ, highlighting that these areas of difficulty cannot simply be attributable to the generally diminished overall level of intellectual ability.

Motor Skills

Prenatal alcohol exposure has been repeatedly linked to impaired motor ability. Any consideration of a diagnosis of FASD involves the assessment of both gross and fine motor skills. Children with FASD typically show deficits in fine motor coordination, specifically complex fine motor skills, whereas adults have been found to show deficits in motor function, especially on measures of balance and fine motor control (Connor et al. 2006). Persons with FASD have also been found to have deficits in postural balance, especially when somatosensory input is manipulated (Roebuck et al. 1998). Although difficulties in motor skills and function are common among persons with FASD, a consistent pattern of deficits has yet to be established.

Social

Children with FASD and PAE often seem to experience social difficulties, such as in forming reciprocal peer relationships, perceiving or responding to social cues, and exhibiting consideration for others. These struggles may lead to instances of social withdrawal, bullying, and poor social judgement, rejection, and victimization. Behaviours associated with aggression, disruptiveness, hyperactivity, and poor conduct and behavioural control have been cited as well. These types of difficulties likely contribute to the high rates of secondary social concerns such as dependency, mental health issues, dangerous sexual conduct, substance use, academic failure, professional problems, and legal troubles (Kully-Martens et al. 2012). These indicators of the mismatch between children with FASD and PAE and their environments are further reflected in significant difficulties in social competence, social problems, and externalizing behaviour problems. Data from caregiver and teacher reports of adaptive functioning and behaviour suggest that children with FASD display social functioning problems that are more pronounced than would simply be predicted by their lower levels of intellectual functioning (Thomas et al. 1998; Jirikowic et al. 2008), and that they increase with age.

The pervasiveness of the social problems among children with FASDs was highlighted in a study of 52 children aged 7–11 years with and without PAE who were tested with a structured interview measure of social information processing about 18 videotaped vignettes of children in different social scenarios involving group entry and provocation (McGee et al. 2009). The responses of the children who had been exposed to alcohol in utero were considered maladaptive on a range of types of responses across both types of scenarios. Their scores on these measures correlated with their scores on the Test of Problem Solving, which also were diminished in relation to those of the children who had been exposed to alcohol prenatally.

The social problems observed in this population are potentially explained by multiple mechanisms. For example, difficulties in executive functions have been found to predict social skills problems both at home and in school. Thus, the difficulties in social problem-solving observed among adolescents with PAEs may be explained by the correlation between difficulties in executive function and problem solving. Social problem-solving difficulties have also been shown to be correlated with those in social information processing.

Sensory processing disorders can contribute to the exhibition of behavioural and functional disruptions, although the relationship between difficulties in sensory regulation and social skill problems remains unclear. One suggestion is that the deficits in sensory processing may impact the ability of children with FASD to adaptively respond to their environments, including social domains and interactions. Atypicality in the prefrontal cortex among those with PAE may partially explain social skills difficulties since damage to the prefrontal cortex has repeatedly been associated with long-term social difficulties. Children with FASD have also been shown to have widespread white matter atypicalities, which may disrupt the networks of connections necessary for social development. From a behavioural perspective, problems in theory of mind, understanding the unique perspectives and thoughts of others, have also been implicated in the social struggles of children with FASD.

Familial

A diagnosis of FASD has also been shown to have profound impacts on the child's family as their parents and siblings must learn to adapt to their needs to cope with their struggles. This relationship is influenced by the quality of care received, as well as by the warm, secure attachment, and strength of the bond between the parties. Child maltreatment and a child's success in learning affective and behavioural regulation from their caregivers are also significant influences. If the problems a child experiences as a result of their FASD are responded to inappropriately, poor adaptive function and behavioural problems will continue.

As is the case with many of the other groups considered in this volume, one of the chronic strains on the families is the financial toll, as the cost of supporting an individual with FASD over the course of their life is in the millions of dollars (Lupton et al., 2004). During childhood and adolescence, special education support is often needed. The financial burden can even escalate in adulthood as individuals with FASD are often unable to maintain full employment and sometimes not even able to independently care for themselves. In these situations, the cost of everyday living expenses are often incurred by the family for virtually the entire lifespan.

Risk and Protective Factors

Children with FASDs are marked by the risk factor of PAE and are likely to also be affected by prenatal exposure to cigarettes and other drugs, as well as family and socioeconomic factors. For young children a 'difficult temperament', characterized by high levels of negative affect, hard-to-read behavioural cues, and difficulty sleeping may all exacerbate the risk factors they face. Children and youth with FASDs commonly show all these difficulties (O'Connor 2001; Kable & Coles 2004; Haley et al. 2006; Troese et al. 2008). Conversely, as is the case with many at-risk groups, certain personal characteristics such as an engaging manner, intact areas of development, and high social motivation have been shown to facilitate more positive developmental outcomes (Olson et al. 2009).

The protective factors for children from all family types (birth, adoptive, foster) include an early diagnosis and high-quality caregiving. Additionally, from the caregiver's perspective, positive perceptions of the relationship between child and caregiver and improved knowledge and practices with regard to FASD have been identified as protective. Specifically, in the context of foster families, caregivers who are able to provide the necessary support, have appropriate personality for raising a child with FASD, and have a thorough understanding of FASD are seen as protective. At the level of the larger social system, support from family, neighbours, community, and social services is important (Olson & Montague 2011).

The stigma surrounding both substance use disorders and FASDs is a barrier to the care and treatment of individuals with these conditions. For example, the findings from a 2020 study by the Canadian FASD Research Network indicated that the stigma of both substance use and having a child with a FASD fostered by the media and health professionals may lead some women to social isolation and a refusal to disclose their history of substance use, thereby diminishing the likelihood of positive outcomes for both mother and child.

Educational Considerations

School-based and academic difficulties are commonly reported for children with FASD by both their parents and teachers who highlight struggles with tasks and subjects that require higher order thinking, problem solving, and cognitive organization. The impact of specific challenges common to FASD on children's learning is outlined in Table 5.1.

Interventions

As is the case with virtually all developmental disabilities, early intervention is considered key to interventions with persons with FASDs. This is largely due to the increased plasticity and amenability of younger children's brains. Also, early interventions help to reframe families' thinking, prepare them for their child's developmental course, and help them access various services. The broad and varied nature of the difficulties associated with FASD has significantly hindered the development of clinically validated interventions thereby leading to considerable distress and stress among the parents as they try to find and access the most appropriate treatments for their children. In this section, we provide some general overviews of some promising approaches to intervention.

Table 5.1 Challenges common to children with FASD and their impact on learning

Areas of Difficulties	Potential Impact on Learning
Processing Speed	– Inconsistent understanding and incomplete intake of course content. – Slow production of course work.
Gross and/or Fine Motor Skills	– Difficulty using tools like scissors, pencils, markers, etc. – Difficulty writing and poor letter formation. – Difficulties with physical education.
Self-Regulation	– Hyperactivity. – Inattentiveness. – Disruptive behaviour.
Executive Function	– Difficulty in planning and project management. – Difficulty with strategy shifting. – Difficulty synthesizing information, generalizing, and forming conclusions.
Language	– Difficulty understanding social communication conventions. – Difficulty in interpreting nonverbal cues. – Difficulty in understanding prosody. – Difficulty following conversations.
Visuospatial Abilities	– Disorganization. – Difficulty remembering the location of classrooms, one's schedule, or steps to a given task. – Poor page-scanning abilities.

Relationship Considerations

Relationship-focused interventions are designed to support and improve early parent–child relationships to reduce stress in the family. Based in the developmental literature, the emphasis is on establishing a stable care-giving environment. In some cases, the children are moved to new homes. When implemented early in the child's life, these interventions can help to deepen the child's sense of attachment security as well as the mutual regulation between the caregiver and the child. This intervention approach often involves regular home visits by a nurse or mental health professional to educate and support the caregivers in providing a secure environment and to encourage them to focus on the emotional needs that underly their child's difficult behaviours and challenges.

In addition, infant and early childhood mental health programmes are firmly rooted in attachment theory with a focus on improving the attachment security between the children and their caregivers. Parents and caregivers are taught to read their child's cues and appropriately soothe their distress, provide support, and foster their child's exploration and independence. As the children grow, the goals of proper limit-setting and caregiver monitoring are introduced to the parents. In general, these types of interventions are designed to facilitate positive parenting and caregiving styles, with the goal of teaching skills and tools to better handle the challenging behaviours associated with the FASDs.

INTERVENTIONS IN AN INTERNATIONAL CONTEXT

Specific cultural and political contexts pose potential barriers to the implementation of effective interventions. Despite a World Health Organization (WHO) initiative for a global strategy to address alcohol use, especially among pregnant women, and increased knowledge worldwide about the perils of drinking during pregnancy, many places in the world do not have the scientific or professional expertise to implement interventions. In addition, scepticism about the teratogenic effects of alcohol on foetuses, the lack of stigma about drinking during pregnancy in certain parts of the world, and limited availability and accessibility of programmes all combine to keep the numbers of children with FASD high and their outcomes poor. This highlights the need for a societal two-pronged approach to FASD that includes both the prevention of FASD and facilitating intervention when it occurs. The intervention also must be at least two-pronged with one focused on the individual and the receipt of interventions beginning as early as possible in the child's life and the other in addressing bigger societal issues including dismantling both prevailing narratives of pathology and barriers to care.

SUMMARY

Foetal alcohol spectrum disorders (FASDs) represent an umbrella of conditions for which the diagnoses, with the exception of FAS, are based on the confirmation of this prenatal exposure to alcohol (PAE). Thus, children with FASD are an entirely unique group among children classified with a developmental disability. Whereas other conditions arise from the child's genetics or inherent physiology, FASDs are entirely a consequence of the actions of another person – the drinking of alcohol by the biological mother during pregnancy – and are therefore entirely preventable.

The consequences of FASD cut across virtually every aspect of functioning and, as a result, are associated with general developmental delays. Accordingly, attempts to identify specific areas of problems must be contextualized within the context of this general developmental delay. For example, common reports of co-occurrence with ADHD need to be reconsidered as attention difficulties reflect general developmental level, even if they are lower as compared to chronological age. Yet, problems in certain cognitive domains, especially executive functions, as well as in the areas of language and social development, continue to reflect concerns for families, teachers, and other professionals throughout the lifespan.

As we conclude this chapter, we note that the research is almost exclusively focused on challenges, or areas of difficulty, among children with FASD in order to highlight potential foci of intervention, but that scholars and practitioners alike are beginning to revise the narrative in order to emphasize strengths. As an example, in a critical review of 19 studies, most of which were about the lived experiences of adults with FASD, Flannigan et al. (2021) cited intrinsic strengths, such as those related to strong self-awareness, receptiveness to support, capacity for human connection, perseverance through challenges, and hope for the future. They highlight that this type of strengths-based approach is essential to developing research, practice, and policy that is optimal for promoting positive outcomes.

Reflective Questions

1. How is FASD unique among developmental disabilities?
2. What strategies can be used to prevent FASD?
3. What do parents and teachers need to consider when discussing the strengths and challenges of children with FASD?
4. What are some of the social issues that may contribute to the unique development of children with FASD?
5. What are some impacts of FASD on the family throughout the lifespan?
6. What are some ways that the 'whole child' approach is particularly relevant to children with FASD?
7. What are some of the characteristics associated with FASD? What developmental factor(s) must be considered when discussing these characteristics?
8. If you were responsible for supporting a teacher with a student with FASD in their class, what would you want to tell them?
9. Why is FASD presented on a spectrum? What does this mean?

Recommended Videos

This video describing FASD:

https://www.fasdhub.org.au/fasd-information/understanding-fasd/

Some videos on the importance of supports in individuals with FASD and the importance of a diagnosis in individuals with FASD:

https://www.hss.gov.nt.ca/en/services/ensemble-troubles-causes-alcoolisation-f%C5%93tale

A three-minute video on executive functioning and how executive functioning skills develop in children:

https://www.youtube.com/watch?v=CYi2EzPkErs

A TedTalk on executive functioning:

https://www.youtube.com/watch?v=qAC-5hTK-4c

REFERENCES

Adebiyi, B. O., & Mukumbang, F. C. (2021). A pooled prevalence of fetal alcohol spectrum disorders in South Africa: a systematic review and meta-analysis protocol. *Archives of Public Health = Archives Belges de Santé Publique, 79*(1), 156–156. https://doi.org/10.1186/s13690-021-00679-0.

American Academy of Pediatrics (2018). *Fetal Alcohol Spectrum Disorders.* https://www.aap.org/en/patient-care/fetal-alcohol-spectrum-disorders/.

Astley, S. J., & Clarren, S. K. (1999) *Diagnostic guide for fetal alcohol syndrome and related conditions: the 4-Digit Diagnostic Code.* 2nd ed. Seattle: University of Washington Publication Services.

Badry, D., & Harding, K. (2020). Fetal alcohol spectrum disorder and child welfare. *Canada FASD Research Network*, 1–9. https://canfasd.ca/wp-content/uploads/publications/FASD-and-Child-Welfare-Final.pdf.

Brown, J. M., Bland, R., Jonsson, E., & Greenshaw, A. J. (2019). The standardization of diagnostic criteria for fetal alcohol spectrum disorder (FASD): Implications for research, clinical practice and population health. *Canadian Journal of Psychiatry/Revue Canadienne de Psychiatrie, 64*(3), 169–176. https://doi.org/10.1177/0706743718777398.

Burack, J. A., Evans, D. W, Russo, N., Napoleon, J. S., Goldman, K. J., & Iarocci, G. (2021). Developmental perspectives on the study of persons with intellectual disability. *Annual Review of Clinical Psychology, 17,* 339–363.

Burack, J. A., Russo, N., Gordon Green, C., Landry, O., & Iarocci, G. (2016). Developments in the developmental approach to intellectual disability. In D. Cicchetti (ed.), *Developmental Psychopathology (Vol. 3): Maladaptation and Psychopathology* (pp. 1–67). New York: Wiley.

The Canada FASD Research Network. (2020, February). *Mothers' Experiences of Stigma: Multi-level Ideas for Action.* https://canfasd.ca/wp-content/uploads/publications/Mothers-Experiences-of-Stigma-final.pdf.

Carney, L. J., & Chermak, G. D. (1991). Performance of American Indian children with Fetal Alcohol Syndrome on the test of language development. *Journal of Communication Disorders, 24*(2), 123–134. https://doi.org/10.1016/0021-9924(91)90016-C.

Centers for Disease Control and Prevention. (2021). *Basics about FASDs.* Centers for Disease Control and Prevention. https://www.cdc.gov/ncbddd/fasd/facts.html.

Centers for Disease Control and Prevention. (2011). Fetal Alcohol Spectrum Disorders (FASDs). Retrieved from http://www.cdc.gov/ncbddd/fasd/facts.html.

Chudley, A. E., Conry, J., Cook, J. L., Loock, C., Rosales, T., LeBlanc, N., & Public Health Agency of Canada's National Advisory Committee on Fetal Alcohol Spectrum Disorder (2005). Fetal alcohol spectrum disorder: Canadian guidelines for diagnosis. *Canadian Medical Association Journal, 172*(5 Suppl), S1–S21. https://doi.org/10.1503/cmaj.1040302.

Coles, C. D., Platzman, K. A., Raskind-Hood, C. L., Brown, R. T., Falek, A., & Smith, I. E. (1997). A comparison of children affected by prenatal alcohol exposure and attention deficit, hyperactivity disorder. *Alcoholism: Clinical and Experimental Research, 21*(1). https://doi.org/10.1097/00000374-199702000-00022.

Coles, C. D., Platzman, K. A., Lynch, M. E., & Freides, D. (2002). Auditory and visual sustained attention in adolescents prenatally exposed to alcohol. *Alcoholism, Clinical and Experimental Research*, *26*(2), 263–271. https://doi.org/10.1111/j.1530-0277.2002.tb02533.x.

Coles, C. D., Kable, J. A., & Taddeo, E. (2009). Math performance and behavior problems in children affected by prenatal alcohol exposure: intervention and follow-up. *Journal of Developmental and Behavioral Pediatrics*, *30*(1), 7–15. https://doi.org/10.1097/DBP.0b013e3181966780.

Cook, J. L., Green, C. R., Lilley, C. M., Anderson, S. M., Baldwin, M. E., Chudley, A. E., Conry, J. L., LeBlanc, N., Loock, C. A., Lutke, J., Mallon, B. F., McFarlane, A. A., Temple, V. K., & Rosales, T. (2016). Fetal Alcohol Spectrum Disorder: A guideline for diagnosis across the lifespan. *Canadian Medical Association Journal*, *188*(3), 191–197. https://doi.org/10.1503/cmaj.141593.

Connor, P. D., Sampson, P. D., Bookstein, F. L., Barr, H. M., & Streissguth, A. P. (2000). Direct and indirect effects of prenatal alcohol damage on executive function. *Developmental Neuropsychology*, *18*(3), 331–354. https://doi.org/10.1207/S1532694204Connor.

Connor, P. D., Sampson, P. D., Streissguth, A. P., Bookstein, F. L., & Barr, H. M. (2006). Effects of prenatal alcohol exposure on fine motor coordination and balance: a study of two adult samples. *Neuropsychologia*, *44*(5), 744–751. https://doi.org/10.1016/j.neuropsychologia.2005.07.016.

Davis, K. M., Gagnier, K. R., Moore, T. E., & Todorow, M. (2013). Cognitive aspects of fetal alcohol spectrum disorder. *Wiley Interdisciplinary Reviews: Cognitive Science*, *4*(1), 81–92. https://doi.org/10.1002/wcs.1202.

DeJoseph, M. (2011). Improving outcomes in adolescents and adults with fetal alcohol spectrum disorders. In S. A. Adubato & D. E. Cohen (eds), *Prenatal Alcohol Use and Fetal Alcohol Spectrum Disorders: Diagnosis, Assessment and New Directions in Research and Multimodal Treatment*. Bentham Science Publishers. https://doi.org/10.2174/97816080503141110101.

Denny, L., Coles, S., & Blitz, R. (2017). Fetal alcohol syndrome and fetal alcohol spectrum disorders. *American Family Physician*, *96*(8), 515–522.

Dörrie, N., Föcker, M., Freunscht, I., & Hebebrand, J. (2014). Fetal alcohol spectrum disorders. *European Child & Adolescent Psychiatry*, *23*(10), 863–875. https://doi.org/10.1007/s00787-014-0571-6.

Flannigan, K., Wrath, A., Ritter, C., McLachlan, K., Harding, K. D., Campbell, A., Reid, D., & Pei, J,. (2021). Balancing the story of fetal alcohol disorder: A narrative review of the literature. *Alcohol: Clinical and Experimental Research*, 45(12): 2448–2464. doi: 10.1111/acer.14733.

Guerri, C., Bazinet, A., & Riley, E. P. (2009). Fetal alcohol spectrum disorders and alterations in brain and behaviour. *Alcohol and Alcoholism*, *44*(2), 108–114. https://doi.org/10.1093/alcalc/agn105.

Gupta, K. K., Gupta, V. K., & Shirasaka, T. (2016). An update on fetal alcohol syndrome-pathogenesis, risks, and treatment. *Alcoholism, Clinical and Experimental Research*, *40*(8), 1594–1602. https://doi.org/10.1111/acer.13135.

Haley, D. W., Handmaker, N. S., & Lowe, J. (2006). Infant stress reactivity and prenatal alcohol exposure. *Alcoholism: Clinical and Experimental Research, 30*(12), 2055–2064. https://doi.org/10.1111/j.1530-0277.2006.00251.x.

HealthyChildren.org (2018). *Fetal Alcohol Spectrum Disorders.* American Academy of Pediatrics. https://www.healthychildren.org/English/health-issues/conditions/chronic/Pages/Fetal-Alcohol-Spectrum-Disorders.aspx.

Jirikowic, T., Kartin, D., & Olson, H. C. (2008). Children with fetal alcohol spectrum disorders: A descriptive profile of adaptive function. *Canadian Journal of Occupational Therapy, 75*(4), 238–248. https://doi.org/10.1177/000841740807500411.

Jones, K. L. (2011) The effects of alcohol on fetal development. *Birth Defects Research C: Embryo Today, 93*(1), 3–11. https://doi.org/10.1002/bdrc.20200.

Jones, K. L., & Smith, D. W. (1973). Recognition of the fetal alcohol syndrome in early infancy. *Lancet (London, England), 302*(7836), 999–1001. https://doi.org/10.1016/s0140-6736(73)91092-1.

Jones, K. L., Smith, D. W., Ulleland, C. N., & Streissguth, A. P. (1973) Pattern of malformation in offspring of chronic alcoholic mothers. *Lancet 301,* 1267–1271.

Kable, J. A., & Coles, C. D. (2004). The impact of prenatal alcohol exposure on neurophysiological encoding of environmental events at six months. *Alcoholism: Clinical and Experimental Research, 28*(3), 489–496. https://doi.org/10.1097/01.ALC.0000117837.66107.64/

Kable, J. A., Coles, C. D., & Taddeo, E. (2007). Socio-cognitive habilitation using the math interactive learning experience program for alcohol-affected children. *Alcoholism: Clinical and Experimental Research, 31*(8), 1425–1434. https://doi.org/10.1111/j.1530-0277.2007.00431.x.

Kully-Martens, K., Denys, K., Treit, S., Tamana, S., & Rasmussen, C. (2012). A review of social skills deficits in individuals with fetal alcohol spectrum disorders and prenatal alcohol exposure: profiles, mechanisms, and interventions. *Alcoholism: Clinical and Experimental Research, 36*(4), 568–576. https://doi.org/10.1111/j.1530-0277.2011.01661.x.

Lane K. A., Stewart, J., Fernandes, T., Russo, N., Enns, J. T., & Burack J. A (2014). Complexities in understanding attentional functioning among children with fetal alcohol spectrum disorder. *Front Hum Neurosci. 7*(8) 1–8. doi: 10.3389/fnhum.2014.00119.

Larroque, B., & Kaminski, M. (1998). Prenatal alcohol exposure and development at preschool age: main results of a French study. *Alcoholism: Clinical and Experimental Research, 22*(2), 295–303. https://doi.org/10.1111/j.1530-0277.1998.tb03652.x.

Lupton, C., Burd, L., & Harwood, R. (2004). Cost of fetal alcohol spectrum disorders. *American Journal of Medical Genetics, 127C*(1), 42–50. https://doi.org/10.1002/ajmg.c.30015.

Maier, S. E., & West, J. R. (2001). Drinking patterns and alcohol-related birth defects. *Alcohol Research & Health, 25*(3), 168–174.

Mattson, S. N., Riley, E. P., Gramling, L., Delis, D. C., & Jones, K. L. (1997). Heavy prenatal alcohol exposure with or without physical features of fetal alcohol syndrome leads to IQ deficits. *The Journal of Pediatrics, 131*(5), 718–721. https://doi.org/10.1016/S0022-3476(97)70099-4.

Mattson, S. N., Calarco, K. E., & Lang, A. R. (2006). Focused and shifting attention in children with heavy prenatal alcohol exposure. *Neuropsychology, 20*(3), 361–369. https://doi.org/10.1037/0894-4105.20.3.361.

Mattson, S. N., Bernes, G. A., & Doyle, L. R. (2019). Fetal alcohol spectrum disorders: a review of the neurobehavioral deficits associated with prenatal alcohol exposure. *Alcoholism: Clinical and Experimental Research, 43*(6), 1046–1062. https://doi-org.proxy3.library.mcgill.ca/10.1111/acer.14040.

May, P., Blankenship, J., Marais, A. S., et al. (2013). Approaching the prevalence of the full spectrum of fetal alcohol spectrum disorders in a South African population-based study. *Alcoholism: Clinical and Experimental Research 37*, 818–830.

May, P. A., Baete, A., Russo, J., Elliott, A. J., Blankenship, J., Kalberg, W. O., Buckley, D., Brooks, M., Hasken, J., Abdul-Rahman, O., Adam, M. P., Robinson, L. K., Manning, M., & Hoyme, H. E. (2014). Prevalence and characteristics of fetal alcohol spectrum disorders. *Pediatrics, 134*(5), 855–866. https://doi.org/10.1542/peds.2013-3319.

May, P. A., Gossage, J. P., Kalberg, W. O., Robinson, L. K., Buckley, D., Manning, M., & Hoyme, H. E. (2009). Prevalence and epidemiologic characteristics of FASD from various research methods with an emphasis on recent in-school studies. *Developmental Disabilities Research Reviews, 15*(3), 176–192. https://doi.org/10.1002/ddrr.68.

May, P. A., Chambers, C. D., Kalberg, W. O., Zellner, J., Feldman, H., Buckley, D., ... Hoyme, H. E. (2018). Prevalence of fetal alcohol spectrum disorders in 4 us communities. *Obstetrical & Gynecological Survey, 73*(7), 385–387.

McGee, C. L., Bjorkquist, O. A., Price, J. M., Mattson, S. N., & Riley, E. P. (2009). Social information processing skills in children with histories of heavy prenatal alcohol exposure. *Journal of Abnormal Child Psychology, 37*(6), 817–30. https://doi.org/10.1007/s10802-009-9313-5.

McGee, C. L., Fryer, S. L., Bjorkquist, O. A., Mattson, S. N., & Riley, E. P. (2008). Deficits in social problem solving in adolescents with prenatal exposure to alcohol. *The American Journal of Drug and Alcohol Abuse, 34*(4), 423–431. https://doi.org/10.1080/00952990802122630.

Nanson, J. L., & Hiscock, M. (1990). Attention deficits in children exposed to alcohol prenatally. *Alcoholism: Clinical and Experimental Research 14*(5), 656–661. https://doi.org/10.1111/j.1530-0277.1990.tb01223.x.

O'Connor, M. J. (2001). Prenatal alcohol exposure and infant negative affect as precursors of depressive features in children. *Infant Mental Health Journal, 22*(3), 291–299. https://doi.org/10.1002/imhj.1002.

Olivier, L, Curfs, L. M. G., & Viljoen, D. L. (2016). Fetal alcohol spectrum disorders: Prevalence rates in South Africa. *South African Medical Journal, 106*, 103–106.

O'Connor, M. J., Frankel, F., Paley, B., Schonfeld, A. M., Carpenter, E., Laugeson, E. A., & Marquardt, R. (2006). A controlled social skills training for children with fetal alcohol spectrum disorders. *Journal of Consulting and Clinical Psychology, 74*(4), 639–648.

Olson, H. C., Brooks, A., Quamma, J. (2005). Efficacy of a new model of behavioral consultation for families raising school-aged children with FASD and behavior problems. *Alcoholism: Clinical and Experimental Research 28*(Suppl. 5): 718.

Olson, H. C., Oti, R., Gelo, J., & Beck, S. (2009). 'Family matters:' Fetal alcohol spectrum disorders and the family. *Developmental Disabilities Research Reviews, 15*(3), 235–249. https://doi.org/10.1002/ddrr.65.

Olson, H. C., & Montague, R. A. (2011). An innovative look at early intervention for children affected by prenatal alcohol exposure. In S. A. Adubato & D. E. Cohen (eds), *Prenatal*

Alcohol Use and Fetal Alcohol Spectrum Disorders: Diagnosis, Assessment and New Directions in Research and Multimodal Treatment. Bentham Science Publishers. https://doi.org/10.2174/97816080503141110101.

Petrenko, C. L. M., & Alto, M. E. (2017). Interventions in fetal alcohol spectrum disorders: an international perspective. *European Journal of Medical Genetics, 60*(1), 79–91. https://doi.org/10.1016/j.ejmg.2016.10.005.

Roebuck, T.M., Simmons, R.W., Mattson, S.N., & Riley, E.P. (1998). Prenatal exposure to alcohol affects the ability to maintain postural balance. *Alcoholism: Clinical and Experimental Research 22*(1), 252–258. https://doi.org/10.1111/j.1530-0277.1998.tb03646.x.

Russo, N., Kaplan, E., Wilson, J., Criss, A., & Burack. J. A. (2021). Choices, challenges, and constraints: A pragmatic examination of the limits of mental age matching in empirical research. *Development and Psychopathology, 33*, 727–738.

Streissguth, A., Barr, H., Kogan, J., & Bookstein, F. (1996). *Understanding the Occurrence of Secondary Disabilities in Clients with Fetal Alcohol Syndrome (FAS) and Fetal Alcohol Effects (FAE).* Final Report to CDC Grant No. R04/C CR008515. Seattle: University of Washington School of Medicine.

Streissguth, A. P., Barr, H. M., Sampson, P. D., Darby, B. L., & Martin, D. C. (1989). IQ at age 4 in relation to maternal alcohol use and smoking during pregnancy. *Developmental Psychology, 25*(1), 3–11. https://doi.org/10.1037/0012-1649.25.1.3.

Thomas, S. E., Kelly, S. J., Mattson, S. N., & Riley, E. P. (1998). Comparison of social abilities of children with fetal alcohol syndrome to those of children with similar IQ scores and normal controls. *Alcoholism: Clinical and Experimental Research, 22*(2), 528–533. https://doi.org/10.1111/j.1530-0277.1998.tb03684.x.

Thorne, J. C. (2017). Accentuate the negative: Grammatical errors during narrative production as a clinical marker of central nervous system abnormality in school-aged children with fetal alcohol spectrum disorders. *Journal of Speech, Language, and Hearing Research, 60*(12), 3523–3537. https://doi.org/10.1044/2017_JSLHR-L-17-0128.

Troese, M., Fukumizu, M., Sallinen, B. J., Gilles, A. A., Wellman, J. D., Paul, J. A., ... Hayes, M. J. (2008). Sleep fragmentation and evidence for sleep debt in alcohol-exposed infants. *Early Human Development, 84*(9), 577–585. https://doi.org/10.1016/j.earlhumdev.2008.02.001.

Uban, K. A., Bodnar, T., Butts, K., Sliwowska, J. H., Comeau, W., & Weinberg, J. (2010). Direct and indirect effects mechanisms of alcohol teratogenesis: Implications for understanding alterations of brain and behavior in FASD. In E. P. Riley, S. Clarren, J, Weinberg, & E. Jonsson (eds), *Fetal Alcohol Spectrum Disorder: Management and Policy Perspectives of FASD* (pp. 71–108). Wiley-VCH Verlag GmbH & Co. KGaA. https://doi.org/10.1002/9783527632510.ch5.

6
NEUROGENETIC SYNDROMES AND RARE DISORDERS ASSOCIATED WITH INTELLECTUAL DISABILITY

> ### Learning Objectives
>
> After reading this chapter, you should be able to:
>
> - Learn about the definition of rare disorders and why this designation is important
> - Learn about the history behind neurogenetic syndrome research
> - Learn about contemporary issues related to the diagnosis of neurogenetic conditions associated with ID
> - Learn about the phenotypic outcomes associated with specific neurogenetic conditions, including fragile X syndrome, Williams syndrome, Smith-Magenis syndrome, Prader-Willi syndrome, and Angelman syndrome

Both social and biological factors are important for understanding intellectual disability (ID). ID is a social phenomenon in that it is defined by people, like clinicians and researchers, using human-made measures, like IQ tests and adaptive behaviour interviews. The social nature of ID can also be observed through the evolving definitions of ID, based on changes in cultural awareness and insight. However, there are often complex underlying biological factors that lead to ID, and we are living through a time when we are rapidly discovering more about the biology of ID from one year to the next.

In this chapter, we will learn about the intersection between biology and ID by describing what we currently know about specific genetic conditions that lead to ID. These conditions are often called 'neurogenetic syndromes' and they fall under the broader category of 'rare disorders'. We will examine these constructs in greater depth below, but there are two important ideas to keep in mind: (1) our knowledge base regarding the link between syndromes and outcomes has transformed the field of ID research, and (2) the technological advances that uncover these links have accelerated our rate of discovery, especially within the last decade.

WHAT IS A RARE DISORDER?

Many biological causes of ID are rare disorders. The term 'rare disorder' is defined differently, depending on where you live in the world. In Europe, a rare disorder (termed 'rare disease') is defined as a condition that occurs at a rate of 1 in every 2,000 people or fewer (Moliner & Waligora 2017). In the United States (US), the definition focuses on the total number of people with the diagnosis; the US definition of a rare disorder is one that occurs in fewer than 200,000 individuals (Rare Diseases Act of 2002).

The *rare disorder* designation may seem arbitrary, but it has societal importance. First, while individual conditions may be rare, recent analyses suggest that 3.5–5.9% of the world population has a rare disorder, which translates to between 263 and 446 million people across the globe (Wakap et al. 2020). This means that, while each of these disorders may be rare, many people have rare disorders and their collective needs are an important societal concern. In addition, in some countries, the 'rare disorder' designation has been tied to incentives to develop new treatments through legislation. This legislative prioritization has been welcome news to people with rare conditions and their loved ones, but it was not always this way. Prior to the 1980s, many individuals were diagnosed with rare disorders, but there were very few treatments or supports available for them because of the costly nature of research and the perceived lack of potential profit from research into conditions with a relatively smaller prevalence. It was only after a great deal of activism from families and professionals that legislation was passed in several countries that aimed to incentivize scientific innovation in the treatment of smaller populations of individuals with rare conditions (e.g. Orphan Drug Act of 1983 in the US). The conditions associated with ID that we will examine in this chapter, for the most part, meet criteria for the various definitions of rare disorders. They have identifiable genetic causes and impact neurodevelopment (nervous system development), which is why they are referred to as neurogenetic syndromes.

NEUROGENETIC SYNDROMES ASSOCIATED WITH ID

Research on neurogenetic syndromes and ID has grown tremendously over the past 50 years. An important origin of this work can be found in Zigler's influential 'two group' approach to ID, which distinguished those individuals with ID who had identifiable, biological causes of ID from those who did not (Zigler 1967). Zigler observed that when a biological cause of ID was identifiable, ID was generally more pronounced, and IQ scores tended to be on the lower end of the ID continuum.

This original insight set in motion wide-reaching discoveries that are now a central aspect of ID research. In 1988, Burack, Hodapp, and Zigler made the case that the aetiology (cause) of ID is critical to consider, and that the study of specific aetiologies of ID could provide new insight to explain individual differences among people with ID. This new paradigm for understanding ID was a catalyst for intensive research endeavours that aimed to describe the link between biological conditions, especially syndromes with genetic causes, to patterns of strength and challenge across many aspects of development (Burack 1990; Dykens 1995; Hodapp 1997).

A Word on Terminology

There have been several different terms used in this area of study, including 'genomic disorders', 'genetic aetiologies', 'genetic syndromes', and 'neurogenetic syndromes'. We use the term neurogenetic syndrome here because it captures three important elements: (1) 'neuro' refers to the involvement of the nervous system and neurodevelopment, which is important when considering the presence of ID; (2) 'genetic' refers to the presence of a change in chromosomes or genes that influences neurodevelopment; and (3) 'syndrome' refers to the presence of a range of symptoms that are present together. In the case of ID-related conditions, this can refer to the presence of congenital birth defects, biomedical diagnoses, sensory impairments, and many other co-occurring outcomes.

Behavioural phenotypes

The original work from Zigler, Burack, Hodapp, and like-minded colleagues like Elisabeth Dykens (1995) has led to an entire field of study, called 'behavioural phenotype' research. The term *behavioural phenotype* refers to the collection of developmental, behavioural, and clinical outcomes that are more likely to be present when someone is diagnosed with a specific neurogenetic syndrome. As a testament to the importance of this area of study to the field of ID research, the Society for the Study of Behavioural Phenotypes was established in 1987, and its annual conferences are attended by researchers and clinicians from around the world.

Behavioural phenotypes are considered *probabilistic*, which means that not every person with a specific syndrome will show all aspects of the outcomes reported at the group level (Dykens 1995). However, people with a genetic condition are more likely to show aspects of the phenotypic pattern than people who do not have the genetic condition (Dykens 1995), and therefore a syndrome places people at higher risk for certain outcomes, which can inform intervention and educational planning in important ways. In the second half of this chapter, we will learn about findings from behavioural phenotype research into several neurogenetic syndromes. You will see that the genetic changes that cause neurogenetic syndromes have far-reaching effects on a range of developmental domains, and that different neurogenetic syndromes are linked to both shared and unique characteristics (Hodapp 1997).

GENETIC FACTORS THAT LEAD TO NEUROGENETIC SYNDROMES

There are several categories of genetic changes that can lead to neurogenetic syndromes. Understanding these types of changes requires a foray into material that you have likely encountered in your human biology classes. It may be helpful to have access to your old textbooks if your memories of chromosomes, genes, and cell division are a little bit hazy.

Chromosomal Causes of ID

Some neurogenetic syndromes are caused by a change in the total number of chromosomes that a person has in their genome. Recall from your previous human biology classes that most humans have 46 chromosomes in the nucleus of their cells; 23 are inherited from a biological mother and 23 are inherited from a biological father. Before fertilization, when meiotic cell division is taking place in the biological parents' reproductive organs to generate gametes (egg or sperm), alterations in the number of chromosomes can occur, leading to an egg or a sperm with 22 or 24 (or more) chromosomes. When fertilization takes place that involves a gamete with greater or fewer than 23 chromosomes; this leads to an embryo with greater or fewer than 46 chromosomes, often either 45 or 47, in the nucleus of each cell. Sometimes chromosomal changes happen after fertilization, during the earliest stages of embryonic cell division. This can lead to *mosaicism*, wherein some of the cells in the developing embryo have a chromosomal number change and some do not.

Trisomy

One type of a chromosomal neurogenetic condition is a *trisomy*, which occurs when an embryo develops with three copies of a specific chromosome instead of two. For example, Down syndrome is most frequently caused by trisomy 21, or the presence of three copies of chromosome 21 instead of two (see Chapter 4 for more information on Down syndrome). In most cases, Down syndrome is caused by the presence of an extra copy of chromosome 21 in the egg that is fertilized, which is linked to the fact that Down syndrome is associated with advanced maternal age.

Monosomy

Other types of chromosomal neurogenetic conditions involve inheriting only one copy of a chromosome instead of two, which is called a *monosomy*. Turner syndrome is a monosomy syndrome that occurs when only one X chromosome is present (Trolle et al. 2016) and no Y chromosome is inherited. While Turner syndrome does not usually lead to pronounced levels of ID, there are many cognitive and social-emotional challenges that may result from this monosomy condition, as well as a range of biomedical outcomes (Trolle et al. 2016).

Uniparental Disomy

In a small number of chromosomal neurogenetic syndromes, the total number of chromosomes is typical (46), but an individual inherits two copies of a chromosome from one biological parent and no copies from the other biological parent. This phenomenon is called a *'uniparental disomy'*. It might seem surprising that a uniparental disomy would lead to an ID-related outcome because the total number of chromosomes is 46 and there are two copies of each autosome (non-sex chromosome). However, scientists have discovered that genes are expressed differently based on whether they are inherited from a biological mother or father, a phenomenon called 'genomic imprinting' (Monk, Mackay, Eggermann, Maher, & Riccio 2019). Prader-Willi syndrome and Angelman syndrome are examples of genomic imprinting in neurogenetic syndromes. More on those two conditions can be found in the latter part of this chapter.

Copy Number Variations

Neurogenetic syndromes associated with ID can also be caused by 'copy number variations' (CNVs; Shaikh 2017). CNVs take place when segments of genes are either deleted (they are missing from a chromosome), duplicated (there are extra copies of genes on a chromosome), or changed in some other way (Shaikh 2017). CNVs vary greatly in size, from 1 kilobase (1,000 nucleotide bases) to several megabases (millions of nucleotide bases). In many cases, CNVs occur as *de novo* mutations, which means that they occur newly and were not carried in the genes and chromosomes of the biological parent. The *de novo* mutations can be newly present in gametes that are fertilized or they can happen after fertilization (Vissers, Gilissen, & Veltman 2016).

Monogenic Disorders

Many neurogenetic syndromes caused by CNVs involve a collection of genes that are either missing or duplicated. Some neurogenetic syndromes, however, are caused by changes to just one gene, and they are called 'monogenic disorders'. For example, fragile X syndrome is caused by changes to one gene on the X chromosome (*FMR1*), but these changes lead to an important set of outcomes across many aspects of cognitive, social, and behavioural development (Hagerman et al. 2017; see corresponding section below). New technologies have made it possible to identify many more monogenic disorders than we had previously known about (Doble et al. 2020), which is helping medical providers find causes for ID in cases that were previously unexplained.

Inherited Versus Non-Inherited Neurogenetic Conditions

The neurogenetic conditions that cause ID can be divided into two categories: inherited and non-inherited, or *de novo,* conditions. When a neurogenetic condition is inherited, that means that one or both biological parents already carried some version of the genetic features that cause ID in their genome. In some cases, a biological parent may have a premutation, or a less pronounced set of genetic changes in their own DNA, and the changes become more pronounced in their biological child. Some biological parents may carry a balanced translocation, where genetic material within their own genome was rearranged, not leading to any observable outcomes for them, but leading to observable outcomes in their offspring. In other cases, a biological parent may carry a recessive gene associated with ID that they do not express, but that may be expressed in their offspring if they mate with someone else who also carries the same recessive gene. The other category of neurogenetic conditions is non-inherited, or *de novo*, which means that the genetic changes that cause ID are new and took place for the first time during meiosis before fertilization or mitosis after fertilization.

Keeping Track of New Discoveries

Recent work suggests that over 700 genes in the human genome are linked to ID, many of which are involved in CNV-related conditions (Vissers et al. 2016). These conditions are tracked in a database called 'Online Mendelian Inheritance in Man' or OMIM. OMIM originally began as a written book that served as a catalogue for the various outcomes observed in medical settings (Hamosh et al. 2021). When genetic discoveries were made, they were added to OMIM as well, leading to a catalogue of both genotypes and phenotypes that are relevant for diagnosing a range of conditions. The original book was published in 1966, and it contained 1,486 entries. As a demonstration of the remarkable amount of research that has taken place over the past 50 years, the 2021 online version of OMIM catalogues approximately 16,400 genes and includes 9,300 phenotypic outcomes (Hamosh et al. 2021). It is used by more than 20,000 people per day to identify specific genetic conditions in patients, to learn about different diagnoses, and to learn about genes associated with specific conditions (Hamosh et al. 2021). The neurogenetic syndromes that are caused by CNVs presented in the latter part of this chapter are each listed in OMIM and have been assigned a unique OMIM identifier number.

THE ROAD TO DIAGNOSIS

There are many different paths that families may take in their journey towards finding a diagnosis for a family member with ID. In some neurogenetic conditions, like Down syndrome, diagnosis may take place prenatally (during pregnancy). Periodic ultrasound and screening tests are available throughout pregnancy that can identify early signs of atypical physical and neurodevelopment, which might lead to the decision to pursue more comprehensive evaluations, and even diagnostic tests that can be performed on foetal or placenta cells through amniocentesis or chorionic villi sampling (American College of Obstetricians and Gynecologists, 2016). For a more in-depth discussion of the Down syndrome diagnosis experiences, see Chapter 4.

Other conditions, like fragile X syndrome, can be screened for at birth when families have concerns about risk for this condition. There is a growing movement toward including fragile X syndrome in the panel of standard newborn screening tests in the US (Tassone 2014; Okoniewski et al. 2019). Advocates for more universal screening believe that it can help parents and health care providers plan early intervention services during a critical window of opportunity, the first few years of life. But because fragile X is an inherited neurogenetic condition, newborn screening can have implications for other family members who have not given their consent for testing. This had led to a discussion of various ethical considerations regarding a universal approach to identification and diagnosis (Bailey, Skinner, Davis, Whitmarsh, & Powell 2008).

In many cases, however, the detection of developmental delays and differences may unfold over the course of early childhood. In these circumstances, families often search for causes of their child's developmental delays, which leads to a sort of investigative journey. This journey can involve a range of evaluations, including physical examinations, brain imaging, and screening for metabolic conditions (Patel, Cabral, Ho, & Merrick 2020). Additional pregnancy factors may also be considered, including premature birth, potential exposure to toxic substances, maternal infection and illness, and nutrition (Vissers et al. 2016). Increasingly, however, a central aspect of this diagnostic journey involves genetic testing.

Genetic Testing Technology

The earliest forms of genetic testing in ID-related conditions took place through a microscope. Using a *karyotyping* approach, scientists discovered that certain chromosomal changes could be detected visually, such as with the diagnosis of Down syndrome (Lejeune, Turpin, & Gautier 1959). Karyotyping was also used to describe visually observable changes in the appearance of the X chromosome in what is now called fragile X syndrome (Lubs 1969). The 1990s brought about an increase in the use of *fluorescence in situ hybridization (FISH)* and other associated techniques that tested DNA directly for the presence of specific neurogenetic conditions. FISH testing uses fluorescent dyes that bind to a specific DNA sequence and then cells are viewed under a microscope with a particular type of light to identify the presence of specific sequences of interest. Using this approach made it possible for researchers and clinicians to test for specific neurogenetic conditions, like Williams syndrome, when a genetic cause of ID was suspected (Vissers et al. 2016).

The subsequent arrival of DNA *microarray analysis* technology, which became more widespread in the 2000s, made it possible for scientists to sequence thousands of genes at the same time (Vissers et al. 2016). This approach, sometimes described as 'DNA chip' technology, involves preparing slides that contain a large number of DNA spots from a patient and from a control sample. The analysis then compares the DNA expression of the patient samples with the DNA expression of the control samples using a unique type of scanner. This type of comparison approach makes it possible to detect the over- or under-expression of specific genes in the patient DNA, and has facilitated the discovery of many new CNV syndromes (Coughlin, Scharer, & Shaikh 2012).

Next Generation Sequencing

The 2010s brought about the use of *next generation sequencing (NGS)*, which has newly transformed our ability to detect underlying genetic causes of ID. NGS techniques involve breaking down patient DNA into fragments and using computational models to compare DNA segments to a reference sequence. Current NGS techniques have revolutionized genetic testing because they can sequence DNA quickly and without great expense (Slatko, Gardner, & Ausubel 2018). This technological advance is having a real-world impact on families of children seeking diagnoses. A recent study demonstrated that use of NGS technologies significantly reduces average healthcare costs for families of children with ID (Vrijenhoek et al. 2018). Having used this type of genetic testing in their diagnostic journey, families reported spending less time focused on health care issues and they also reported fewer hospitalizations for their child (Vrijenhoek et al. 2018).

Why is a Genetic Diagnosis Important?

As we have discussed, when a child demonstrates early developmental delays, there is often an evaluation process that aims to identify a cause. More and more, this evaluation process has begun to include the search for an underlying genetic diagnosis (Moeschler & Shevell 2014). The American Academy of Pediatrics has endorsed this type of genetic evaluation for a variety of child and family outcome-related reasons (Moeschler & Shevell 2014). A diagnosis can help families manage and understand symptoms, especially those that may be unusual or difficult to interpret. For example, in a condition like Smith-Magenis syndrome (see section below) that is associated with challenging and self-injurious behaviours, having a diagnosis can help families interpret their child's behaviour as a part of the phenotypic expression of a deletion on chromosome 17 (Smith & Gropman 2021). Families can then work with clinicians to address those challenging behaviours from a phenotype-informed stance.

Having a diagnosis can also positively impact overall parent and family well-being (Moeschler & Shevell 2014). A diagnosis can help families understand their child's prognosis and therefore plan more effective interventions and treatments (Moeschler & Shevell 2014). In addition, a diagnosis can help families understand the likelihood of recurrence in future pregnancies and make decisions about family planning. Importantly, a diagnosis can help families find social-emotional support through connecting with families of children with the same condition who can relate to their experiences (Moeschler & Shevell 2014). Being able to describe shared experiences can alleviate some of the isolation and psychological stress associated with parenting a child with a rare condition.

Finally, a diagnosis may also help researchers to better meet the needs of children with the same condition in the future. The fields of intervention and educational science have increasingly begun to use findings from neurogenetic syndrome research to develop novel syndrome-informed interventions. These approaches are developed with a specific phenotypic pattern of strengths and challenges in mind, and aim to capitalize on areas of strength while supporting areas of vulnerability commonly observed in a particular syndrome (Lemons et al. 2018). In addition, new syndrome-informed approaches take a more anticipatory stance, recognizing that certain outcomes are more likely in a particular neurogenetic syndrome group, and developing targeted interventions for infants and young children that aim to strengthen foundations in those areas from the earliest stages (Fidler et al. 2021). In this way, seeking and establishing a specific syndrome diagnosis makes it possible for researchers to know more about the range of outcomes and the unique patterns of functioning that may be associated with a given syndrome, which can lead to more personalized and more effective treatment and intervention approaches.

SPECIFIC NEUROGENETIC CONDITIONS ASSOCIATED WITH ID

We have now discussed the definitions of *rare disorder* and *neurogenetic syndrome*, and we have learned about how and why families may seek and arrive at a diagnosis for a child who is demonstrating developmental delays. We now turn to the wealth of new information that has become available regarding specific neurogenetic syndromes. Several decades of research have helped our field gain more in-depth accounts of a variety of neurogenetic syndromes, and we will examine a few of these conditions below. It is important to remember, however, that there are many other neurogenetic conditions that are under-researched, and that impact developmental outcomes in pronounced ways just as the conditions listed below. It is also important to remember that advanced genetic testing technology has led to the discovery of new rare conditions each year, and these conditions likely will involve complex phenotypic profiles that have yet to be examined. *Note: This textbook includes a comprehensive chapter on Down syndrome, the most common neurogenetic condition associated with ID. You are encouraged to read the in-depth account of Down syndrome in Chapter 4.*

Fragile X Syndrome

Fragile X syndrome (FXS) is a monogenic condition, which means that it is caused by only one affected gene, called *FMR1*. It is the most common inherited cause of ID, occurring in approximately 1 in every 7,000 males, and 1 in every 11,000 females (Crawford et al., 2020). FXS is an X-linked disorder, which means that the gene involved in FXS is found on the X chromosome. This has important implications for how FXS is inherited.

As you may remember from human biology class, the genome of biological females contains two X chromosomes and the genome of biological males contains an X and a Y chromosome. This leads to a sex-related phenomenon, where biological males who inherit an X chromosome with the FXS mutation will be more impacted than biological females, who are likely to have inherited an unaffected X chromosome alongside the affected X chromosome. In terms of ID, this leads to a sex-related disparity wherein the vast majority of males with FXS meet criteria for ID, compared with only 30% of females (de Vries et al. 1998; Hartley et al. 2011; Hagerman et al. 2017).

FXS is caused by the expansion of a part of the *FMR1* gene, which contains a repetition of the nucleotides cytosine (C) and guanine (G) in the order of CGG. In the general population, the CGG sequence on *FMR1* is repeated less than 55 times in a row, but in individuals with FXS, there are over 200 CGG repeats found in this region (Hagerman et al. 2017). This causes a disruption in the production of an important protein, called FMRP. FMRP plays an important role in brain development and functioning, and this disruption leads to ID-related outcomes in FXS (Crawford et al. 2020). It is also important to note that when between 55 and 200 CGG repeats are present on *FMR1*, this is called a fragile X syndrome 'premutation', which leads to a different set of outcomes than FXS (Crawford et al. 2020). Recent NGS testing has also brought about the discovery of deletions in *FMR1*, which also impact the production of FMRP, causing outcomes similar to those who have FXS based on the CGG repeat presentation (Quartier et al. 2017).

Phenotypic Outcomes Associated with FXS

FXS predisposes individuals to a distinct phenotypic pattern of outcomes. During infancy, feeding and motor delays are often observed in this population (Hagerman et al. 2017). A range of behavioural and psychiatric features are often present during childhood and adolescence, including tantrums, aggressive behaviour, and impulsivity (Wheeler, Raspa, Bishop, & Bailey 2016). During early childhood, a range of social features often emerge, including difficulty making eye contact and an aversion to being touched by other people (Hagerman et al. 2017; Rais, Binder, Razak, & Ethell 2018). Individuals with FXS are at elevated likelihood for demonstrating anxiety symptoms (Hagerman et al. 2017; Ezell et al. 2019) and co-occurring autism spectrum disorder, which occurs in over half of males with FXS (Harris et al. 2008).

Families of children with FXS report elevated stress levels, especially when a child demonstrates more challenging behaviours. At a stakeholder meeting that incuded researchers, professionals, and family members of individuals with FXS, attendees described a greater need for resources for families (Riley, Mailick, Berry-Kravis, & Bolen 2017). Desired resources include help with accessing educational, social, and health-related services. There was also consensus among stakeholders that there was a need for more family-focused interventions in this population (Riley et al. 2017). These sentiments underscore the wide-ranging impact of the alteration of just one gene on one chromosome and the indirect effect of this monogenic condition on families and communities. When understood from this perspective, it is clear that a somewhat rare condition like FXS requires a great deal of research attention to address the needs of individuals with this condition and their families.

Williams Syndrome

Williams syndrome (WS; also known as Williams Beuren syndrome) is another CNV disorder that is caused by a deletion in a specific region on chromosome 7. The size of the deletion in WS is relatively small, between 1.5 to 1.8 MB, usually including between 26 and 30 genes in a region that includes the gene *ELN*. *ELN* is a gene that encodes for the protein elastin, an important protein for connective tissue in humans. A deletion of this gene is linked to some of the biomedical challenges associated with WS, like cardiovascular abnormalities (Collins 2018). Usually, WS results from a *de novo* mutation (Morris & Braddock 2020). Recent genetic analyses have uncovered additional, smaller deletions in this region that vary from the usual WS deletion, and outcomes associated with these variants differ (Morris & Braddock 2020).

The prevalence of WS is approximately 1 in every 7,500 (Strømme, Bjømstad, & Ramstad 2002), which leads to a designation as a rare disorder. Individuals with WS tend to have specific facial features, with a broad forehead and short nose (Morris & Braddock 2020), and they are at elevated risk for biomedical conditions such as cardiovascular anomalies and hypercalcemia, especially during early childhood (Morris & Braddock 2020).

Phenotypic Outcomes Associated with WS

WS has been the focus of research attention for several decades because of unique phenotypic features related to social skills (https://www.youtube.com/watch?v=M6n4z0XjPh4&t=166s), language acquisition (https://www.youtube.com/watch?v=7pyNe2TBQi8), and cognition (https://www.youtube.com/watch?v=EgJVTRfwcAU) (Mervis & Velleman 2011; Thurman & Fisher 2015). Although the majority of individuals with WS have ID, there are notable phenotypic patterns of strength and challenge associated with this condition. A great deal of research has focused on describing an interpersonal style often observed in individuals with WS, which involves strong social motivation and frequent social initiations (Thurman & Fisher 2015). Additional research has described a unique language acquisition profile associated with WS, which can involve stronger phonological processing skills, but weaker comprehension skills (Mervis & Velleman 2011; see Chapter 9 for more information on language subsystems). Although verbal and phonological processing skills may be relatively stronger among many individuals with WS, visuospatial processing skills are known to be an area of distinct vulnerability (Miezah et al. 2021). It is also interesting to note that, in the presence of verbal and phonological processing skills, many individuals with WS have hyperacusis, or hypersensitivity to certain sounds (John & Mervis 2010).

In terms of psychiatric diagnoses, children with WS are at elevated risk for attention deficit and hyperactivity disorder (Leyfer, Woodruff-Borden, Klein-Tasman, Fricke, & Mervis 2006). They are also at risk for elevated rates of anxiety, but usually these symptoms are nonsocial in nature (Leyfer et al. 2006). A subgroup of children with WS may demonstrate autism features and meet criteria for autism spectrum disorder, despite the high social motivation reported on the group level (Klein-Tasman, Phillips, Lord, Mervis, & Gallo 2009).

Outcomes associated with WS are varied. Some people with WS live independently in adulthood and some receive some form of post-secondary education (Howlin & Udwin 2006). However, many adults with WS rely on supports for activities of daily living to some degree and many continue to live with their families of origin into adulthood (Howlin & Udwin 2006).

One area of specific concern is that social disinhibition may place adults with WS at risk for manipulation or being taken advantage of (Thurman & Fisher 2015). A strong motivation to create social connections coupled with the presence of ID can make it difficult for many people with WS to discern whether someone is being genuine or whether they may have less than honorable motives. Interventions that promote social decision-making skills to avoid such situations are often recommended for people with WS in order to increase independence and reduce social vulnerability (Thurman & Fisher, 2015).

Smith-Magenis Syndrome

Another syndrome that has a CNV genetic origin is Smith-Magenis syndrome (SMS), which is caused by a deletion on chromosome 17 (Smith & Gropman 2021). SMS is a rare disorder, occurring at a rate of 1 in every 15,000 to 25,000 (Greenberg et al. 1991), and generally involves a unique facial appearance. Though SMS is linked to ID in most cases, behavioural hallmarks of SMS include high rates of aggression, sleep disturbance, co-occurring ADHD, and repetitive, stereotyped behaviour (Poisson et al. 2015). Stereotyped behaviour can be observed in the form of repetitive hand and arm motions that are common to people with SMS, but often repetitive behaviours in this population can be self-injurious, including self-biting and self-hitting (Smith & Gropman 2021). Self-injury becomes more frequent throughout childhood in many individuals with SMS, and the number of different types of self-injury increase with age as well (Finucane, Dirrigl, & Simon 2001).

In addition to the safety risk to the person with SMS that results from self-injurious behaviour, this behavioural feature poses specific challenges to family members and caregivers (Nag, Hoxmark, & Nærland 2019). When parents of children with SMS were interviewed in a recent study, many voiced concerns about the lack of effective strategies for helping their child reduce these behaviours, reporting that they do not have adequate understanding and knowledge about how to support their child (Nag et al. 2019). Some parents also reported that many professionals working with their child were not well-versed in the behaviour patterns associated with SMS, and that they tended to receive recommendations that were not effective (Nag et al. 2019). These responses highlight the importance for families to identify their child's diagnosis, but also for professionals to become educated regarding the phenotypic profiles associated with specific genetic conditions, like SMS.

Prader-Willi and Angelman Syndromes

The neurogenetic syndromes that were examined in this section can all be considered CNVs of different varieties. We now focus our attention on two syndromes that involve complex sets of features. Though they are two distinct syndromes with different phenotypic outcomes, we examine Prader-Willi syndrome (PWS) and Angelman syndrome (AS) together because of their linked genetic cause. PWS and AS are both caused by missing genetic material in a specific region on chromosome 15 (Buiting 2010). When this was discovered, scientists were confused about why missing the same genetic information could lead to such different syndromes. They then examined the importance of parental origin—was genetic information missing from the maternal chromosome 15 (inherited from biological mother) or the paternal chromosome 15 (inherited from biological father)? Researchers found that the deletion associated with PWS-related features was found on the paternal chromosome 15, and that features associated with AS were always caused by missing genetic material on the maternal chromosome 15 (Butler & Palmer 1983; Knoll et al. 1989).

Additional scientific discovery led to the knowledge that the missing genetic information on chromosome 15 for each syndrome can be caused either by a deletion (only a piece of the chromosome is missing) or by a uniparental disomy. Earlier in this chapter, we learned that uniparental disomies take place when two of a certain chromosome are inherited from one biological parent and none are inherited from the other biological parent. Scientific discovery led to the insight that PWS can be caused when someone inherits two maternal chromosome 15s, and AS can be caused when someone inherits two paternal chromosome 15s.

Phenotypic Outcomes in PWS & AS

Though they share a related origin, these two syndromes predispose individuals to very different developmental trajectories. PWS occurs in 1 in every 10–30,000 individuals (Emerick & Vogt 2013) and is associated with mild to moderate levels of ID. A prominent feature of PWS is hyperphagia, or uncontrollable eating behaviour. Hyperphagia sets the stage of obesity-related health challenges for people with PWS, which is often accompanied by food-related ideation, or obsessive thinking about food (McAllister, Whittington, & Holland 2011). Interestingly, early development in PWS is often associated with lack of interest in food (McAllister et al. 2011). However, between the ages of two and five years, many children with PWS become fixated on food and the hyperphagia generally becomes observable (McAllister et al. 2011). Eating behaviour in PWS has been linked to an atypical response of 'feeling full' after eating that most people experience (McAllister et al. 2011).

In contrast, the majority of people with Angelman syndrome demonstrate severe levels of ID (Williams, Driscoll, & Dagli 2010). With an occurrence of 1 in 12–20,000, many people with AS are minimally verbal and have pronounced motor challenges (Williams et al. 2010). They are also known to demonstrate frequent happy emotional displays and laughter, as well as excited hand-flapping (Williams et al. 2010). Researchers aiming to understand why there are such differences between these related syndromes have found that different genes are impacted, despite the fact that both disorders are caused by missing genetic material in the same region of chromosome 15 (Buiting 2010). The contrast between these two conditions has given us a greater understanding of 'genomic imprinting' or how genes inherited from paternal versus maternal DNA are expressed differently in our genome.

Treatments for PWS include both biomedical and behavioural approaches to manage challenging behaviours (Butler, Miller & Forster 2019). Feeding interventions during infancy aim to address early sucking behaviour and may involve tube feeding (Butler et al. 2019). Some recommendations include supports for maintaining physical activity and dietary counseling to address hyperphagia (Butler et al. 2019). To address challenging behaviour, a variety of approaches are recommended, including applied behaviour analysis, cognitive behaviour therapy, social skills training, and the use of medication (Butler et al. 2019). For AS, primarily pharmacological approaches are currently being researched to address the cognitive and motor delays associated with this condition. Yet the need for more empirically based intervention approaches is needed for this population. A recent study highlighted the range of therapeutic priorities from a parental perspective, including expressive communication, seizures, behaviour challenges, and cognition (Wilgoss et al. 2021).

SUMMARY

This chapter offered a glimpse into the complex and rapidly changing landscape of rare disorders and neurogenetic syndromes associated with ID. On the one hand, hard work and advocacy has brought the challenges associated with these rare conditions to the societal level, and has led to important legislative victories that promote research advances. Biotechnological changes have continued to improve the identification and diagnosis of rare disorders, which can then be understood more comprehensively with research on behavioural phenotypes and biomedical outcomes. Leading organizations like the American Academy of Pediatrics have strongly endorsed the importance of genetic testing to identify aetiologies of ID.

At the same time, we have seen that each condition is associated with a unique combination of areas of strength and vulnerability, and families often struggle to find the right treatments and services to meet the needs of their child. With such a large and growing number of ID-related neurogenetic syndromes identified, it can be difficult for families to find professionals who have specific knowledge regarding a child's rare condition, which can lead to a sense of isolation and lack of support. As this field continues to innovate, it is clear that technological advances from a genetic perspective must be complemented by advances in our social fabric, so that more tailored support systems are available for the sizable percentage of people who have rare disorders and their families.

Reflective Questions

1. What are the advantages of knowing the genetic causes of ID for family members?
2. What are the advantages of knowing the genetic causes of ID for researchers?

3   What are the advantages of knowing the genetic causes of ID for interventionists?
4   Imagine receiving a rare disorder diagnosis for a loved one. What information would you want to know? What questions would you want researchers to answer?

REFERENCES

American College of Obstetricians and Gynecologists. (2016). Practice bulletin no. 162: Prenatal diagnostic testing for genetic disorders. *Obstetrics & Gynecology, 127*(5), e108-e122. doi:10.1097/AOG.0000000000001405.

Bailey, D. B., Skinner, D., Davis, A. M., Whitmarsh, I., & Powell, C. (2008). Ethical, legal, and social concerns about expanded newborn screening: fragile X syndrome as a prototype for emerging issues. *Pediatrics, 121*(3), e693–e704. doi:10.1542/peds.2007-0820.

Buiting, K. (2010). Prader–Willi syndrome and Angelman syndrome. Paper presented at the *American Journal of Medical Genetics Part C: Seminars in Medical Genetics.*

Burack, J. A., Hodapp, R. M., & Zigler, E. (1988). Issues in the classification of mental retardation: Differentiating among organic etiologies. *Journal of Child Psychology and Psychiatry, 29*, 765–779.

Burack, J. A. (1990). Differentiating mental retardation: The two-group approach and beyond. *Issues in the Developmental Approach to Mental Retardation*, 27–48.

Butler, M. G., Miller, J. L., & Forster, J. L. (2019). Prader-Willi syndrome-clinical genetics, diagnosis and treatment approaches: an update. *Current Pediatric Reviews, 15*(4), 207–244.

Butler, M. G., & Palmer, C. G. (1983). Parental origin of chromosome 15 deletion in Prader-Willi syndrome. *Lancet, 1*(8336), 1285–1286.

Collins, R. T., II. (2018). Cardiovascular disease in Williams syndrome. *Current Opinion in Pediatrics, 30*(5), 609–615. doi:10.1097/MOP.0000000000000664.

Coughlin, C. R., Scharer, G. H., & Shaikh, T. H. (2012). Clinical impact of copy number variation analysis using high-resolution microarray technologies: advantages, limitations and concerns. *Genome Medicine, 4*(10), 1–12.

Crawford, H., Abbeduto, L., Hall, S. S., Hardiman, R., Hessl, D., Roberts, J. E., ... Oliver, C. (2020). Fragile X syndrome: An overview of cause, characteristics, assessment and management. *Paediatrics and Child Health.* doi:10.1016/j.paed.2020.08.007.

de Vries, B., Halley, D., Oostra, B. A., & Niermeijer, M. F. (1998). The fragile X syndrome. *Journal of Medical Genetics, 35*(7), 579–589. doi:10.1136/jmg.35.7.579.

Doble, B., Schofield, D., Evans, C.-A., Groza, T., Mattick, J. S., Field, M., & Roscioli, T. (2020). Impacts of genomics on the health and social costs of intellectual disability. *Journal of medical genetics, 57*(7), 479–486.

Dykens, E. M. (1995). Measuring behavioral phenotypes: Provocations from the' new genetics.'. *American Journal on Mental Retardation.*

Emerick, J. E., & Vogt, K. S. (2013). Endocrine manifestations and management of Prader-Willi syndrome. *International Journal of Pediatric Endocrinology, 2013*(1), 1–10. doi:10.1186/1687-9856-2013-14.

Ezell, J., Hogan, A., Fairchild, A., Hills, K., Klusek, J., Abbeduto, L., & Roberts, J. (2019). Prevalence and predictors of anxiety disorders in adolescent and adult males with autism spectrum disorder and fragile X syndrome. *Journal of Autism and Developmental Disorders, 49*(3), 1131–1141. doi:10.1007/s10803-018-3804-6.

Fidler, D. J., Schworer, E. K., Needham, A., Prince, M., Patel, L., Will, E. A., & Daunhauer, L. A. (2021). Feasibility of a syndrome-informed micro-intervention for infants with Down syndrome. *Journal of Intellectual Disability Research, 65*(4), 320-339. doi:10.1111/jir.12814.

Finucane, B., Dirrigl, K. H., & Simon, E. W. (2001). Characterization of self-injurious behaviors in children and adults with Smith-Magenis syndrome. *American Journal on Mental Retardation, 106*(1), 52–58. doi:10.1352/0895-8017(2001)106<0052:COSIBI>2.0.CO;2.

Greenberg, F., Guzzetta, V., de Oca-Luna, R. M., Magenis, R., Smith, A., Richter, S., ... Lupski, J. (1991). Molecular analysis of the Smith-Magenis syndrome: a possible contiguous-gene syndrome associated with del(17)(p11.2). *American Journal of Human Henetics, 49*(6), 1207.

Hagerman, R. J., Berry-Kravis, E., Hazlett, H. C., Bailey, D. B., Moine, H., Kooy, R. F., ... Mandel, J. L. (2017). Fragile X syndrome. *Nature Reviews Disease Primers, 3*(1), 1–19. doi:10.1038/nrdp.2017.65.

Harris, S. W., Hessl, D., Goodlin-Jones, B., Ferranti, J., Bacalman, S., Barbato, I., ... Hagerman, R. J. (2008). Autism profiles of males with fragile X syndrome. *American Journal on Mental Retardation, 113*(6), 427–438. doi:10.1352/2008.113:427–438.

Hartley, S. L., Seltzer, M. M., Raspa, M., Olmstead, M., Bishop, E., & Bailey Jr, D. B. (2011). Exploring the adult life of men and women with fragile X syndrome: results from a national survey. *American Journal of Intellectual and Developmental Disabilities, 116*(1), 16–35. doi:10.1352/1944-7558-116.1.16.

Hodapp, R. M. (1997). Direct and indirect behavioral effects of different genetic disorders of mental retardation. *American Journal on Mental Retardation, 102*(1), 67–79.

Howlin, P., & Udwin, O. (2006). Outcome in adult life for people with Williams syndrome–results from a survey of 239 families. *Journal of Intellectual Disability Research, 50*(2), 151–160. doi:10.1111/j.1365-2788.2006.00775.x.

John, A. E., & Mervis, C. B. (2010). Sensory modulation impairments in children with Williams syndrome. *American Journal of Medical Genetics Part C: Seminars in Medical Genetics, 154C*(2), 266–276. doi:10.1002/ajmg.c.30260.

Klein-Tasman, B. P., Phillips, K. D., Lord, C. E., Mervis, C. B., & Gallo, F. (2009). Overlap with the autism spectrum in young children with Williams syndrome. *Journal of Developmental & Behavioral Pediatrics, 30*(4), 289–299. doi:10.1097/DBP.0b013e3181ad1f9a.

Knoll, J. H., Nicholls, R., Magenis, R., Graham Jr, J., Lalande, M., Latt, S., ... Reynolds, J. F. (1989). Angelman and Prader-Willi syndromes share a common chromosome 15 deletion but differ in parental origin of the deletion. *American Journal of Medical Genetics, 32*(2), 285–290.

Lejeune, J., Turpin, R., & Gautier, M. M. (1959). Le mongolisme, premier exemple d'aberration autosomique humaine. *Annales de genetique, 1*(2), 41–49.

Lemons, C. J., King, S. A., Davidson, K. A., Puranik, C. S., Al Otaiba, S., & Fidler, D. J. (2018). Personalized reading intervention for children with Down syndrome. *Journal of School Psychology, 66*, 67–84. doi:10.1016/j.jsp.2017.07.006.

Leyfer, O. T., Woodruff-Borden, J., Klein-Tasman, B. P., Fricke, J. S., & Mervis, C. B. (2006). Prevalence of psychiatric disorders in 4 to 16-year-olds with Williams syndrome. *American Journal of Medical Genetics Part B: Neuropsychiatric Genetics, 141*(6), 615–622. doi:10.1002/ajmg.b.30344.

Lubs, H. A. (1969). A marker X chromosome. *American Journal of Human Genetics, 21*(3), 231.

McAllister, C., Whittington, J., & Holland, A. (2011). Development of the eating behaviour in Prader–Willi Syndrome: advances in our understanding. *International Journal of Obesity, 35*(2), 188–197. doi:10.1038/ijo.2010.139.

Mervis, C. B., & Velleman, S. L. (2011). Children with Williams syndrome: language, cognitive, and behavioral characteristics and their implications for intervention. *Perspectives on Language Learning and Education, 18*(3), 98–107. doi:10.1044/lle18.3.98.

Miezah, D., Porter, M., Rossi, A., Kazzi, C., Batchelor, J., & Reeve, J. (2021). Cognitive profile of young children with Williams syndrome. *Journal of Intellectual Disability Research*. doi:10.1111/jir.12860.

Moeschler, J. B., & Shevell, M. (2014). Comprehensive evaluation of the child with intellectual disability or global developmental delays. *Pediatrics, 134*(3), e903–e918. doi:10.1542/peds.2014-1839.

Moliner, A. M., & Waligora, J. (2017). The European Union policy in the field of rare diseases. In *Rare Diseases Epidemiology: Update and Overview* (pp. 561–587): Springer.

Monk, D., Mackay, D. J., Eggermann, T., Maher, E. R., & Riccio, A. (2019). Genomic imprinting disorders: Lessons on how genome, epigenome and environment interact. *Nature Reviews Genetics, 20*(4), 235–248.

Morris, C. A., & Braddock, S. R. (2020). Health care supervision for children with Williams syndrome. *Pediatrics, 145*(2). doi:10.1542/peds.2019–3761.

Nag, H. E., Hoxmark, L. B., & Nærland, T. (2019). Parental experiences with behavioural problems in Smith–Magenis syndrome: The need for syndrome-specific competence. *Journal of Intellectual Disabilities, 23*(3), 359–372. doi:10.1177/1744629519847375.

Okoniewski, K. C., Wheeler, A. C., Lee, S., Boyea, B., Raspa, M., Taylor, J. L., & Bailey, D. B. (2019). Early identification of fragile X syndrome through expanded newborn screening. *Brain Sciences, 9*(1), 4.

Patel, D. R., Cabral, M. D., Ho, A., & Merrick, J. (2020). A clinical primer on intellectual disability. *Translational Pediatrics, 9*(Suppl 1), S23–S35. doi:10.21037/tp.2020.02.02.

Poisson, A., Nicolas, A., Cochat, P., Sanlaville, D., Rigard, C., de Leersnyder, H., … Demily, C. (2015). Behavioral disturbance and treatment strategies in Smith-Magenis syndrome. *Orphanet Journal of Rare Diseases, 10*(1), 111. doi:10.1186/s13023-015-0330-x.

Quartier, A., Poquet, H., Gilbert-Dussardier, B., Rossi, M., Casteleyn, A.-S., des Portes, V., … Redin, C. (2017). Intragenic FMR1 disease-causing variants: a significant mutational mechanism leading to Fragile-X syndrome. *European Journal of Human Genetics, 25*(4), 423–431. doi:10.1038/ejhg.2016.204.

Rais, M., Binder, D. K., Razak, K. A., & Ethell, I. M. (2018). Sensory processing phenotypes in fragile X syndrome. *American Society for Neurochemistry, 10*, 1–19. doi:10.1177/1759091418801092.

Rare Diseases Act of 2002, 42 U.S.C. 281, Pub. L. No. 107–280 (6 Nov. 2002).

Riley, C., Mailick, M., Berry-Kravis, E., & Bolen, J. (2017). The future of fragile X syndrome: CDC stakeholder meeting summary. *Pediatrics, 139*(Supplement 3), S147–S152. doi:10.1542/peds.2016-1159B.

Rotaru, D. C., Mientjes, E. J., & Elgersma, Y. (2020). Angelman syndrome: from mouse models to therapy. *Neuroscience, 445*, 172–189.

Shaikh, T. H. (2017). Copy number variation disorders. *Current Genetic Medicine Reports, 5*(4), 183–190. doi:10.1007/s40142-017-0129-2.

Slatko, B. E., Gardner, A. F., & Ausubel, F. M. (2018). Overview of next-generation sequencing technologies. *Current Protocols in Molecular Biology, 122*(1), e59. doi:10.1002/cpmb.59.

Smith, A. C. M., & Gropman, A. L. (2021). Smith–Magenis Syndrome. In J. C. Carey, A. Battaglia, D. Viskochil, & S. B. Cassidy (eds), *Cassidy and Allanson's Management of Genetic Syndromes* (pp. 863–893).

Strømme, P., Bjømstad, P. G., & Ramstad, K. (2002). Prevalence estimation of Williams syndrome. *Journal of Child Neurology, 17*(4), 269–271. doi:10.1177/088307380201700406.

Tassone, F. (2014). Newborn screening for fragile X syndrome. *JAMA Neurology, 71*(3), 355–359.

Thurman, A. J., & Fisher, M. H. (2015). The Williams syndrome social phenotype: Disentangling the contributions of social interest and social difficulties. In *International Review of Research in Developmental Disabilities* (Vol. 49, pp. 191-227): Elsevier.

Trolle, C., Nielsen, M. M., Skakkebæk, A., Lamy, P., Vang, S., Hedegaard, J., ... Gravholt, C. H. (2016). Widespread DNA hypomethylation and differential gene expression in Turner syndrome. *Scientific Reports, 6*(1), 1–14. doi:10.1038/srep34220.

Vissers, L. E., Gilissen, C., & Veltman, J. A. (2016). Genetic studies in intellectual disability and related disorders. *Nature Reviews Genetics, 17*(1), 9–18.

Vrijenhoek, T., Middelburg, E. M., Monroe, G. R., van Gassen, K. L., Geenen, J. W., Hövels, A. M., ... Frederix, G. W. (2018). Whole-exome sequencing in intellectual disability; cost before and after a diagnosis. *European Journal of Human Genetics, 26*(11), 1566–1571. doi:10.1038/s41431-018-0203-6.

Wakap, S. N., Lambert, D. M., Olry, A., Rodwell, C., Gueydan, C., Lanneau, V., ... Rath, A. (2020). Estimating cumulative point prevalence of rare diseases: analysis of the Orphanet database. *European Journal of Human Genetics, 28*(2), 165–173.

Wheeler, A., Raspa, M., Bishop, E., & Bailey, D., Jr. (2016). Aggression in fragile X syndrome. *Journal of Intellectual Disability Research, 60*(2), 113–125. doi:10.1111/jir.12238.

Williams, C. A., Driscoll, D. J., & Dagli, A. I. (2010). Clinical and genetic aspects of Angelman syndrome. *Genetics in Medicine, 12*(7), 385–395. doi:10.1097/GIM.0b013e3181def138.

Willgoss, T., Cassater, D., Connor, S., Krishnan, M. L., Miller, M. T., Dias-Barbosa, C., ... & Bichell, T. J. (2021). Measuring what matters to individuals with Angelman syndrome and their families: Development of a patient-centered disease concept model. *Child Psychiatry & Human Development, 52*(4), 654–668.

Zigler, E. (1967). Familial mental retardation: A continuing dilemma. *Science, 155*(3760), 292–298.

PART III
DEVELOPMENTAL DISABILITIES

PART III
DEVELOPMENTAL DISABILITIES

7
AUTISM SPECTRUM DISORDER (OR DIFFERENCE)
Features, Identification, and Screening

> **Learning Objectives**
>
> After reading this chapter, you should be able to:
>
> - Outline the current criteria for formally identifying ASD
> - Briefly describe how current identification systems relate to their historical context
> - Give a critical summary of the different instruments currently used to assess and measure the behavioural profile of individuals on the autism spectrum
> - Demonstrate a critical awareness of the strengths and weaknesses of the processes used to formally identify autism and of the instruments used to assess it

The set of behavioural differences often referred to as 'Autism Spectrum Disorder' (ASD) affects the developmental trajectory of an individual's behavioral adaptation to the world. It is present from birth, although not usually identified until the second or third year and persists across the entire life span from birth to old age. Accurate and reliable identification and assessment are at the heart of the study of ASD: planning for and provision of autism-appropriate services depends crucially on the identification and estimates of prevalence of affected individuals in the general population. Formulation of assistive strategies depends on research into their effectiveness, which requires not only accurate identification of target individuals but also on the development of instruments that are not only accurate and reliable but also are sensitive to changes in clinical features. Scientific investigations of underlying mechanisms not only depend on the recruitment of adequately characterized participants but also on an understanding of the fundamental nature or underlying causes of the behavioural features. This interdependence between accurate documentation of defining features and understanding of underlying mechanisms means the ideas discussed in the present chapter will be better understood when read in conjunction with Chapter 8 on theories of ASD. Moreover, it is important to be aware both that current frameworks and associated procedures for the identification of autism have not emerged out of the blue but have developed over time and will continue to develop in the future and also that 'autism' most probably does not stop at the somewhat arbitrary cutoff points set up to define clinical 'cases' but may also spill over into the rest of the population. It should also be noted at this point that many of the ideas discussed in this chapter derive from the strongly medical/disease-oriented model of ASD that has predominated in the past. As a consequence, some terminology (e.g. diagnosis, clinical features, pathology) will inevitably be used. The present author acknowledges the growing awareness that autism might better be viewed from a perspective of neurodiversity (see Pellicano & den Houting 2022), which, quite rightly, argues against a pathologizing of autistic people and should appropriately acknowledge the viewpoint and experiences of autistic people themselves (see Milton 2014). Therefore, I have in the main attempted to use non-pathologizing language whist at the same time attempted neither to deny the past nor to re-write history.

This chapter will first outline the main clinical features as defined by traditional and still widely used systems of identification together with a brief overview of some of the commonly used instruments used to identify and screen for autism from this perspective. The chapter will conclude by providing some critical reflections on the material covered in the earlier sections.

HISTORICAL BACKGROUND

The set of conditions we now refer to as ASD was first included in the third edition of the American Psychiatric Association's *Diagnostic and Statistical Manual of Mental Disorders* (DSM-III, American Psychiatric Association, 1980). However, although this was the first systematic description aimed at formal identification, it was not the first description of the condition we now call autism. Many earlier first-hand accounts describe individuals who in retrospect were probably on the autism spectrum (Frith 2003; Wing 2013) and would have met the criteria set out in any of the incarnations of the DSM. Examples include Itard's *Wild Boy of Aveyron* (Itard 1802/1962; Lane 1976, dramatized in François Truffaut's 1970 film *L'Enfant Sauvage*) or Melanie Klein's description of a boy – 'Dick' – she described as being devoid of affect, not upset at being separated from his parents and as treating her like a piece of furniture (Klein 1930/1975, cited in Hobson 1990). There is also quite an industry that has attempted retrospectively to diagnose major historical figures such as the philosopher Immanuel Kant, the concert pianist Glenn Gould, or the poet W. B. Yeats as having ASD (Houston & Frith 2000; Lyons & Fitzgerald 2005). Both the first-hand accounts and the retrospective 'diagnoses' are all possible only through the lens of our current systems of identification, which have their origins in the systematic accounts of two psychiatrists, Leo Kanner (Kanner 1943) and Hans Asperger (Asperger 1944, 1991), whose observations continue to influence the thinking of clinicians, scientists and the general population. Kanner's article was the first clinical description of 11 children he encountered in his professional practice and who were characterized by what he called *autistic disturbances of affective contact*. Much of the behavioural profile painted by Kanner – social difficulties and repetitive behaviour – survives in in the current version of the DSM (DSM-5, American Psychiatric Association, 2013), albeit in a modified form. Other features considered by Kanner to be important, such as repetitive and stereotyped play, are now subsumed under the heading of restrictive and repetitive interests and behaviours, as are sensory sensitivities and resistance to change. And Kanner's identification of affective (emotional) difficulties prominent in the title of his paper, especially emotion in social relationships, is less evident in DSM-5 although it remains an important focus of autism-related research (Ben Shalom, Bowler, Gaigg, & Delmonte in preparation; Bird & Cook 2013).

For almost 40 years, Kanner's view of autism dominated attempts to identify and understand the condition until the seminal epidemiological work of Wing and Gould (1979), which brought the work of Hans Asperger to the attention of the wider world. Asperger (1944, 1991) described four adolescents who, although in many respects were different from Kanner's patients, nevertheless shared with them several striking characteristics. Asperger's cases had neither intellectual nor language disabilities, yet he was of the opinion that they exhibited marked atypicalities in social interaction as well as highly intense or focused interests that were pursued almost to the exclusion of all other activities with little apparent desire to share these interests with other people. It is this disconnectedness from other people and the presence of repetitive behaviour (manifested by specialized interests in Asperger's cases) that led Wing (1981) to conclude that far from representing two distinct conditions, Kanner's and Asperger's cases represented different points on an *autistic continuum* (later to become an *autistic spectrum*) ranging from the most obvious cases of the kind described by Kanner to individuals who would not attract a clinical diagnosis. All parts of the spectrum were characterized by what Wing (1981) called a *triad of impairments* [sic] in social interaction, communication, and imagination as well as repetitive behaviours. But perhaps most important from the perspective of developmental psychopathology was Wing's contention that 'autism' could really only be identified by reference to the developmental history of the child, which should document clear evidence of reduced levels of symbolic play, repetitive behaviour and characteristic, atypical interactions with others. The genius of Wing's contribution lies in the way she saw a link between what at first sight appear to be very different behavioural profiles. Like Kanner, she noticed that the developmental history of children who fitted the clinical picture he described had a particular patterning of early development characterized by what she called 'social impairment' (Wing & Gould 1979) which led to atypical patterns of communication with others. She also noticed, like Kanner, that they had a tendency to repetitive behaviours which had an adverse effect on the development of symbolic and imaginative play. But she also observed that this developmental pattern could be observed in individuals like those described by Asperger, as well as people who might not have precisely met either Kanner's or Asperger's criteria. This common behavioural patterning has paved the way to our conceptions of autism as defined in current diagnostic frameworks. Wing's insight has also had the consequence of enabling us to see 'autism' or ASD as a spectrum of different yet similar conditions that are linked by common underlying processes operating across disparate patterns of observable signs and reported symptoms. And it is this view that has prefigured and informed later diagnostic schemes from DSM-III and the eleventh edition of the World Health Organisation's *International Classification of Diseases and Related Health Problems* (ICD-11; World Health Organisation 2018) through to DSM-5 (American Psychiatric Association 2013). Although there have been other diagnostic schemes (see Chapter 1 of Bowler 2007 and Chapters 1 and 2 of Boucher 2017 for more detail on past diagnostic frameworks), most of these are of purely historical interest, and in any case, overlap to such an extent with current DSM and ICD schemes that we have chosen in the next section to focus principally on the DSM-5 framework.

As mentioned at the outset, our conceptualization of ASD has in recent years been radically altered by the *neurodiversity* movement, which tends to reject the pathologization of atypical behaviour. Instead, advocates of neurodiversity see such behaviour as an individual's attempt to adapt to a world that they experience differently from others. In some ways, it is ironic that the broadening of the boundaries of the medical/diagnostic category of autism has resulted in the labelling as autistic of individuals who can articulate their own experience of autism and advocate for a more inclusive account of the condition in terms of neurodiversity rather than pathology.

But whatever perspective we take, two issues need constantly to be borne in mind, First, that ASD is a complex and diverse set of conditions that frequently occur in conjunction with other patterns of difference, most notably intellectual and language disabilities, anxiety, or ADHD. Second, despite decades of research into the biological bases of ASD, it remains a *behaviourally defined* set of conditions that can only be identified on the basis of a rigorous determination of the co-occurrence of a specific set of behavioural clinical features and, most importantly, their patterning across the early years of development. And from the perspective of the traditional, biomedical model, such a diagnostic evaluation can be reliably carried out only in the context of direct observation and interaction with the individual and with someone familiar with their early developmental history. The alternative, neurodiversity-oriented perspective, increasingly questions the necessity to have an outsider (a non-autistic person) to 'label' an individual as having autism, and accepts that someone can self-identify as autistic on the basis of their own experience and of information they themselves have gathered from others about themselves (see, for example Pellicano & den Houting, 2022).

CURRENT SYSTEMATIC APPROACHES TO IDENTIFICATION

At present, the majority of individuals with ASD are identified by means of two broad frameworks: the *Diagnostic and Statistical Manual (DSM)* of the American Psychiatric Association and the *International Classification of Diseases (ICD)* of the World Health Organisation. The most recent DSM formulation of the behavioural profile of ASD, and the one which we describe in this section, is the 5th edition of the DSM (DSM-5; American Psychiatric Association 2013). The ICD scheme, especially its most recent version, ICD-11 (World Health Organisation 2018) mirrors quite closely the DSM scheme, although there are some differences (see Wilson, Gillan, Spain, Robertson, et al. 2013 for further discussion). DSM-5 represents a refinement of earlier versions of the DSM dating back to the first version to include the term *Autistic Disorder* – the third edition (DSM-III, American Psychiatric Association, 1980 – note the change from Roman to Arabic numerals).

DSM-5 proposes a single category of *Autism Spectrum Disorder* where an individual must, either currently or by history, meet the criteria set out in Table 7.1 (taken from American Psychiatric Association, 2013 with permission).

Table 7.1 DSM-5 criteria for Autism Spectrum Disorder

A. *Persistent deficits in social communication and social interaction* across multiple contexts, as manifested by the following, currently or by history (examples are illustrative, not exhaustive, see text):
   1. Deficits in social-emotional reciprocity, ranging, for example, from abnormal social approach and failure of normal back-and-forth conversation; to reduced sharing of interests, emotions, or affect; to failure to initiate or respond to social interactions.
   2. Deficits in nonverbal communicative behaviours used for social interaction, ranging, for example, from poorly integrated verbal and nonverbal communication; to abnormalities in eye contact and body language or deficits in understanding and use of gestures; to a total lack of facial expressions and nonverbal communication.
   3. Deficits in developing, maintaining, and understanding relationships, ranging, for example, from difficulties adjusting behaviour to suit various social contexts; to difficulties in sharing imaginative play or in making friends; to absence of interest in peers.
B. *Restricted, repetitive patterns of behaviour, interests, or activities*, as manifested by at least two of the following, currently or by history (examples are illustrative, not exhaustive; see text):
   1. Stereotyped or repetitive motor movements, use of objects, or speech (e.g., simple motor stereotypies, lining up toys or flipping objects, echolalia, idiosyncratic phrases).
   2. Insistence on sameness, inflexible adherence to routines, or ritualized patterns or verbal nonverbal behaviour (e.g., extreme distress at small changes, difficulties with transitions, rigid thinking patterns, greeting rituals, need to take same route or eat food every day).
   3. Highly restricted, fixated interests that are abnormal in intensity or focus (e.g., strong attachment to or preoccupation with unusual objects, excessively circumscribed or perseverative interest).
   4. Hyper- or hyporeactivity to sensory input or unusual interests in sensory aspects of the environment (e.g., apparent indifference to pain/temperature, adverse response to specific sounds or textures, excessive smelling or touching of objects, visual fascination with lights or movement).
C. Symptoms must be present in the early developmental period (but may not become fully manifest until social demands exceed limited capacities or may be masked by learned strategies in later life).
D. Symptoms cause clinically significant impairment in social, occupational, or other important areas of current functioning.
E. These disturbances are not better explained by intellectual disability (intellectual developmental disorder) or global developmental delay. Intellectual disability and autism spectrum disorder frequently co-occur; to make comorbid diagnoses of autism spectrum disorder and intellectual disability, social communication should be below that expected for general developmental level.

The clinician making the diagnosis must rate not only the presence or absence but also the severity of the impairment under each of these headings.

Reflective Exercise

Science is not always a linear process

People are often tempted to contrast 'the latest research' or 'the latest findings' or 'current thinking' with earlier findings, as if the mere fact of one thing occurring after another gives it epistemological superiority over what went before. This is often the case: the history of science is full of examples of later findings superseding earlier ones. The Greek astronomer Ptolemy thought that the sun and the planets revolved around the Earth, whereas (thanks to Tycho Brahe, Copernicus and Galileo among others) we now know that this is not the case. But sometimes, later findings that contradict earlier ones are in actual fact wrong, and the earlier ones were correct all along (it used to be argued that the physical limitations of telephone lines made video telephone communication impossible, yet people now regularly use video chat over the internet, which in part uses the same telephone lines that were previously deemed to be incapable of carrying such information). It also sometimes happens that neither the 'earlier' nor the 'later' accounts are true, necessitating a complete re-formulation of the issue in question. An example of this is our conceptualization of light, which used to be thought of as consisting of waves, then as streams of particles (aspects of its behaviour is consistent with one or the other), but is now thought to be a set of complex particles with associated wave functions of a kind that is difficult for the layperson to imagine.

These considerations are as true for systems of identifying atypicalities such as ASD as they are for empirical findings that describe or attempt to explain ASD and its underlying causal mechanisms. It might be useful to speculate what the current science of autism might look like had we moved from a 'broad brush' view (such as the one we have now) to a more focussed one such as that exemplified in Kanner's account. Or you might like to speculate on the implications for autism research of a neurodiversity perspective that acknowledges that some autistic people might prefer to self-identify rather than go to another person to be diagnosed.

The guidelines accompanying DSM-5 stress that an evaluation must take account of developmental and cultural appropriateness of the behaviours being evaluated and that must the severity of these behaviours as well as the level of support an individual requires (descriptors), ranging from 'requiring support', 'requiring substantial support' to 'requiring very substantial support' must be noted. Moreover, the guidelines also stipulate that an individual must meet criteria under all of the headings listed in Table 7.1 in order to be identified as having ASD. It should also be specified whether or not there is an accompanying intellectual or language impairment or an accompanying genetic syndrome or whether there was any developmental regression, where already acquired skills were lost (specifiers). DSM-5, in contrast to earlier classification schemes, also allows for the possibility of including co-occurring behavioural differences such as OCD or ADHD as specifiers when ASD is identified. Prior to DSM-5, evaluators had to make a choice as to which term to use when a child met criteria for ASD and another condition, something that DSM-5 no longer requires.

The range of behavioural profiles codified by DSM-5 must provide evidence either *currently* or *by history* of:

1. Social communication difficulties including difficulties in initiating and maintaining social relations as well as in the patterning of social communication, both verbal and non-verbal. This is something Wing (1996) has called *social impairment* [sic], a term which provides a neat shorthand for the kinds of difficulties encompassed in this aspect of the DSM. In Chapter 8, we discussed how this feature of ASD continues to form the basis of many attempts to work out the underlying mechanisms that might cause the condition.
2. Restricted and repetitive behaviours, which not only include obviously repetitive motor and vocal behaviours but also include interests that take up a large part of an individual's life to the exclusion of other activities, such as cataloguing information on train timetables or zoological taxonomic systems. Included here are sensory sensitivities, such as under- or over-reactivity to sensory stimuli in all modalities or atypically strong interests in particular sensory stimuli. Again, in Chapter 8, we will discuss the implications for developing explanatory theories of ASD of grouping these two (arguably quite different) features under a single diagnostic heading.

Differences between DSM-5 and Earlier Versions of the DSM

Perhaps the most obvious difference between DSM-5 and its two predecessors is that the earlier versions catalogued autism-related difficulties under three headings – social interaction, communication, and restricted and repetitive behaviours – whereas DSM-5 combined the first two into 'Deficits in Social Communication and Social Interaction' (see Table 7.1). This change was in accord with DSM-5's conceptualization of ASD as a single disorder varying in severity and behavioural profile rather than a cluster of related conditions. In this respect, DSM-5's requirement for an individual to meet criteria under all headings represents an improvement over earlier schemes. DSM-IV, for example, tended to list sets of areas of difficulty, grouped under broad headings, but requiring only a subset to be present in order to warrant a diagnosis. For example, in the previous version of the DSM (DSM-IV-TR, the text revision of DSM-IV, American Psychiatric Association 1994), part of the requirement for a diagnosis involved an individual having at least two of the following characteristics under the heading *Qualitative Impairment in Social Interaction*:

(a) marked impairment in the use of multiple non-verbal behaviours such as eye-to-eye gaze, facial expression, body postures, and gestures to regulate social interaction

(b) failure to develop peer relationships appropriate to developmental level

(c) a lack of spontaneous seeking to share enjoyment, interests or achievements with other people (e.g. by a lack of showing, bringing or pointing out objects of interest)

(d) lack of social or emotional reciprocity.

It is easy to see how a large sample of individuals might contain individuals scoring on (a+b), (a+c), (a+d), (b+c), (b+d), (c+d), (a+b+c), (a+c+d) or (b+c+d). So, two individuals who received a 'DSM diagnosis of ASD' might present quite a different clinical picture and require quite different kinds of support. Similarly, a researcher wishing to test a large sample of 'participants who met DSM-IV criteria' could end up with quite a diverse group (2,027 diagnostic sub-combinations according to Evers, Maljaars, Carrington, et al. 2020), with possible repercussions on their performance on the measures the researcher was interested in. Keen-eyed readers will have noticed that a similar criticism can be levelled at the evidential requirements in DSM-5 for section B – Restricted, repetitive patterns of behaviour, interests, or activities, where two out of four types of behaviour need only be present). The authors of DSM-5 argue that the decision rules in DSM-5 should, in theory, eliminate this possibility and lead to more reliable diagnosis and more homogenous samples for inclusion in research.

This last point reflects the hopes of the framers of DSM-5 that the new criteria would reduce inconsistency in findings and the often widely varying levels of performance that have dogged much research into ASD. However, by solving one set of problems, the changes brought about by DSM-5 might well have generated new ones. For example, the changes may make the pooling of data in meta-analyses more, rather than less problematic. In meta-analyses, data from studies of a particular topic (say working memory) that might have been carried out several years or decades apart are combined in an attempt to get a better estimate of strengths and difficulties because there is a larger participant base. In general, larger samples produce more reliable results because noise is reduced in the data. But the inclusion of samples recruited using different diagnostic schemes might well have the unintended consequence of increasing rather than decreasing noise and thereby diminishing the chance of finding an overall effect in a meta-analysis. This is a speculation that has some support in recent studies (e.g. Bennett & Goodall 2016) and to which we will return in our later discussion of the broader autism phenotype.

Meta-Analysis

Meta-analysis is a systematic method of pooling data from several studies that investigate the same research question. By pooling data from a number of studies, the resulting estimates of the size of between-group effects are more reliable than those from individual studies because they are based on a larger sample of individuals. Selection of studies for inclusion in a meta-analysis are drawn up before the analysis is conducted in order to eliminate possible bias. In the case of ASD research, an important selection criterion is the adequate characterization of participant diagnosis. Recent meta-analyses into ASD have been limited to participants with a DSM-IV, DSM-5 or ICD-10 diagnosis (Demetriou, Lampit, Quintana, et al. 2018; Desaunay, Briant, Bowler, et al. 2020).

A good guide to conducting a meta-analysis can be found in Field and Gillett (2010).

Identifying ASD in the Very Young and the Very Old

There is wide consensus that to be identified as having ASD, there should be first-hand evidence of the presence of behavioural features before the age of three years, but this raises two distinct considerations. The first is the question of the earliest age at which ASD can be identified. The second is whether it can be reliably identified in adulthood or old age, when reliable information about developmental history is lacking because people who can give reliable first-hand accounts are no longer available. The question of later-life identification is a complex one which has only relatively recently been acknowledged in ASD. As such, any answers are likely to change as research evolves. Further discussion can be found in Bowler, Geurts, & Howlin (2019) and Brugha, Bankart, Scott, et al. (2011).

By contrast, the question of how early a reliable identification can be made is the subject of active research in several centres and there is growing evidence that a stable identification can be made before the age of three years in high-likelihood groups such as younger siblings of children with autism (Ozonoff, Young, Landa, et al. 2015) and after 14 months of age in the general population (Pierce, Gazestani, Bacon, Barnes, et al. 2019). In a later section, we will discuss some of the instruments used to screen infants in order to identify those at greater likelihood of developing ASD.

Controversies Surrounding DSM-5

DSM-5 made two major changes to previous diagnostic practice. The first of these was to subsume two hitherto separate conditions – *Pervasive Developmental Disorder Not Otherwise Specified* (PDD-NOS) and Asperger Disorder/Asperger's syndrome under the umbrella of ASD. DSM-5 further recommends that individuals with established DSM-IV diagnoses of these conditions should be classified as having DSM-5 Autism Spectrum Disorder. The dropping of PDD-NOS and Asperger Disorder/Asperger's syndrome as separate diagnostic categories has not gone unchallenged. Tsai and colleagues (Tsai 2013; Tsai & Ghaziuddin 2014) argue that despite many studies that show no differences among these three conditions, there exists sufficient evidence to support the case for keeping them diagnostically separate. And Smith and Jones (2020) have found evidence of dissatisfaction over the loss of identity among individuals who were no longer considered to have a DSM-IV designation of Asperger's syndrome as a consequence of the changes from DSM-IV to DSM-5.

The second change was to create a new condition called *Social Communication Disorder* (SCD). This is characterized by difficulties with the socially appropriate use of language and non-verbal communication – with the *pragmatics* of language and communication – without the requirement for restrictive and repetitive behaviours and interests required for ASD. Historically, a condition that came to be known as *semantic-pragmatic disorder* was first identified as 'semantic-pragmatic syndrome without autism' by Rapin and Allen (1983) and since then debate has waxed and waned as to whether or not the condition was a facet of the autism spectrum or a condition apart (see Bishop & Rosenbloom 1987; Bishop 1989; Lister Brook & Bowler 1992; Bishop & Norbury 2002). Recent research tends to the conclusion that SCD is not a separate entity but should be considered as lying 'on the borderlands of the autism spectrum (Mandy, Wang, Lee, & Skuse 2017) or having more in common with the Broad Autism Phenotype (Flax, Gwin, Wilson, et al. 2019).

International Classification of Diseases (ICD-11, World Health Organisation 2018)

The inclusion of conditions such as pervasive developmental disorder and Asperger's syndrome (or Asperger Disorder) as separable conditions within the autism spectrum and their subsequent re-integration within the spectrum seen in the move from DSM-IV to DSM-5 is also mirrored in the latest version of the other main framework for identifying autism-related conditions – the eleventh edition of the *International Classification of Diseases* (ICD-11, World Health Organisation, 2018). The earliest mention of autism in this system occurred in ICD-8 (World Health Organisation, 1968) which listed 'infantile autism' as a condition alongside schizophrenia. From 1993 until 2018, ICD-10 set out criteria that were largely similar to those of DSM-IV and DSM-IV TR (see Wilson et al., 2013 for further discussion). After over ten years of deliberation, ICD-11 was released in June 2018 and in most respects it mirrors the changes brought about by DSM-5: a reduction from three to two the number of headings under which difficulties are counted and the re-inclusion of conditions such as pervasive developmental disorder and Asperger's Syndrome.

In sum, recent frameworks for the identification of ASD have in common the listing of behavioural features of a different developmental pathway that is characterized by difficulties in social communication and restricted and repetitive behaviours and interests. The criteria for evaluating the presence and degree of these difficulties vary with the person's age and overall level of development, and whether the difficulties can require greater or lesser provision of support structures for the individual. The diagnosis and classification of ASD has always engendered lively debate (see Volkmar & McPartland 2014 for a thorough and accessible review), and DSM-5 itself has attracted its fair share of commentary, not all of it positive (Barker & Galardi 2015). Moreover, every change from one framework to another raises clinical and scientific challenges, some of which are unintended, unexpected or unintentional (Tsai 2013; Smith & Jones 2020). Nevertheless, although the intention was for the behavioural profile painted by DSM-5 of individuals on the autism spectrum to be sufficiently clear and detailed to enable the development of reliable diagnostic procedures to base management, educational interventions, and scientific research on a firm basis, it has given rise to some unforeseen consequences that will be discussed in a later section.

DIAGNOSTIC ASSESSMENT AND MEASUREMENT INSTRUMENTS

It should always be borne in mind that the identification of ASD can only be made on the basis of a direct evaluation, which should comprise a detailed developmental history together with direct observation of the person who needs the designation of autism. From a more biomedical diagnostic perspective, this will involve a clinician observing and interviewing the relevant people. A neurodiversity perspective will also accept a person's own evaluation of their experienced difficulties and developmental trajectory. In this section, we will discuss a range of the more commonly used instruments that help in this process, ranging from standardized and validated interview and observation schedules through to self- and parent/caregiver-report questionnaires as well as personal accounts of autistic persons themselves.

'Gold Standard' Instruments: The Autism Diagnostic Interview (ADI) and the Autism Diagnostic Observation Schedule (ADOS)

In parallel with the increasing refinement of frameworks for identification of ASD has been the development of reliable and valid procedures for assessing whether or not individuals meet criteria for the condition specified in the framework. Instruments that are generally considered to be 'gold standard' in this regard are the *Autism Diagnostic Interview – Revised* (ADI-R, Lord, Rutter, & LeCouteur 1994) and the *Autism Diagnostic Observation Schedule* (ADOS-2, Lord, Rutter, Di Lavore, Risi, Gotham, & Bishop 2012). The ADI-R is suitable for individuals aged from about 18 months through to adulthood and consists of a structured, 93-item interview with an individual's parents or other person who knows the individual well, covering their family background, developmental history, and the areas of social communication, special interests, sensory sensitivities, and repetitive behaviours. Informants' answers are rated and aggregated under the headings *Language and Communication, Reciprocal Social Interaction, and Restricted and Repetitive Stereotyped Behaviours and Interests*. Individual behaviours are rated on a scale from '0' denoting absence of the behaviour to '3' denoting extreme evidence of the behaviour, with additional scores for atypicalities in other areas or absence of information. Scores are summed under each of the three headings just described and entered into an algorithm that yields cutoff scores which determine whether an individual can be given an ASD diagnosis. In a review of the psychometric properties of the ADI, Zander, Willfors, Berggren, et al. (2017) report acceptable levels of sensitivity, specificity, test-retest, and inter-rater reliability (IRR) for the ADI-R when used by investigators trained to research reliability. In their own study, Zander et al. (2017) found similarly acceptable levels in clinicians working in the Swedish health service.

Because the ADI's initial development was closely allied to DSM-IV diagnostic criteria, concerns were raised that it might identify fewer children if DSM-5 were required. However, studies such as that by Huerta et al. (2012) have shown that the ADI coupled with the ADOS (see later) results in the majority (91%) of children already identified by DSM-IV also met DSM-5 criteria for ASD.

The *Autism Diagnostic Observation Schedule* (ADOS-2, Lord et al. 2012), as its name implies, is a structured schedule of tasks designed to create situations in which someone on the autism spectrum is likely to behave in a characteristic manner. The original version of the ADOS (Lord, Risi, Lambrecht, et al. 2000) consisted of four modules each designed to assess people at different ages and language abilities from 18 months to adulthood. The revised version (ADOS-2) added a toddler module, aimed at 12–30-month-old children who do not consistently use speech (Luyster, Gotham, Guthrie, Coffing, et al. 2009). The other modules are suitable for children over 31 months who have no phrase speech (Module 1), children who have phrase speech and can move around (Module 2), older children (Module 3) and adolescents and adults (Module 4). A list of the tasks from the Toddler Module, which are appropriate for a non-verbal, 18-month-old child, is given in Table 7.2. For all modules, the instructions stipulate that the participant may not be given direct instruction on how to perform a task but can be given what the authors call 'presses' to elicit certain responses or actions from the participant. Responses are rated on a scale ranging from 0, denoting no evidence of autism-related atypicality through to 3, denoting definite evidence of behaviour that interferes with social interaction and when all the activities are rated, the scores collated and an algorithm then are used to determine whether or not the DSM criteria are met. Both the equipment required and the instructions to participants are varied and complex. Moreover, the scoring requires a great deal of judgement on the part of the examiner. For example, some items, such as responding to own name in the toddler module are often scored on the basis of a single observation. Other, summary items,

Table 7.2 Activities from the Toddler and the Adolescent/Adult Modules of the ADOS-2

Toddler Module	Module 4 (adolescent/adult)
1. Free Play	1. Construction task (optional)
1a. Free Play – Ball	2. Telling a story from a book
2. Blocking Toy Play	2. Description of a picture (optional)
3. Response to Name	4. Conversation and reporting
4. Bubble Play	5. Current work or school (optional)
4a. Bubble Play – Teasing Toy Play	6. Social difficulties and annoyance
5. Anticipation of a Routine with Objects	7. Emotions
5a. Anticipation of a Routine with Objects – Unable Toy Play	8. Demonstration task
6. Anticipation of a Social Routine	9. Cartoons
7. Response to Joint Attention	10. Break
8. Responsive Social Smile	11. Daily living (optional)
9. Bathtime	12. Friends, relationships, and marriage
9a. Bathtime – Ignore	13. Loneliness
10. Functional and Symbolic Imitation	14. Plans and hopes
11. Snack	15. Creating a story

Source: Taken from the ADOS-2 with permission.

by contrast require synthesis of observations over a variety of situations in order to rate quality of social responses or quality of social overtures on a scale from 0 (no abnormality) through 3 (abnormality definitely present). The complexity of administration and scoring mean that examiners need to be trained to a high degree of reliability, which has resulted in high levels of inter-rater reliability (IRR) (intra-class correlations ranging from 0.79 to 0.98) between two highly trained research raters (Lord, Rutter, DiLavore, et al. 2012). In a multi-site study of clinicians, Zander et al. (2017) report lower but nonetheless satisfactory overall IRR across the four modules (0.74–0.83) but accompanied by some low values on particular items. A further study by Kamp-Becker, Albertowski, Becker Ghareman, et al. (2018) found that good reliability depends on the degree of clinical diagnostic experience and expert supervision available to the rater.

Although neither the ADOS nor the ADOS-2 can on their own provide an identification of ASD, they can be used in conjunction with the ADI-R and a clinical differential diagnostic interview to support a reliable identification (National Institute for Health and Clinical Excellence 2013). However, a decision can be made on whether criteria for a diagnosis of autistic disorder or autism spectrum are met can be made by reference to cutoff scores derived from an algorithm provided by the developers of the instrument (Lord et al. 2012). Medda, Cholemkery, and Freitag (2019) review a wide range of studies of sensitivity and specificity on the ADOS and conclude that the introduction of the revised algorithm for the ADOS-2 resulted in estimates of sensitivity and specificity either increasing or remaining the same. Medda et al.'s (2019) own study of a large German sample found good sensitivity (0.70–0.93) but more variable specificity (0.20–0.94) in differentiating autism from non-ASD cases.[1]

Other Instruments: The DISCO and the 3Di

The *Diagnostic Interview for Social and Communication Disorders* (DISCO, Wing, Leekam, Libby, et al. 2002) is a semi-structured interview designed to elicit from parents or carers a picture of the patterning of an individual's behaviours. The interview is the final formalization of a clinical interview developed by Wing and colleagues (Wing & Gould 1978, 1979) based on her conceptualization of autism which sees it as a spectrum of related conditions all driven by a triad of social, symbolic, and communicative difficulties accompanied by restrictive and repetitive behaviours. Although this dimensional view of autism pre-dates the more categorical view that prevailed until DSM-IV, it anticipates by several decades the more dimensional view encompassed in DSM-5. Algorithms can be applied to data from the DISCO to yield DSM-IV and ICD-10 characterizations (Leekam, Libby, Wing, Gould, & Taylor 2002; Kent, Carrington, LeCouteur, et al. 2013). In addition to covering topics on the core features of autism, the

---

[1] Some specificity and sensitivity values of 1.00 were reported for sub-samples with small numbers of participants.

more than 300 questions in the interview schedule also aim to gain a complete picture of an individual's strengths, weaknesses and needs in relation to their overall developmental level, making it a tool that goes beyond simple formulation of the behavioural profile.

The *Developmental, Dimensional and Diagnostic Interview* (3Di, Skuse, Warrington, Bishop, Chowdhury, et al. 2004) also adopts a dimensional view of ASD. This computer-based tool is what the authors describe as a hybrid between a structured and a semi-structured interview designed to overcome the limitations of both these approaches. The questions cover the full range of domains of difficulty associated with ASD. A particular advantage of the instrument is that it does not cluster questions from different domains of interest, thus making it less likely that informants answer in a particular way in order to achieve a desired outcome. Computerization also enables 'skip' decisions to be made automatically, for example by automatically dropping questions about the details of the child's language if they have already been recorded as non-verbal. Computerization also means that a diagnosis and formulation can be made available immediately at the end of the interview. Although originally developed as a dimensional measure of autistic traits, providing information that went beyond that measured by the ADI-R, the information it collects has been reliably used to generate a DSM-IV and more recently DSM-5 (see Mandy, Clarke, McKenner, et al. 2018) as well as confirming the two-factor 'dyad' model of ASD advocated by DSM-5 (Mandy, Charman, & Skuse 2012; Slappendel et al. 2016). Since its original development, other versions of the instrument have been developed: a short version consisting of 53 items (3Di-SV; Santosh et al. 2009) an adult version (3Di-Adult; Mandy et al. 2018).

Other Screening Instruments

The time required to administer either the ADI-R, the ADOS-2, the DISCO, and to a lesser extent the 3Di, and the consequent cost implications for research and clinical budgets has led to the quest for faster methods of confirming formal identification that do not unduly sacrifice reliability or validity. In addition, because ASD cannot be reliably identified in children under about 18 months of age (Pierce, Gazestani, Bacon, Barnes, et al. 2019), a variety of instruments are used, some of which have been specifically developed for the purpose to help identify children prospectively at risk for ASD. A third set of instruments follows the logic of a spectrum or dimensional view of autism, which implies that lower-intensity features may be present in the general population. A selection of all three types of measure is set out in Table 7.3. As with many of the measures discussed earlier on, none of these can be used as substitutes for a proper evaluation based on direct observation and interview with a someone who knows the person being assessed. But they are useful when used either as a screen for referral for more systematic identification procedures, or to rule out accidental inclusion of autistic participants in non-autistic comparison groups. As with all measurement instruments that aim to inform a decision on whether an individual comes under one category or another (in this case 'is likely to have autism' or 'is unlikely to have autism'), questions of *sensitivity* (the accuracy of the

Table 7.3 Brief methods of measuring ASD-related behavioural features

Early Screening Instruments for Infants

Ages and Stages Questionnaire (Squires & Bricker 2009).

Checklist for Autism in Toddlers/Modified Checklist for Autism in Toddlers (CHAT/M-CHAT: Baird et al. 2000; Robins et al. 2014).

Screening Instruments: Toddlers to Adulthood

Autism Symptom Dimensions Questionnaire (ASDQ, Frazier et al. 2023).

Autism Spectrum Screening Questionnaire (ASSQ) – revised extended version (ASSQ-REV, Kopp & Gillberg 2011)

Childhood Autism Rating Scale (CARS: Schopler et al. 1980, 1988).

Social Responsiveness Sale (SRS/SRS-2: Constantino & Gruber 2012).

Social Communication Questionnaire (SCQ: Rutter, Bailey, & Lord 2003).

Screening Instruments: General Population

Autism Spectrum Quotient (Baron-Cohen, Wheelwright, Martin, & Clubley 2001).

Broad Autism Phenotype Questionnaire (Hurley, Losh, Parlier, et al. 2007).

The Comprehensive Autistic Trait Inventory (CATI): development and validation of a new measure of autistic traits in the general population (English et al. 2021).

The Ritvo Autism Asperger Diagnostic Scale – Revised (RAADS-R). Ritvo et al. (2011).

---

instrument in correctly identifying individuals with the condition) and *specificity* (the instrument's accuracy in identifying individuals who do not have the condition) are paramount. It is possible to successfully identify all individuals with ASD by simply giving the entire population the label 'autistic'. But this would mis-identify over 98% of people who do not have ASD. In the context of screening, an important concept is that of *positive predictive* value (PPV) which is a function of specificity and sensitivity and indexes the extent to which positive predictions turn out to be actual cases.

Further discussions of the issues of sensitivity and specificity can be found in Chapter 3.

The *Checklist for Autism in Toddlers* (CHAT, Baird, Charman, Baron-Cohen, et al. 2000) started out as a 23-item parental questionnaire for use with 16- to 30-month-old children. Although the instrument had high sensitivity, its specificity was low and subsequent revisions (Modified Checklist for Autism in Toddlers, M-CHAT; Robins, Fein, Barton, et al. 2001 and Modified Checklist for Autism in Toddlers – Revised with Follow-Up, M-CHAT R/F; Robins, Casagrande, Barton, et al. 2014). A recent meta-analysis by Yuen, Penner, Carter, et al. (2018) concluded that when used with 18- and 24-month-old children with developmental concerns, the M-CHAT has moderate sensitivity but low specificity, with poorer accuracy in children aged 18 months. Charman & Gotham's (2013) review of screening instruments in ASD report low PPV (0.25–0.79) for this instrument.

The *Childhood Autism Rating Scale* (Schopler et al. 1980, 1988) is one of the oldest observational scales in which ratings are made on the basis of observations of the person being assessed. Because the original instrument was developed in the context of children with additional intellectual disability, a newer version, the CARS2 (Schopler et al. 2010) was developed to include non-intellectually disabled individuals. CARS2 retains the original CARS (re-named the CARS2-ST) for use with the original target population. Although it is not a instrument for formal identification, scores can be interpreted by a trained clinician in terms of different levels of severity of autism. Moon, Hwang, Shin, et al. (2019) in a meta-analysis report the CARS as having good inter-rater reliability (0.9), acceptable sensitivity (0.86), but lower specificity (0.79). In a study of 2- to 4-year-old toddlers, Cheblowski, Green, Barton, & Fein (2010) report that the CARS had an acceptable PPV (0.85) when a cutoff score was used.

The *Social Responsiveness Scale* (SRS, Constantino et al. 2003) is a questionnaire measure aimed at parents, teachers or other adults familiar with the individual being assessed. In this respect, it differs from the CARS, which requires direct observation. The latest version, SRS-2 (Constantino & Gruber 2012) comprises four versions suitable for pre-school (ages 2.5–4.5 years), school age (ages 4–18 years) and adult (age 19+) groups. The 65 questions cover five treatment subscales: Social Awareness, Social Cognition, Social Communication, Social Motivation, and Restricted interests and Repetitive Behaviours. Total scores can be used as a measure of severity of social communication difficulty. In a study comparing parent and teacher ratings on the SRS with evaluations based on the ADOS and ADI-R, Aldridge, Gibbs, Schmidhofer et al. (2012) found high sensitivity (0.94 for parents; 0.84 for teachers) but much lower specificity (0.08 and 0.41). This, together with Charman & Gotham's (2013) review showing only a single study reporting a PPV of 0.63 suggests that caution should be exercised in the use of this instrument as the sole assessment of the presence of autism.

Social Communication Questionnaire (SCQ; Rutter et al. 2002) is a 40-item parent questionnaire measure based on the ADI-R. It has two versions, one covering current behaviour and the other covering behaviour over an individual's lifetime. In a review of the sensitivity and specificity research, Charman and Gotham (2013) conclude that sensitivity is acceptable in most studies (0.70–0.88 for school aged children) but lower specificity were found (0.54–0.79). PPV values are low to moderate (0.54–0.79) (Charman & Gotham 2013).

Reflective Exercise

Given that many of the measures produce scores with a cutoff indicating a high likelihood of being 'on the autism spectrum', think about what it means to score just below the cutoff. Are such individuals 'a little bit autistic'? Pushing this a little bit further, is everyone to some extent 'a little bit autistic'? What might this mean for someone coming from a neurodiversity perspective who is contemplating self-identification as an autistic person?

As well, you could think about what this issue might mean for the topics discussed in Chapter 8 and the quest for underlying processes that might explain autism.

NON-CLINICAL AUTISM AND THE BROAD AUTISM PHENOTYPE

The shift from a perspective that saw 'autism' or ASD as a distinct pathological condition or set of conditions to a spectrum or continuum of atypicality raises the question: What features might be exhibited by individuals who do not meet full criteria for formal identification as having autism or experienced by someone who was contemplating self-identifying as autistic? These questions have been further highlighted with the advent of the screening instruments described above, many of which have cutoff scores that indicate the strong possibility of having autism (and by implication, a lower probability of this outcome for people scoring below the cutoff). Right from the start, Kanner (1944) noticed that some of the parents of his cases were rather detached, cold, formal, and obsessive. Considerations like these led to the development of a number of instruments to measure these 'non-clinical' patterns of behaviour that were not severe enough to meet criteria for formal identification. The *Autism Spectrum Quotient* (AQ), developed by Baron-Cohen, Wheelwright, Skinner, Martin, & Clubley (2001) in its original form consisted of a 50-item self-report questionnaire covering *Social Skills, Attention Switching, Attention to Detail, Communication,* and *Imagination*. Participants have to say whether they Definitely Disagree, Slightly Disagree, Slightly Agree or Definitely Agree with each statement.[2] Although different authors (Baron-Cohen et al., 2001; Woodbury-Smith, Robinson, Wheelwright, & Baron-Cohen 2005) have produced cutoff scores indicating a high probability of having autism, the authors are at pains to emphasize that the measure is *not* a diagnostic instrument.

Table 7.4 Sample questions from the AQ together with the areas they assess.

Q.1: I prefer to do things with others rather than on my own. (*social skill*)

Q.2: I prefer to do the same thing over and over again. (*attention switching*)

Q.5: I often notice small sounds when others do not. (*attention to detail*)

Q.7: Other people frequently tell me that what I've said is impolite, even though I think it is polite. (*communication*)

Q.8: When I'm reading a story, I can easily imagine what the characters might look like. (*imagination*)

Source: From Baron-Cohen et al. (2001).

Studies of the genetics of ASD provided more insight into this question. Studies like those of Folstein & Rutter (1977) and Bailey, LeCouteur, Gottesman, et al. (1995) found that identical twin siblings of individuals diagnosed with ASD had a higher chance of being formally identified as having autism than non-identical twin siblings and Bolton, MacDonald, Pickles, et al. (1994) found that non-autistic siblings as well as parents of children who were formally identified as

---

[2] Baron-Cohen et al. (2002) point out that the 4-point scale can be collapsed into an Agree/Disagree scoring system.

autistic (*probands*) exhibited many features characteristic of ASD but not at a level sufficient to meet diagnostic criteria. The thrust of studies like these led to the development of the term *Broad Autism Phenotype (BAP)* as shorthand for the less marked manifestations of the full ASD clinical picture that might be driven by parts of the genetic mechanism of ASD (Bolton, MacDonald, Pickles, et al. 1994). Losh, Childress, Lam, & Piven (2007) describe the BAP as 'a constellation of subtle language, cognitive, social and personality characteristics that parallel the defining features of autism' (p. 424). Because the BAP is highly prevalent in parents of children with ASD (Wheelwright, Auyeung, & Allison 2010), it remains a valuable concept in disentangling genetic contributions to the development of ASD. It also serves as a useful tool to carry out preliminary tests of hypotheses about underlying mechanisms or factors associated with autistic traits by using easier-to-recruit samples of individuals who score highly on BAP measures (see below for discussion of these). However, we need to be cautious about the conclusions we draw about ASD from studies based on samples with high levels of BAP. As Landry and Chouinard (2016) observe, Wheelwright et al. (2010), in addition to finding high levels of BAP in parents of ASD children, also found high levels in some parents who did not have a child with ASD. Landry and Chouinard argue that the BAP may be a *phenocopy* of ASD, which is to say that its characteristic behavioural features may have origins other than the genetic mechanisms thought to drive the development of the full behavioural profile of ASD.

The point to take away from this discussion is that ASD as currently conceptualized is rather different from what it was thought to be even 10 or 20 years ago and tends to still be thought of by the general public, the press, and perhaps politicians. Far from being a single, discrete entity with clear boundaries, ASD is now considered to be a diverse set of complex behavioural differences, all of which share difficulties in relating to the social world and a behavioural repertoire characterized by restrictive and repetitive activities and possible evidence of atypical responses to sensory stimulation. These behavioural differences may or may not be accompanied by intellectual disabilities or language difficulties of varying severity as well as by co-occurring conditions, most notably anxiety and ADHD. It is this changed clinical picture that has been a major contributor to changes in estimates of the prevalence of ASD over the decades.

HOW COMMON IS ASD? THE CHANGING PICTURE OF PREVALENCE

As we have just seen, the way we describe ASD has changed over the decades. The broadening of the diagnostic criteria together with the notion of a continuum between clinical autism and sub-clinical states such as the BAP has inevitably had repercussions on estimates of the proportion of the population who receive an ASD diagnosis. Epidemiologists distinguish between the *incidence* of a condition, which is the number of new cases in a population in a given time period divided by the total number of individuals with the potential to develop the condition and *prevalence*, which refers to the percentage of instances in a given population irrespective of time of identification (Reber, 2012). Because autism is a life-long condition, estimates of prevalence give the most accurate picture of how common ASD is in a given population. Initial prevalence estimates, based on Kanner's or similar criteria, gave a value of 4.5 cases per 10,000 of the population or 0.045% (Lotter 1966). But in a review of epidemiological studies over 30 years later, Wing and Potter (2002) concluded that by the 1990s, after the introduction of DSM-III, prevalence had risen to 15–40 cases per 10,000 or a rate of 0.15 to 0.40%. By the early twenty-first century this figure had risen to 14.6 cases per 1,000 (note the smaller denominator), or a rate of 1.46% (Christen, Bilder, Zahorodny, et al. 2016). These increases in prevalence have attracted considerable press attention around the question of a possible 'epidemic of autism' (Fombonne 2001). A number of studies have explored possible reasons for this apparent increase (see Reber 2012 and Weintraub 2011 for detailed expositions). Rutter (2005) mentions two factors that are partly responsible for the increase. The first is heightened awareness of autism among clinicians and education professionals, resulting in more routine screening for ASD in the general population of toddlers and young children. The second is that the concept of 'autism' is now much wider, with the result that many individuals who now receive a diagnosis of ASD would not have done so 20 or 30 years ago. The findings of a recent report from the *Morbidity and Mortality Weekly Report* of the Centers for Disease Control and Prevention in the United States of a possible prevalence in eight-year old children of 18.5 cases per 1,000 of the population or one child in 54 (Maenner, Shaw, Baio… Dietz, et al. (2020) point to some possible reasons behind increasing prevalence. The Maenner et al. study ascertained cases by means of a review of case records provided by schools and medical service providers, which are then reviewed by an expert, which means that there was no direct diagnostic evaluation by the investigators. Moreover, part of the ascertainment process involved billing codes provided by the service providers, which raises the possibility that decisions on some individuals with borderline ASD might have been influenced by the fact that a child who receives a formal identification may be eligible for more services than one who does not.

Reflective Exercise

You might like to think about the paradox raised by the increasing prevalence figures talked about here, and our discussion earlier on of the likely *decrease* in number of diagnosed cases consequent on adoption of DSM-5.

IS AUTISM MORE LIKELY IN MEN THAN IN WOMEN?

A raft of epidemiological studies (see Loomes, Hull, & Mandy, 2017) have led to the widely held view expressed in DSM-5 that autism is four times more common in men than in women. This male preponderance has even led to an influential theory of the cause of autism as resulting from an extreme male brain (Baron-Cohen 2002). However, recent research has considerably altered our image of the sex ratio of people receiving an autism diagnosis. Loomes et al.'s (2017) meta-analysis of 54 studies established a male–female ratio close to 3:1 in those studies that actively ascertained cases of ASD in a given population. This figure contrasted with a ratio closer to 4:1 for those studies that tested only those already formally identified as having ASD. The authors conclude from this discrepancy that there may be a diagnostic bias in that women and girls who meet criteria for ASD often do not receive a diagnosis, a conclusion that has given rise to some debate in the literature. For example, Kaat, Shui, Ghods et al. (2020) report few sex differences in ADOS or ADI-R scores, with any such differences being small and conclude that there is little in the way of sex-related bias in the identification of ASD. Ratto (2020) takes issue with these conclusions, highlighting what she terms the inherent tautology in the failure to find sex biases in measures that have been developed and standardized using relatively homogenous samples with a high proportion of males. Ratto argues that the criteria derived from such samples are not likely to be met by someone who was not in the standardization group and, therefore, stands a high chance of not meeting criteria. She further argues that the development and standardization of diagnostic and measurement instruments must be carried out with groups that are far more inclusive both of gender, cultural, and sociodemographic factors, as well as of wider manifestations of autism as expressed in the autism community.

The changing sex ratio in ASD has given rise to a growing literature arguing that autism in women might in fact be experienced and exhibited differently from men in some fundamental way (Dworzynski, Ronald, Bolton, & Happé 2012; Baldwin & Costley 2016; Egerton & Carpenter 2016; Dean, Harwood, & Kasari 2017). Many contributors to this debate argue that this different expression results from a high level of compensation, camouflaging, and 'passing as normal' in women, which results in their under-representation in the epidemiological literature (see Chapter 8, and Livingston & Happé 2017; Fombonne 2020; for further discussion). Moreover, authors such as those just listed argue that the fact of female autism being different should prompt a re-consideration of the core defining features of ASD in a way that makes the identification process more inclusive, not only of hitherto less evident forms of ASD but also of its varying manifestations among different cultural groups. This is an argument made by Ratto (2020) and discussed above. Re-working the diagnostic conceptual framework along these lines will inevitably result in more people being identified, thereby increasing the prevalence figures still further.

Insofar as it reduces the exclusion of groups hitherto overlooked in autism research, the development of a more inclusive re-casting of the conceptual framework for identification carries other dangers that mean it should be engaged in with a certain degree of circumspection. It will, as we have just seen, be likely to lead to further inflation of prevalence estimates but it also raises some thorny conceptual issues. At the outset, we were at pains to point out that ASD is currently a behaviourally defined phenomenon the presence of which is inferred from a rigorous identification of specific behaviour patterns. We need to be careful, therefore, when extending the category of ASD to groups whose behaviour patterns differ from the canonical ones reflected in the current diagnostic criteria. It is tempting to take an *essentialist* position (Popper 1959) by assuming that there is an 'autism' that underlies the DSM criteria albeit an 'autism' that may reveal itself differently in some individuals or groups, for example, women or girls. However, in the absence of a measure of 'autism' that is independent of the patterning of behaviour, we need to be careful about the extent to which we can push the boundaries of the existing behavioural descriptors. If behaviour pattern 'X' (for example, the one first described by Kanner, 1943) is found predominantly in males and is given the label 'autism', when a group of women who self-identify as 'having autism' yet show a behaviour pattern that might resemble 'X' to a certain extent, can we legitimately say that these women 'have autism' in the same way as the men? In the absence of a marker for 'autism' that is independent of the behaviour pattern, this is not an easy question to settle. It touches closely on the issue of the validity of psychiatric classification systems and the nature of psychopathological categories (Jablensky, 2016; Scadding, 1996) and which we will return to shortly.

Another important consideration raised by the changing criteria for identifying ASD has been elegantly illustrated in a recent study by Rødgaard and colleagues (Rødgaard, Jensen, Vergnes, Soulières, & Mottron, 2019). Noting the parallel between diagnostic changes and increasing prevalence rates, these authors conducted a meta-analysis of effect sizes in meta-analyses of empirical studies that compared autistic and non-autistic individuals since the introduction of DSM-III in 1980. They found that for a set of measurements ranging from physical attributes (brain size) to psychological ones (planning, 'theory of mind') there was a statistically significant downward trend that correlated with the change in diagnostic instruments used. Notably, they did not find a similar downward trend in studies of schizophrenia, which, although being a complex, largely behaviourally defined psychopathological condition, has not shown a rise in prevalence similar to that of ASD. This association between diminished effect sizes between autistic and non-autistic individuals has considerable implications on a range of levels. It can affect the evidence base for clinical interventions by diluting individuals with genuine difficulties that need intervention among a larger pool of people whose difficulties are of a lesser order or who have found their own way to deal with their difficulties through compensation (Livingston, Colvert, Social Relationships Study Team, Bolton & Happé 2019). A similar dilution process can affect the way we infer underlying mechanisms when developing explanatory frameworks for autism.

Finally, most of the discussion so far has centred on a positivist set of assumptions that see psychopathological entities including ASD as having a real existence in the world that is independent of scientists, clinicians, carers etc. However, we should always ask ourselves whether categories like 'autism' constitute real entities in the world with an underlying essence (*essentialism* Popper 1959) or are they simply clusters of observable events to which we give a particular name (what Popper (1959) calls *nominalism*)? The positivist stance is developed further in Chapter 8, which deals with the nature of the underlying processes thought to drive the clinical picture outlined in this chapter.

The alternative, less positivist position sees the clinical entities discussed in this chapter (or indeed all objects of knowledge) as being socially constructed (see van Riel 2016 for a general discussion and Maynard & Turowetz 2019 for a discussion in relation to ASD). Although it is temptingly easy to parody such approaches by, for example, imagining that any group of individuals could socially construct their interesting and not-so-interesting characteristics into a psychopathological category and then attempt to wield societal power, such a temptation should be resisted. Rather, it should be simply acknowledged that all understanding is to some extent socially constructed but is ultimately constrained by certain properties of the external world.[3] A good example of how a critical take on social constructivist perspectives can be used to illuminate the diagnostic process in autism can be found in Navon and Eyal (2016) who explore the less-than-perfect yet dynamic relations that exist between diagnostic disease categories on the one hand and our knowledge of the genome on the other. Rather than opting for a 'genetics can explain all' or an 'everything is socially constructed' approach, they adapt and extend Hacking's (1995) idea of 'looping' to explore the dynamic interplay between genetics and *inter alia* autism, where identification of genes that might be associated with autism could potentially specify a particular segment of the population as autistic. However, because autistic people actively respond to being (re-) classified, this has the potential for enlarging or diminishing the pool of people labelled as 'autistic', with knock-on consequences for the identification of further genetic associates of autism. This approach is useful in that it does not deny the utility of taking biological associates of autism seriously (or, by extension, structures and processes such as cognition that mediate between biology and society) but also acknowledges the important role of social processes in terms of the individual's reflexivity and susceptibility to social influences both at an interpersonal and a societal level. It is neatly illustrated in the discussion of sex-differences in the clinical picture of autism presented earlier on.

SUMMARY

You should now be aware that the set of conditions commonly grouped under the term 'Autism Spectrum Disorder', often shorthanded as 'autism' is characterized by a unique cluster of behavioural features that affect the developmental trajectory of an individual's adaptation to the physical and social world. These have been codified into a number of schemes, two of which – those developed by the APA (DSM) and the WHO (ICD) are the most widely used.

You should also be able to describe a range of ways in which descriptions of this cluster of features have been codified and how these codifications have been operationalized into a range of standardized assessment and screening instruments.

You should also be able to offer some evaluative and conceptually based comment on the strengths and weaknesses of the different systems used for identification and the instruments

---

[3] I remember once taking a seminar with a group of undergraduates, one of whom took an extreme social constructivist position on just about everything. We were on the fourth floor of our building, opposite an apartment block. I invited the group to socially deconstruct gravity so that the student in question could step outside the window and walk across the road to a fourth floor apartment in the building opposite without needing to use any stairs or walk on the street below.

used to put them into practice. In addition, you should be able to demonstrate an awareness of the epistemological context of their development as well as how they might relate to studies of the factors that could determine or alter the direction of the development of autism within the individual and which will be discussed in more detail in Chapter 8.

REFERENCES

Aldridge, F. J., Gibbs, V. M., Schmidhofer, K., & Williams, M. (2012). Investigating the clinical usefulness of the Social Responsiveness Scale (SRS) in a tertiary level autism spectrum disorder specific assessment clinic. *Journal of Autism and Developmental Disorders, 42,* 294–300.

American Psychiatric Association (1980). *Diagnostic and Statistical Manual of Mental Disorders (3rd edn).* Washington, DC: American Psychiaric Association.

American Psychiatric Association (1994). *Diagnostic and Statistical Manual of Mental Disorders (4th edn) Text Revised.* Washington, DC.

American Psychiatric Association (2013). *Diagnostic and Statistical Manual of Mental Disorders (5th edn).* Washington, DC: American Psychiatric Association.

Asperger, H. (1944). Die 'autistische Psychopathen' im Kindesalter. *Archiv für Psychiatrie und Nervenkrankheiten, 117,* 76–136.

Asperger, H. (1991). Autistic psychopathy in childhood (trans. U. Frith). In U. Frith (ed.), *Autism and Asperger Syndrome,* Cambridge: Cambridge University Press.

Bailey, A. Le Couteur, A., Gottesman, I., Bolton, P., Simonoff, E., Yuzda, E., & Rutter, M. (1995). Autism as a strongly genetic disorder: evidence from a British twin study. *Psychological Medicine, 25,* 63–77.

Baird G. (2000). A screening instrument for autism at 18 months of age: a 6-year follow-up study. *Journal of the American Academy of Child and Adolescent Psychiatry, 39,* 694–702.

Baird, G., Charman, T., Baron-Cohen, S., Cox, A., Swettenham, J., Wheelwright, S., & Drew, A. (2000). A screening instrument for autism at 18 months of age: a 6-year follow-up study. *Journal of the American Academy of Child and Adolescent Psychiatry. 39* (6): 694–702.

Baldwin, S., & Costley, D. (2016). The experiences and needs of female adults with high-functioning autism spectrum disorder. *Autism, 20,* 483–495.

Barker, K., & Galardi, T. R. (2015). Diagnostic domain defense: Autism Spectrum Disorder and the DSM-5. *Social Problems, 62,* 120–140.

Baron-Cohen S. (2002). The extreme male brain theory of autism. *Trends in Cognitive Science, 6,* 248–254.

Baron-Cohen, S., Wheelwright, S., Skinner, R., Martin, J., & Clubley, E. (2001). The Autism-Spectrum Quotient (AQ): Evidence from Asperger Syndrome/high-functioning autism, males and females, scientists and mathematicians. *Journal of Autism and Developmental Disorders, 31,* 5–17.

Ben Shalom, D., Bowler, D. M., Gaigg, S. B., & Delmonte, M. (in preparation). Alexithymia in autism: intrinsic feature or comorbidity? To be submitted to *Autism.*

Bennett, M., & Goodall, E. (2016) A meta-analysis of DSM-5 autism diagnoses in relation to DSM-IV and DSM-IV-TR. *Review Journal of Autism and Developmental Disorders, 3,* 119–124.

Bird, G., & Cook, R. (2013). Mixed emotions: the contribution of alexithymia to the emotional symptoms of autism. *Translational Psychiatry*, 3, e285.

Bishop, D. V. M. (1989). Autism, Asperger's Syndrome and semantic-pragmatic disorder: Where are the boundaries? *British Journal of Disorders of Communication*, 24, 107–121.

Bishop, D. V. M., & Rosenbloom, L. (1987). Classification of childhood language disorders. In W. Yule & M. Rutter (eds), *Language Development and Disorders. Clinics in Developmental Medicine* (No. 101/102). London: MacKeith Press.

Bishop, D. V., and C. F. Norbury (Oct. 2002). Exploring the borderlands of autistic disorder and specific language impairment: a study using standardised diagnostic instruments, *Journal of Child Psychology and Psychiatry, and Allied Disciplines*. 43, 917–929.

Bolton, P., MacDonald, H., Pickles, A., Rios, P., Goode, S., Crowson, M., Bailey, A., & Rutter, M. (1994). A case-control family history study of autism. *Journal of Child Psychology and Psychiatry*, 35, 877–900.

Boucher, J. (2017). *The Autistic Spectrum: Characteristics, Causes and Practical Issues 2nd Edition*. London: Sage.

Bowler, D. (2007). *Autism Spectrum Disorders: Psychological Theory and Research*. Chichester, UK: Wiley.

Bowler, D. M., Geurts, H. & Howlin, P. A. (2019). Special issue on 'Growing Older with Autism'. *Research in Autism Spectrum Disorders*. 63, 1–78.

Brugha, T. S., Bankart, J., Scott, F., et al. (2011) Epidemiology of autism spectrum disorders in adults in the community in England. *Archives of General Psychiatry*, 68, 459–65

Charman, T., & Gotham, K. (2013). Measurement issues: screening and diagnostic instruments for autism spectrum disorders – lessons from research and practise. *Child and Adolescent Mental Health*, 18, 52–64.

Cheblowski, C., Green, J. A., Barton, M. L., & Fein, D. (2010). Using the Childhood Autism Rating Scale to diagnose autism spectrum disorders. *Journal of Autism and Developmental Disorders*, 40, 787–799.

Christensen, D. L., Bilder, D. A., Zahorodny, W., Pettygrove, S., Durkin, M. S., et al. (2016). Prevalence and characteristics of autism spectrum disorder among 4-year-old children in the Autism and Developmental Disabilities Monitoring Network. *Journal of Developmental and Behavioral Pediatrics*, 37, 1–8.

Constantino, J. N., Davis, S. A., Todd, R. D., Schindler, M. K., Gross, M. M. et al. (2003). Validation of a brief quantitative measure of autistic traits: comparison of the social responsiveness scale with the autism diagnostic interview-revised. *Journal of Autism and Developmental Disorders*, 33, 427–433.

Constantino, J. N., & Gruber, C. P. (2012). *Social Responsiveness Scale, Second Edition (SRS-2)*. Torrance, CA: Western Psychological Services.

Dean, M., Harwood, R., & Kasari, C. (2017). The art of camouflage: Gender differences in the social behaviors of girls and boys with autism spectrum disorder. *Autism*, 21(6), 678–689.

Demetriou, E. A., Lampit, A., Quintana, D. S., Naismith, S. L., Song, Y. J. C., Pye, J. E., … Guastella, A. J. (2018). Autism spectrum disorders: A meta-analysis of executive function. *Molecular Psychiatry*, 23, 1198–1204.

Desaunay, P., Briant, A. R., Bowler, D. M... & Guillery-Girard, B. (2020). Memory in autism spectrum disorder: A Meta-analysis of experimental studies. *Psychological Bulletin, 146*, 377–410.

Dworzynski, K., Ronald, A, Bolton, P., & Happé, F. (2012). How different are girls and boys above and below the diagnostic threshold for autism spectrum disorders? *Journal of the American Academy of Child and Adolescent Psychiatry, 51*, 788–797.

Egerton, J., & Carpenter, J. (2016). *Girls and Autism: Flying under the Radar.* London: National Association for Special Educational Needs.

English, M. C. W., Gignac, G. E., Visser, T. A. W., et al. (2021). The Comprehensive Autistic Trait Inventory (CATI): development and validation of a new measure of autistic traits in the general population. *Molecular Autism, 12:* 37.

Evers, K., Maljaars, J., Carrington, S. J., Carter, A. S., Happé, F., Steyaert, J., Leekam, S. R., & Noens, I. (2020). How well are DSM-5 diagnostic criteria for ASD represented in standardized diagnostic instruments? *European Child and Adolescent Psychiatry,* doi: https://0-doi-org.wam.city.ac.uk/10.1007/s00787-020-01481-z.

Field, A. P., & Gillett, R. (2010). How to do a meta-analysis. *British Journal of Mathematical and Statistical Psychology, 63*, 665–694.

Flax, J., Gwin, C., Wilson, S., Fradkin, Y., Buyse, S., & Brzustowicz, L. (2019). Social (pragmatic) communication disorder: another name for the Broad Autism Phenotype? *Autism, 23*, 1982–1992.

Folstein, S., & Rutter, M. (1977). Infantile autism: a genetic study of 21 twin pairs. *Journal of Child Psychology and Psychiatry, 25*, 63–77.

Fombonne, E. (2001). Is there an epidemic of autism? *Pediatrics, 107*, 411–413.

Fombonne, E. (2020). Editorial: camouflage and autism. *Journal of Child Psychology and Psychiatry, 61*, 735–738.

Frazier, T. W., Dimitropoulos, A., Abbeduto, L., et al. (2023). The autism symptom dimensions questionnaire: development and psychometric evaluation of a new, open-source measure of autism symptomatology. *Developmental Medicine and Child Neurology,* in press.

Frith, U. (2003). *Autism: Explaining the Enigma* (2nd edn). Oxford: Blackwell.

Hacking, I. (1995). The looping effects of human kinds, in D. Sperber, D. Premack, & A. J. Premack (eds), *Causal Cognition: A Multidisciplinary Debate, Symposia of the Fyssen Foundation* (pp. 351–94). New York: Oxford University Press.

Hobson, R.P. (1990). On psychoanalytic approaches to autism, *American Journal of Orthopsychiatry, 60*, 324–336.

Houston, R., & Frith, U. (2000). *Autism in History: The Case of Hugh Blair of Borgue.* Oxford, UK: Blackwell.

Huerta M, Bishop SL, Duncan A, Hus V, and Lord C. (2012). Application of DSM-5 criteria for autism spectrum disorder to three samples of children with DSM-IV diagnoses of pervasive developmental disorders. *American Journal of Psychiatry 169*, 1056–1064.

Hurley, R. S. E., Losh, M., Parlier, M., Reznick, J. S., & Piven, J. (2007). The Broad Autism Phenotype Questionnaire. *Journal of Autism and Developmental Disorders, 37*, 1679–1690.

Itard, J-M. G. (1802/1962). *The Wild Boy of Aveyron.* New York: Meredith Company.

Jablensky, A. (2016). Psychiatric classifications: validity and utility. *World Psychiatry, 15*, 26–31.

Kaat, A. J., Shui, A. M., Ghods, S. S., Farmer, C. A., et al. (2020). Sex differences in scores on standardized measures of autism symptoms: a multisite integrative analysis. *Journal of Child Psychology and Psychiatry,* in press.

Kamp-Becker, I., Albertowski, K., Becker, J. Gahremann, M. Langmann, A., et al. (2018). Diagnostic accuracy of the ADOS and ADOS-2 in clinical practice. *European Child and Adolescent Psychiatry, 27,* 1193–1207.

Kanner, L. (1943). Autistic disturbances of affective contact. *Nervous Child, 2,* 217–250.

Kanner, L. (1944). Early infantile autism. *The Journal of Pediatrics, 25,* 211–217.

Kent, R. G., Carrington, S. J., Le Couteur, A., Gould, J., Wing, L., et al. (2013). Diagnosing autism spectrum disorder: who will get a DSM-5 diagnosis. *Journal of Child Psychology and Psychiatry, 54,* 1242–1250.

Kopp, S., & Gillberg, C. (2011). The Autism Spectrum Screening Questionnaire (ASSQ)-Revised Extended Version (ASSQ-REV): an instrument for better capturing the autism phenotype in girls? A preliminary study involving 191 clinical cases and community controls. *Research in Developmental Disabilities, 32,* 2875–2888.

Landry, O., & Chouinard, P. A. (2016). Why we should study the broader autism phenotype in typically developing populations. *Journal of Cognition and Development, 17,* 584–595.

Lane, H. (1976). *The Wild Boy of Aveyron.* Cambridge, MA: Harvard University Press.

Leekam, S. R., Libby, S. J., Wing, L., Gould, J., & Taylor, C. (2002). The Diagnostic Interview for Social and Communication Disorders: algorithms for ICD-10 childhood autism and Wing and Gould autistic spectrum disorder. *Journal of Child Psychology and Psychiatry, 43,* 327–342.

Lister Brook, S., & Bowler, D. M. (1992). Autism by another name? Semantic and pragmatic impairments in children. *Journal of Autism and Developmental Disorders, 22,* 61–81.

Livingston, L. A., Colvert, E., The Social Relationships Study Team, Bolton, P., & Happé, F. (2019). Good social skills despite poor theory of mind: exploring compensation in autism spectrum disorder. *Journal of Child Psychology and Psychiatry, 60,* 102–110.

Livingston, L. A. & Happé, F. (2017). Conceptualising compensation in neurodevelopmental disorders: reflections from autism spectrum disorder. *Neuroscience and Biobehavioral Reviews, 80,* 729–742.

Loomes, R. Hull, R., & Mandy, W. P. L. (2017). What is the male-to-female ratio in Autism Spectrum Disorder? A systematic review and meta-analysis. *Journal of the American Academy of Child and Adolescent Psychiatry, 56,* 466–474.

Lord, C., Risi, S., Lambrecht, L., Cook, E.H., Leventhal, B.L., DiLavore, P.C., …& Rutter, M. (2000). The Autism Diagnostic Observation Schedule-Generic: A standard measure of social and communication deficits associated with the spectrum of autism. *Journal of Autism and Developmental Disorders, 30,* 205–223.

Lord, C., Rutter, M., & Le Couteur, A. (1994). Autism Diagnostic Interview-Revised: a revised version of a diagnostic interview for caregivers of individuals with possible pervasive developmental disorders. *Journal of Autism and Developmental Disorders, 24,* 659–685.

Lord, C., Risi, S., Lambrecht, L., Cook, E. H., Leventhal, B. L., DiLavore, P. C., & Rutter, M. (2000). The Autism Diagnostic Observation Schedule–Generic: A standard measure of social and communication deficits associated with the spectrum of autism. *Journal of Autism and Developmental Disorders, 30,* 205–223.

Lord, C., Rutter, M., DiLavore, P.C., Risi, S., Gotham, K., & Bishop, S.L. (2012). *Autism Diagnostic Observation Schedule, Second Edition (ADOS-2) Manual Part I: Modules 1–4*, Torrance, CA: Western Psychological Services.

Losh, M., Childress, D., Lam, K., & Piven, J. (2008). Defining key features of the broad autism phenotype: a comparison across parents of multiple- and single-incidence autism families. *American Journal of Medical Genetics, Part B (Neuropsychiatric Genetics), 147B*, 424–433.

Lotter, V. (1966). Epidemiology of autistic conditions in young children: I. Prevalence. *Social Psychiatry, 1*, 124–137.

Luyster, R. Gotham, K. Guthrie, W. Coffing, M. Petrak, R., et al. (2009). The Autism Diagnostic Observation Schedule–Toddler Module: a new module of a standardized diagnostic measure for autism spectrum disorders. *Journal of Autism and Developmental Disorders, 39*, 1305–1320.

Lyons, V., & Fitzgerald, M. (2005). *Asperger's Syndrome: A Gift or a Curse?* New York, NY: Nova Science Publishers Inc.

Maenner, M. A., Shaw, K. A., Baio, E. S., Washington, A. M.... & Dietz, P. M. (2020). Prevalence of autism spectrum disorder among children aged 8 years – autism and developmental disabilities monitoring network, 11 sites, united states, 2016. *MMWR Surveillance Summaries, 69*(4), 1–12.

Mandy, W. P., Charman, T. & Skuse, D. H. (2012). Testing the construct validity of proposed criteria for DSM-5 autism spectrum disorder. *Journal of the American Academy of Child and Adolescent Psychiatry, 51*, 41–50.

Mandy, W. Clarke, K., McKenner, M., Strydom, A., Crabtree, J., et al. (2018). Assessing autism in adults: an evaluation of the Developmental Dimensional and Diagnostic Interview – Adult version (3Di-Adult). *Journal of Autism and Developmental Disorders, 48*, 1–12.

Mandy, W., Wang, A., Lee, I., & Skuse, D. (2017). Evaluating social (pragmatic) communication disorder. *Journal of Child Psychology and Psychiatry, 58*, 1166–1175.

Maynard D. W., & Turowetz, J. (2019). Doing abstraction: Autism, diagnosis and social theory. *Sociological Theory, 37*, 89–116.

Medda, J. E., Cholemkery, H., & Freitag, C. M. (2019). Sensitivity and specificity of the ADOS-2 algorithm in a large German sample. *Journal of Autism and Developmental Disorders, 49*, 750–761.

Milton, D. E. M. (2014). Autistic expertise: a critical reflection on the production of knowledge in autism studies. *Autism, 18*, 794–802.

Moon, S. J., Hwang, J. S., Shin, A. L., Kim, J. Y., et al. (2019). Accuracy of the Childhood Autism Rating Scale: a systematic review and meta-analysis. *Developmental Medicine and Child Neurology, 61*, 1030–1038.

National Institute for Health and Care Excellence (2013). Autism: the management and support of children and young people on the autism spectrum, *Clinical Guideline 170* (accessed 31 Jan. 2016 at http://guidance.nice.or.uk/CG170).

Navon, D., & Eyal, G. (2016). Looping genomes: diagnostic change and the genetic makeup of the autism population. *American Journal of Sociology, 121*, 1416–1471.

Ozonoff, S., Young, G. S., Landa, R. J. ... & Iosif, A-M. (2015). Diagnostic stability in young children at risk for autism spectrum disorder: a baby siblings research consortium study. *Journal of Child Psychology and Psychiatry, 56*, 988–998.

Pellicano, E. & den Houting, J. (2022). Annual research review: shifting from 'normal science' to neurodiversity in autism sciences. *Journal of Child Psychology and Psychiatry, 63,* 381–396.

Pierce, K., Gazestani, V. H., Bacon, E., Barnes, C. C.,...& Courchesne, E. (2019). Evaluation of the diagnostic stability of the early autism spectrum disorder phenotype in the general population starting at 12 months. *JAMA Pediatrics, 173 (6),* 578–587.

Popper, K. R. (1959). *The Logic of Scientific Discovery.* London: Hutchinson.

Rapin, I. and Allen, D. A. (1983) Developmental language disorders: nosological considerations. In: Kirk, U. (ed.), *Neuropsychology of Language, Reading and Spelling.* New York: Academic Press.

Ratto, A. B. (2020). Commentary: What's so special about girls on the autism spectrum? – a commentary on Kaat et al. (2020). *Journal of Child Psychology and Psychiatry,* in press.

Reber, M. E. (2012). Epidemiology of autism. In M. E. Reber (ed.), *The Autism Spectrum.* Cambridge: Cambridge University Press, pp. 34–58.

Riel, R. van (2016). What is constructionism in psychiatry? From social causes to psychiatric classification. *Frontiers in Psychiatry, 7,* 1–13.

Ritvo, R. A., Ritvo, E. R., Guthrie, D., et al. (2011). The Ritvo Autism Asperger Diagnostic Scale-Revised (RAADS-R): A Scale to Assist the Diagnosis of Autism Spectrum Disorder in Adults: An International Validation Study, *Journal of Autism and Developmental Disorders, 41,* 1076–1089.

Robins, D. L., Casagrande, K., Barton, M., Chen, C. M., Dumont-Mathieu, T., & Fein D. (2014). Validation of the modified checklist for autism in toddlers, revised with follow-up (M-CHAT-R/F). *Pediatrics, 133 (1),* 37–45. doi:10.1542/peds.2013-1813

Robins D. L., Fein D., Barton M. L., & Green, J. A. (2001). The Modified Checklist for Autism in Toddlers: an initial study investigating the early detection of autism and pervasive developmental disorders. *Journal of Autism and Developmental Disorders, 31,*131–144.

Rødgaard, E-M., Jensen, K, Vergnes, J-N., Soulières, I., & Mottron, L. (2019). Temporal changes in effect sizes of studies comparing individuals with and without autism. A meta-analysis. *JAMA Psychiatry, 76,* 1124–1132.

Rutter, M. (2005). Incidence of autism spectrum disorders: changes over time and their meaning. *Acta Paediatrica, 94,* 2–15.

Rutter, M., Bailey, A., & Lord, C. (2002). *Social Communication Questionnaire.* Torrance, CA: Western Psychological Services.

Santosh, P.J., Mandy, W. P. L,, Puura, K., Kaartinen, M., Warrington, R., & Skuse, D. H. (2009) The construction and validation of a short form of the developmental, diagnostic and dimensional interview. *European Child and Adolescent Psychiatry 18,* 521–524.

Scadding, J. G. (1996). Essentialism and nominalism in medicine: logic of diagnosis in disease terminology. *The Lancet, 348,* 594–596.

Schopler, E., Reichler, R., & DeVellis, R. (1980). Toward objective classification of childhood autism: childhood autism rating scale (CARS). *Journal of Autism and Developmental Disorders, 10,* 91–103.

Schopler, E., Reichler, R. & Rochen Renner, B. (1988). *The Childhood Autism Rating Scale.* Torrance, CA: Western Psychological Services.

Schopler, E., Van Bourgondien, M., Wellman, G., & Love, S. (2010). *Childhood Autism Rating Scale* (2nd edn). Los Angeles, CA: Western Psychological Services.

Skuse, D., Warrington, R., Bishop, D., Chowdhury, U., Lau, J., Mandy, W., & Place, M. (2004). The developmental, dimensional and diagnostic interview (3di): a novel computerized assessment for autism spectrum disorders. *Journal of the American Academy of Child and Adolescent Psychiatry, 43*, 548–558.

Slappendel, G., Mandy, W., van der Ende, J., Verhulst, F. C., van der Sijde, A., Duvekot, J., Skuse, D., & Greaves-Lord, K, (2016) Utility of the 3Di short version for the diagnostic assessment of autism spectrum disorder and compatibility with DSM-5. *Journal of Autism and Developmental Disorders, 46*, 1834–1846.

Smith, O. & Jones, S. C. (2020). 'Coming out' with autism: identity in people with an Asperger's diagnosis after DSM-5. *Journal of Autism and Developmental Disorders, 50*, 592–602.

Squires, J., & Bricker, D. (2009). *Ages & Stages Questionnaires®, Third Edition (ASQ- 3™). A Parent-Completed Child-Monitoring System.* Baltimore, MD: Paul H. Brookes Publishing Co.

Tsai, L. (2013). Asperger's disorder will be back. *Journal of Autism and Developmental Disorders, 43*, 2914–2942.

Tsai, L., & Ghaziuddin, M. (2024). DSM-5 ASD moves forward into the past, *Journal of Autism and Developmental Disorders,44,* 321–330.

Van Riel, R. (2016). What is constructionism in psychiatry? From social causes to psychiatric classification. *Frontiers in Psychiatry, 7*, 57.

Volkmar, F. R., & McPartland, J. C. (2014). From Kanner to DSM-5: autism as an evolving diagnostic concept. *Annual Review of Clinical Psychology, 10*, 193–212.

Walker, A. & Fitzgerald, M. (2006). *Unstoppable Brilliance: Irish Geniuses and Asperger's Syndrome.* Liberties Press, Dublin

Weintraub, K. (2011). Autism counts. *Nature, 479 (7371)*, 22–24.

Wheelwright, S., Auyeung, B., Allison, C., & Baron-Cohen, S. (2010). Defining the broader, medium and narrow autism phenotype among patients using the Autism Spectrum Quotient (AQ). *Molecular Autism, 17*, 1–10.

Wilson, C. E., Gillan, N., Spain, D., Robertson, D., et al., (2013). Comparison of ICD-10R, DSM-IV-TR and DSM-5 in an adult autism spectrum disorder diagnostic clinic. *Journal of Autism and Developmental Disorders, 43*, 2515–2525.

Wing, L. (1981). Asperger's syndrome: A clinical account. *Psychological Medicine, 11*, 115–129.

Wing, L. (1996). *The Autistic Spectrum: A Guide for Parents and Professionals.* London: Constable.

Wing, L. (2013). Feral children. In Volkmar, F. R. (ed.), *Encyclopedia of Autism Spectrum Disorders.* New York: Springer.

Wing, L., & Gould, J. (1978). Systematic recording of behaviours and skills of retarded and psychotic children. *Journal of Autism and Childhood Schizophrenia, 8*, 79–97.

Wing, L., & Gould, J. (1979). Severe impairments of social interaction and associated abnormalities in children: Epidemiology and classification. *Journal of Autism and Developmental Disorders, 9*, 11–29.

Wing, L., & Potter, D. (2002). The epidemiology of autistic spectrum disorders: is the prevalence rising? *Mental Retardation and Developmental Disabilities Reviews, 8*, 151–161.

Wing, L., Leekam, S. R., Libby, S. J., Gould, J., & Larcombe, M. (2002). The diagnostic interview for social and communication disorders: Background, inter-rater reliability and clinical use. *Journal of Child Psychology and Psychiatry and Allied Disciplines, 43*, 307–325.

Woodbury-Smith, M. R., Robinson, J., Wheelwright, S., & Baron-Cohen, S. (2005). Screening adults for Asperger Syndrome using the AQ: a preliminary study of its diagnostic validity in clinical practice. *Journal of Autism and Developmental Disorders, 35*, 331–335.

World Health Organisation. (1968). *International Classification of Diseases – 8th Edition*. Geneva: WHO.

World Health Organisation. (1993). *International Classification of Diseases – 10th Edition*. Geneva: WHO.

World Health Organisation. (2018). *International Classification of Diseases – 11th Edition*. Geneva: WHO.

Yuen, T., Penner, M., Carter, M. T., Szatmari, P., & Ungar, W. J. (2018). Assessing the accuracy of the Modified Checklist for Autism in Toddlers: a systematic review and meta-analysis. *Developmental Medicine and Child Neurology, 60*, 1093–1100.

Zander, E., Willfors, C., Berggren, S., Coco, C., et al. (2017). The interrater reliability of the Autism Diagnostic Interview – Revised (ADI-R) in clinical settings. *Psychopathology,*

8
AUTISM SPECTRUM DISORDER
Psychological Theories and Explanations

> ### Learning Objectives
>
> After reading this chapter, you should be able to:
>
> - Describe a range of empirically-based, psychological approaches to understanding ASD
> - Critically evaluate each of these approaches in terms of a range of broader conceptual dimensions
> - Assess the adequacy of each approach in relation to the diversity inherent in the autistic population
> - Demonstrate using supporting evidence how individuals with autism can compensate for their difficulties and show how this compensation can have repercussions for the kinds of theoretical explanations that can be developed

It is sometimes forgotten that the identification of what is formally referred to as Autism Spectrum Disorder (ASD) but perhaps better thought of as Autism Spectrum *Difference*, is entirely based on systematic observations of behaviour (see Chapter 7 for further elaboration), with little or no reference to possible underlying causes or mechanisms. Indeed, the current criteria as set out in widely used frameworks such as DSM-5 (American Psychiatric Association 2013) or ICD-11 (World Health Organisation 2018) do not refer to underlying causal mechanisms nor do they attempt to offer any frameworks to explain why the observed patterns of behaviour arise. Yet, whether for reasons of natural scientific curiosity or in an attempt to identify ways of helping autistic individuals, scientists, clinicians and others have gone beyond simple observation and classification of behaviours in an attempt to identify underlying structures, processes or mechanisms that might point to causes or explanations of the observable patterns of behaviour. These explanations can be pitched at different levels ranging from the biological (neurotransmitters, neuronal assemblies, brain structures and their interactions) to basic psychological processes (attention, perception, or learning), cognitive processes and their higher-order manifestations (memory, mental state understanding, language) right through to psychosocial processes such as interpersonal interactions and wider societal processes. In this chapter, we focus principally on attempts to account for the clinical picture of ASD from psychological and cognitive perspectives.

A FRAMEWORK FOR ANALYSING AND EVALUATING THEORIES

At first sight, the detail of the different contributions that psychological science has made to our understanding of ASD can seem bewildering. So, to make sense of this complexity, it can help to have a framework within which to organize and evaluate, compare and contrast as well as to understand the different theoretical accounts better. In developing this framework, we first need to step back and reflect on what a psychological account of ASD should ideally provide. We need to ask what we might legitimately expect these accounts to offer over and above the diagnostic formulation in terms of accurate descriptions of behaviour. Will a particular psychological account *explain* the behavioural pattern or simply *redescribe* it in different terms? This distinction between redescription and explanation will become clearer as the discussion develops but for now we should try to avoid thinking of them as a pair of mutually exclusive categories. Rather, they are two ends of a continuum where a particular theory will fall towards one or other end.

We also need to ask whether our explanations should be constructed within a causal hierarchy where some levels of explanation can be considered to be more fundamental in some way than others. For example, a particular clinical feature such as repetitive behaviour can result from damage to the frontal lobes of the brain, leading to the conclusion that it is the brain that has causal primacy and that effective intervention should be targeted there. By contrast, radically behaviourist forms of psychological science take as given the fact that organisms behave, with the task of accounting for the structure and patterning of that behaviour being seen as being a function of the organism's history of rewards and punishments determined by its own action in a particular environment (Skinner 1938, 1954). This view advocates the primacy of the environment in which the organism acts. According to this account, a complete understanding of any individual's behaviour can therefore be reached by reference to that particular individual's specific history of the operation of broad principles of action–reward relations, without the need to invoke any additional underlying mechanisms, neural or otherwise. Theories that adopt a more cognitive or cognitive neuroscience perspective, as do nearly all of the accounts discussed in this chapter, conceptualize the patterning of behaviour as the product of a hierarchy of mechanisms, systems, and processes, which mediate the relation between patterns of behaviour and activity in the brain. Here, causal power may lie at any or all of these levels.

Two of the best expositions of this last approach are David Marr's analysis of the process of vision (Marr 1982) where he proposes three levels of analysis of any psychological process, and Morton and Frith's (1995) explicit structural-causal analysis of developmental delay and difference (see also Frith, Morton, & Leslie 1991). Here, we will focus on Marr's scheme because its more abstract analysis avoids the trap of ending up saying that people with ASD behave the way they do because they are autistic. The first of Marr's levels – the *computational* level – refers to what the system can do; the problems it can solve. This could be thought of as the behavioural capabilities of the organism. The second, *algorithmic* level (sometimes called the *representational* level) concerns the structured processes and representations the system needs to build up in order to perform actions at the previous, algorithmic level. This level could be thought of as referring to the cognitive structures a person needs in order to engage in certain kinds of behaviour. The third level in Marr's scheme is the *implementational* or *physical* level; the machinery that makes the two other levels possible. For our purposes, this can be thought of as the brain, its associated structures and operations. This analysis, illustrated in Figure 8.1, explicitly or implicitly informs the majority of the accounts considered in this chapter, and its characteristics, together with the explanation-(re-)description dimension alluded to above, form an important framework within which the various accounts can be analysed and evaluated. A logical extension of Marr's account would be to dispense with the algorithmic level altogether and explain behaviour directly in terms of brain structures and processes. Morton and Frith (1995) acknowledge that for some developmental differences (they cite the example of tics in Tourette's syndrome) a direct link from the biological to the behavioural might be warranted. They also acknowledge that for many conditions, including ASD, such an extreme reductionist approach is less warranted even if it is often an unwritten sub-text of many more biologically oriented attempts to gain a deeper understanding of ASD.

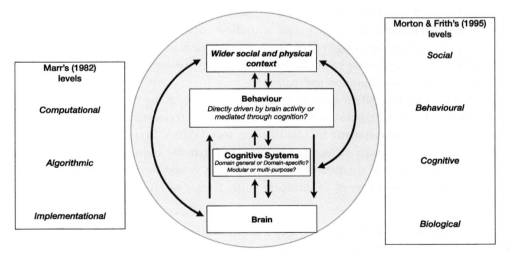

Figure 8.1 Levels of analysis used in explanations of autism

Source: Author's own graphic based on ideas contained in Marr (1982) and Morton and Frith (1995).

Theories that are broadly based on Marr's algorithmic or Morton and Frith's cognitive level of analysis can also be thought about in two other important ways. First, we can ask about how these theories conceptualize the interfaces between operation of the cognitive level both upwards to behaviour and downwards towards biology.[1] Second, we need to ask how a particular theory conceptualizes the *organization* of the cognitive level. Such organization can range from a single, general-purpose set of processes that apply across all kinds of sensory material (visual, auditory, tactile, kinaesthetic) and that functionally organized behaviour, such as language, numerical calculation, navigation, or social interaction represent specific clusterings of the operation of these general processes. A contrasting framework sees the cognitive level as organized as *modular* processes that are specifically dedicated to processing information relevant to a particular domain of experience and action. This contrast between *domain-general* and *modular* or *domain-specific* views of the operation of Marr's algorithmic or cognitive level of analysis has important implications for Marr's other two levels. Strict modularist positions such as that initially proposed by Fodor (1983) view the dedicated operation of modular systems at the algorithmic level as being directly reflected at the neural level, although this claim has been subsequently toned down (see Fodor 2000). Less modular, more domain-general approaches argue that a given psychological function, such as language, or calculation or memory, which are defined at the behavioural (computational), level may result from a range of operations at both the cognitive (algorithmic) and brain (implementational) level. These characterizations may seem a little abstract at present, but will become clearer when we come to discuss individual theoretical accounts in more detail. They may also appear to have little practical utility or application to the everyday lives of autistic individuals. However, this is far from the case. Much research effort (and money!) is expended on the premise that to 'fix' the disordered behaviour patterns of autistic individuals, we need to identify what is 'wrong' with their brains and not worry about hypothetical entities that might be thought to mediate brain–behaviour interactions. Even if you are a proponent of this extremely reductionist viewpoint, by the end of this chapter you might have a more nuanced opinion on the matter.

A final consideration when looking at ways of explaining the behaviour patterns that define ASD is the starting point of a particular theoretical framework. Does the framework start from a given characteristic of ASD (such as social difficulties) or does it start from a psychological process (such as learning or memory) that has been studied in the general population? Examples of the first of these approaches would be to explain difficulties in social communication in terms of difficulty with 'Theory of Mind' (Baron-Cohen, Leslie,

---

[1] The use of the terms 'upwards' and 'downwards' here is entirely arbitrary, and could just as easily be reversed, or thought of as 'leftwards or rightwards' or vice versa (it depends on how you draw the diagram). It is not meant to imply that the brain is more fundamental to, or inferior to the other levels.

& Frith 1985), or to explain restricted and repetitive behaviours in terms of particular patterns of executive dysfunction (Hill 2004a, b). An example of the second approach would be memory, which although not a defining clinical feature of ASD, has been described as being atypical in clinical accounts right back to Kanner (1943) and is now known to present a characteristic ASD-related patterning (Boucher, Mayes, & Bigham 2008; Desaunay, Briant, Bowler et al. 2020) with important knock-on effects on a range of other psychological processes (see Bowler, Gaigg, & Lind 2011).

To summarize, attempts to go beyond the behavioural descriptions of the defining clinical picture can be thought of as lying somewhere in a multidimensional space defined by the following dimensions:

1. The extent to which a theoretical system offers an *explanation* or a *redescription* of the behavioural picture of ASD.
2. The nature of the factors that give rise to and influence the development of patterned behaviour, and whether these are external (environmental, reward/punishment) or internal to the organism (constitutional, organic (including brain) processes).
3. The *direct* or *mediated* nature of the relations between behaviour and the factors that influence it. In other words, are there real or hypothetical structures that can be inferred from the patterning of behaviour and which can be used as explanatory constructs?
4. Whether these mediating constructs can be related to a different level of analysis that can be placed in a causal hierarchy.[2]
5. The extent to which the mediating constructs are dedicated to a particular behaviour pattern (modular, domain-specific) or operate across a range of behaviours (domain-general).
6. Whether the chosen starting point for an explanation is rooted in specific clinical features (diagnostic or otherwise) of ASD, or starts with well-established constructs elucidated in the study of wider typical and atypical populations.

Figure 8.2 attempts to set out these dimensions in a way that helps you to grasp the fact that they are axes of a multidimensional space, which, although not orthogonal (i.e. completely independent) can to some extent vary independently. It is important that you should see this framework as a heuristic to aid understanding rather than as something that is set in stone. Not all of these dimensions are relevant for every single theoretical account described in this chapter, and many of the accounts lie somewhere along particular dimensions rather than at

---

[2] The most common way this is done in the context of ASD is to think of behaviour as being driven by a cognitive process that is instantiated in the brain. But we might just as easily think as behaviour being driven by systematic reward systems that are driven by societal structures that sustain the existence of marginalized groups. This last view is less widespread but not completely unknown in autism research (see Maynard & Turowetz 2019) and should not be dismissed out of hand.

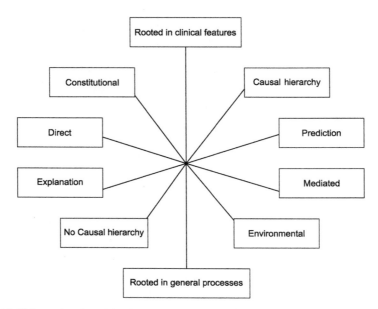

Figure 8.2 Multidimensional analytical space reflecting different explanatory approaches to autism
Source: Author's own graphic.

one or other end. A key dimension in terms of evaluating theoretical accounts (of any difference, not just of autism) is the extent to which those accounts simply describe (or re-describe) particular aspects of the phenomenon or whether they offer an explanation in terms of other entities or mechanisms. There is not space here to go into this important distinction, but a good summary of the issues can be found in Bechtel and Wright (2009).

CURRENT PSYCHOLOGICAL ACCOUNTS OF ASD

Social, Emotional and Interpersonal Accounts

From the perspective of a neurotypical person, one of the most striking features of individuals with ASD of whatever level of accompanying intellectual disability is atypicality in social communication. It is not surprising, therefore, that this is one of the key criteria for a formal identification of ASD (APA 2013; see Chapter 7) and that it has attracted a large share of research attention. The very title of Kanner's original series of case reports (*Autistic disturbances of affective contact*, my emphasis) indicates a difficulty with understanding emotion and its knock-on effects on social relatedness. Since then, a considerable body of literature investigating autism and emotion has grown up, with varied and at times complex results. When grappling with this complex literature, it is helpful to keep in mind the considerable changes in the identification of ASD that have taken place over the eight decades since Kanner's observations, especially the changes that have occurred since the 1990s. Up until then, the consensus was that people identified as having ASD (largely pre-DSM, or DSM-III (APA 1980) or DSM-IV, APA 1994) had difficulties understanding facial, vocal, and bodily expressions of emotion. In a series of elegant and well-controlled studies by Hobson and colleagues in the United Kingdom and Sigman and colleagues in the United States (e.g. Sigman, Kasari, Kwon, & Yirmiya 1992) demonstrated that children and adolescents with ASD, many of whom had a co-occurring intellectual disability, performed less well than matched comparison participants on a number of tasks requiring an ability to discriminate emotional aspects of facial expressions, vocalizations, actions, or body postures. See Chapter 3 of Bowler (2007), for further discussion of this research.

Hobson (1993) argued that autistic individuals' atypical responses to expressions of emotions in others were likely to be constitutional in origin[3] and that they disrupted the *affective patterning of self-other relationships* that was necessary for the kind of understanding of self and other needed for typical psychological development (see Hobson 1991, 2002). In later writings (Hobson & Hobson 2007) he and his colleagues argue that an autistic developmental trajectory results from difficulties in interpersonal relatedness that is a consequence of the reduced identification with the other. This reduced identification occurs because of difficulties in emotional understanding that Hobson thought were necessary for the construction of self and other (Hobson 2002). Interestingly, in terms of the framework set out in Figures 8.1 and 8.2, Hobson's account links behaviours that are characteristic of ASD directly to the wider social environment, while at the same time anchoring them in a constitutional difficulty that centres around sensitivity to emotional expression and its role in the regulation of interpersonal interaction.

The broadening of the clinical picture of ASD resulting from the widening of diagnostic criteria for ASD (see Chapter 7) has led to a nuancing of the conclusion that autistic individuals show reduced performance on emotion recognition tasks. A meta-analysis of 48 papers by Uljarevic and Hamilton (2013) report reduced emotion recognition of the basic emotions of sadness, anger, surprise, fear, and disgust in autistic participants with an overall corrected effect size of -0.41, which is generally interpreted as a small effect size (Lakens 2013). Meta-analyses and review articles (e.g. Harms, Martin, & Wallace 2010) can be helpful in identifying broad trends in a population, but well-conducted individual studies that produce unexpectedly counter-trend results can also help us to understand possible mechanisms that underlie performance on tasks such as emotional recognition. For example, Williams and Happé (2010) asked mildly intellectually disabled adolescents with and without autism to define, and then describe an appropriate situation and then recognize from a film clip, a set of 'basic' (happiness, anger, sadness, etc.) and 'self-conscious' (pride, shame, embarrassment, etc.) emotions.

---

[3] Although Hobson did not specify the precise details of the constitutional causes of difficulties in emotional understanding, he argued that anything that disrupts the emotional modulation of adult–child interaction can give rise to an autism-like behavioural profile and gives the example of congenital blindness in this regard (Hobson & Bishop 2003).

They found no overall group differences in ability to define, describe, or recognize either basic or self-conscious emotions in self or other.

But the relation between verbal mental age (VMA) and emotional processing differed across the groups. VMA correlated positively with the *quality of self-reports* of basic and self-conscious emotions in the ASD but not the comparison group. By contrast, VMA correlated with neither basic nor self-conscious emotion *recognition* in the ASD group. For the comparison participants, VMA correlated only with the self-conscious emotions. Findings such as these are important because by showing a different pattern of correlations across groups, in the absence of an overall group difference in performance, they suggest that there might be different underlying mechanisms driving autistic and non-autistic individuals' processing of emotion. This conclusion is further supported by Harms et al.'s, (2010) review of the role of demographic and methodological factors in emotion processing recognition in ASD, which concludes that although not all studies report ASD-related difficulty in processing expressions of emotion, there is ample evidence to suggest that even in the absence of group differences, a range of methodologies (eye-tracking; Pelphrey, Morris, McCarthy, & Labar 2007; brain imaging: Ashwin, Baron-Cohen, Wheelwright, O'Riordan, & Bullmore 2007) have shown that the successful decoding of expressions of emotion can result from different underlying mechanisms in individuals with autism.

This conclusion is further refined in a study of self-conscious emotions in autistic adolescents (Jankowski & Pfeifer 2021) who were asked to rate video clips of singers' state of pride or embarrassment when they were performing under circumstances that were more or less likely to engender these emotions. Unlike the majority of earlier studies, Jankowski and Pfeifer not only asked participants to rate emotions that were congruent with the emotion being rated (e.g. singing badly and acting in an embarrassed manner) but also when they were incongruent (e.g. singing well but acting embarrassed).

In addition to demonstrating that their autistic participants were capable of accurately rating both positively and negatively valenced emotions, they were also more likely to infer incongruent emotions when the circumstances suggested them. The researchers conclude from this that although non-intellectually disabled people with autism have little difficulty in rating and empathizing with bodily expressed self-conscious emotion, they appear to be more sensitive to situational aspects of that expression and that this might result from their relying on learned social rules in order to compensate for difficulties in this domain. This observation that similar behavioural outcomes might be driven by different underlying, compensatory, mechanisms in some domains chimes with the findings of the Williams and Happé (2010) study described above as well as earlier work by Hobson (1986). These findings exemplify the theme of compensation that will recur throughout this chapter and will be discussed at length in a final section.

Another dimension has been added to the way we think of emotion in autism by research into a condition known as *alexithymia*. Alexithymia is a difficulty in reading emotions in self and other (Berthoz & Hill 2005) and is reported as being more common in individuals with an ASD diagnosis (c50%, Berthoz & Hill 2005; Kinnaird, Stewart, & Tchanturia 2019) than in the general population (c10%, Berthoz, Pouga, & Wessa 2011). Because it is also found in other conditions such as schizophrenia (Henry, Bailey, von Hippel, et al. 2010) and depression (Li, Zhang, Guo, & Zhang 2015), researchers such as Bird and colleagues (Bird & Cook 2013; Bird, Silani, Brindley, White, et al. 2010; Cook, Brewer, Shah, & Bird 2013) have suggested that it might also simply be a co-occurring factor, independent of autism and that many of the emotion-related difficulties that are considered to be important markers in the identification of autism (even if they are not *criteria*; see Chapter 7), are in fact manifestations of co-occurring alexithymia. In support of this argument, they provide evidence that alexithymia (whether or not it co-occurs with ASD) is associated with atypical functioning of the insular cortex of the brain, often called the 'interoceptive cortex' because of its involvement in the process of awareness of internal bodily (including emotional) states (Bird, Silani, Brindley, et al. 2010). When adults with and without ASD are shown videos of emotional and non-emotional interactions between people, the ratio between fixations to the actors' eyes relative to their mouths (a measure of emotion sensitivity) correlates with a measure of alexithymia (the Toronto Alexithymia Scale, TAS, Bagby, Parker, & Taylor 1994) but not a measure of autism severity (Autism Diagnostic Observation Schedule; Lord, Risi, Lambrecht, et al. 2000; Bird, Press, and Richardson 2011). And when participants with and without ASD observed a familiar other person receiving a painful electric shock, activation of the anterior insula did not differ between participants with and without ASD but did correlate with levels of alexithymia to the same extent in both participant groups (Bird, Silani, Brindley, et al. 2010). A study from a different research group (Scheerer, Boucher, & Iarocci 2021) found that a measure of alexithymia accounted for variation in social competence in children with and without ASD, supporting the view that social difficulties more widely conceived – not simply the understanding of emotions – are associated with alexithymia both in the presence and the absence of ASD.

We should be careful, however in unquestioningly equating alexithymia with interoception, or in regarding all measures of interoception as equivalent. In a series of studies, Nicholson and colleagues (Nicholson, Williams, Carpenter, & Kallitsounaki 2019; Nicholson, Williams, Grainger, Christensen, Calvo-Merino, & Gaigg 2018) found that although interoception as measured by heartbeat tracking (Schandry 1981) and accuracy in tracking breathing rate (Murphy, Catmur, & Bird 2018) appears to be diminished in children with ASD, it is intact in adults even when they had clinically significant levels of alexithymia. Nicholson et al. (2019) conclude that there appears to be a developmental progression in autistic individuals' awareness of their internal bodily states, which improves over time. However, the capacity to relate such awareness to reports of their own emotions, such as is measured by alexithymia questionnaires (e.g. the Toronto Alexithymia Scale, TAS-20; Bagby, Parker, & Taylor 1994) appears to be decoupled, at least in some individuals with autism. This might explain persisting difficulties in processing emotion in self and in others, but also warrants caution in equating higher-level, questionnaire measures of alexithymia with more direct, physiological measures of alexithymia. It would be interesting to repeat Nicholson et al.'s studies using neuroimaging measures of insular activities such as those used by Bird and colleagues described earlier.

Despite the uncertainties in the literature, the suggestion that part of the behavioural picture of ASD might be explained by a condition (alexithymia) that operates independently of autism is important and informative and helps to shed some light on how we understand the overall picture of ASD. If the claim that altered emotional sensitivity and empathy (which are often thought of as behavioural markers of ASD, see Cook et al. 2013) are, in fact independent of it is true, then we may need to re-evaluate those theoretical accounts of autism (such as that of Hobson, discussed above), which see difficulty with emotional relatedness as having a central, causal role in its development. Moreover, if it is possible to have ASD *without* having alexithymia, we need to reflect on what non-emotion- or empathy-related features need to be present in order to meet the criteria for identification of ASD, as well as formulate a theory of how these features develop. In other words, we need to ask what a non-alexithymic autistic person would look like and how this patterning of their behaviour came about.

Reflective Exercise

At this point it might be worth looking back at Figures 8.1 and 8.2 and asking yourself the following questions:

1. Where do you see the alexithymia account fitting in to these schemes?
2. In what ways does it explain, rather than re-describe, what we see in the behavioural profile of ASD?
3. What further investigations do you think would be needed in order to improve its Explanatory potential?

ACCOUNTS IN TERMS OF DIFFICULTIES IN UNDERSTANDING OTHER MINDS

As we saw Chapter 7, autistic individuals are defined by what are called 'persistent deficits [sic] in social communication and social interaction' (DSM-5; American Psychiatric Association 2013) and even if, as we have just seen, the emotional aspects of social communication difficulties might not be unique to ASD, there is another parallel, body of research into non-affective aspects of social functioning. Various terms have been used to describe, conceptualize and attempt to explain these difficulties. 'Theory of Mind (ToM, Baron-Cohen, Leslie, & Frith 1985), Mentalizing (Frith 2001), Mental State Understanding (MSU), have each been used with varying degrees of precision and rigour but all of them are based on the idea that human social interaction implies some kind of understanding that other people understand the world in ways that are different from one's own. Moreover, grasping this difference involves the inference of unseen mental states that can be used to predict another person's behaviour. Once an individual has grasped this fact, they can be said to be able to mentalize, to be capable of MSU or to possess a ToM.

Figure 8.3 Schematic illustration of 'Sally-Anne' task

Source: Simon Baron-Cohen, Alan M. Leslie, and Uta Frith, Does the autistic child have a 'theory of mind'?, *Cognition* 21(1), copyright Elsevier 1985. Republished under STM conditions.

In the context of ASD, the seminal study that launched the ToM-difficulty account of autism was that of Baron-Cohen, Leslie, and Frith (1985) which used a version of Wimmer and Perner's (1983) unexpected transfer task (see Figure 8.3 – illustration of Sally-Anne task) to show that children with ASD and moderate intellectual disability were less able than typically developed children or those with Down syndrome at grasping a protagonist's false belief (about the location of a marble that the protagonist had hidden, when the marble had been moved without the protagonist's knowledge). The pervasive and persistent impact of this finding – the terms 'impaired Theory of Mind' or 'Theory of Mind deficit' continue to be shorthand in the field – stems from a number of factors. The theoretical background to the study is particularly elegant and powerful. In a landmark paper on the development of the cognitive underpinnings of pretence in typical infants, Leslie (1987) astutely observed that the computational demands of pretending that a block of wood is a car (something toddlers can do effortlessly and autistic children only with difficulty (Baron-Cohen, 1987; Jarrold, Boucher & Smith, 1993), developing it late if at all) are identical to those engaged in by someone observing Sally when she falsely believes that her marble is in the basket when it actually is in the box (see Figure 8.3). Leslie argued that this mechanism was modular in the way we discussed earlier on, which meant that Baron-Cohen et al.'s (1985) evidence that children who have difficulty engaging in pretence (because they are autistic) also have difficulty understanding mental states because they have a differently functioning Theory of Mind module. Further research showing that autistic children could pass tests of false non-mental representations such as false photographs (Leekam & Perner 1991) or drawings (Charman & Baron-Cohen 1992), reinforced this view of a *specific deficit* [sic] *in mental state understanding* (Baron-Cohen 1995) in autism. Extreme modularist versions of this position, which see computational modules as instantiated in the brain, have driven the quest for the neural mechanisms underlying the (lack of) 'Theory of Mind' in autism (Frith 2001; Baribeau, Dupuis, Paton, Hammill, et al. 2019).

As is often the case in psychological science, what initially appears to be a neat, clear and often helpful theoretical framework rapidly becomes more complex on further investigation. The version of the '"ToM-Deficit" account of autism is no exception difficulty is called into question, when in studies using more sophisticated methodologies that more adequately controlled for task complexity (e.g. Bowler, Briskman, Gurvidi, & Fornells-Ambrojo 2005; Iao & Leekam 2014), autistic children's performance on mental state and non-mental state tasks was found to be equivalent. These studies show that it is factors such as task complexity or predicting the behaviour of agents that are difficult for autistic people and not mental state understanding per se. It is likely that an autistic person's difficulty in understanding minds is just one aspect of a more general problem in understanding many complex situations they might find themselves in.

Reflective Exercise

You might like to think about the contrasting implications of a modularist versus a more domain-general account of mental state understanding for the design and development of interventions with autistic individuals.
1. Which one would be more likely to generalize to a wider set of difficulties?
2. Is there any existing literature that might inform your thinking?

Regardless of how the findings of impaired false belief understanding were interpreted, their scope is limited by the fact that not all individuals with autism appear to have difficulty in this area. For example, a range of studies showed that Bowler (1992) found that older children, adolescents, and adults on the autism spectrum had no difficulty with higher-order mental state reasoning of the 'John thinks Mary thinks...' kind (see Perner & Wimmer 1986). These findings highlighted the need to develop measures that were more appropriate for older, non-intellectually disabled children as well as adults with autism and there is now a wide range of so-called 'advanced' tests of Theory of Mind available (see Brewer, Young, & Barnett 2017 for review). From the outset, it is important to remain aware of what these tests claim to measure and what they might actually be measuring. As we have seen with the Sally-Anne task, and will shortly see with the more advanced measures, even if a test is referred to as a 'Theory of Mind measure' or a 'mentalizing measure', it might not be assessing any of these concepts or, more importantly, may be assessing them in typically developed individuals but assessing something quite different in people with autism.

An early alternative to false belief-type measures of mental state understanding was Happé's *Strange Stories Test* (Happé 1994; White, Hill, Happé, & Frith 2009), recently upgraded to a film version – the *Strange Stories Film Task* (Murray, Johnston, Cunnane, Kerr, et al. 2017). This test is firmly rooted in the view that mental states are 'special' and that as such, they present particular difficulties for individuals on the autism spectrum. It comprises a number of verbal scenarios requiring participants to answer questions about situations centred either on psychological situations such as a Lie, a White Lie, a Joke, a Double Bluff, etc. (see Happé 1994 for more details) or about stories centred on physical components such as the effect of different kinds of weather on the unfolding of a scenario. There is now a large body of evidence showing that autistic individuals have difficulty on the first kind of stories but not the second (Chung, Barch, & Straube 2014), reinforcing the view of a differently functioning 'Theory of Mind' in autistic individuals. However, we need to be careful about such claims. In common with many areas of autism research, they rely on the assumption of an exact equivalence between the 'mental state' and the 'non-mental-state' tasks, which might not always be the case in practice. Sometimes the non-mental-state story is easier (see Bowler 2007: 44–45 for an example) meaning that the mentalizing 'problem' is simply a difficulty with performing inherently harder tasks irrespective of their mental state content. And as with the false belief measure discussed earlier, if we can find a control task that does not involve mental state reasoning yet is equally difficult for autistic people, then the problem cannot be fundamentally one of mental state understanding, but may be more pervasive than that. This is not a trivial methodological point. It goes to the very heart of what we mean when we say that autistic individuals have a specific difficulty with mental state understanding, or that their difficulties in other areas result from problems with mentalizing.

Another measure that aims to tackle the problem of quantifying mentalizing deficits in older, less intellectually disabled autistic individuals has centred on asking participants to describe short video animations. The *Frith-Happé Animations Test* (Abell, Happé, & Frith 2000, www.youtube.com/watch?v=qH1O6l6FDq0) grew out of early work by Heider and Simmel (1944, www.youtube.com/watch?v=VTNmLt7QX8E) who noted that people from the general population often gave anthropomorphic descriptions couched in mental state language when describing films of animated geometric shapes. In the *Frith-Happé Animations Task,* people are asked to describe three sets of animations similar to those of Heider and Simmel. One set depicts random motion of the animated elements, the second depicts interactions of the elements that depend on physical relations among them, and the third set depicts interactions that could be construed as involving one element acting in response to the mental state of the other. These animations have been used in a wide range of studies, reviewed by White, Coniston, Rogers, and Frith (2011), who also developed a more objective scoring system designed to overcome the rather subjective and time-consuming scoring method of the original test. This and other studies have revealed that autistic adults are less able to classify the animations into those that typical individuals tend to describe as physical or mental interactions. These findings have generally been taken as further confirmation of the view that autistic individuals are characterized by difficulties in understanding other minds. However, as with the two classes of measure discussed earlier (False Belief-type measures and Strange Stories-type measures), this conclusion permits of several other interpretations.

In order to go beyond a simple redescription of the observation that autistic people do not give the same responses to the 'Theory of Mind' animations as do neurotypical people, we need to specify the characteristics of stimuli that produce this difference and identify the mechanisms that might drive it. This move from re-description to explanation is much more difficult to do but is vital if the measure is to have any explanatory power, that is to say to re-describe autistic behaviour in a way that links with processes beyond mere performance on the test. In an attempt to do this, Bowler and Thommen (2000) asked children with and without autism to describe the Heider and Simmel animation and found that the autistic children were poorer than non-autistic children at identifying the chase scene in the original Heider and Simmel (1944) animation. They interpreted this in the context of the work of Rochat, Morgan and Carpenter (1997), who found that typical infants developed the capacity to discriminate chases only when they had mastered *protodeclarative pointing* at nine months of age. In protodeclarative pointing, an infant points to an object of interest and alternates gaze between the object and another person; it is characteristically absent from the development of autistic children (Baron-Cohen 1989; Toth, Munson, Meltzoff, & Dawson 2006). Bowler and Thommen concluded that a more fundamental difficulty for many autistic individuals might be in seeing contingency in patterns of activity of elements that were not visibly physically connected to each other as when one element of an animation chases another distant element which is trying to escape the first.

A third, widely used measure of mentalizing is the *Reading the Mind in the Eyes* (RMET) test developed by Baron-Cohen (Baron-Cohen, Jolliffe, Mortimore, & Robertson, 1997; Baron-Cohen, Wheelwright, Hill, Raste, & Plumb 2001) in an effort to develop an appropriate test for older and more intellectually able participants. The theoretical and empirical rationale for this test is rooted in early work by Baron-Cohen and colleagues that argues for the importance of an individual's awareness of another person's eye gaze direction in determining the contents of that person's mind (Baron-Cohen 1995; Baron-Cohen, Campbell, Karmiloff-Smith, Grant, & Walker 1995; Khalid, Deska, & Hugenberg 2016). The RMET that resulted from this work consists of a series of 36 pictures of the eye region of the face together with four 'mental state terms' such as *confused, angry, regretful, thoughtful, happy, sad…* one of which the participant had to select. It is widely used as an implicit measure of mental state understanding in both autism and other conditions such as schizophrenia (Oliver, Moxon-Emre, Lai, et al. 2021), healthy ageing (Kynast, Quinque, Polyakova, et al. 2020), Alzheimer's disease (Yi, Zhao, Zhang, et al. 2020) among others. In addition to being thought of as a less explicit measure, several investigators have argued that it measures 'affective' rather than 'cognitive' understanding of mental states. Oakley, Brewer, Bird, and Catmur (2016) capture this neatly when they argue that in autistic individuals, understanding mental states is separate from understanding emotions, which is driven more by alexithymia than by autism and produce evidence showing that the RMET is an emotional recognition rather than a Theory of Mind test.

Reflective Exercise

Again, at this point it might be worth looking back at Figures 8.1 and 8.2 and apply the following questions to Happé's strange stories, the Happé-Frith animations and Baron-Cohen's RMET. It might be helpful to carry out a literature search to see if you can find any relevant material.

1 Where do you see the 'Strange Stories', the 'Animations', or the RMET fitting in to these frameworks?
2 In what ways do the three accounts explain, rather than re-describe, what we see in the clinical picture of ASD?
3 What further investigations do you think would be needed in order to improve their explanatory potential?

The three approaches to measuring mentalizing just described, along with many others, have been used in large numbers of studies aimed at refining descriptions of the behavioural profile of autistic individuals, establishing neural, cognitive, and wider adaptive/behavioural correlates in autistic individuals and have been important in generating and maintaining the narrative that autism is at least in part, a difficulty with 'mentalizing'. This conclusion is reinforced by a recent study by Brewer, Young, and Barnett (2017), who validated their own *Adult-Theory-of-Mind* (A-ToM) measure against the *Strange Stories Test* described above, and the *Frith-Happé Animations Test*. Although they were able to derive a social interaction measure from the A-ToM that reliably distinguished their autistic from their non-autistic sample, thus reinforcing the idea that autism is characterized by mentalizing difficulties, the patterns of intercorrelations among the mentalizing measures differed in the two groups. They were higher and correlated with verbal and non-verbal IQ in the autistic group in a way that was not found for the non-autistic group, suggesting that the autistic group may have been solving the problems set by the measurement instruments in radically different ways from the typical participants. This capacity to arrive at solutions to problems via different routes has been known for quite some time ('logico-affective states, Hermelin & O'Connor 1985; 'hacking out'; Bowler 1992; Happé 1995) and raises the whole question of whether or not autistic individuals engage in compensatory strategies to achieve what appear to be typical levels of performance. This is a theme to which we will return at the end of this chapter.

It is clear from this brief overview that our understanding of what constitutes Theory of Mind or mentalizing difficulties in autism has changed quite a bit since the 1980s. We have come a long way from a specific neurocognitive modular mechanism dedicated understanding representational mental states to more general, arguably less precise, descriptive allusions to an individual's capacity to infer unobservable entities (thoughts, beliefs, feelings) on the basis of another person's behaviour. This shift may or may not be a good thing, but it is important to be clear about its implications for the framework outlined at the start of this chapter. The overarching idea of a 'difficulty in understanding other minds' is of immense clinical value. It renders an autistic person's puzzling behaviour less puzzling to a non-autistic observer. But if this understanding is to succeed in providing pointers to underlying mechanisms that might become the targets of intervention strategies, we need to be clear about what exactly we refer to when speaking about mentalizing, or indeed any other construct we refer to in an explanatory manner.

ACCOUNTS ROOTED IN NON-SOCIAL ASPECTS OF THE CLINICAL PICTURE

The second major set of behavioural features noted in formal descriptions of ASD and reflected in frameworks such as DSM and ICD (see Chapter 7) are those relating to sensory sensitivity and restricted and repetitive behaviours (RRBs). As with social-communicative difficulties, researchers have looked outside ASD to seek potentially useful paradigms to explain these defining characteristics. In this section, we will discuss two widely used paradigms – *Executive Functions* (EF) and *Weak Central Coherence* (WCC).

Executive Function Accounts

Damasio and Maurer's (1978) observation of a similar patterning of behaviour in autism and in people with lesions of the frontal lobe of the brain led to a programme of research into a particular set of phenomena, broadly considered under the heading of executive functions (see Pennington & Ozonoff 1996; Russell 1997; Hill 2004a,b; Demetriou, Lampit, Quentana, et al. 2018; Xie, Sun, Yang, & Guo 2021), impairment of which is characteristic of frontal lobe damage. Early measures of EF emerged from clinical studies of the behaviour of individuals with damage to the frontal lobes (Roberts, Robbins, & Weiskrantz 1998; Stuss & Knight 2002) and many of the concepts and assessment instruments still in use today stem from these or even earlier studies. Later developments in the form of more systematic experimental work have led to a more differentiated conceptualization EF, leading scientists to the view that EF is a cluster of 'high-level cognitive processes that, through their influence on lower-level processes, enable individuals to regulate their thoughts and actions during goal-directed behaviour' (Friedman & Miyake 2017: 187). The range of processes comprising EF all involve some degree of disengagement from the current situation in order to regulate behaviour in relation to some future goal. This includes inhibition, working memory,[4] set switching, and cognitive flexibility. At a higher level, the coordinated operation of these processes results in effective planning and strategic behaviour. To give a flavour of some of the issues raised by an EF account of autism, we now consider in more detail two tasks that are widely used in the area of autism research – the so called 'Tower' tasks (Shallice 1982; Hughes, Russell, & Robins 1994) that assess planning, and the Wisconsin Card Sorting Test (WCST. Heaton, Chelune, Talley, et al. 1993; Jones 2013), which is generally thought to assess perseveration and cognitive flexibility

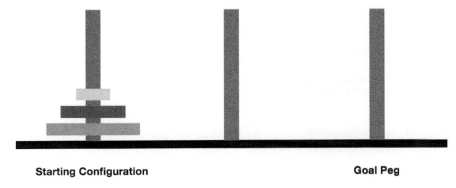

Figure 8.4 'Tower of Hanoi' task: starting configuration

Source: Author's own graphic.

---

[4] It is important to bear in mind that the concept of working memory (Baddeley 2007) has multiple memory components in addition to the central executive, which is the relevant component here.

Both parental reports and experimental investigations reveal that planning is an aspect of EF that poses widespread difficulty for autistic individuals (Olde Dubbelink, & Geurts 2017). These difficulties are captured by performance on tasks like the Tower of London (Shallice 1982), Tower of Hanoi or Stockings of Cambridge (Hughes et al. 1994) in which participants have to move objects (either physically or on a screen) from one configuration to a different one while respecting specific rules. On average, autistic individuals' performance is characterized by more errors and longer task times. In the simplest Tower of Hanoi for example (Figure 8.4), the rule is to reproduce on the goal (right-hand) peg, the configuration of discs seen on the starting peg by moving only one disc at a time and never placing a larger disc on a smaller one. Even when autistic individuals' performance is comparable to non-autistic comparison participants, they often appear to use a more visually rather than verbally mediated strategy (Williams, Bowler, & Jarrold 2012). When participants were asked to engage in *articulatory suppression* (repetition of a word such as 'Saturday' while performing the task) the performance of the non-autistic participants was adversely affected to a greater extent than that of the autistic participants, suggesting that the latter group were less reliant on an internal dialogue to perform the task than were the typical participants. This shows how ASD participants can use a cognitive strength (visuo-spatial skills) to compensate for an underlying difficulty in using language to mediate a complex task.

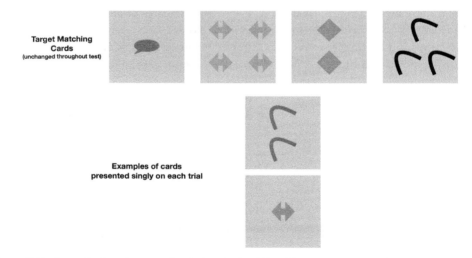

Figure 8.5 Layout of cards according to the logic of the Wisconsin Card Sorting Test

Source: Author's own drawing based on descriptions given in Heaton et al. (1993)

In another EF test – the WCST – that has revealed widespread autism-related difficulties, participants are asked to match a sequence of individually presented cards with one of a set of four target cards, which remain visible throughout the test. Both target and test cards vary along the dimensions of colour, shape, and number. The instructions are minimal; participants are given

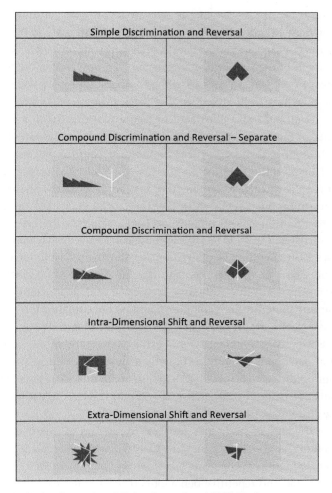

Figure 8.6 Layout of Intradimensional-Extradimensional Shift Task

Source: Author's own drawing based on description given in Downes et al. (1989)

a card and asked which of the four target cards it can best be matched with. On the first trial, the experimenter rewards a shape match which, crucially, the participant is not told about and has to discover by trial and error. After ten correct trials, the experimenter, unbeknownst to the participant, switches the criterion to number, and after ten more correct responses, to colour, then back to shape, and so on. The principle of the task is illustrated in Figure 8.6. Although there is some variability in results, individuals from across the autism spectrum generally show some degree of difficulty on measures of perseveration and set-shifting on this test (Landry & Al-Taie 2016; Westwood, Stahl, Mandy, & Tchanturia 2016). Because the WCST arose out of the clinical need to systematically elicit and document behavioural difficulties following brain injury, it is not always clear precisely what is measured by the task and so, what conclusions we can legitimately draw in order to go beyond simple redescription. To begin to address this problem, Hughes and colleagues employed tasks such as the *Intradimensional-Extradimensional Shift* (IEDS) component of the Cambridge Automated Neuropsychological Test Battery (CANTAB, Fray & Robbins 1999), which teases apart the component processes thought to be tapped by the WCST. The IEDS task (fully described in Geurts, Corbett, & Solomon 2009 and Yearsley, Gaigg, Bowler, et al. 2021 and illustrated in Figure 8.6) consists of a sequence of visual discrimination tasks of increasing difficulty ranging from simple discrimination between two coloured shapes through more complex discriminations requiring the participant to ignore irrelevant material (white line patterns) on the screen. Whilst the earlier stages of the task require participants to shift their attention from one set of coloured shapes to another, i.e. *within* a dimension (intra-dimensional shift: ID), the crucial later stages involve participants having to shift their attention *between* dimensions from coloured shapes to white line patterns and back (extra-dimensional shift: ED). Although the consensus view is that autistic individuals have difficulties with cognitive flexibility and set-shifting as operationalized by this task (e.g. Ozonoff, Cook, Coon, et al. 2004; Kouklari, Tsermentseli, & Monks 2018), there are sufficient conflicting results (e.g. Yerys, Antezana, Weinblatt, et al. 2015; Gooskens, Bos, Mensen, et al. 2019) to warrant some further exploration and reconceptualization of this diversity of outcome. In a review of the area, Geurts et al. (2008) argued that more consideration needs to be given to sample sizes, comorbid conditions such as ADHD and more precise, conceptually based experimental paradigms in order to provide a clearer account of the patterning of EF across age and comorbidities. Geurts et al. (2008) also argue that we need a better understanding of the mechanisms that drive this patterning and how it relates to the broader behavioural profile of ASD (see also Kenworthy, Yerys, Anthony, et al. 2008).

As an example of the kind of study that attempts to respond to Geurts et al's observations, Hogeveen, Krug, Elliott, et al. (2018) compared children with ASD and typical development on parent reports of attention problems (*Child Behavior* Checklist: CBCL; Achenbach & Rescorla 2001) and restricted and repetitive behaviours (*Repetitive Behavior Scale – Revised:* RBS-R; Bodfish, Symons, & Lewis 1934) and an experimental measure, the *Continuous Performance Task* (AX-CPT, Chatham, Frank, & Munakata 2009). This last task rapidly presents children cue–response sequences where, in 70% of trials, when the child sees picture 'A' followed by picture 'X' they press the 'target' button. If 'A' is followed by 'Y' (10% of trials) or 'B' followed by 'X' or 'Y' (10% each), they should press the 'non-target' button. Their hypothesis was that autistic participants should show diminished *proactive control* (slower reaction times and higher error rates on AY trials compared to all other trial types) and that this would correlate with the clinical features measured by the RBS-R and the CBCL. Both the reaction time and the error rate data showed no between-groups difference in proactive control but higher levels of proactive control were associated with reduced attention difficulties and, paradoxically, associated with increased RRBs (we would expect high levels of proactive control to predict *reduced* RRBs). Hogeveen et al. speculate that this paradoxical finding might result from a greater difficulty for the autistic participants to modify a well-learned response (AX) in conditions where this has to be modified rapidly.

This study is important for several reasons. The task is very simple, making few demands on the participant. It models the kinds of situations encountered in real life, where existing knowledge has to be deployed rapidly in response to fast-changing circumstances (think of what happens in a social interaction). By showing correlations with 'real-life' measures of the autistic behavioural profile, it points 'upwards' in the scheme outlined in Figures 8.1 and 8.2. The paradoxical association of good task performance and increased RRBs is in fact a strength, as it falsifies one of the authors' predictions, leading to a re-conceptualization that generates further hypotheses. The task also lends itself to more neurally focused investigations (see Gordon, Krug, Wulff, et al. 2021) to explore the brain systems that might be associated with the task. The study also neatly illustrates how an absence of group differences on a variable of interest need not mean the task or measures derived from it are not informative. It is the *patterning* of the data and their relation to other measures that matters.

The importance of the patterning of data is illustrated in another study in which a mathematical model was developed of a measure that we have already discussed – the IEDS task with a view to further testing some of the conclusions that have been drawn about performance on this task. Starting from an a priori analysis of the learning processes necessary for non-random performance on the task, Yearsley et al. (2021) proposed a mathematical model that included the parameters of attention switching, learning from reward and learning from punishment. They then demonstrated that this model could successfully simulate the kinds of performance we would predict under particular parameter configurations, for example, a performance fall-off at the *Extradimensional Shift* stage when the attention switching parameter is reduced. But parameter manipulation also revealed that high attention switching could also reduce performance in the earlier (*Intradimensional Shift* stages of the task and that poor ED performance could also result from low levels of the learning from punishment parameter, patterns that are not seen in real-life atypical groups. However, when IEDS data from large sample of autistic adults (n = 42) and comparison participants (n = 40) were run through the model, although performance on various task outcome measures did not differ significantly between groups, the best single predictor of task progression in both groups was the learning from punishment parameter, which in turn was correlated with general intelligence in both the ASD and typical comparison group. Yearsley et al. went on to fit existing published data from participants with ASD, schizophrenia and intellectual disability to the model and found broadly similar results to those from their own dataset, namely that learning from punishment significantly predicted progression through the task. Attention switching (or cognitive flexibility), which is traditionally thought to drive autism-related patterns of responding on this task (Westwood et al. 2016) did not significantly predict performance.

The conceptual approach outlined in Yearsley et al.'s study is important because it provides a way of revealing atypicality-specific patterns in underlying processes that are not readily apparent from standard analyses of the data but which may operate even in the absence of group differences in overall performance. What is also clear from Yearsley et al.'s analysis is that processes like reduced learning from punishment appear not to be specific to ASD but are found in other groups such as Intellectual Disability and schizophrenia. The fact that they are readily amenable to investigation at the neural level (Argyelan, Herzallah, Sako, et al. 2020) and can, as in the Hogeveen et al. study described earlier, be correlated with real-life patterns of clinically significant behaviour, leaves open the possibility of trans-diagnostic research that has the potential to gain a comprehensive picture that links neural processes to real-life behaviour across different types of psychological or behavioural differences.

Reflective Exercise

The Hogeveen et al. (2018) and the Yearsley et al. (2020) studies are good examples of how variations in behaviour at one level of analysis can be accounted for by changes at a different level.

It might be helpful to speculate about causal direction here. For example do the 'parameters' identified by Yearsley et al. cause changes in IEDS performance, or is it the latter that causes the former? Or are they both caused by some third factor?

You could also think about ways that these speculations could be tested out empirically?

If measures on any psychological construct are to be of practical value, they must in some way predict everyday patterns of behaviour that are thought to be driven by that construct. In their reviews of EF measures, Geurts et al. (2009) and Kenworthy et al. (2008) lament both the lack of consistency of EF findings in ASD research and the scarcity and unreliability of research that links EF measures with reports of the everyday difficulties faced by autistic individuals. In the preceding paragraphs, we have seen how a lack of group difference might not be so great a problem as might be imagined, and how systematic patterns of variability in task performance might be highly informative. But Kenworthy et al. (2008) make the point that most experimental and many psychometric assessments of EF are carried out either under conditions that are unfeasibly resource- and time-intensive, or that are highly controlled in ways that maximize good performance in autistic individuals and do not mirror the messiness of real life. They propose adopting more 'ecologically valid' methods of assessment and adopt Franzen & Wilhelm's (1995) dimensions of *verisimilitude* – the extent to which task demands mirror those of everyday life and *veridicality* – the extent to which a measure correlates with measures of everyday functioning. Among the ecologically valid measures reviewed is the *Behavioral Assessment of the Dysexecutive Syndrome* (BADS, Wilson, Evans, Emslie, Alderman, & Burgess, 1998), a battery of six tests, some of which are carried out in real-life settings and others which, although carried out in the clinic, closely model real-life problems. The BADS also includes two versions of a dysexecutive questionnaire, one to be completed by the participant, the other by someone who knows the participant well.

A similar questionnaire based measure of EF is the *Behavior Rating Inventory of Executive Functioning* (BRIEF, Gioia, Isquith, Guy, & Kenworthy, 2000), which contains eight clinical scales that can be grouped into a *Metacognition* and a *Behavioral Regulation* index. There are versions that can be administered by parents, teachers, or by the autistic person themselves. Kenworthy et al. (2008), in a review of the measure, conclude that it has both ecological validity and can be used to test hypotheses both about the unitary or fractionable nature of EFs as well as to explore possible underlying reasons for particular patterns of performance in different participant groups. What is worth noting at this point is the parallel in studies of EF with investigations of mentalizing discussed in an earlier section, where there has been a shift from more precise, lab-based, experimental measures of the constructs under consideration to quicker, broader, some would say less precise measures that are more appropriate to an everyday context. What needs to be kept in mind is the nature of what is being measured by the two approaches and how this can be understood within the broader conceptual framework outlined in Figures 8.1 and 8.2.

Given the wide variability in the clinical picture of ASD as currently defined, it is perhaps not surprising that there is considerable diversity of EF findings in this group. Nonetheless, there are EFs such as planning, set-shifting and perseveration that pose widespread difficulties across the spectrum (Pennington & Ozonoff 1996; Russell 1997; Hill 2004a, b; Demetriou et al. 2018; Xie et al. 2021) and others, such as inhibition which seem to be broadly intact even if there are circumstances, such as on a complex task, where they can be elicited (see van den Bergh, Scheeren, Begeer, Koot, & Geurts 2014). There are multiple reasons for inconclusive sets of experimental findings ranging from poor conceptualization of the parameter being measured, through poor operationalization of the function in terms of experimental task, to participant factors such as level of global intellectual ability or capacity to use compensatory strategies which can lead to similar behavioural outcomes using different underlying mechanisms. We have seen from the previous paragraph that it is also important to keep in mind the sometimes contrasting requirements of real-life or applied research and laboratory-based investigations. Applied research tends to want measures of executive processes that yield outputs that enable the identification of everyday areas of difficulty and possible ways of remediating them. Laboratory-based research can contrast with this approach, being more focused on the conceptualization of underlying constructs and their identification by means of highly controlled experiments that sometimes have the unintended consequences of eliminating the messiness and complexity that gives rise to the difficulties in the first place. Recent developments, such as mathematical modelling, may well help to increase the overlap between these two approaches by placing less emphasis on the need to find 'differences' and 'deficits' and use performance variability to build a better picture of underlying processes that drive executive behaviour. Such an approach has the additional advantage of helping us to situate autistic difference in a framework such as the RDoC (Cuthbert & Insel 2013; Mandy 2018) that cuts across different patterns of behavioural difference.

Accounts in Terms of Sensory, Perceptual, and Conceptual Organization and Coherence

Many first-hand accounts by autistic people themselves describe heightened sensory sensitivity, sensory overload, and distortion (Williams 1994; Grandin 2005). The current version of the *Diagnostic and Statistical Manual* (DSM-5) describes unusual responses to or interest in sensory aspects of the environment, echoing the observations of clinicians going right back to Kanner (Kanner 1943; Talay-Ongan & Wood 2000). Kanner also noted a strong tendency to attend to details and ignore the higher level meanings of stimuli, especially in relation to their context, a conclusion that was confirmed empirically by Hermelin and O'Connor (1970) who concluded from a large programme of empirical work that autistic children sometimes had difficulty encoding stimuli meaningfully. More recent reviews of the clinical and experimental literature on autistic individuals' tendency to respond atypically to sensory stimuli (Happé & Frith 2006; Takayanagi, Kawasaki, Shinomiya, et al. 2021; Van der Hallen, Chamberlain, de-Wit, & Wagemans 2018) conclude that although some findings have been robustly replicated, others are more sensitive to minor procedural variations across studies.

Among the more robustly replicated phenomena are those related to so called 'islets of ability' (Lockyer & Rutter 1970), which have been interpreted as manifestations of autistic individuals' superior processing of spatially organized material (DeMeyer, Barton, Alpern, et al. 1974) and which contribute to uneven profiles of performance on psychometric tests[5] (see Dawson, Soulières, Gernsbacher, & Mottron 2007; Soulières, Dawson, Gernsbacher, & Mottron 2011 for further discussion). Islets such as peaks in performance on the *Children's Embedded Figures Test* (Witkin, Oltman, Raskin, et al. 1971), the Block Design sub-test of the *Wechsler Intelligence Scale for Children* (see Figure 8.7a and 8.7b for illustrations of the kinds of stimuli used in these tasks) and *Homograph Reading* (Happé 1997; Leekam & Lopez 2003) have produced robust autism-related effects and continue to be canonical reference points in this area (Happé & Frith 2006; Van der Hallen et al. 2018; Takayanagi et al. 2021).

The Children's Embedded Figures Test measures the time it takes a child to identify a simpler shape within a larger, more complex shape; autistic children have been shown to be both faster and more accurate on the task (Shah & Frith 1983). In the Block Design test, participants have to reproduce a complex geometric pattern using blocks that contain fragments of that pattern. Shah and Frith (1993) confirmed autistic children's on-average superior performance on this task and showed that pre-segmenting the target pattern did not enhance the performance

---

[5] These islets can sometimes amount to savant syndrome, which is more prevalent in the autistic than in the general population (Howlin, Goode, Hutton, & Rutter 2009). Although it forms part of the general, layperson's stereotype of autism – the central character played by Dustin Hoffman in the 1988 film *Rain Man* was an autistic savant with exceptional calculation skills – its relative rarity should make us cautious about using it as a model for autistic functioning more generally.

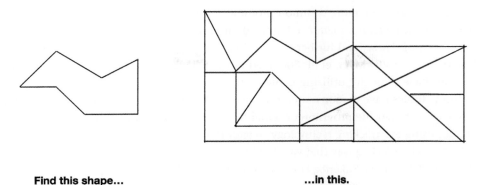

Find this shape... ...in this.

Figure 8.7a Embedded figures task

Source: Author's own drawing based on descriptions given in Witkin et al. (1971).

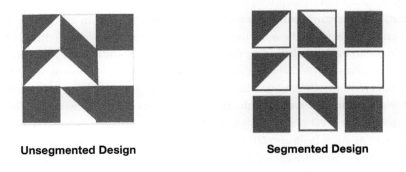

Unsegmented Design   Segmented Design

Blocks

Figure 8.7b Segmented and unsegmented versions of the block design task

Source: Authors own drawing based on descriptions given in Shah and Frith (1993).

of the autistic children in the same way as for the typical children, concluding that autistic children seemed to be able to pre-segment the target image in a way that the typical children could not. The Homograph Reading test measures the extent to which children can appropriately pronounce words that have the same spelling (e.g. *lead*) but have different pronunciation depending on the context (taking the dog for a walk vs a heavy weight). Whereas autistic children tend to give the more common pronunciation, regardless of context, providing the context before the target homograph eliminated this difference (Frith & Snowling 1983; Snowling & Frith 1986). These, and further studies (Jolliffe & Baron-Cohen 1997; López & Leekam 2003; Burnette, Mundy, Myer, et al. 2005) led to the widespread conclusion that individuals with autism have difficulty utilizing context to regulate their ongoing behaviour. However, more recent studies have demonstrated that autistic difficulties in homograph reading could be attenuated through the provision of semantic primes (Hala, Pexman, & Glenwright 2007) and studies using eye tracking technology suggest that autistic individuals alter their reading strategies in such tasks in a way that variably influences their susceptibility to the effect (Brock and Bzishvili 2013; Brock, Sukenik, & Friedmann 2017; Roch, Cain, & Jarrold 2021). Roch et al. (2021) used eye-tracking methodology to show that the task was more complex than earlier researchers had suspected, even for typically developed individuals.

The large number of empirical studies that have flowed from the clinical observations of atypical perceptual and conceptual processing in autism has led to several attempts to develop a systematic theoretical formulation with greater power to explain the unique patterning of autistic behaviour. Among the most influential of these formulations is Frith's (1989) proposition that autistic cognition, including difficulty with understanding other minds, resulted from *Weak Central Coherence* (WCC) or a diminished drive to integrate diverse sources of information into coherent, meaningful wholes. Having WCC meant that an autistic individual would have difficulty 'seeing the wood for the trees'. WCC can operate across a range of phenomena ranging from lower-level perceptual organization such as visual illusions (Happé 1996; Manning, Morgan, Allen, & Pellicano 2017) or face perception (Stanti, Ichijo, Catmur, & Bird 2021) through to higher level conceptual material such as narrative comprehension (Nuske & Bavin 2011) and concept formation (Mercado, Chow, Church, & Lopata 2020).

Frith's initial formulation of WCC (Frith 1989) as asserting that autistic people hardly ever saw the 'big picture' was re-worked into an account that spoke of a detail-focused 'cognitive style' that can account for many of the non-social atypicalities (both strengths *and* weaknesses) seen in autistic individuals (Frith & Happé 1994; Frith 2003; Happé & Frith 2006). According to this account, WCC as a cognitive style is considered to be independent of 'Theory of Mind' although it may contribute to social difficulties because detail focus may lead to atypical perceptions of objects such as faces (Nomi & Uddin 2015) or situations. Such atypical reactions can sometimes be interpreted by a neurotypical observer as odd or different.

The advantage of WCC theory was that it provided a falsifiable[6] framework to drive research that was hitherto based on clinical observations and anecdotes relating to ASD-related atypical

---

[6] The philosopher Karl Popper (Popper, 1965) argued that science is not just about gathering evidence in support of a proposition; to be scientific, propositions should be falsifiable, i.e. have the potential to be proved wrong. He cites the proposition 'all swans are white' as an example. No matter how many white swans are observed, doubt will still remain about the truth of the proposition. But observing a single black swan can show it to be false. Observing a black swan forces us to revise our theory of swans, thereby progressing our knowledge.

sensory and perceptual processes. Other research began to yield results that placed constraints on the predictive power of WCC theory. Plaisted, O'Riordan, & Baron-Cohen (1998a) used WCC theory to predict diminished performance by autistic children on a *conjunctive visual search* task, which measured a speed of target identification in an array when the target combines the features of the other elements of the array. Imagine a matrix of red letters S and T and green letters X. Participants were asked to locate the single red coloured X – i.e. that consists of a *conjunction* of the features of the other stimuli (the letter value of the X and the colour of the Ss and Ts). However, contrary to the predictions of WCC theory, Plaisted and colleagues' autistic children were significantly faster at this task. In another experiment, Plaisted, O'Riordan, and Baron-Cohen (1998b) taught children with and without autism to learn to discriminate between pairs of patterns of circles. Their capacity to discriminate was then assessed on new stimuli that were related to those they were first trained on as well as on new stimuli that were unrelated to those. Whereas typical, comparison children's discrimination performance was higher on the related stimuli (i.e. they benefited from prior exposure) that of the autistic children did not. Plaisted et al. argued that this was because the autistic children, because of their enhanced capacity for perceptual discrimination, were not sufficiently aware of the similarity between the related stimuli to those used in the initial training and so did not benefit from that training. These and other findings led to a formulation of autistic difficulty in terms of *reduced generalization* and *enhanced discrimination*.

A parallel approach to the opposition between detail focus and the 'bigger picture' that is central to WCC theory has proposed that autistic people experience difficulty in structuring stimuli hierarchically; their difficulty is one of *hierarchization* (Mottron, Burack, Iarocci, Belleville, & Enns, 2003; Deruelle, Rondan, Gepner, & Fagot 2006; Soroor, Mokhtari, & Pouretemad 2021). An example of hierarchically organized stimuli are those developed by Navon (1977) and illustrated in Figure 8.8. Navon figures consist of large symbols (in this case the letters A and H made up of smaller symbols that could be either the same as or different from the larger symbol). When participants rapidly presented with one of the items in Figure 8.8 are asked to identify whether or not a particular letter is present, neurotypical participants are slower at identifying the local letter when the global letter is different (i.e. when they are asked if the letter 'H' is there when a large 'A' made up of small 'H's is presented). Although WCC theory would predict that this *global interference* should be less in evidence in ASD, the data are contradictory. In a meta-analysis of 56 studies, Van der Hallen, Evers, Brewaeys, et al. (2015) did not identify either enhanced local nor diminished global processing in ASD groups but they did find that ASD participants were reliably slower at processing information at the global level, particularly in circumstances where there was conflicting information at the local level. This and other meta-analyses (e.g. Muth, Hönekopp, & Falter 2014) shows that the difficulty with global processing in autistic individuals is relatively small and easily affected by minor procedural differences in different studies. What does emerge however is the sense of an autism-related difficulty in relating information at one level to information at the other. What remains a point of debate, however, is the question of whether autistic individuals have difficulty conceptualizing a global configuration by integrating local elements, as WCC theory advocates, or do they have enhanced or 'hyper-functioning' local processing that results in its taking precedence over the global configuration when a choice needs to be made?

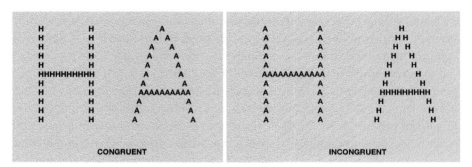

Figure 8.8 Stimuli used in the Navon task

Source: Author's own graphic based on descriptions given in Navon (1977).

This last point highlights the rationale behind a series of alternatives to WCC theory that are grounded in the idea that the fundamental difficulty experienced by autistic individuals is perceptual, that is to say, in the organization of incoming sensory information. *Enhanced Perceptual Functioning Theory* (EPF, Mottron, Dawson, Soulières, Hubert, & Burack, 2006), proposes that autistic individuals' lower-level perceptual functioning is enhanced in a manner that, as it were, out-competes information at the more global level. This theory accounts for findings where autistic individuals have been shown capable of processing information at the global level (Plaisted, Swettenham, & Rees 1999; Koldewyn, Jiang, Weigelt, & Kanwisher 2013) and is also consistent with the conclusions of Van der Hallen et al.'s (2015) meta-analysis described in the last paragraph. An important aspect of these conclusions is that although autistic individuals *are* capable of processing information at the global level, they often do so only when prompted in some way. An interesting and potentially quite subversive spin-off of the EPF theory is Mottron's (2004) idea of autism as being a 'different intelligence' (*une autre intelligence*). Starting from the block design islet of ability described earlier on, Mottron and his colleagues demonstrate how non-verbal, visuo-spatial measures of intelligence such as the Ravens Matrices (Raven, Raven, & Court 1998) can under estimate the ability of children and adults with autism when compared with more verbal and less visuo-spatial measures such as the Wechsler scales of intelligence (Dawson, Soulières, Gernsbacher, & Mottron 2007) although this might be limited to individuals with a global IQ of more than 85 (Bölte, Dziobek, & Poutska 2009). This characterization of autistic intelligence being rooted to a greater extent in perceptual detail has implications for the way autistic individuals construct an image of the world upon which they base their patterns of adaptive behaviour. The challenge posed by this conceptualization is to marry up what we know about the patterning of adaptive behaviour in autistic individuals with assessments of the extent to which their response to stimuli is locally rather than globally driven.

A more recent set of attempts to see the phenomena of WCC in autism, as well as autistic cognition more generally, as perceptual in nature is based on Bayesian accounts of perceptual processing (Palmer, Lawson, & Hohwy 2017). The broad principle of Bayesian decision theory is that when we are faced with a decision on how to respond to new information, we generally have recourse to *prior* beliefs or representations that have been built up from previous experience of similar pieces of information. Comparison between the incoming information and the prior representation results in a decision either to update the prior, resulting in a reciprocal modification of both the prior and the incoming information or to treat the incoming information as something completely new. Applying these principles to perceptual processing in autism, Pellicano and Burr (2014) argued that although sensory processing per se is not atypical in autism, there is an atypical Bayesian organization of sensations into perceptions through the comparison[7] of the incoming sensory information with the existing prior representation. Autistic people have what Pellicano and Burr call 'hypo-priors', i.e existing representations that have less influence on incoming information, which results in the incoming stimulus being seen 'as it is' rather than being altered to reinforce an existing prior representation. As Brock (2014) observes, Pellicano and Burr's account represents a mathematical formalization of ideas on diminished influence of context on perception that were first set out by earlier researchers such as Rimland's (1964: 179) conclusion that autism resulted from an impaired ability to relate new stimuli to remembered experience, Hermelin and O'Connor's (1970: 129) view of autism as a 'failure to encode stimuli meaningfully' or more recent accounts in terms of diminished top-down processing or sensitivity to context in autism (Ropar & Mitchell 2002; Mitchell, Mottron, Soulières, & Ropar 2010).

Ropar and Mitchell compared the performance of autistic adolescents with moderate intellectual disabilities with that of appropriately matched comparison groups on a task that required them to view a circle that was slanted (thus appearing as an ellipse). Participants had to adjust a shape on a computer screen so that it matched the ellipse that they saw. They did this both before and after seeing that the viewed ellipse was actually a slanted circle. Although both autistic and non-autistic participants tended to exaggerate the 'circularity' of the ellipse, the autistic participants did this to a lesser extent than the other groups even when they knew that the ellipse was a slanted circle. Although Ropar and Mitchell conclude that this finding points to attenuated 'top-down' processing in autism at a perceptual level, they warrant caution about over-generalizing this to a general difficulty with conceptual processing.

Pelicano and Burr's idea that atypical perceptual processing of sensory information lay at the heart of a wide range of atypical autistic cognition has been taken up by several other researchers who have attempted to ground the concepts of Bayesian theory in brain processes (Friston, Lawson, & Frith, 2013; van Boxtel & Lu 2013; van de Cruys et al. 2014; see Palmer

---

[7] The words 'decide', 'compare', or 'evaluate' should not be taken as necessarily implying that these processes are conscious. Indeed, at this level of processing, they are likely to happen without conscious awareness.

et al. 2017 for review). Common to these accounts is the idea of *predictive coding* derived from computational neuroscience, in which the brain is seen as a device that compares the results of what it predicts will happen with what actually happens. Inevitably, this comparison results in *prediction errors* since not all predictions can be completely accurate. This account also proposes that the brain represents the precision of its predictions, which will affect the way in which future predictions operate. Faced with noisy incoming stimuli, predictions that are too broad – which are imprecise – will 'accept' quite a wide range of incoming stimuli as confirming the prediction whereas narrow, over-precise predictions will result in frequent prediction violations causing the organism to respond differently even to quite small stimulus variations. But it is prediction precision that regulates the relative influence of top-down and bottom-up processes in cognition (Friston 2008).

There is currently considerable debate and no easy consensus about whether autism results from reduced or enhanced prediction errors (Friston et al. 2013; Lawson, Rees, & Friston 2014; van de Cruys et al. 2014). However, despite the currently inconclusive state of Bayesian accounts of autism, the overall approach has features that point to its being an advance on earlier frameworks. We have already seen how it is consistent with demonstrations of autistic individuals' behaviour being governed by lower-level perceptual features of their environment rather than by higher-level conceptual abstractions. But in so doing, it has generated an explanatory framework that can be been drawn upon to explain a wider variety of psychological phenomena seen in ASD. These include heightened sensory reactivity (Tavassoli, Bellesheim, Siper, et al. 2016), reduced susceptibility to some visual illusions (Chouinard, Royals, Landry, & Sperandio 2018), restricted and repetitive behaviours (Palmer et al. 2017: 535) intolerance of uncertainty (Wigham, Rodgers, South, McConachie, & Freeston 2015), action prediction (Amoruso, Narzisi, Pinzono, et al. 2019) to name but a few (see Palmer et al. 2017 for further discussion). There is also growing neural evidence that is consistent with aspects of the theory (Coll, Whelan, Catmur, & Bird. 2020). But more importantly, the account is based on a view of brain functioning that reflects an organism's adaptation to its environment. This gives it the potential to help us gain a greater understanding of the development of autistic individuals both over short time periods, such as learning new information in a specific task or longer ones in terms of the development of life-span developmental trajectories.

Other Psychological Processes

So far, our discussion has centred on the main psychological formulations specifically aimed at increasing our understanding of autism-characteristic patterns of behaviour. But there are difficulties in other areas of psychological science, such as attention, learning, and memory, which although they are not in any way autism specific difficulties, can show patterns of functioning that help achieve a greater understanding of ASD. Attentional difficulties in the form of *monotropism* – the tendency of an autistic individual to over-focus their attention on one part of their environment to the virtual exclusion of all others – have been suggested by autistic scientists themselves as an account of the different ways they experience the world (Murray, Lesser, & Lawson 2005). The example of punishment sensitivity discussed above in relation to certain EF processes (Yearsley et al. 2021) is another good example of how atypicality in a specific simple learning process can give rise to patterns of task performance characteristic of autism. Ullman and Pullman (2017) have suggested that some autistic individuals may rely on declarative memory to navigate the social world and there is ample evidence that shows atypicalities in this domain (Boucher & Bowler 2008; Boucher et al. 2012; Desaunay et al. 2020). Autistic individuals have a specific pattern of memory performance in which poorer performance relative to typical comparison participants is seen on 'unsupported' memory tasks such as free recall but undiminished performance on 'supported' tasks such as recognition and cued recall. But even intact behavioural performance can be accompanied by atypical neural activity (Gaigg, Bowler, Ecker, et al. 2015; Massand, Jemel, Mottron, & Bowler 2013), a finding that has potential for explaining atypical or unexpected patterns of performance in other areas of functioning. This example provides a testable framework to explore how difficulties with the social world might be driven by atypical memory functioning, which itself might be the result of atypicalities in other areas of functioning such as attention or perception.

The last paragraph has raised two ideas that have been the topic of a lively ongoing discussion in the early 2020s autism literature: the question of compensation (Livingston & Happé 2017) and the related construct camouflaging (Fombonne 2020) and which are also discussed in Chapter 7. Although related, the two constructs should not be completely conflated. In an attempt to account for the well-documented phenomena of 'growing out of the clinical picture of ASD' (Lord, Bishop, & Anderson 2015; Georgiades & Kasari 2018), late diagnosis of autism (implying earlier life compensation for difficulties; Lai & Baron-Cohen 2015) and the lower incidence of autism in women (Loomes, Hull, & Mandy 2017; see also discussion in Chapter 7), Livingston and Happé (2017) define compensation as 'the process contributing to improved behavioural presentation of a neurodevelopmental disorder [sic], despite persisting core deficit(s) [sic] at cognitive and/or neurobiological levels' (p. 739). The discovery by Massand et al. (2013) of intact recognition memory performance in autistic adults accompanied by ERP signals that differed from those of typical individuals is a good example of atypical neural activity resulting in typical behavioural performance. This different operation of a neural configuration that probably operates automatically and without conscious awareness should not be confused with the kinds of deliberate, consciously formulated changes in behaviour in order to 'fit in' that are reported in qualitative studies such as Bernadin, Mason, Lewis, and Kanne's (2021) qualitative account of the self-reports of autistic adolescents. The whole question of the precise nature of compensation and camouflaging, how they should be measured and their degree of overlap is currently a hot topic in autism research (see Lai, Hull, Mandy, et al. 2021; Williams 2021). What is clear, however, is that apparently typical levels of overt performance by autistic individuals, both in real life and on some laboratory tasks, can mask very atypical underlying processes. Moreover when overt performance is atypical, some autistic individuals manage to alter their behaviour so as to stand out less.

The discussion around compensation and camouflaging as well as the wider question of heterogeneity of findings in autism research have highlighted the need for different approaches to understanding the psychological and neuropsychological aspects of autism and its development. If we look again at Figure 8.1, one way to interpret it is simply to see the patterning of behaviour as the 'thing to be explained', preferably in terms of entities at the lower levels[8] in the diagram. These entities can be conceptualized at the cognitive or neural (or lower) level and could be thought of as the 'drivers' of autistic behaviour. On this view, helping autistic individuals would involve a 'find it and fix it' approach. But such an approach needs to be taken cautiously. Just because we find something 'different' does it necessarily have to be fixed? This is not, ultimately a scientific question but one that touches on politics and morality (see Pellicano, Fatima, Hall, et al. 2022 for a further discussion in the context of autism).

As we have seen in the previous paragraphs, although we can re-describe autism-specific patterns of behaviour in terms of a set of constructs such as 'theory of mind' or executive functions or 'central coherence, participants' performance on many of the tasks used to measure these constructs can be accounted for in terms of a different set of broader, lower-level processes such as attention, perception, learning, or memory. This is not to say that we should jettison the first set of concepts in favour of the second, or to try to preferentially instantiate one or other of them at a different hierarchical level. Rather, we should regard concepts from whichever of the two sets as placeholders that have different utility for different purposes and see all of them as manifestations of particular states of a more dynamic system. An example of this can be found in Bowler et al.'s (2005) attempt to re-cast false belief understanding as one of many facets of complex reasoning as formalized by Halford's (1992) account of typical development in terms of relational complexity. Bowler (2007) described the potential of dynamic systems theory (DST; Smith & Thelen 2003) in relation to ASD, ideas that have been taken up at a more neural level of analysis by Johnson and colleagues (Johnson, Gliga, Jones, & Charman 2015a; Johnson, Jones, & Gliga 2015b; Johnson 2017). Johnson, Charman, Pickles, & Jones (2021) have set out a framework based on systems neuroscience (similar to DST; Ahn, Tewari, Poon, & Phillips 2006) to gain a better empirical and conceptual grip on the conduct of prospective and longitudinal studies of neurodevelopmental disorders including ASD. They argue that a whole brain, systems neuroscience perspective, which looks at emergent properties over time gives a better account of the existing evidence, which does not support the idea of simple, mechanistic causal pathways across developmental time. They counsel against the kind of simplistic reductionist approaches which are common in some biomedically oriented quests for intervention targets. As an alternative, Johnson et al. propose a systems neuroscience-based framework to explore the evolution of atypical behaviour over time and outline its application to two often highly co-occurring developmental conditions – attention deficit hyperactivity disorder (AHD) and ASD (Leyfer, Folstein, Bacalman, et al. 2006).

---

[8] Following the way Figure 8.1 is drawn – see footnote 1.

Johnson et al.'s (2021) developmental systems-oriented analysis of developmental disorder has the further advantage of being transdiagnostic. Historically, classification systems based on the medical model have tended to create hermetic categories of psychopathological conditions which meant that scientists tended to focus on explaining 'their' disorder. Indeed, earlier versions of the DSM (III & IV – American Psychiatric Association 1980, 1994) precluded the possibility of a person receiving two diagnoses. Clinicians' intuitions that this is not always possible have now been respected; the DSM-5 (American Psychiatric Association 2013) now allows an individual to be thought of as having both ASD *and* ADHD, for example (see Chapter 7 for more on formal identification). This loosening of the diagnostic boundaries is a reflection of a wider move away from discrete categories and towards formulations in terms of patterns of processes – social, behavioural, cognitive, neural, genetic … that has now been formulated in the Research Domain Criteria framework (RDoC, Cuthbert & Insel 2013). This framework was developed out of a dissatisfaction with existing psychiatric diagnostic categories and although firmly set within a biomedical model, shows a more sophisticated understanding of the systemic nature of the way the different levels of analysis interact that holds considerable promise for our understanding of developmental behavioural difference in general (more detail on RDoC can be found on www.nimh.nih.gov/research/research-funded-by-nimh/rdoc).

SUMMARY

It should be clear from a reading of this chapter and Chapter 7 that both scientific endeavour and clinical practice change over time, and different aspects of these two domains sometimes change at different rates. Attempts to reconcile the behavioural picture of ASD with psychological science have had to respond to theoretical and conceptual changes both in applied practice and in the science of psychology. Over the past six decades we have seen our concept of 'autism' change from a very rare, specific condition of children to a broad spectrum of superficially dissimilar conditions that collectively affect over 1% of the population. Over the same period, the science of psychology has moved in and out of radical behaviourism, cognitivism, cognitive neuropsychology that suggested strict localization of behavioural functions in the brain through to sophisticated mathematical modelling of behavioural and neural functions (for an enlightening summary of some of these issues in the context of autism, see Happé & Frith 2020). Against this background, the present chapter has set out to achieve two broad aims: to give an overview of the main, currently actively researched attempts to account for the patterning of behaviour seen in ASD and to provide a conceptual framework to enable evaluation of these approaches.

You should now have a good grasp of the structure, evidence base and current research status of what have historically become the three canonical attempts to re-describe and explain the clinical pattern of ASD in psychological terms – the 'ToM'/Mentalizing account, the EF account and accounts cast in terms of perceptual and conceptual coherence. Combined with the evaluative framework, you should be able to provide a critical commentary on the strengths and weaknesses of these three accounts.

Additionally, you should be able to outline a growing alternative to the historically dominant theoretical accounts – one that is expressed in terms of systems neuroscience. You should be able to outline its relevance for a more inclusive research programme that is aimed at conceptualizing ASD in a truly developmentally focused way.

REFERENCES

Abell, F., Happé, F., & Frith, U. (2000). Do triangles play tricks? Attribution of mental states to animated shapes in normal and abnormal development. *Cognitive Development*, 15, 1–16.

Achenbach, T. M., & Rescorla, L. (2001). *Manual for the ASEBA School-age Forms and Profiles: An Integrated System of Multi-informant Assessment*. Burlington, VT: Research Center for Children, Youth, and Families.

Ahn, A. C., Tewari, M., Poon, C.-S., & Phillips, R. S. (2006). The limits of reductionism in medicine: Could systems biology offer an alternative? *PLoS Medicine*, 3, e208.

American Psychiatric Association (1980). *Diagnostic and Statistical Manual of Mental Disorders (3rd edn)*. Washington, DC: American Psychiaric Association.

American Psychiatric Association (1994). *Diagnostic and Statistical Manual of Mental Disorders (4th edn). Text Revised*. Washington, DC.

American Psychiatric Association (2013). *Diagnostic and Statistical Manual of Mental Disorders (5th edn)*. Washington, DC: American Psychiatric Association.

Amoruso, L., Narzisi, A. Pinzino, M. et al. (2019). Contextual priors do not modulate action prediction in children with autism. *Proceedings of the Royal Society, B, 286,* 20191319.

Argyelan, M., Herzallah, M., Sako, W. et al. (2020). Dopamine modulates striatal response to reward and punishment in patients with Parkinson's disease: a pharmacological challenge fMRI study. *Neuroreport*, 29, 532–540.

Ashwin, C., Baron-Cohen, S., Wheelwright, S., O'Riordan, M., & Bullmore, E. T. (2007). Differential activation of the amygdala and the 'social brain' during fearful face-processing in Asperger Syndrome. *Neuropsychologia*, 45, 2–14.

Baddeley, A. D. (2007). *Working Memory, Thought and Action*. Oxford: Oxford University Press.

Bagby, R. M., Parker, J. D., & Taylor, G. J. (1994). The twenty-item Toronto alexithymia scale–II. Convergent, discriminant, and concurrent validity. *Journal of Psychosomatic Research*, 38(1), 33–40.

Baribeau, D. A., Dupuis, A., Paton, T. A., Hammill, C., et al. (2019). Structural neuroimaging correlates of social deficits are similar in autism spectrum disorder and attention-deficit/hyperactivity disorder: analysis from the POND Network. *Translational Psychiatry*, 9, 72.

Baron-Cohen, S. (1987). Autism and symbolic play. *British Journal of Psychology*, 5, 139–148.

Baron-Cohen, S. (1989). Perceptual role-taking and protodeclarative pointing in autism. *British Journal of Developmental Psychology*, 7, 113–127.

Baron-Cohen, S. (1995). *Mindblindness*. Cambridge, MA.: MIT Press.

Baron-Cohen, S., Campbell, R., Karmiloff-Smith, A., Grant, J., & Walker, J. (1995). Are children with autism blind to the mentalistic significance of the eyes? *British Journal of Developmental Psychology, 13*, 379–398.

Baron-Cohen, S., Leslie, A., & Frith, U. (1985). Does the autistic child have a 'theory of mind'?, *Cognition, 21*, 37–46.

Baron-Cohen, S., Jolliffe, T., Mortimore, C., & Robertson, M. (1997). Another advanced test of theory of mind: evidence from very high functioning adults with autism or Asperger syndrome. *Journal of Child Psychology and Psychiatry and Allied Disciplines, 38*, 813–822.

Baron-Cohen, S., Wheelwright, S., Hill, J., Raste, Y., & Plumb, I. (2001). The 'Reading the Mind in the Eyes' Test revised version: a study with normal adults, and adults with Asperger syndrome or high-functioning autism. *Journal of Child Psychology & Psychiatry, 42*, 241–251.

Bechtel, W. & Wright, C. D. (2009). What is psychological explanation? In J. Symons (ed.), *The Routledge Companion to the Philosophy of Psychology* (pp. 113–130).

Bernadin, C. J., Mason, E., Lewis, T., & Kanne, S. (2021). 'You must become a chameleon to survive': adolescent experiences of camouflaging. *Journal of Autism and Developmental Disorders*, in press.

Berthoz, S., & Hill, E. L. (2005). The validity of using self-reports to assess emotion regulation abilities in adults with autism spectrum disorder. *European Psychiatry, 20*, 291–298.

Berthoz, S., Pouga, L., & Wessa, M. (2011). Alexithymia from the social neuroscience perspective *The Oxford Handbook of Social Neuroscience*. New York: Oxford University Press.

Bird, G., & Cook, R. (2013). Mixed emotions: the contribution of alexithymia to the emotional symptoms of autism. *Translational Psychiatry, 3*, e285.

Bird, G., Press, C., & Richardson, D. C. (2011). The role of alexithymia in reduced eye fixation in autism spectrum conditions. *Journal of Autism and Developmental Disorders, 41*, 1556–1564.

Bird, G., Siliani, G., Brindley, R., White, S., et al. (2010). Empathic brain responses in insula are modulated by levels of alexithymia not autism. *Brain, 133*, 1515–1525.

Bodfish, J. W., Symons, F. J., & Lewis, M. H. (1999). *The Repetitive Behavior Scale*. Morganton, NC: Western Carolina Center Research Reports.

Bölte, S., Dziobek, I., & Poustka, F. (2009). Brief report: the level and nature of autistic intelligence revisited. *Journal of Autism and Developmental Disorders, 39*, 678–682.

Boucher, J. & Bowler, D. M. (eds). (2008). *Memory in Autism*. Cambridge: Cambridge University Press.

Boucher, J., Mayes, A., & Bigham, S. (2012). Memory in autistic spectrum disorder. *Psychological Bulletin, 138*(3), 458–496.

Bowler, D. M. (1992). 'Theory of Mind' in Asperger's syndrome. *Journal of Child Psychology and Psychiatry, 33*, 877–893.

Bowler, D. (2007). *Autism Spectrum Disorders: Psychological Theory and Research*. Chichester, UK: Wiley.

Bowler, D. M., Briskman, J. A. Gurvidi, N., & Fornells-Ambrojo, M. (2005). Autistic and non-autistic children's performance on a non-social analogue of the false belief task. *Journal of Cognition and Development, 6*, 259–283.

Bowler, D. M., Gaigg, S. B., & Lind, S. E. (2011). Memory in autism: binding, self and brain. In I. Roth & P. Rezaie (eds), *The Autism Spectrum: Research Reviews*. Milton Keynes: Open University Press.

Bowler, D. M., & Thommen, E. (2000). Attribution of mechanical and social causality to animated displays by children with autism. *Autism, 4*, 147–171.

Brewer, N., Young, R. L., & Barnett, E. (2017). Measuring Theory of Mind in adults with autism spectrum disorder. *Journal of Autism and Developmental Disorders, 47*, 1927–1941.

Brock, J. (2014). Combining the old and the new: Bayesian and predictive coding accounts of autistic cognition. *The Psychologist, 27*, 750–753.

Brock, J. & Bzishvili, S. (2013). Deconstructing Frith and Snowling's homograph-reading task: implications for autism spectrum disorders. *Quarterly Journal of Experimental Psychology, 66*, 1764–1773.

Brock, J., Sukenik, N., & Friedman, N. (2017). Individual differences in autistic children's homograph reading: evidence from Hebrew. *Autsm and Developmental Language Impairments, 2*, 1–10.

Burnette, C. P., Mundy, P. C., Meyer, J. A., et al. (2005). Weak central coherence and its relation to theory of mind and anxiety in autism. *Journal of Autism and Developmental Disorders, 35*, 63–73.

Charman, T., & Baron-Cohen, S. (1992). Understanding drawings and beliefs: a further test of the metarepresentation theory of autism. *Journal of Child Psychology and Psychiatry, 33*, 1105–1112.

Chatham, C. H., Frank, M. J., & Munakata, Y. (2009). Pupillometric and behavioral markers of a developmental shift in the temporal dynamics of cognitive control. *Proceedings of the National Academy of Sciences of the United States of America, 106*, 5529–5533.

Chouinard, P. A., Royals, K. A., Landry, O., & Sperandio, I. (2018). The Shepard illusion in reduced in children with an autism spectrum disorder because of perceptual rather than attentional mechanisms. *Frontiers in Psychology, 9*, 2452.

Chung, Y. S., Barch, D., & Strube, M. (2014). A meta-analysis of mentalizing impairments in adults with schizophrenia and autism spectrum disorder. *Schizophrenia Bulletin, 40*, 602–616.

Coll, M-P., Whelan, E., Catmur, C., & Bird, G. (2020). Autistic traits are associated with atypical precision-weighted integration of top-down and bottom-up neural signals. *Cognition, 199*, 104236.

Cook, R., Brewer, R., Shah, P., & Bird, G. (2013). Alexithymia, not autism, predicts poor recognition of emotional facial expressions. *Psychological Science, 24*, 723–732.

Cuthbert, B. N., & Insel, T. R. (2013). Toward the future of psychiatric diagnosis: the seven pillars of RDoC. *BMC Medicine, 11*, 126.

Damasio, A. R., & Maurer, R. G. (1978). A neurological model for childhood autism. *Archives of Neurology, 35*, 777–786.

Dawson, M., Soulières, I., Gernsbacher, M. A., & Mottron, L. (2007). The nature and level of autistic intelligence. *Psychological Science, 18*, 657–662.

DeMeyer, M., Barton, S., Alpern, G. D., Kimberlin, C., Allen, J., Yang, E., & Steele, R. (1974). The measured intelligence of autistic children. *Journal of Autism and Childhood Schizophrenia, 4*, 42–60.

Demetriou, E. A., Lampit, A., Quintana, D. S., Naismith, S. L., Song, Y. J. C., Pye, J. E., … Guastella, A. J. (2018). Autism spectrum disorders: A meta-analysis of executive function. *Molecular Psychiatry*, *23*, 1198–1204.

Deruelle, C., Rondan, C., Gepner, B., & Fagot, J. (2006). Processing of compound visual stimuli by children with autism and Asperger syndrome. *International Journal of Psychology*, *41*(02), 97–106.

Desaunay, P., Briant, A. R., Bowler, D. M., Ring, M., Gérardin, P., Baleyte, J-M., Guénolé, F., Eustache, F., Parienti J. J., & Guillery-Girard, B. (2020). Memory in autism spectrum disorder: A meta-analysis of experimental studies. *Psychological Bulletin*, *146*, 377–410.

Downes, J. J., Roberts, A. C., Sahakian, B. J., Evenden, J. L., Morris, R. G., & Robbins, T. W. (1989). Impaired extra-dimensional shift performance in medicated and unmedicated Parkinson's disease: Evidence for a specific attentional dysfunction. *Neuropsychologia*, *27*, 1329–1343.

Fodor, G. (1983). *The Modularity of Mind*. Cambridge, Mass: MIT Press.

Fodor, G. (2000). *The Mind Doesn't Work That Way: The Scope and Limits of Computational Psychology*. Cambridge, Mass: MIT Press.

Fombonne, E. (2020). Editorial: camouflage and autism. *Journal of Child Psychology and Psychiatry*, *61*, 735–738.

Franzen, M. D., & Wilhelm, K. L. (1996). Conceptual foundations of ecological validity in neuropsychology. In R. J. Sbordone, & C. J. Long (eds), *Ecological Validity of Neuropsychological Testing* (pp. 91–112). Delray Beach: GR, St Lucie.

Fray, P. J., & Robbins, T. W. (1999). CANTAB battery: Proposed utility in neurotoxicology. *Neurotoxicologyand Teratology*, *18*, 499–504.

Friedman, N. P., & Miyake, A. (2017). Unity and diversity of executive functions; individual differences as a window on cognitive structure. *Cortex*, *86*, 186–204.

Friston, K. (2008). Hierarchical models in the brain. *PLoS Comput. Biol.* 4:e1000211.

Friston, K.J., Lawson, R., & Frith, C.D. (2013). On hyperpriors and hypopriors: comment on Pellicano and Burr. *Trends in Cognitive Sciences*, *17*, 1.

Frith, U. (1989). *Autism: Explaining the Enigma*. Oxford: Blackwell.

Frith, U. (2001). Mind blindness and the brain in autism. *Neuron*, *32*, 969–979.

Frith, U. (2003). *Autism: Explaining the Enigma* (2nd edn). Oxford: Blackwell.

Frith, U., & Happé, F. (1994). Autism – beyond theory of mind. *Cognition*, *50*, 115–132.

Frith, U., & Snowling, M. (1983). Reading for meaning and reading for sound in autistic and dyslexic children. *British Journal of Developmental Psychology*, *1*, 329–342.

Frith, U., Morton, J., & Leslie, A. M. (1991) The cognitive basis of a biological disorder: autism. *Trends in Neurosciences*, *14*, 433–438.

Gaigg, S. B., Bowler, D. M., Ecker, C., Calvo-Merino, B., & Murphy, D. (2015). Atypical relational encoding processes contribute to attenuated recollection in autism. *Autism Research*, *8*, 317–327.

Georgiades, S., & Kasari, C. (2018). Reframing optimal outcomes in autism. *JAMA Pediatr. 172*, 716–717.

Geurts, H. M., Corbett, B., & Solomon, M. (2009) The paradox of cognitive flexibility in autism. *Trends in Cognitive Science 13*, 74–82.

Gioia, G. A., Isquith, P. K., Guy, S., & Kenworthy, L. (2000). *BRIEF: Behavior Rating Inventory of Executive Function*. Odessa, FL: Psychological Assessment Resources.

Gooskens, B., Bos, D. J., Mensen, V.T., Shook, D. A., et al. (2019): No evidence of differences in cognitive control in children with autism spectrum disorder or obsessive-compulsive disorder: An fMRI study. *Developmental Cognitive Neuroscience 36*, 100602.

Gordon, A., Krug, M. K., Wulff, R., et al. (2021). Components of executive control in autism spectrum disorder: a functional magnetic resonance imaging examination of dual-mechanism accounts, *Biological Psychiatry: Cognitive Neuroscience and Imaging, 6*, 792–801.

Grandin T. (2005). A personal perspective of autism. In Volkmar, F. R., Paul, R., Klin, A., & Cohen, D. (eds), *Handbook of Autism and Pervasive Developmental Disorders. Volume 3*. New Jersey: Wiley, pp. 1276–1286.

Hala, S., Pexman, P. M., & Glenwright, M. (2007). Priming the meaning of homographs in typically developing children and children with autism. *Journal of Autism and Developmental Disorders, 37*, 329–340.

Halford, G. S. (1992). *Children's Understanding: The Development of Mental Models*. Hillsdale, N.J.: L. Erlbaum.

Happé, F. G. E. (1994). An advanced test of theory of mind: understanding of story characters' thoughts and feelings by able autistic, mentally handicapped and normal children and adults. *Journal of Autism and Developmental Disorders, 24*, 129–154.

Happé, F. G. E. (1995). The role of age and verbal ability in the Theory of Mind task performance of subjects with autism. *Child Development, 66*, 843–855.

Happé, F. G. E. (1996). Studying weak central coherence at low levels: children with autism do not succumb to visual illusions: a research note. *Journal of Child Psychology and Psychiatry, 37*, 873–877.

Happé, F. G. E. (1997). Central coherence and theory of mind in autism: reading homographs in context. *British Journal of Developmental Psychology, 15*, 1–12.

Happé, F. G. E., & Frith, U. (2006). The weak central coherence account: detail-focused cognitive style in autism spectrum disorders. *Journal of Autism and Developmental Disorders, 36*, 5–25.

Happé, F. G. E., & Frith, U. (2020). Annual research review: looking back to look forward – changes in the concept of autism and implications for future research. *Journal of Child Psychology and Psychiatry, 61*, 218–232.

Harms, M. B., Martin, A., & Wallace, G. L. (2010). Facial emotion recognition in autism spectrum disorders: a review of behavioral and neuroimaging studies. *Neuropsychology Review, 20*, 290–322.

Heaton, R. K., Chelune, G. J., Talley, J. L., Kay, G. G., & Curtis, G. (1993). *Wisconsin Card Sorting Test Manual: Revised and Expanded*. Odessa: FL: Psychological Assessment Resources.

Heider, F. & Simmel, M. (1944). An experimental study of apparent behavior. *American Journal of Psychology, 57*, 243–249.

Henry, J. D., Bailey, P. E., von Hippel, C., Rendell, P. G., & Lane, A. (2010). Alexithymia in schizophrenia. *Journal of Clinical and Experimental Neuropsychology, 32*, 890–897.

Hermelin, B. & O'Connor, N. (1970). *Psychological Experiments with Autistic Children*. Oxford: Pergamon Press.

Hermelin, B., & O'Connor, N. (1985). Logico-affective states and nonverbal language. In E. Schopler & G. B. Mesibov (eds), *Communication Problems in Autism*. NY: Plenum Press.

Hill, E. L. (2004a). Executive dysfunction in autism. *Trends in Cognitive Sciences, 8*, 26–32.

Hill, E. L. (2004b). Evaluating the theory of executive dysfunction in autism. *Developmental Review, 24*, 189–233.

Hobson, J. A. & Hobson, R. P. (2007). Identification: the missing link between joint attention and imitation? *Development and Psychopathology, 19*, 411–431.

Hobson, R. P. (1991). Against the theory of theory of mind. *British Journal of Developmental Psychology, 9*, 33–51.

Hobson, R. P. (1993). *Autism and the development of mind*. Hove: Lawrence Erlbaum.

Hobson, R.P. (2002). *The Cradle of Thought*. Oxford: Oxford University Press.

Hobson, R. P. (1993). *Autism and the Development of Mind*. Hove, Sussex: Erlbaum.

Hobson, R. P. (1986). The autistic child's appraisal of expressions of emotion: a further study. *Journal of Child Psychology and Psychiatry, 27*, 671–680.

Hobson, R. P. (2002). *The Cradle of Thought*. London: Macmillan.

Hobson, R. P. & Bishop, M. (2003). The pathogenesis of autism: insights from congenital blindness. *Philosophical Transactions of the Royal Society, London, Series B, 358*, 335–344.

Hogeveen, J., Krug, M. K., Elliott, M. V., et al. (2018). Proactive control as a double-edged sword in autism spectrum disorder. *Journal of Abnormal Psychology, 127*, 429–435.

Howlin P., Goode S., Hutton J., & Rutter, M. (2009). Savant skills in autism: psychometric approaches and parental reports. *Philosophical Transactions of the Royal Society of London. Series B, Biological Sciences. 364 (1522)*, 1359–1367.

Hughes, C., Russell, J., & Robbins, T. W. (1994). Evidence for executive dysfunction in autism. *Neuropsychologia, 32*, 477–492.

Iao, L-S., & Leekam, S. R. (2014). Nonspecificity and theory of mind: new evidence from a nonverbal fals-sign task and children with autism spectrum disorders. *Journal of Experimental Child Psychology, 122*, 1–20.

Jankowski, K. F. & Pfeifer, J. H. (2021). Self-conscious emotion processing in autistic adolescents: Over-reliance on learned rules during tasks with heightened perspective-taking demands may serve as compensatory strategy for less reflexive mentalizing. *Journal of Autism and Developmental Disorders,* online first, January 2021.

Jarrold, C., Boucher, J. & Smith, P. (1993). Symbolic play in autism: a review. *Journal of Autism and Developmental Disorders, 23*, 281–307.

Johnson, M.H. (2017). Autism as an adaptive common variant pathway for human brain development. *Developmental Cognitive Neuroscience, 25*, 5–11.

Johnson, M. H., Charman, T., Pickles, A. & Jones, E. H. (2021). Annual Research Review: Anterior Modifiers in the Emergence of Neurodevelopmental Disorders (AMEND)—a systems neuroscience approach to common developmental disorders. *Journal of Child Psychology and Psychiatry, 62*, 612–630.

Johnson, M. H., Gilga, T., Jones, E., & Charman, T. (2015a). Annual research review: Infant development, autism, and ADHD–early pathways to emerging disorders. *Journal of Child Psychology and Psychiatry, 56*, 228–247.

Johnson, M. H., Jones, E. J., & Gilga, T. (2015b). Brain adaptation and alternative developmental trajectories. *Development and Psychopathology, 27*, 425–442.

Jolliffe, T., & Baron-Cohen, S. (1997). Are people with autism and Asperger syndrome faster than normal on the embedded figures test? *Journal of Child Psychology and Psychiatry, 38*, 527–534.

Jones C.R.G. (2013) Wisconsin Card Sorting Test (WCST). In Volkmar F. R. (eds), *Encyclopedia of Autism Spectrum Disorders*. New York: Springer.

Kanner, L. (1943). Autistic disturbances of affective contact. *Nervous Child, 2*, 217–250.

Kenworthy, L., Yerys, B. E., Anthony, L. G., & Wallace, G. L. (2008). Understanding executive control in autism spectrum disorders in the lab and in the real world. *Neuropsychology Review, 18*, 320–338.

Khalid, S., Deska, J. C., & Hugenberg, K. (2016). The eyes are windows to the mind: direct gaze triggers the ascription of others' minds. *Personality and Social Psychology Bulletin, 42*, 1666–1677.

Kinnaird, E., Stewart, C., & Tchanturia, K. (2019). Investigating alexithymia in autism: A systematic review and meta-analysis. *European Psychiatry, 55*, 80–89.

Koldewyn, K., Jiang, Y. V., Weigelt, S., & Kanwisher, N. (2013). Global/local processing in autism: not a disability, but a disinclination. *Journal of Autism and Developmental Disorders, 43*, 2329–2340.

Kouklari, E. C., Tsermentseli, S., & Monks, C. P. (2018). Everyday executive function and adaptive skills in children and adolescents with autism spectrum disorder: Cross-sectional developmental trajectories. *Autism and Developmental Language Impairments, 3*, 1–16.

Kynast, J., Quinque, E-M., Polyakove, M., et al. (2020). Mindreading from the eyes declines with aging – evidence from 1,603 subjects. *Frontiers in Aging Neuroscience, 12*, 500416.

Lai, M.-C., & Baron-Cohen, S. (2015). Identifying the lost generation of adults with autism spectrum conditions. *Lancet Psychiatry 2*, 1013–1027.

Lai, M-C., Hull, L., Mandy, W., et al. (2021). Commentary: 'Camouflaging' in autistic people – reflection on Fombonne (2020). *Journal of Child Psychology and Psychiatry, 62*, 1037–1041.

Lakens, D. (2013). Calculating and reporting effect sizes to facilitate cumulative science: a practical primer for *t*-tests and ANOVAs, *Frontiers in Psychology*, 2013, 4, 863.

Landry, O. & Al-Taie, S. (2016). A meta-analysis of the Wisconsin card sorting test in autism. *Journal of Autism and Developmental Disorders, 46*, 1220–1235.

Lawson, R. P., Rees, G., & Friston, K. J. (2014). An aberrant precision account of autism. *Frontiers in Human Neuroscience, 8*, 302.

Leekam, S. & Lopez, B. (2003). Do children with autism fail to process information in context? *Journal of Child Psychology and Psychiatry, 44*, 285–300.

Leekam, S., & Perner, J. (1991). Does the autistic child have a metarepresentational deficit? *Cognition, 40*, 203–318.

Leslie, A. M. (1987). Pretense and representation: the origins of 'theory of mind'. *Psychological Review, 94*, 412–426.

Leyfer, O. T., Folstein, S. E., Bacalman, S., Davis, N. O., Dinh, E., et al. (2006). Comorbid psychiatric disorders in children with autism: interview development and rates of disorders. *Journal of Autism and Developmental Disorders, 36*, 849–861.

Li, S. W., Zhang, B., Guo, Y. F., & Zhang, J. P. (2015). The association between alexithymia asassessed by the 20-item Toronto Alexithymia Scale and depression: a meta-analysis. *Psychiatry Research, 227*, 1–9.

Livingston, L. A. & Happé, F. (2017). Conceptualising compensation in neurodevelopmental disorders: reflections from autism spectrum disorder. *Neuroscience and Biobehavioral Reviews, 80*, 729–742.

Lockyer, L. & Rutter, M. (1970) A five to fifteen year follow-up study of infantile psychosis: IV. patterns of cognitive ability. *British Journal of Social and Clinical Psychology, 9*, 152–163.

Loomes, R. Hull, R., & Mandy, W. P. L. (2017). What is the male-to-female ratio in Autism Spectrum Disorder? A systematic review and meta-analysis. *Journal of the American Academy of Child and Adolescent Psychiatry, 56*, 466–474.

Lord, C., Bishop, S., & Anderson, D. (2015). Developmental trajectories as autism phenotypes. *American Journal of Medical Genetics, C, Seminars in Medical Genetics 169*, 198–208.

López, B. & Leekam, S. (2003). Do children with autism fail to process information in context? *Journal of Child Psycology and Psychiatry, 44*, 285–300.

Lord, C., Risi, S., Lambrecht, L., Cook, E. H., Leventhal, B. L., DiLavore, P. C., et al. (2000). The autism diagnostic observation schedule-generic: A standard measure of social and communi- cation deficits associated with the spectrum of autism. *Journal of Autism and Developmental Disorders, 30*(3), 205–223.

Mandy, W. (2018). The Research Domain Criteria: a new dawn for neurodiversity research. *Autism, 22*, 642–644.

Manning, C., Morgan, M. J., Allen, C. T. W., & Pellicano, E. (2017). Susceptibility to Ebbinghaus and Müller-Lyer illusions in autistic children: a comparison of three different methods. *Molecular Autism, 8*, 16.

Marr, D. (1982). *Vision: A Computational Investigation into the Human Representation and Processing of Visual Information.* San Francisco: W. H. Freeman and Company.

Massand, E., Jemel, B., Mottron, L., & Bowler, D. (2013). ERP correlates of recognition memory in autism spectrum disorder. *Journal of Autism and Developmental Disorders, 43*, 2038–2047.

Maynard, D. W., & Turowetz, J. (2019). Doing abstraction: autism, diagnosis and social theory. *Sociological Theory, 37*, 89–116.

Mercado, E., Chow, K., Church, B. A., & Lopata, C. (2020). Perceptual category learning in autism spectrum disorder: truth and consequenes. *Neuroscience and Biobehavioral Reviews, 118*, 689–703.

Mitchell, P., Mottron, L., Soulières, I., & Ropar, D. (2010). Susceptibility to the Shepard illusion in participants with autism: Reduced top-down influences within perception? *Autism Research, 3*, 113–119.

Morton, J., & Frith, U. (1995). Causal modelling: a structural approach to developmental psychopathology: In D. Cicchetti & D. J. Cohen (eds), *Developmental Psychopathology: Theory and Methods.* New York: Wiley, 1, 357–390.

Mottron, L. (2004). *L'autisme: une autre intelligence.* Bruxelles: Mardaga

Mottron, L., Burack, J. A., Iarocci, G., Belleville, S., & Enns, J. T. (2003). Locally oriented perception with intact global processing among adolescents with high-functioning autism: Evidence from multiple paradigms. *Journal of Child Psychology and Psychiatry, 44*(6), 904–913.

Mottron, L., Dawson, M., Soulieres, I., Hubert, B., & Burack, J. (2006). Enhanced perceptual functioning in autism: An update, and eight principles of autistic perception. *Journal of Autism and Developmental Disorders, 36*, 27–43.

Murphy, J., Catmur, C., & Bird, G. (2018). Alexithymia is associated with a multidomain, multidimensional failure of interoception: Evidence from novel tests. *Journal of Experimental Psychology: General, 147*(3), 398.

Murray, K., Johnston, K., Cunnane, H., Kerr, C., et al. (2017). A new test of advanced theory of mind: the 'strange stories film task' captures social processing differences in adults with autism spectrum disorders. *Autism Research, 10*, 1120–1132.

Murray, D., Lesser, M., & Lawson, W. (2005). Attention, monotropism and the diagnostic criteria for autism. *Autism, 9*, 139–156.

Müth, A., Hönekopp, J., & Falter, C. M. (2014). Visuo-spatial performance in autism: a meta-analysis. *Journal of Autism and Developmental Disorders, 44*, 3245–3263.

Navon, D. (1977). Forest before trees: the precedence of global features in visual perception. *Cognitive Psychology, 9*, 353–383.

Nicholson, T. M., Williams, D. M., Carpenter, K., & Kallitsounaki, A. (2019). Interoception is impaired in children, but not adults, with autism spectrum disorder. *Journal of Autism and Developmental Disorders, 49*, 3625–3637.

Nicholson, T. M., Williams, D. M., Grainger, C., Christensen, J. F., Calvo-Merino, B., & Gaigg, S. B. (2018). Interoceptive impairments do not lie at the heart of autism or alexithymia. *Journal of Abnormal Psychology, 127*(6), 612.

Nomi, J. S., & Uddin, L. Q. (2015). Face processing in autism spectrum disorders: from brain regions to brain networks. *Neuropsychologia, 71*, 201–216.

Nuske, H. J., & Bavin, E. L. (2011). Narrative comprehension in 4–7 year old children with autism: testing the weak central coherence account. *International Journal of Language and Communication Disorders, 46*, 108–119.

Muth, A., Hönekopp, J., & Falter, C. M. (2014). Visuo-spatial performance in autism: a meta-analysis. *Journal of Autism and Developmental Disorders, 44*, 3245–3263.

Oakley, B. F. M., Brewer, R., Bird, G., & Catmur, C. (2016). Brief Report: Theory of mind is not theory of emotion: a cautionary note on the Reading the Mind in the Eyes Test. *Journal of Abnormal Psychology, 125*, 818–823.

Olde Dubbelink, L. M. E. & Geurts, H. M. (2017). Planning skills in autism spectrum disorder across the lifespan: a meta-analysis and meta-regression. *Journal of Autism and Developmental Disorders, 47*, 1148–1165.

Oliver, L. D., Moxon-Emre, I., Lai, C., et al. (2021). Social-cognitive performance in schizophrenia spectrum disorders compared with autism spectrum disorder: a systematic meta-analysis and meta-regression. *JAMA Psychiatry, 78*, 281–292.

Ozonoff, S., Cook, I., Coon, H., et al. (2004): Performance on Cambridge Neuropsychological Test Automated Battery subtests sensitive to frontal lobe function in people with ASD disorder: evidence from the collaborative programs of excellence in autism network. *Journal of Autism and Developmental Disorders, 34*, 139–150.

Palmer, C. J., Lawson, R. P., & Hohwy, J. (2017). Bayesian approaches to autism: towards volatility, actin and behavior. *Psychological Bulletin, 143*, 521–542.

Pellicano, E., & Burr, D. (2012). When the world becomes 'too real': A Bayesian explanation of autistic perception. *Trends in Cognitive Sciences, 16,* 504–510.

Pellicano, E, Fatima, Hall, G., Heyworth, M., Lawson, W., Lilley, R., Mahony, J., & Stears, M. (2022). A capabilities approach to understanding and supporting autistic adulthood. *Nature Reviews Psychology, 1,* 624–639.

Pelphrey, K. A., Morris, J. P., McCarthy, G., & Labar, K. S. (2007). Perception of dynamic changes in facial affect and identity in autism. *Social Cognitive and Affective Neuroscience, 2,* 140–149.

Pennington, B. F., & Ozonoff, S. (1996). Executive function and developmental psychopathology. *Journal of Child Psychology and Psychiatry, 37,* 51–87.

Perner, J., & Wimmer, H. (1986). 'John *thinks* that Mary *thinks* that...' attribution of second-order beliefs by 5–10 year old children, *Journal of Experimental Child Psychology, 39,* 437–471.

Plaisted, K. C., O'Riordan, M. A. F., & Baron-Cohen, S. (1998a). Enhanced visual search for a conjunctive target in autism: a research note. *Journal of Child Psychology and Psychiatry, 39,* 777–783.

Plaisted, K. C., O'Riordan, M., & Baron-Cohen, S. (1998b). Enhanced discrimination of novel, highly similar stimuli by adults with autism during a perceptual learning task. *Journal of Child Psychology and Psychiatry, 39,* 765–775.

Plaisted, K., Swettenham, J., & Rees, L. (1999). Children with autism show local precedence in a divided attention task and global precedence in a selective attention task. *The Journal of Child Psychology and Psychiatry and Allied Disciplines, 40,* 733–742.

Popper, K. (1965). *Conjectures and Refutations: The Growth of Scientific Knowledge.* New York: Basic Books.

Raven J, Raven J. C., & Court J. H. (1998) *Standard Progressive Matrices. Raven Manual.* Oxford: Oxford Psychologists Press.

Rimland, B. (1964). *Infantile Autism: The Syndrome and Its Implication for a Neural Theory of Behavior.* London: Methuen.

Roberts, A. C., Robbins, T. W., & Weiskrantz, L. (eds) (1998) *The Prefrontal Cortex; Executive and Cognitive Functions.* Oxford: Oxford University Press.

Roch, M., Cain, K., & Jarrold, C. (2021). Reading for comprehension in individuals with Down syndrome, autism spectrum disorder and typical development: similar or different patterns of ability? *Brain Sciences, 11,* 828.

Rochat, P., Morgan, R., & Carpenter, M. (1997). Young infants' sensitivity to movement information specifying social causality. *Cognitive Development, 12,* 441–465.

Ropar, D. & Mitchell, P. (2002). Shape constancy in autism: the role of prior knowledge and perspective cues. *Journal of Child Psychology and Psychiatry, 43,* 647–653.

Russell, J. (1997). *Autism as an Executive Disorder.* Oxford: Oxford University Press.

Schandry, R. (1981). Heart beat perception and emotional experience. *Psychophysiology, 18*(4), 483–488.

Scheerer, N. E., Boucher, T. Q., & Iarocci, G. (2021). Alexithymia is related to poor social competence in autistic and non-autistic children. *Autism Research, 14,* 1252–1259.

Shah, A., & Frith, U. (1983). An islet of ability in autism: a research note. *Journal of Child Psychology and Psychiatry, 24,* 613–620.

Shah, A., & Frith, U. (1993). Why do autistic individuals show superior performance on the block design task? *Journal of Child Psychology and Psychiatry, 34,* 1351–1364.

Shallice, T. (1982). Specific deficits in planning. *Philosophical Transactions of the Royal Society of London, 298,* 199–209.

Sigman, M. D., Kasari, C., Kwon, J. H., & Yirmiya, N. (1992). Responses to the negative emotions of others by autistic, mentally retarded, and normal children. *Child Development, 63,* 796–807.

Skinner, B. F. (1938). *The Behavior of Organism: A Scientific Analysis.* New York: Appleton-Century.

Skinner, B. F. (1954). *Science and Human Behavior.* New York: Simon & Schuster.

Smith, L. B., & Thelen, E. (2003). Development as a dynamic system. *Trends in Cognitive Science, 7,* 343–348.

Snowling, M., & Frith, U. (1986). Comprehension in hyperlexic readers. *Journal of Experimental Chld Psychology, 42,* 392–415.

Soroor, G., Mokhtari, S. & Pouretemad, H. (2021). Priming global processing strategy improves the perceptual performance of children with autism spectrum disorders. *Journal of Autism and Developmental Disorders,* in press.

Soulières, I., Dawson, M., Gernsbacher, M. A., & Mottron, L. (2011). The nature and level of autistic intelligence II: what about Asperger syndrome? PLoS One, 6(9), e25372.

Stanti, M., Ichijo, E., Catmur, C., & Bird, G. (2021). Face memory and face perception in autism. *Autism.* In press.

Stuss, D. T., & Knight, R. T. (2002). *Principles of Frontal Lobe Function.* Oxford: Oxford University Press.

Takayanagi, M., Kawasaki, Y., Shinomiya, M., et al. (2021). Review of cognitive characteristics of autism spectrum disorder using performance on six subtests on four versions of the Wechsler Intelligence Scale for Children, *Journal of Autism and Developmental Disorders,* Online, March 2021

Talay-Ongan, A & Wood, K. (2000). Unusual sensory sensitivities in autism: A possible crossroads. *International Journal of Disability, Development, and Education, 47,* 201–211.

Tavassoli, T, Bellesheim, K, Siper, P. M., et al. (2016). Measuring sensory reactivity in autism spectrum disorder: application and simplification of a clinician-administered sensory observation scale. *Journal of Autism and Developmental Disorders, 46,* 287–293.

Toth, K., Munson, J., Meltzoff, A. N., & Dawson, G. (2006). Early predictors of communication development in young children with autism spectrum disorder: Joint attention, imitation, and toy play. *Journal of Autism and Developmental Disorders,* 36(8), 993–1005.

Uljarevic, M., & Hamilton, A. (2013). Recognition of emotions in autism: a formal meta-analysis. *Journal of Autism and Developmental Disorders, 43,* 1517–1526.

Ullman, M. T., & Pullman, M. Y. (2015). A compensatory role for declarative memory in neurodevelopmental disorders. *Neuroscience and Biobehavioral Revews, 51,* 205–222.

van Boxtel, J. J. A., & Lu, H. (2013). Impaired global, and compensatory local, biological motion processing in people with high levels of autistic traits. *Frontiers in Psychology, 4,* 209.

Van de Cruys, S., Evers, K., Van der Hallen, R., Van Eylen, L., Boets, B., de-Wit, L., & Wagemans, J. (2014). Precise minds in uncertain worlds: Predictive coding in autism. *Psychological Review, 121,* 649–675.

Van den Bergh, S. F. W. M., Scheeren, A. M., Begeer, S., Koot, H. M., & Geurts, H. M. (2014). Age related differences in executive functioning problems in everyday life of children and adults in the autism spectrum. *Journal of Autism and Developmental Disorders, 44,* 1959–1971.

Van der Hallen, R., Evers, K., Brewaeys, K., Van den Noortgate, W. & Wagemans, J. (2015). Global processing takes time: a meta-analysis on local-global visual processing in ASD. *Psychological Bulletin, 141*, 549–573.

Van der Hallen, R., Chamberlain, R, de-Wit, L., & Wagemans, J. (2018). Superior disembedding in children with ASD: new tests using abstract, meaningful and 3D contexts. *Journal of Auitsm and Developmental Disorders, 48*, 2478–2489.

Westwood, H., Stahl, D., Mandy, W. & Tchanturia, K. (2016). The set-shifting profiles of anorexia nervosa and autism spectrum disorder using the Wisconsin Card Sorting Test: a systematic review and meta-analysis. *Psychological Medicine, 46*, 1809–1827.

White, S., Coniston, D., Rogers, R., & Frith, U. (2011). Developing the Frith-Happé animations: a quick and objective test of Theory of Mind for Adults with Autsim. *Autism Research, 4*, 149–154.

White, S., Hill, E., Happé, F., & Frith, U. (2009). Revisiting the strange stories: revitalizing mentalizing impairments in autism. *Child Development, 80*, 1097–1117.

Wigham, S., Rodgers, J., South, M., McConachie, H., & Freeston, M. (2015). The interplay between sensory processing abnormalities, intolerance of uncertainty, anxiety and restricted and repetitive behaviours in autism spectrum disorder. *Journal of Autism and Developmental Disorders, 45*, 943–952.

Williams D. (1994). *Somebody Somewhere*. New York: Doubleday.

Williams, D., Bowler, D. M., & Jarrold, C. (2012). Inner speech is used to mediate short-term memory, but not planning, among intellectually high-functioning adults with autism spectrum disorder. *Development and Psychopathology, 24*, 225–239.

Williams, D., & Happé, F. (2010). Recognising social and non-social emotions in self and others: a study of autism. *Autism, 14*, 285–304.

Williams, Z. J. (2021). Commentary: the construct validity of 'camouflaging' in autism: psychometric considerations and recommendations for future research – reflection on Lai et al. (2020). *Journal of Child Psychology and Psychiatry,* in press.

Wilson, B. A., Evans, J. J., Emslie, H., Alderman, N., & Burgess, P. (1998). The development of an ecologically valid test for assessing patients with a dysexecutive syndrome. *Neuropsychological Rehabilitation, 8*, 213–288.

Wimmer, H. & Perner, J. (1983). Beliefs about beliefs: representation and constraining function of wrong beliefs in young children's understanding of deception. *Cognition, 13*, 103–128.

Witkin, H. A., Oltman, P. K., Raskin, E., & Kapp, S. (1971). *A manual for the Embedded Figures Test*. Consulting Psychologists Press, California.

World Health Organisation. (2018). *International Classification of Diseases – 11th Edition*. Geneva: WHO.

Xie, R., Sun, X., Yang, L., & Guo, Y. (2021). Characteristic executive dysfunction for high-functioning autism sustained to adulthood. *Autism Research, 13*, 2102–2121.

Yearsley, J. M., Gaigg, S. B., Bowler, D. M., Ring, M., & Haenschel, C. (2021). What can performance on the IEDS task tell us about attention shifting in clinical groups? *Autism Research, 14*, 1237–1251.

Yerys, B. E., Antezana, L., Weinblatt R., et al. (2015). Neural correlates of set-shifting in children with autism. *Autism Research 8*, 386–397.

Yi, Z. Q., Zhao, P. W., Zhang, H., et al. (2020). Theory of mind in Alzheimer's disease and amnestic mild cognitive impairment: a meta-analysis. *Neurological Sciences, 41*, 1027–1039.

9
LANGUAGE AND COMMUNICATION

> ### Learning Objectives
>
> After reading this chapter, you should be able to:
>
> - Understand the distinctions between communication and language and their importance for people with ID
> - Learn about communication skill acquisition in ID and its implications for early intervention
> - Learn about subsystems of language and their presentations in different ID conditions
> - Learn about effective interventions to support the development of speech, language, and communication in people with ID

Communication is a fundamental aspect of human behaviour. The ability to signal one's thoughts, feelings, knowledge, desires, and other mental states is essential for our relationships with others and to navigate the world around us. Humans use a range of modalities to communicate: spoken words, gestures, eye gaze, and written figures. We use these skills in an infinite number of combinations to convey a vast array of meanings. Communication connects us to others, and it helps us transcend our immediate surroundings through shared meaning and ideas.

In the general population, communication skills are acquired during early childhood in almost seamless ways. Though the processes that support early language and communication are quite complex, most early acquisition takes place through ongoing social interaction without a child's awareness of these processes, and with little effortful intention on the part of the communicators and language users in their environment. However, when the acquisition of communication skills occurs at a slower rate, or when difficulties are observed in specific aspects of language acquisition, the impact on everyday life can be evident, and modifications and supports become important. Many people with ID experience difficulties with the development of language and communication skills. Understanding the nature of these skills is a vital step toward supporting outcomes and well-being in this population.

LANGUAGE VERSUS COMMUNICATION: WHAT IS THE DIFFERENCE?

Though the terms *language* and *communication* are often used interchangeably, they refer to different constructs. Difficulties with language acquisition and difficulties with communication skills necessitate different approaches to intervention and supports for people with ID who may be facing delays in these areas. Before entering into an exploration of language and communication in individuals with ID, a brush up on basic definitions will be helpful.

Communication

Let's begin with the term *communication*. Communication refers to the process of sending meaningful information from one entity to another. It is a broad term that is not limited to humans, or even to the signals that living things send to one another. A remote control sends signals to a television. Cellular phones send information to cell phone towers. These non-human signals can be considered communication, too.

For humans, communication serves as a foundation for the development of social relationships, with the onset of early cries at birth and social smiles during the first few months, both setting our social relationships in motion. Human communication signals come in a wide variety of forms throughout the lifespan. Walking by someone in the hall, looking at them, and waving your hand in their direction is a form of communication. In Western cultures, it signals a warm greeting, especially if accompanied by a facial display that includes flexing your mouth muscles into a smile. Alternatively, if you walk by someone in the hall, look in their direction, and then quickly look down while passing them, you are also sending a clear communicative signal as well, though not necessarily a warm and friendly one. The important issue is that no words need to be exchanged when communicating in this way.

Nonverbal communication in humans is expressed through different parts of our bodies. As humans, we often use eye gaze to communicate. A child can send a signal by looking at their caregiver, looking at something that is interesting to them, and even by alternating their gaze between something of interest and their caregiver (called 'joint attention', which will be discussed later in this chapter). Humans also communicate with their hands through the use of gestures. Gestures can be used to indicate all sorts of things: how large or small something is, where something is across the room, to ask people to be quieter, and to cross our arms in protest. We even gesture with our heads, as in the West one might nod in agreement and shake their head in disagreement. All of this takes place without the use of words, though we often integrate our gestures with words and other communicative forms, like vocalizations and eye gaze. Of course, as humans, one of our distinguishing forms of communication is through words and combinations of words, and we will get to that topic in the next section. But it is important to recognize that words and sentences are just one way to communicate, and the human communication repertoire is far more complicated than combinations of spoken or written words.

Language

If 'communication' refers to the information sent from one entity to another, then what does 'language' refer to? Many scholars describe that language is a system of symbols that humans use to communicate with one another. These symbols take several forms – often they are spoken, though language can be expressed via gesture as well, as in sign language. Humans have evolved to use this symbolic system to communicate an almost infinite range of ideas, thoughts, and perspectives. We can use language to describe what's in our immediate environment, for example, a freshly baked cookie that we are about to eat. But we can also use language to describe outrageous, unlikely, and imaginary ideas, like a castle filled with freshly baked cookies that has a never-ending dipping fountain of milk.

More recently in human history, language became something that could be conveyed through written squiggles and drawings, which we now call letters. Right now, you are visually encoding a set of squiggles on this printed page (or on this computer screen) and interpreting them as standing in for real things out in the world. If I type the word 'elephant', and I ask you to close your eyes and envision an elephant, you can conjure up a mental image of an elephant. All of that took place with the use of symbols – there was no actual elephant that was present in front of you, no one said the word 'elephant' out loud. All that you were presented with was a set of squiggles that English language users agree stands in for a large mammal that has a trunk. All of these ideas were conveyed through symbols on the page, which represented an idea of something that exists in the real world.

Language vs Communication

Why make a distinction between language and communication when learning about people with ID? The answer is that challenges in these areas require different approaches for intervention and support. Difficulties with the development of word combination skills or conjugating present/past tense require a different set of teaching and intervention strategies than difficulties with sharing attention with a social partner. The remarkable and complex nature of communication and language in humans means that a vast range of well-informed and targeted strategies are needed to support these skills in all of their complexity.

COMMUNICATION DEVELOPMENT IN PEOPLE WITH ID

Early Social Communication

The development of communication, and specifically social communication, is a fundamental part of the infant, toddler, and preschool years. Several key milestones are relevant for individuals with ID. The first is what Colwyn Trevarthen and colleagues call the onset of 'primary intersubjectivity' (Trevarthen & Aitken 2001). This is a term that describes the early development of social relatedness between an infant and their early social partners, most often parents and caregivers. The term *intersubjectivity* refers to the ability to share your internal, mental state – your subjective state – with another person. The ability to regard other people as social beings, as opposed to other inanimate objects in their environment, is an essential part of infant communication, however basic it may seem. *Primary* indicates that we are referring to the earliest forms of sharing one's mental state between an infant and a social partner. This usually takes place in the form of face-to-face emotional signalling between an infant and their caregivers, or in a 'dyad'. This dyadic signalling often involves one member of the dyad initiating an exchange by sending an emotional signal, like a smile from a caregiver, with the infant responding with a vocalization or emotional display, which then elicits a response, in a sort of dance. There is a turn-taking element to this process that reflects the infant's recognition that they are sending and receiving signals with another person.

In typical development, these signalling skills usually emerge between the ages of 3–6 months. In some children who later receive a diagnosis of ID, the onset of these skills can be delayed. In children with ID who have co-occurring autism spectrum disorder (ASD), the development of intersubjectivity may be an area where early features are observable (Leekam, López, & Moore 2000). The lack of dyadic communication may result from differences in the way an infant orients to social stimuli (Dawson et al. 1998).

After an infant develops face-to-face dyadic communication skills, the next set of early social communication milestones fall under the umbrella of 'secondary intersubjectivity' (Trevarthen & Aitken 2001). These skills generally develop between 9–13 months in infants without disabilities and constitute a change in early communication from face-to-face interactions to communication about objects, people, and events outside of the dyad. It is often referred to as 'triadic' communication, because it involves sending communicative signals between an infant and a social partner about a third entity.

Nonverbal Requesting

Triadic communication has two main categories. In one category, called 'nonverbal requesting', an infant uses their newfound eye contact, gesture, and vocalization skills to achieve a desired end state, or as a means to an end. An infant who wants a toy that is out of reach may point to the toy, look at their caregiver, and vocalize, as if to say '(please) bring that to me.' As they continue to develop these skills, the same infant might alternate their gaze between the toy and the caregiver while pointing at the toy, as if to say, 'here's what I want you to get for me'. Nonverbal requesting is used for regulating others' behaviour, and in many ways, it is one of the earliest forms of problem solving that an infant develops.

Joint Attention

There is another form of triadic communication that is used for entirely different purposes. Rather than using their eye contact, gesture, and vocalization to achieve a desired end state, infants can also use these exact communicative behaviours for the purpose of social sharing, through *joint attention*. An infant who is with a caregiver in the park and observes an interesting creature with wings and a beak that is flying overhead might point to the winged creature, vocalize, and then look at their caregiver. The purpose of this communication is not to get the caregiver to do something about the bird overhead. The infant is not asking the caregiver to go bring the bird to them from the sky. Instead, the goal of this type of triadic communicating is to share an experience with their caregiver, as if to say, 'did you see what I just saw? Are you experiencing what I am experiencing?' In other words, early triadic communication in the form of joint attention serves as a way to include others in one's own experiences.

Secondary intersubjectivity is contingent upon the development of key non-verbal communication forms, including eye contact, gesture, and vocalization. Though they may occur in isolation, for example, vocalizing about a toy or pointing to it, often these three communicative behaviours are integrated together, with an infant pointing to an object, looking at their caregiver and nonverbally vocalizing. Regardless of its form, the ability to bring in others to one's early experiences is the ideal context for so many important early developmental opportunities. In particular, for the purposes of this chapter, joint attention is an important facilitator of language acquisition. Joint attention interactions are often when caregivers provide new labels for objects, which allows an infant to acquire a vocabulary for the things they see and engage with in their environments.

Early Communication in Individuals with ID

Overall developmental delays are often accompanied by delays in communication skill acquisition as well. This means that most children who are later diagnosed with ID likely acquired communication milestones later than TD children. These delays necessitate careful intervention planning to provide young children who are likely to demonstrate ID with opportunities to build early communication foundations and to avoid prolonged early experiences with barriers to communication. However, an additional important consideration is whether some or all early communication skills are more delayed than would be anticipated based on overall developmental status. If this is the case, it may be important to target specific skills more intensively with interventions, and possibly to evaluate a child for co-occurring neurodevelopmental conditions, like ASD.

Learning more about the communication skill acquisition profile associated with various ID-related conditions can help guide education, treatment, and intervention in this population. For example, there is converging evidence suggesting that most children with Down syndrome (DS) meet primary and secondary intersubjective milestones in line with their overall developmental status (Hahn, Brady, & Versaci 2019; Fidler, Philofsky, Hepburn, & Rogers 2005). However, one aspect of triadic communication appears to be more delayed in young children with DS: the onset of nonverbal requesting (Fidler et al. 2005). Toddlers and preschoolers with DS on average demonstrate equivalent amounts of joint attention to their developmentally equated counterparts without DS, but they show fewer nonverbal requesting initiations (Fidler et al. 2005). Because joint attention behaviours generally develop with competence in many children with DS; it is likely that challenges with nonverbal requesting are a reflection of difficulties with the foundations of goal-directed behaviour, and not necessarily difficulties with triadic communication. It is noted here that the profile of stronger joint attention than requesting skills pertains to children with DS who do not have co-occurring ASD.

Other conditions associated with ID are associated with specific patterns of performance in early nonverbal communication. Children with Williams syndrome, a neurogenetic syndrome caused by a microdeletion on chromosome 7, often show difficulties with the acquisition of joint attention, despite strong foundations in early social orienting (Lincoln, Searcy, Jones, & Lord 2007). Though many young children with Williams syndrome show competence in other critical social foundations, like eye contact and sharing their enjoyment with another person via facial display and eye gaze, many show difficulties with the initiation of joint attention with another person (Lincoln et al. 2007). Unlike other children at similar developmental levels, young children with Williams syndrome may not direct their social partner's attention to something of interest, and they may be less likely to show their social partner a toy that they enjoy. This is another example of a complex early communication profile, as was observed in young children with DS; some aspects of early social communication appear to develop with strength in young children with Williams syndrome, while other areas are in need of additional supports.

This exploration of early social communication suggests that young children with neurogenetic syndromes associated with ID can present with a variety of early skills and abilities, and that a one-size-fits-all approach to treatment is less likely to impact outcomes than a more tailored approach. But this work also suggests that there are links between diagnosis and outcomes that can guide intervention and help identify which areas may be in greater need of targeted supports. Using a syndrome-informed approach to early communication intervention may make it possible to monitor development in an anticipatory way and provide early enrichments for areas that appear to be emerging with delays in their earliest manifestations during infancy and toddlerhood.

LANGUAGE DEVELOPMENT IN ID

Language Overview

In the previous section, we learned about early communication milestones. During the first few years of development, children rely on their eyes and hands to communicate with social partners, but in this context, an additional communicative modality is establishing its earliest foundations as well: language.

Language can be thought of as a system because it is formed of many different components that all contribute to its understanding and production. In fact, there are five subsystems of language that are developing in tandem during early typical development as children acquire this skillset. Several of these subsystems, including *phonology*, *morphology*, and *syntax*, involve the development of the forms of language – the ways that we combine sounds, parts of words, whole words, and word combinations to conform to a specific language. The other subsystems, *semantics* and *pragmatics*, primarily involve the development of the meaning conveyed when we use language. Each of these language subsystems contribute critical ingredients to the fluent use of language. Difficulties with the acquisition of one of these subsystems can pose considerable communication challenges to a person with ID.

Phonology

Phonology refers to the rules for the use of sounds that are blended together to formulate spoken utterances. These rules vary from language to language and are generally what makes one language sound different from another. For spoken languages, phonological rules and constraints can be observed on many levels. The first involves the range of speech sounds that are used in a given language. These speech sounds are called 'phonemes', and while many languages share phonemes in common, there is variation in the range of phonemes commonly used across languages (International Phonetic Association 1999). Many languages include phonemes that are produced at the front of the mouth, called bilabials, like *b*, *p*, and *m*. However, some languages feature speech sounds that are found less frequently across languages, like the trill of the *rr* sound in Spanish. Through early exposure to a native language, infants begin to recognize, distinguish, and produce the phonemes that are found in their early environments, and this flexibility becomes more constrained during later childhood.

In addition to the range of speech sounds, or phonemes, that a language possesses, phonology also involves additional components, like the rules regarding how speech sounds are combined to make words in a particular language. Phonology also refers to the prosody, or the melodic contours that we assign to our speech when we talk. We often ignore these nuances, but the intonation and pitch changes that accompany the delivery of spoken language can provide additional layers of information that are critical for meaningful communication. One can internally conjure the difference in prosody between the statement 'We're having sandwiches for lunch.' versus the question 'We're having sandwiches for lunch?' The rising pitch contour that accompanies the question provides the listener with the understanding that the speaker is asking for clarification, even when they are not able to annotate their utterance with a question mark.

Speech and speech sounds are important for language use and are often thought of as the main component of language. However, language can be expressed through other modalities aside from speech. Though most languages are spoken, language can also be gesture-based, as in sign language. Sign languages have many hallmarks of a spoken language that we will learn about below, but they do not involve phonology. For this reason, phonology can be understood to be a salient, but not an essential, language subsystem.

Phonology in ID

Because speech delays are common among children with ID, the topic of early phonological development is often of interest to interventionists and educators. When speech delays are present, it may be helpful to conduct a phonemic inventory, wherein the range of phonemes produced by a child can be analysed. This type of assessment will examine the percentage of consonants produced correctly, and whether phonological processes are present, like assimilation (changing a consonant to be similar to another consonant within the same word), consonant deletions, and syllable changes. Investigating these skills can help answer questions regarding whether phonological development is delayed in ways that are comparable to chronologically younger counterparts at similar developmental stages, or whether specific phonological challenges are observed beyond what would be anticipated for overall developmental status. In one study comparing boys with fragile X syndrome to those with Down syndrome, boys with fragile X syndrome were found to show phonological performances aligned with their overall development, but boys with Down syndrome showed patterns of performance that were more unique (Roberts et al. 2005). More than half of the boys with Down syndrome engaged in frequent 'cluster reduction', or the substitution of a combination of consonants with fewer consonants (e.g. *swing* is replaced with *sing*), while only 8% of boys with fragile X syndrome demonstrated this pattern. Careful monitoring of phonological challenges during early childhood may facilitate more targeted interventions to promote these critical foundations for spoken language use.

Reading in ID. Language is not only spoken (or gestured), but it also takes a written form. The ability to interpret written figures into language for meaning and interpretation is a complex skill that is interconnected with language capabilities. Phonological skills, for example, have relevance not only for speech and articulation, but they are also important for the acquisition of reading and decoding skills. In alphabetic languages, reading and decoding rely upon the ability to perceive and interpret phonemes, and then to link them with specific letters and words. This skill involves *phonological* or *phonemic awareness*, and it is now understood to be a key source of variability in childhood literacy outcomes (Melby-Lervåg, Lyster, & Hulme 2012). Even when elevated likelihood of phonological skill challenges is present, as for children with Down syndrome and those with cerebral palsy, phonological skills are associated with decoding words (Peeters, Verhoeven, Van Balkom, & De Moor 2008; Lemons & Fuchs 2010). Phonemic awareness skills among individuals with mild ID may be impacted by limitations in the amount of verbal information that they can hold in their temporary memory (Schuchardt, Maehler, & Hasselhorn 2011). Recent meta-analysis work has demonstrated that children with ID who experience well-crafted, multicomponent reading interventions make gains in this academic foundational area (Afacan, Wilkerson, & Ruppar 2018).

Morphology and Syntax

One of the many astounding features of human language is the fact that our thoughts and ideas can be conveyed in an infinite number of ways through the combination of words into sentences and utterances. This combining property of language is the result of two important language subsystems, called morphology and syntax. They are sometimes combined in language research, in the study of *morphosyntactic development*. These two subsystems, though they are closely related, each offer something unique and important to the development of language skills and will be described as such below.

Morphology

The building blocks of language involve the use of words that serve as symbols that stand in for objects, events, and other ideas or representations that someone may carry in their mind. We generally think of these symbols as coming in the form of whole words, like 'basketball' or 'dunk'. But from a language development perspective, we can break down parts of language into smaller units of meaning, called *morphemes*. Morphemes come in various forms. They can be whole words, like 'baseball' or 'catch'. They can also come in the form of the additions that we make to words that convey meaning, called *grammatical morphemes*. In English, when we want to convey that there is more than one of something (pluralize), we often add on the grammatical morpheme of -*s*. By adding -*s* to the end of the word 'baseball', I am able to signify that I am referring to at least two or more small, stitched spheres that can be thrown from one person to another. Grammatical morphemes are also commonly used to convey verb tense, or when something happened. In English, these modifications are made to verbs usually by adding the suffix -*ed*. Just by adding -ed to the word 'walk', I can convey to the listener or reader that the walking that I am referring to took place before the present moment. Of course, there are exceptions to these morphological rules in English, and we learn as we acquire the English language that we should not apply the -s morpheme when pluralizing the words 'foot' and 'goose', and many other irregular plural forms. We also learn not to apply the -ed rule to the verbs 'run', 'speak', and 'break'. It takes some experience in the language environment to sort through the rules and the exceptions, but for the most part, typically developing children are able to acquire a language's morphological rules and the exceptions to those rules by simply engaging with ongoing language use in their natural environments.

Syntax

Another closely related subsystem of language that contributes to our communicative abilities is syntax, which refers to the ways that we order words together into longer utterances or sentences. The order of words into sentences greatly impacts the ultimate meaning generated. Consider the sentence 'The girl ate the pizza.' The ordering of those five words conveys important information about the subject of the sentence (the girl), the object of the sentence (the pizza), and the action in the sentence (she ate it). But one small change can be made in syntax by reordering the words into the sentence 'The pizza ate the girl.' Those same five words now connote something completely different. All of the words are the same. All of the morphological rules and phonological rules have remained the same. The only difference in this sentence relates to the ordering of the words. And yet a completely different, and ultimately absurd, meaning is generated by that one small syntactic change.

Morphology and Syntax in ID

Studies of morphosyntactic development in individuals with ID are somewhat sparse. Those existing studies are generally focused on specific diagnostic groups, as observed throughout this chapter. Based on this work, we can observe a range of profiles of unique features and differing ability levels in the acquisition of grammatical morphemes across different ID-related conditions. Children with Williams syndrome, for example, show competencies in the use of morphological rules, like the use of -ed for past tense (Clahsen & Almazan 1998). However, they tend to demonstrate difficulty with irregular conjugations of past tense (e.g. 'went' or 'gave'; Clahsen & Almazan 1998). Importantly, grammatical abilities have been linked to underlying neuropsychological processes in many individuals with ID. Aspects of short-term memory, or the ability to briefly retain verbal input, is associated with grammar skills in children with Williams syndrome (Robinson, Mervis, & Robinson 2003). Linking underlying information processing skills to language outcomes may hold the key to treatments that support strong underlying skill components.

Semantics

The next subsystem introduces an important ingredient into the use of language – the ability to mean something. As we discussed at the beginning of this chapter, language involves symbols that we use in order to communicate. The symbols that we use, whether they are spoken, gestured, or written, stand in for, or represent, objects, events, and ideas that exist (or are imaginary). In order for the symbolic system to work, the critical ingredient of *meaning* must be a driving force. But how do we develop the ability to use symbols to mean things?

Our earliest experiences with using symbols to mean things happen when we acquire our first words. Consider a typically developing 12-month old playing with a caregiver. The caregiver may reach into a toy bin and present a round object that bounces. The caregiver may hold up the object, look at the infant, and then say the word 'ball' with excitement. In that moment, the infant has the opportunity to make an association between the round object that bounces and the sounds that are made when the caregiver says 'ball'. At that moment, or over the course of the next few interactions with a round, bouncing object that a caregiver labels 'ball', that infant can map on the sound symbol with the object itself. Without knowing it, this infant is developing *lexical semantics,* or the meaning of words.

Developing semantic skills is not just about mapping labels onto objects. It also involves understanding the organizational structure of how that object (or event) relates to other things. As children acquire language, they are also learning about the world around them and come to understand that the world contains different categories of things. We first may learn about dogs and cats, and how they differ from one another. But soon enough, we also come to learn that they both belong to a higher-level category of 'animals', and that dogs and cats have more in common with one another than dogs and tables. Being able to organize the world that we are learning about into this type of structure is often called semantic organization.

Semantics in ID
Challenges in the development of semantics in children with ID can be examined from a variety of perspectives. For children with ID, semantic challenges may result from disruptions

in retrieving information from the organizational structure. Early in development, this can be observable in a child's use of nonspecific words and excessive pauses in their speech (Sheng 2014). These skills are supported by underlying neuropsychological processes, like working memory. Children who have shorter verbal working memory spans may experience greater difficulty with remembering new words and representing the context extensively enough to map a new meaning on to the novel word presented. This relationship between verbal working memory and vocabulary skills has been reported in boys with fragile X syndrome (Pierpont, Richmond, Abbeduto, Kover, & Brown 2011). Early visual attention skills also predict vocabulary acquisition during infancy and toddlerhood in fragile X syndrome (Kover, McCary, Ingram, Hatton, & Roberts 2015). Understanding the unique profiles and underlying factors that contribute to semantic skill acquisition can provide essential information for anticipatory intervention approaches that can strengthen foundations from the outset, and support increased semantic skill acquisition during the earliest stages of development.

Pragmatics

The complex skills involved in the development of phonology, syntax, morphology, and semantics stand on their own as remarkable structures that children without disabilities acquire through ongoing natural interactions in the social environment. But there is one more important component involved in language acquisition – the ability to use language in purposeful ways in the social world. The social use of language is called *pragmatics*, and it refers to all of the complex (and often unspoken) rules that determine our ability to navigate interactions with others. At earlier developmental stages, pragmatics involve understanding how to begin and end a conversation, understanding how speaking to a grown-up may be different from speaking to a peer, and learning how to take turns in a conversation to maintain a social interaction. Later on, pragmatics can also include the use of jokes, sarcasm, the use of figurative expressions, and the ability to know how to adjust your language use based on the context that you are in (giving a presentation versus hanging out with friends).

Pragmatics in Individuals with ID

The development of pragmatic language use intersects with developing social abilities, and in particular, social cognition. Social cognition refers to our ability to think about the social world and understand other people's mental states in ways that inform our own social behaviour. Pragmatic language use is reliant upon an individual's ability to think about the social partner to whom they are directing their communication, and their ability to understand norms and expectations about appropriate ways of relating. TD children build pragmatic skills throughout the course of their childhood years, and it is likely that pragmatic skills are similarly acquired in line with overall developmental capabilities in those with ID. However, the presence of co-occurring conditions, such as autism spectrum disorder (ASD), may further impact the acquisition of pragmatic skills (Martin, Losh, Estigarribia, Sideris, & Roberts 2013). ASD is a diagnosis that influences social communication. Though other structural aspects of language may be acquired in many individuals with ASD, the pragmatic use of language across a range of social situations may be influenced by the presence of ASD.

In comparison to other language subsystems, there has been substantial research into the development of pragmatic language skills across different conditions associated with ID. Often pragmatic difficulties are accompanied by repetitive language use, wherein an individual may remain focused on a narrow topic repetitively. Individuals with Williams syndrome (Laws & Bishop 2004) and males with fragile X syndrome (Murphy & Abbeduto 2007) demonstrate a greater likelihood for this type of repetitive style. The pragmatic language profile associated with Williams syndrome is particularly of interest, as many people with this condition demonstrate elevated levels of social motivation, but this does not necessarily translate into more advanced social pragmatic skills. In fact, increased social interest during childhood may lead to excessive attention to the affective tone of their social partner, rather than the content of their speech, and therefore may not choose socially informed responses during interactions (Fidler, Hepburn, Most, Philofsky, & Rogers 2007). Another unique feature to the pragmatic profile of children with WS relates to social disinhibition, often in the context of relating to strangers. While social pragmatics often involve a less socially gregarious tone with unfamiliar people, individuals with Williams syndrome may adopt the social strategies of relating to an old friend when engaging with strangers (Bellugi, Lichtenberger, Mills, Galaburda, & Korenberg 1999).

Individuals with fragile X syndrome also demonstrate unique pragmatic language outcomes. Perseverative speech, or the repetition of specific phrases, words, and sounds, also interferes with the development of pragmatic language skills in individuals with fragile X syndrome. These pragmatic language difficulties are increased by the presence of co-occurring ASD (Klusek, Martin, & Losh 2014), and may be influenced by the increased likelihood of social anxiety observed in this population. In addition to demonstrating more repetitive speech patterns, males with fragile X syndrome are prone to use language that is tangential, on topics that do not necessarily follow directly from the conversational flow (Sudhalter & Belser 2001).

Summary

As we contemplate each of the critical components of language acquisition, from speech sounds to word meanings to social judgement and appropriate language use, it is astonishing how the majority of children are able to acquire language seamlessly so early in development. A close examination of each subsystem helps us appreciate just how complex language is, and it also helps us appreciate how challenging it might be to acquire language skills in the face of intellectual and cognitive processing challenges. Growth in our understanding of the unique language presentations associated with specific conditions associated with ID offers the promise that we may be able to tailor interventions in more precise ways to greater effects. In the next section, we consider treatment innovations that aim to facilitate language development in people with ID.

COMMUNICATION AND LANGUAGE INTERVENTIONS IN ID

Interventions to Promote Early Social Communication

Early social communication skills are in many ways the 'launching pad' of later language and social relatedness skills. In addition to facilitating our social relationships and connecting us to those in our home and community environments, early social communication skills play a critical role across a range of important skill areas. Joint attention skills predict language acquisition (Bono, Daley, & Sigman 2004; Kasari, Gulsrud, Freeman, Paparella, & Hellemann 2012) and nonverbal requesting is associated with early problem solving (Fidler et al. 2005). Because of these important links, intervening to promote the foundational strength of social communication during the infant and toddler years is likely to yield powerful effects on later developmental outcomes in children with conditions associated with ID.

Naturalistic Developmental Behavioural Interventions (NBDIs)

Over the past several decades, separate clinical research teams have developed strategies to enhance early social-communication foundations, yielding impactful results across a range of techniques and approaches. Recently, intervention scientists have sought to understand the underlying core factors that these approaches have in common. These similar components have been examined closely and a new over-arching category of interventions has been named 'Naturalistic Developmental Behavioural Interventions' or NBDIs (Schreibman et al. 2015). Though different NBDI intervention programmes may vary in their execution, most NBDIs are implemented in everyday settings, like a child's home or school. NBDIs often target foundational skills, like joint attention and requesting, that can propel a child forward in their acquisition of a broad range of skills (Schreibman et al. 2015). Many NBDI intervention activities are embedded in daily routines or in play and include toys and other objects that are of intrinsic interest to the child. NBDIs are structured so that both the child and the interventionist contribute to social interactions.

JASPER is an NBDI that targets the critical foundational skills of joint attention, as well as the important related skill areas of symbolic play, engagement, and regulation (www.kasarilab.org/treatments/jasper). This intervention approach has been implemented with children with ASD in both clinical and educational settings. Daily JASPER intervention for two months has been shown to increase both joint attention frequency and language skills in the form of increased utterance length (Chang et al. 2016). Gains have been shown to be maintained at follow-up visits, suggesting that even after the intervention is implemented, children continue to initiate these important behaviours.

Early Start Denver Model (ESDM) is another NBDI that has strong empirical support. Designed for young children with elevated likelihood for autism spectrum disorder, ESDM involves a developmental approach that is relationship based, and that involves elements of behavioural learning techniques (Rogers et al. 2012). When implemented at a high intensity by ESDM-trained therapists, children at who have an elevated likelihood for autism demonstrate fewer autism-related features two years post-treatment. Though a high intensity of intervention may pose numerous barriers in terms of time and cost, a cost-benefit analysis has demonstrated that subsequent reductions in the services and supports needed for ESDM participants offset the costs of early intervention.

An additional core feature of NBDIs is the use of behavioural approaches to support developmental skill acquisition (Schreibman et al. 2015). They are often structured so that a clear connection can be made by the child between their behaviour and contingent rewarding experiences. These contingencies often take place in the context of predictable day-to-day contexts, like play or activities of daily living. In addition, NBDIs frequently employ natural contingencies. This means that interactions are designed with a direct connection between the motivator for producing a new or desired behaviour and the new/desired behaviour being acquired. A child who is learning the word 'ball', and begins to produce the phonemes for the word 'ball', would receive a play break with a ball, and not an unrelated experience, like listening to music.

NBDIs are generally codified with explicit manualized procedures for implementation and require training and implementation at designated levels of fidelity. And importantly, the goals set in NBDIs are targeted towards the child's developmental needs, and careful data are collected within and across sessions to monitor the effectiveness of the intervention over time.

Early Language Intervention

Interventions that aim to support the acquisition of language skills have been categorized as either *targeted* or *comprehensive* (Hampton & Kaiser 2016). Targeted intervention for children with disabilities involve a focus on specific skill areas, such as speech, receptive language, or expressive language. Comprehensive interventions take a wider view and aim to build spoken language through the strengthening of underlying skills, such as cognition, play, imitation, and motor development. In a meta-analysis of early language interventions for children with ASD, it was found that a combination of parent and clinician delivery yielded the most pronounced gains relative to community treatment (Hampton & Kaiser 2016). Other dimensions, however, such as how much of the intervention received, did not seem to influence the impact of the intervention.

An important topic of research in language intervention relates to the role of parenting behaviour, and the opportunity to build parenting skills that will then support child language acquisition. Two categories of parenting behaviours are known to facilitate language use for children with disabilities: parental responsivity to child behaviours and parental modelling of language use (Heidlage et al. 2020). Responsivity behaviours include facilitating turn taking, responding to child initiations for shared attention, and responding with words to their child's vocalizations (Heidlage et al. 2020). Modelling behaviours include providing labels for objects during joint attention providing more complex language examples through rephrasing their child's speech (Heidlage et al. 2020). Positive effects have been demonstrated for dimensions like expressive vocabulary for interventions that involve book reading with a social partner and interventions that involve play and social routines (Heidlage et al. 2020).

SUMMARY

In this chapter, we have explored the complex landscape of communication and language development for individuals with ID. These skills serve as an important bridge between the individual and their social surroundings, and can serve as a key facilitator of the development of many additional skill areas that promote adaptation and independence. In developing an understanding of the 'ingredients' necessary for competent communication and language use, we can observe just how many foundational skill areas converge to achieve early milestones like first words. We can appreciate the fluidity with which language acquisition skills are acquired in the general population of children, and we can also develop targeted strategies to address areas of vulnerability in individuals with delays, such as those at elevated likelihood to demonstrate ID. There is little doubt that the next generation of researchers and practitioners in this area will continue to refine our understanding and innovate with more and more effective teaching and intervention practices.

Reflective Questions

1. What is the difference between communication and language? Why is this distinction important?
2. What are the different forms of communication that do not involve language during early childhood? Why do you think they are important for acquiring language skills?
3. Which subsystems of language do you think would be most important to address to support outcomes for people with ID?
4. Why is intervention to support communication and language skills important for children with ID?

REFERENCES

Afacan, K., Wilkerson, K. L., & Ruppar, A. L. (2018). Multicomponent reading interventions for students with intellectual disability. *Remedial and Special Education*, 39(4), 229–242.

Bellugi, U., Lichtenberger, L., Mills, D., Galaburda, A., & Korenberg, J. R. (1999). Bridging cognition, the brain and molecular genetics: evidence from Williams syndrome. *Trends in Neurosciences*, 22(5), 197–207.

Bono, M. A., Daley, T., & Sigman, M. (2004). Relations among joint attention, amount of intervention and language gain in autism. *Journal of Autism and Developmental Disorders, 34*(5), 495–505.

Chang, Y. C., Shire, S. Y., Shih, W., Gelfand, C., & Kasari, C. (2016). Preschool deployment of evidence-based social communication intervention: JASPER in the classroom. *Journal of Autism and Developmental Disorders, 46*(6), 2211–2223.

Clahsen, H., & Almazan, M. (1998). Syntax and morphology in Williams syndrome. *Cognition, 68*(3), 167–198.

Dawson, G., Meltzoff, A. N., Osterling, J., Rinaldi, J., & Brown, E. (1998). Children with autism fail to orient to naturally occurring social stimuli. *Journal of Autism and Developmental Disorders, 28*(6), 479–485.

Fidler, D. J., Hepburn, S. L., Most, D. E., Philofsky, A., & Rogers, S. J. (2007). Emotional responsivity in young children with Williams syndrome. *American Journal on Mental Retardation, 112*(3), 194–206.

Fidler, D. J., Philofsky, A., Hepburn, S. L., & Rogers, S. J. (2005). Nonverbal requesting and problem-solving by toddlers with Down syndrome. *American Journal on Mental Retardation, 110*(4), 312–322.

Hahn, L. J., Brady, N. C., & Versaci, T. (2019). Communicative use of triadic eye gaze in children with down syndrome, autism spectrum disorder, and other intellectual and developmental disabilities. *American Journal of Speech-Language Pathology, 28*(4), 1509–1522.

Hampton, L., & Kaiser, A. (2016). Intervention effects on spoken-language outcomes for children with autism: a systematic review and meta-analysis. *Journal of Intellectual Disability Research, 60*(5), 444–463.

Heidlage, J. K., Cunningham, J. E., Kaiser, A. P., Trivette, C. M., Barton, E. E., Frey, J. R., & Roberts, M. Y. (2020). The effects of parent-implemented language interventions on child linguistic outcomes: A meta-analysis. *Early Childhood Research Quarterly, 50*, 6–23.

International Phonetic Association. (1999). *Handbook of the International Phonetic Association: A guide to the use of the International Phonetic Alphabet*: Cambridge University Press.

Kasari, C., Gulsrud, A., Freeman, S., Paparella, T., & Hellemann, G. (2012). Longitudinal follow-up of children with autism receiving targeted interventions on joint attention and play. *Journal of the American Academy of Child & Adolescent Psychiatry, 51*(5), 487–495.

Klusek, J., Martin, G. E., & Losh, M. (2014). A comparison of pragmatic language in boys with autism and fragile X syndrome. *Journal of Speech, Language, and Hearing Research, 57*(5), 1692–1707.

Kover, S. T., McCary, L. M., Ingram, A. M., Hatton, D. D., & Roberts, J. E. (2015). Language development in infants and toddlers with fragile X syndrome: change over time and the role of attention. *American Journal on Intellectual and Developmental Disabilities, 120*(2), 125–144. doi:10.1352/1944-7558-120.2.125

Laws, G., & Bishop, D. V. (2004). Pragmatic language impairment and social deficits in Williams syndrome: a comparison with Down's syndrome and specific language impairment. *International Journal of Language & Communication Disorders, 39*(1), 45–64.

Leekam, S. R., López, B., & Moore, C. (2000). Attention and joint attention in preschool children with autism. *Developmental Psychology, 36*(2), 261.

Lemons, C. J., & Fuchs, D. (2010). Phonological awareness of children with Down syndrome: Its role in learning to read and the effectiveness of related interventions. *Research in Developmental Disabilities, 31*(2), 316–330.

Lincoln, A. J., Searcy, Y. M., Jones, W., & Lord, C. (2007). Social interaction behaviors discriminate young children with autism and Williams syndrome. *Journal of the American Academy of Child & Adolescent Psychiatry, 46*(3), 323–331.

Martin, G. E., Losh, M., Estigarribia, B., Sideris, J., & Roberts, J. (2013). Longitudinal profiles of expressive vocabulary, syntax and pragmatic language in boys with fragile X syndrome or Down syndrome. *International Journal of Language & Communication Disorders, 48*(4), 432–443.

Melby-Lervåg, M., Lyster, S.-A. H., & Hulme, C. (2012). Phonological skills and their role in learning to read: a meta-analytic review. *Psychological Bulletin, 138*(2), 322.

Mervis, C. B., & Klein-Tasman, B. P. (2000). Williams syndrome: cognition, personality, and adaptive behavior. *Mental Retardation and Developmental Disabilities Research Reviews, 6*(2), 148–158.

Murphy, M. M., & Abbeduto, L. (2007). Gender differences in repetitive language in fragile X syndrome. *Journal of Intellectual Disability Research, 51*(5), 387–400.

Peeters, M., Verhoeven, L., Van Balkom, H., & De Moor, J. (2008). Foundations of phonological awareness in pre-school children with cerebral palsy: the impact of intellectual disability. *Journal of Intellectual Disability Research, 52*(1), 68–78.

Pierpont, E. I., Richmond, E. K., Abbeduto, L., Kover, S. T., & Brown, W. T. (2011). Contributions of phonological and verbal working memory to language development in adolescents with fragile X syndrome. *Journal of Neurodevelopmental Disorders, 3*(4), 335–347. doi:10.1007/s11689-011-9095-2

Roberts, J. E., Long, S. H., Malkin, C., Barnes, E., Skinner, M., Hennon, E. A., & Anderson, K. (2005). A comparison of phonological skills of boys with fragile X syndrome and Down syndrome. *Journal of Speech, Language, and Hearing Research, 48*(5), 980–995. doi:10.1044/1092-4388(2005/067)

Roberts, J. E., Mirrett, P., Anderson, K., Burchinal, M., & Neebe, E. (2002). Early communication, symbolic behavior, and social profiles of young males with fragile X syndrome. *American Journal of Speech-Language Pathology*.

Robinson, B. F., Mervis, C. B., & Robinson, B. W. (2003). The roles of verbal short-term memory and working memory in the acquisition of grammar by children with Williams syndrome. *Developmental Neuropsychology, 23*(1–2), 13–31.

Schreibman, L., Dawson, G., Stahmer, A. C., Landa, R., Rogers, S. J., McGee, G. G., ... Bruinsma, Y. (2015). Naturalistic developmental behavioral interventions: Empirically validated treatments for autism spectrum disorder. *Journal of Autism and Developmental Disorders, 45*(8), 2411–2428.

Schuchardt, K., Maehler, C., & Hasselhorn, M. (2011). Functional deficits in phonological working memory in children with intellectual disabilities. *Research in Developmental Disabilities, 32*(5), 1934–1940.

Sheng, L. (2014). Semantic Development in Children With Language Impairments. In P. J. Brooks & V. Kempe (eds), *Encyclopedia of Language Development* (pp. 535–539): SAGE Publications, Inc.

Sudhalter, V., & Belser, R. C. (2001). Conversational characteristics of children with fragile X syndrome: Tangential language. *American Journal on Mental Retardation, 106*(5), 389–400.

Trevarthen, C., & Aitken, K. J. (2001). Infant intersubjectivity: Research, theory, and clinical applications. *Journal of Child Psychology and Psychiatry, 42*(1), 3–48.

10
SPECIFIC LEARNING DISORDER

> ### Learning Objectives
>
> After reading this chapter, you should be able to:
>
> - Review the main theories of Specific Learning Disorder (SLD)
> - Understand risk factors associated with SLD
> - Understand the developmental course of SLD
> - Review the process and challenges of SLD diagnosis
> - Review the pharmacological, psychosocial and academic remedial interventions for SLD

SLD is a neurodevelopment disability associated with atypicalities in the central nervous system that affects an individual's ability to efficiently process verbal and nonverbal information. SLD manifests at the behavioural level as difficulties learning in at least one of the main areas of academic skills (e.g. reading, writing, and mathematics) and persists for at least six months, despite providing intervention and support that focuses on these areas of difficulty. These academic skills should be considerably lower than expected for the chronological age and significantly affect the individual's achievements in their occupation, education, or everyday lives (American Psychiatric Association [APA], 2013).

The onset of SLD is during the school years, but in some people, it might not be identified until later when academic skills fall behind and the child is not able to cope with the demands (e.g. reading or writing long and complicated passages in a limited time). Learning difficulties in SLD cannot be better attributed to intellectual disabilities (estimated IQ scores are within 70 ± 5), general developmental delay, mental, neurological, motor, visual or auditory deficits, or external variables such as economic and environmental issues or insufficient academic instruction (APA, 2013).

Relationship between IQ and SLD

According to DSM-5, SLD affects individuals with normal IQ score (70 ± 5). However, an SLD might also be diagnosed in individuals with below-average IQ if learning challenges are beyond what is expected for their cognitive disabilities (Criterion D; APA, 2013). In addition, IQ measures underestimate the cognitive ability (IQ scores) of individuals with SLD. Since they read less and have difficulty with academic learning, they may not attain the same levels of vocabulary or general information as their TD peers. Therefore, these children might score lower, particularly on the verbal IQ subtests which are often influenced by a student's schooling achievement. For example, those that relate to one's vocabulary development or facts about the world that are attained mostly through reading books (Siegel, Swanson, and Keogh 1990).

In addition, some children with SLD (particularly those with mathematical difficulties) who have challenges in fine motor and visuo-spatial skills cannot receive accurate IQ scores on their Non-Verbal/Performance subtest. These subsets are timed, and the participant achieves a bonus point for performing the tasks more quickly (Picture Organization, Block Design, and Object Assembly). Even though children with SLD can complete the tasks within the given time, they are less likely to obtain the bonus point for the faster performance as compared to their TD peers, and consequently, they might receive lower performance IQ scores Siegel (1988).

People with SLD generally have an average or above IQ score. Therefore, the SLD population includes some intellectually gifted people. Toffalini, Pezzuti, & Cornoldi (2017) examined the controversial idea that learning disorder is associated with giftedness. They showed that an overall intelligence quotient of higher than 130 occurred in less than 1% of children with SLD, which is well below the rate of 2.28% in the typical population. However, when this comparison was made using the General Ability Index (GAI; consists of Verbal Comprehension and Perceptual Reasoning), the rate of giftedness was considerably higher (3.75%) in children with SLD (Toffalini, Pezzuti, & Cornoldi 2017). They suggest that the rate of giftedness in the SLD population depends on how we measure intelligence. Giftedness in this population is very low if we consider the Full-Scale IQ and high when using the GAI as it does not include Working Memory (WM) and Processing Speed (PS) subscales. This is because the WM and PS measures are typically the ones that children with SLD perform poorly on (Giofrè & Cornoldi 2015). WM is the capacity to store and manipulate information in mind for a short time and is a crucial predictor of learning and academic achievements. WM is an essential component of fluid intelligence and can be a good measure for estimating children's potential for learning, as opposed to academic assessments and IQ measures that are affected by the child's knowledge and what they have learned (Alloway et al. 2005; Alloway 2009). However, WM does not reflect the g-factor (i.e. general intelligence) in children with SLD to the extent it does in TD children; these children might have average intelligence regardless of their below-average WM and PS (Giofrè & Cornoldi 2015).

SLD might be present only in one area of learning, such as reading (isolated type) or in multiple areas such as reading, writing, and mathematics (mixed type). Impairment in each domain might occur in various academic sub-skills, including word reading accuracy, reading rate/

fluency or reading comprehension (in the reading domain; also referred to as dyslexia), spelling accuracy, grammar, and punctuation accuracy, clarity or organization of written expression (in the writing domain), and number sense, memorization of arithmetic facts, accurate or fluent calculation, accurate maths reasoning (in the mathematics domain; also referred to as dyscalculia). SLD is identified at three levels of severity, considering the level of support that the individual needs to perform in academic tasks. These levels include mild (student may perform well with accommodation and support), moderate (can complete school activities with support and accommodations and needs at least some intensive individualized teaching) and severe (needs intensive special instructions throughout the years of education, yet might not be able to finish the academic tasks successfully). In addition, challenges in attaining the key academic skills can affect the learning of other school subjects (APA 2013). For example, for a student with reading fluency issues, cognitive resources are spent decoding the words instead of understanding and learning the content (Steinle, Stevens, & Vaughn 2022).

SLD occurs across languages but manifests differently depending on the level of orthographic transparency in each language. In languages with an opaque/deep orthography (e.g. Portuguese, French, Danish, English), several graphemes (symbols) correspond with a single phoneme (sound), and several phonemes correspond with the same grapheme. In transparent/shallow orthography languages (e.g. Finnish, Greek, Italian, Spanish, German), mainly, each grapheme has just one pronunciation. Literacy learning is generally more complex, with more reading errors and less fluency in opaque languages (Seymour, Aro, & Erskine 2003). Also, learning disabilities in opaque languages manifest more severely. For example, a Spanish-speaking child with moderately impaired phonological awareness might achieve reading skills in Spanish with minor challenges, but if the same child were raised in an English-speaking environment and needed to learn English, they would have considerable difficulties in reading (Wagner, Francis, & Morris 2005). Clinical symptoms of SLD vary in opaque and transparent languages. For instance, reading disabilities in English affect accuracy and reading speed, whereas, in the Spanish language, reading problems manifest in reading speed rather than reading accuracy. In other words, Spanish language readers with dyslexia might read accurately but have difficulty finishing timed reading tasks (Serrano & Defior 2008). In Italian, spelling disabilities are more frequent than reading disabilities. As a result of the transparent nature of the Italian language, reading mistakes can be easier to avoid than spelling errors (Toffalini, Giofrè, & Cornoldi 2017).

RISK FACTORS

There is a critical role of genetics in the manifestation of SLD (Gilger, 2001). Learning abilities are impacted by 'candidate genes' (e.g. chromosome 6) that affect the function or structure of the brain. However, more than one gene is involved in developing a SLD, and different genes might be impacted differently in each individual. Also, environmental factors are responsible for about half of the variations in the aetiology of SLD.

For example, extremely low birth weight, prenatal drug effects, anoxia, poor environment after birth and effects of medical treatments increase the risk of learning difficulties. Also, socioeconomic status (SES) factors such as parental unemployment and low level of education are associated with a higher risk of SLD (Gilger 2001; De Rodrigues, Mello, & Fonseca 2006; Sahin, Bozkurt, & Karabekiroglu 2019). Therefore, the coexistence of these environmental factors and genetic factors (e.g. gene mutations) can better explain SLD rather than one single factor (Gilger 2001).

Neuroimaging and electrophysiological research (e.g. evoked responses studies) has explored the relations between SLD and brain dysfunction (Rourke 2005).

A longitudinal study showed that newborns' event-related potential (ERP) might be a valid predictor of later language abilities at 2.5, 3.5, and 5 years old. The findings indicated that the right hemisphere ERPs are associated with receptive language skills at 2.5, and the ERPs from the left hemisphere predict the verbal memory skills at the age of five (Guttorm et al. 2005).

Cognitive risk factors for SLD are underlying impairments associated with learning difficulties, such as slow processing speed, letter knowledge, rapid automatized naming, verbal memory, and working memory as these are key processes that impact learning (Partanen & Siegel 2014; Moll, Göbel, Gooch, Landerl, & Snowling 2016). Also, it is documented that phonological awareness (e.g. recognizing the beginning and end sound of a word) is an essential factor in learning reading skills (Partanen & Siegel 2014), and students with SLD have challenges with phonological processing (Snowling 1995). Therefore, if children (age 5–6 years) score below average in these fundamental skills, they are at risk for developing a SLD (Partanen & Siegel 2014).

PREVALENCE OF SLD

SLD is one of the most prevalent neurodevelopmental disabilities diagnosed in childhood, with a rate of 5–15% (APA 2013). However, the prevalence of SLD differs widely across countries and cultures (e.g. from 1.2% in a Greek to 20% in an Australian study) depending on the epidemiologic study sample sizes, inclusion criteria and different measures and cutoff points used in different studies (Görker 2019). In addition, variation in prevalence rates arises from inadequate definitions and different diagnostic models for diagnosing SLD (see Diagnostic Process section for more information).

The mixed SLD type is the most prevalent subtype (APA 2013; Willcutt et al. 2013; Toffalini, Giofrè, & Cornoldi 2017). Isolated reading disorder, followed by spelling disorder, is more frequent than isolated mathematics disorder, which is infrequent and mostly is comorbid with other types (Butterworth 2004). Comorbidity of mathematics with spelling disorder is more likely than co-occurrence of mathematics and reading disorder. More boys than girls show isolated spelling deficits, and more girls show challenges with arithmetic. Nevertheless, the ratio is balanced in comorbid learning disorders in which three domains are affected (Moll, Kunze, Neuhoff, Bruder, & Schulte-Körne 2014). Diagnosis of SLD is more prevalent in older children

(11–17 years old) and those with lower SES than younger children (3–10 years old) and those with higher SES. In addition, more Black students, followed by White students, are diagnosed with SLD than Hispanic students (Zablotsky & Alford 2020).

GENDER DIFFERENCES IN SLD

According to the Diagnostic and Statistical Manual of Mental Disorders, Fifth Edition (DSM-5), SLD is diagnosed in males more often than in females (ratio 2–3:1), and this difference is not related to factors such as variation in measures, language, race, and SES (APA 2013). As mentioned, few studies found that difficulties in reading and writing are more prevalent in boys, whereas mathematic disorders are more frequent in girls (Bhandari & Goyal 2004; Moll et al. 2014). Similarly, other researchers suggested that males with learning difficulties have more difficulties than females in reading, handwriting, composing, and spelling (Berninger, Nielsen, Abbott, Wijsman, & Raskind 2008). Conversely, a few studies found no significant differences in the isolated reading and mixed SLD between boys and girls (Moll et al. 2014). The different prevalence rate of SLD in males and females seems to be due to a biased identification, not an actual difference in the prevalence of LD (Shaywitz, Shaywitz, Fletcher, & Escobar 1990). They explained that the higher referral rate in male students is due to their behavioural differences (e.g. acting out behaviours) than female students rather than their SLD symptoms.

THE COGNITIVE BASIS OF DIFFERENT SUBTYPES

Even though the DSM-5 views SLD as a single-category diagnosis, it requires using specifiers for the impaired academic domains and sub-skills (reading, written expression or mathematics, or any combination of these domains; APA 2013). Previously, impairment in each domain was considered a separate category of learning disorder (e.g. reading disorder; APA 2000). Studies show similarities and differences in cognitive processing with different SLD subtypes. For example, Toffalini, Pezzuti, and Cornoldi (2017) compared the cognitive profile of four SLD subtypes (deficits in reading, writing, mathematics, or a mixed type) using the Wechsler Intelligence Scale for Children-IV (WISC-IV). They found that deficits in the Cognitive Processing Index (CPI), which consists of Processing Speed (PS) and Working Memory (WM), are shared among all SLD subtypes. All four groups showed scores on the CPI to be one standard deviation (SD) below their General Ability Index (GAI, which consists of Verbal Comprehension and Perceptual Reasoning). As well, WM was the lowest score for all SLD subtypes. The CPI was slightly below average in isolated reading and isolated spelling subtypes, but around 1 SD below in the mixed subtype, indicating that individuals with mixed SLD subtype have more significant deficits in cognitive processing. The GAI was within the normal range for the mathematic disorder but significantly higher than the normative range in spelling and reading LD subtypes, supporting the controversial idea that people with dyslexia have superior visuospatial abilities.

Both dyslexia and dyscalculia share deficits in WM and PS, but dyslexia is mainly associated with poor phonological processing, while dyscalculia is associated with impaired visuospatial abilities (Willcutt et al. 2013; Toffalini, Giofrè, & Cornoldi 2017).

Silver (2008) introduced the input-integration-memory-output model to explain the bases of different variations of SLD. Learning disabilities are caused by deficits in any part of the learning process, including receiving the information (input), processing the information to be understood (integration), storing and retrieving the information (memory), and communicating the information (output).

Input disability involves difficulty with the visual perception (e.g. confusion with subtly different letters such as b and d, challenges with visual figure-ground tasks or depth perception). Also, input disability might arise in auditory perception, such as mishearing similar words such as hair instead of air, issues with distinguishing between the auditory figure from the ground (i.e. what is important to listen to when there are multiple sounds in the environment and slow auditory processing or auditory lag).

Integration disability might appear in sequencing (e.g. reading saw instead of was, difficulty with the order of months of the year), abstraction (e.g. difficulty with understanding subtle meanings of jokes and idioms) and organization (e.g. issues with integrating pieces of information to structure a whole concept, difficulty with time management and planning).

Memory disability in SLD is usually a deficit in short-term memory (visual or auditory) that affects concentration and information storage. Therefore, individuals with SLD might learn new information but cannot easily retain it in their long-term memory without many repetitions.

Output disability is difficulty bringing information out of the brain by oral communications or using muscles. For example, children with SLD might have challenges with in-demand language where the child is required to respond to a question without having the chance to plan and organize their thoughts. Output disability also might be in the form of difficulty using small muscles, i.e. fine motor skills such as handwriting and spelling or large muscles, i.e. gross motor skills such as climbing and swimming (Bhandari & Goyal 2004).

According to the input-integration-memory-output model, each person with SLD has a unique profile consisting of strengths and weaknesses in the aforementioned areas that should be assessed individually.

DIAGNOSIS OF SLD

Even though SLD is considered a disability based on the differences of the central nervous system, evidence of structural brain differences may or may not appear in medical/neurological examination at the individual level. Therefore, diagnosis of SLD relies on psychological, clinical, and academic assessments rather than medical or neurological examinations (Bhandari & Goyal 2004).

Earlier, 'discrepancy theory' was a well-established and accepted model for diagnosing LD. In the previous version of the DSM (IV-TR), LD was identified by a significant discrepancy

(1.5 standard deviations) between the standardized IQ score and standardized achievement scores (APA 2000). However, the research identified this criterion as problematic due to validity and reliability issues. For example, one could not differentiate between low achievements caused by social-emotional factors with those originating from a neurodevelopmental disability (Brueggemann, Kamphaus, & Dombrowski 2008). Also, impaired reading skills might lead to poor performance on IQ tests and certain students with LD might receive lower IQ scores (below their actual cognitive capacities) that are consistent with their level of achievement without meeting the discrepancy criterion (Siegel 1989). Also, children with learning disabilities show the same core impairments in the reading process regardless of their lower or higher IQ scores (Stanovich 2005). Using IQ discrepancy scores as a required factor for diagnosis might be discriminatory to certain students. For Example, IQ is associated with SES and students with a learning disability from lower SES groups might receive lower IQ scores consistent with their low achievements. Therefore, they might be excluded from the diagnosis of SLD and, consequently, not meet the eligibility to receive the services they need (Siegel 1999).

Thus, discrepancy theory is no longer seen as valid, and it was omitted from the SLD diagnostic criteria of the DSM-5; measuring IQ is no longer necessary for diagnosing SLD (APA 2013). Moreover, Siegel (1999) suggested that assessment of IQ does not help predict the success of remedial interventions. She found no significant differences in reading-related tasks in two groups of students with SLD with higher and lower IQ scores, suggesting that higher IQ scores in these children are not associated with better reading. Moreover, one study showed that when a child has an SLD, those with lower IQ might benefit from the remedial programmes more than those with higher IQ scores (Yule 1973).

Another model to guide the diagnosis of SLD, based on the DSM-5, is the 'low achievement' model. In this model, SLD is defined as academic achievement considerably lower than expected for the chronological age. Low achievement is identified by administering standardized academic achievement measures and comprehensive clinical assessment. This criterion can be met confidently when the student scores 1.5 standard deviations below the average range for that age, or more liberally with a higher achievement score (e.g. 1 standard score below the mean) when strong evidence is available from other sources such as clinical assessment, educational history, and school reports. Research suggests that performing at least two standardized achievement tests on the same impaired academic domain can lead to a more confident decision on the low achievement method (Brueggemann et al. 2008).

Response to Intervention (RtI) is another model used to identify SLD. This model measures students' academic performance and responsiveness to interventions. All students with learning difficulties receive intervention, and only those whose academic skills remain below average regardless of the additional intervention support are diagnosed with SLD. RtI is known to be useful for early interventions. However, this method is criticized for its inadequacy in differentiating LD students from others with below-average academic achievements. Furthermore, this model cannot determine if a general education intervention or an intensive individual intervention is needed, how the responsiveness to interventions is measured, or whether the intervention gains are maintained (Vaughn, Linan-Thompson, & Hickman 2003).

Recent studies showed concerns over the complexity of SLD identification and the lack of evidence-based methods professionals use to diagnose SLD (Whittaker & Burns 2019). Depending on the diagnostic model, clinical judgement, and the tests and cutoffs used to measure academic achievements, one student may or may not receive an SLD diagnosis (Embleton 2021). For example, cutoff points for designating a learning disability are necessary for allocating resources, but using strict cutoff points might be discriminatory to certain students who score just above the cutoff. These children might be excluded from accessing services despite having an educational profile and academic needs similar to those slightly below the cutoff point and who receive the services (Fletcher & Miciak 2019).

To overcome the issues with the reliability of SLD identification, Fletcher & Miciak (2019) advise that professionals should consider a range for test scores (confidence intervals) instead of a strict cutoff point and use multiple data points (e.g. different measurements) rather than relying on just one data point or a single criterion. Also, they suggest employing high thresholds for intervention planning, inclusive of a higher number of students with learning difficulties. This consideration will facilitate early inclusive intervention and reduce the chances of false-negative error, in which a student has SLD but is not diagnosed and does not receive interventions. On the other hand, this method might increase the chance of false-positive errors that are less damaging. If a child with learning issues is diagnosed with SLD, they can be pulled out of the intervention programme if further monitoring and assessment reveals an inaccurate diagnosis.

COMORBIDITY

The prevalence of comorbidity with other disorders is very high among individuals with SLD. The presence of additional disorders might impact the manifestation and severity of learning difficulties (e.g. poor social outcomes and response to interventions). Therefore, it is essential to identify the comorbid disorders with SLD.

More than 50% of children with dyslexia meet the criteria for a Specific Language Disorder diagnosis (McArthur, Hogben, Edwards, Heath, & Mengler 2000). Moreover, children with LD often present deficits in motor, sensory, and perceptual areas (Capellini, Coppede, & Valle 2010).

About 31% to 45% of individuals with SLD also have ADHD (DuPaul, Gormley, & Laracy 2013). The high rate of comorbidity between SLD and ADHD may be due to sharing the common nonspecific underlying mechanisms. Finding an isolated developmental disability is rare, and what we diagnose as different conditions are various manifestations of the same difficulties, atypical brain development (Gilger and Kaplan 2001). However, according to DSM-5, ADHD is different from SLD. Even though ADHD is associated with poor academic skills, learning problems in these children are more likely to be secondary to the ADHD symptoms affecting academic performances rather than a specific learning disorder. Regardless, if the criteria are met for both disorders, one can be diagnosed with both. In addition, comorbidity with ADHD puts individuals at a higher risk for academic and mental health issues and poor long-term outcomes (Sexton, Gelhorn, Bell, & Classi 2012).

Prevalence of comorbid symptoms such as anxiety and depression is also high among people with SLD. Learning disorders often place children at risk for stressful educational and relationship experiences that, if not adequately addressed, might lead to psychosocial maladjustment over time (Sorrenti et al. 2019). In some cases, failing to achieve academic success may lead to increased levels of stress or depression for students with SLD (Bender, Rosenkrans, & Crane 1999). SLD is a risk factor for internalizing problems in the early school years and externalizing problems later. In their first years of school, children with SLD may experience school failure and other struggles that might result in low self-esteem (McNulty 2003), whereas behavioural problems in these children are likely to accumulate over time (Halonen, Aunola, & Ahonen 2006; Klassen, Tze, & Hannok 2013; Sorrenti et al. 2019). Children with co-occuring (math and reading) SLD have more extensive achievement struggles than single-deficit groups and, therefore, are more likely to be at risk for internalizing and externalizing problems (Sorrenti et al. 2019). The higher likelihood of psychiatric disorders among people with learning disabilities as compared to their peers (Cooray & Bakala 2005) may be due to a variety of factors some of which may be genetic. However, their negative school and interpersonal experiences are significant stressors that can be reduced if SLD is detected early and children receive adequate support.

Studies found an association between SLDs and suicidal ideation and suicide attempts. For example, in 2012, a Canadian Community Health Survey (n = 21,744) showed a much higher rate of lifetime suicide attempts in individuals with SLD (11.1%) compared to those without (2.7%). In addition, the odds of attempting suicide were 46% higher in adults with SLD despite adjusting for important risk factors (e.g. unfavourable childhood, mental disorders, and substance abuse and SES). Adverse childhood experiences greatly impacted the link between SLD and suicide attempts. Also, exposure to chronic parental domestic violence and having a major depressive disorder were significantly associated with higher odds of suicide attempts (Fuller-Thomson, Carroll, & Yang 2018).

DEVELOPMENTAL COURSE

SLD is diagnosed during school years. However, early signs of SLD manifest in preschool years in different areas of a child's development such as difficulties with motor skills (e.g. hand–eye coordination, balance), language (e.g. unclear speech, delay in expressive and receptive language), attention (e.g. following instructions, focusing), and social skills (e.g. social adaptively, peers' acceptance; Balikci & Melekoglu 2020).

The onset of learning challenges in the form of reading, writing and mathematics disabilities is evident in the early school years, but SLD usually persists and impacts the individual's learning throughout the life span (Wilson et al. 2015) and their functioning and well-being into adulthood. People with SLD struggle with academic achievement and consequently, with obtaining credentials, maintaining employment and financial security, poor self-esteem, mental health, and marital discord (Bonti et al. 2021; Eloranta et al. 2021). Levels of emotional and social adaptation and life outcomes in individuals with learning disabilities differ widely. These differences can be explained by differences in risk factors and adaptive factors, and co-occurring conditions with SLD (Morrison & Cosden 1997). Risk factors might be related to the individual (e.g. impulsivity, hyperactivity or denial of the disability), environment (e.g. lack of flexibility and organization in family, school disruption and failure) or an interaction between the two. On the other hand, individual protective factors (e.g. self-esteem, verbal skills, and awareness about the disability) and environmental protective factors (e.g. good parenting skills, parents' realistic expectations and flexibility, school support) can help protect the individual from the possible adverse outcomes of SLD. Also, there is an association between educational and occupational achievement (employment and income) of adults with SLD in their twenties and their parents' SES and education. Parents' SES contributes to various factors such as financial resources for specialized support and school services and providing employment opportunities for children with SLD (O'Connor & Spreen 1988) that can mitigate the risk of poor outcomes in children with SLD. Also, how the parents and family perceive a child's disability (different beliefs about the etiology of SLD and how it affects a child's future life) may affect the child's vulnerability and emotional challenges. For example, in cultures where reading and numerical skills are highly valued, children with SLD may experience more extensive emotional and social impacts (Morrison & Cosden 1997).

Many students with SLD enrol in college programs, but their persistence and graduation rate is lower than typically developing students (Wagner et al. 2005). Although high school GPA is a significant predictor of college GPA, social integration is the most powerful predictor of academic persistence (intention for graduation). DaDeppo (2009) emphasized the importance of social interaction between the SLD student and the faculty members, peers and connection with the campus community. For example, the perception of SLD students that the campus community cares for them and is interested in them affects their academic persistence. However, social interactions are not a unique predictor of college GPA (DaDeppo 2009; Jorgensen, Budd, Fichten, Nguyen, & Havel 2018).

INTERVENTIONS FOR SLD

Medical Interventions

Many people with learning disabilities use psychotropic medications such as antipsychotics, antidepressants, antianxiety, mood stabilizers, antiepileptic medications, psychostimulants, and opioid antagonists. However, the appropriateness of these medications for behaviour problems has not been sufficiently studied (i.e. studies did not apply randomized controlled trials; Deb 2007). Moreover, since the adverse effects of psychotropic drugs are well documented (Mago 2016), medications should be prescribed with a precise rationale. Also, non-medical interventions should be utilized along with or as a substitute for medications (Deb 2007).

Psychological Interventions

As a result of repeated failure experiences in their academic activities, children with SLD might experience frustration, helplessness, anger, and challenges in interacting and developing solid relationships with peers (Agaliotis & Kalyva 2008; Leichtentritt & Shechtman 2010). Therefore, SLD professionals should focus on psycho-educational interventions and social skills in children with SLD in addition to working on literacy and arithmetic skills (Sorrenti et al. 2019). For example, I Can Succeed (ICS) is a psychological intervention for adolescents with SLD that works on improving the intrapersonal, interpersonal, and school/community areas. ICS helps students understand their strengths and challenges and improve their self-awareness, communication skills, relationships with parents, and self-advocacy skills (i.e. expressing their needs and what can help them). This programme also focuses on improving the connection between the family and school and supporting parents to communicate with school personnel to address the student's school issues. This intervention effectively decreased internalizing and externalizing problems in youth (aged 11–15 years) and significantly increased academic hope and effort (Kopelman-Rubin et al. 2012). Also, studies show that individuals with SLD might benefit from mindfulness meditation techniques (Beauchemin, Hutchins, & Patterson 2008) and Cognitive Behaviour Therapy (Bekirogullari 2018).

Remediation for Learning Academic Skills

The RTI intervention identification model supports early SLD intervention. This model provides all early elementary students with a curriculum that focuses on phonemic awareness, the alphabetic principle, vocabulary, and text comprehension, which can reduce the number of referred students for special education. However, a few students persist in having learning problems despite receiving these high-quality general instructions. This suggests that they should receive interventions that focus on specific areas of weakness and are designed based on a comprehensive assessment of the student.

Similarly, Partanen and Siegel (2014) suggested that learning disabilities are associated with phonological awareness, letter knowledge, rapid automatized naming, and working memory issues. A longitudinal study showed that early interventions targeting these skills could reduce the number of children who identified with SLD in the following school years. All kindergarten children in this study received training for phonological awareness, language development, and early literacy learning. Also, at-risk students received additional individual or group interventions (i.e. activities to improve rhyming, segmenting, sounds, blending sounds, and matching sounds with their letters). In Grade 1–7, the training programme focused on more advanced reading comprehension skills, including making connections to background knowledge, predicting what will happen next, guessing the meaning of unknown words, self-monitoring and self-correcting, recognizing themes, and summarizing and inferring the text. Results showed that 22% of the participants were identified as at-risk for SLD in kindergarten (age 5–6), but only 6% had reading disabilities in grade 7 (age 12–13).

Nayton, Hettrich, Samar, and Wilkinson (2017) summarized the evidence-based interventions for reading disability (RD) in three aspects, including reading accuracy, fluency, and comprehension. Interventions of reading accuracy are focused on improving the deficits in phonological awareness and phoneme-grapheme connections. Examples of these interventions include teaching alphabetic letters and their corresponding sounds, or teaching to break down the words into onset (M in Meat) and rime (eat in Meat). Strategies for improving reading fluency include repeated reading, passage preview and corrective feedback for errors. Repeated reading involves reading a passage (at the student's reading level) multiple times until a specific goal is achieved (e.g. specified number of correct words and errors). This technique improves reading fluency and accuracy and facilitates reading comprehension, and is more effective when applied intensively in 10–20 minute sessions, 3–5 times a week. Corrective feedback is another intervention technique. That is providing immediate feedback when the student misreads or skips a word or overall feedback after finishing a passage, followed by the student's attempt to reread the text and correct the mistakes. Also, the passage preview intervention delivers an example of the passage read aloud (either by a fluent reader or by using an audio player). Then, students can follow along and practice reading after listening. The fluency intervention techniques can be effectively applied by peers partnered with students, using audio recording, adults, teachers, or tutoring volunteers. However, well-trained teachers can deliver the best outcomes.

Another element of RD interventions is reading comprehension, which can employ a text-based or an oral language approach. In a text-based method, students learn skills such as text-monitoring, making and answering questions, summarizing and paraphrasing, and making story maps and graphic organizers. These strategies are more beneficial for secondary students. On the other hand, the oral language approach emphasizes language development, vocabulary development and enriching the language environment. Oral language strategies include analysing similarities and differences and connections between words, repeated exposure to vocabulary, and pre-teaching vocabulary (Nayton et al. 2017).

Methods to improve mathematics disability include verbal strategies (understanding questions' sentences) and visual strategies (placing numbers in diagrams). These interventions can improve problem-solving and solution accuracy. Moreover, working memory is a moderator for the effectiveness of the interventions. The students with higher working memory capacity benefit more from the treatment (Swanson 2015).

Writing intervention strategies improve the writing skills of children with written expression disability. These methods include teaching students to plan, write, and revise (strategy instruction), allowing students to dictate the composition aloud to a person/scribe or on a tape recorder instead of writing by hand, and defining short-term goals such as revising or using certain elements, engaging students in the process of planning (goal setting) and drafting, revising, editing, and publishing their writing for their actual writing needs as they come up (process writing; Nayton et al. 2017).

Interventions are most effective when they are systematic (i.e. structured, planned and repeated sessions), intensive (i.e. with a high level of frequency), and with a lower teacher–student ratio (e.g. group size of 2–7 children). Also, proper timing of the interventions for each developmental stage (e.g. phonemic awareness in early elementary and reading comprehension tasks such as summarizing and paraphrasing secondary years) and applying a multisensory approach (learning by seeing a word, hearing how it sounds and tracing it with finger) are shown to be essential factors in the effectiveness of interventions (Nayton et al. 2017).

Assistive Technology

Applying assistive technology for the education of students with SLD is crucial as they compensate for their disabilities and facilitate learning. Individuals with SLD can benefit from generic technology made for the public (e.g. audio recorders, word processing software, calculators, spell checkers, grammar checkers). In addition, they can use the type of technology designed specifically for people with disabilities (e.g. text-to-speech- software, audio taped school books, interactive videos, and instructional software; Lewis & Lewis 1998; Forgrave 2002). Technology allows individuals with SLD to participate in activities and learn alongside their peers in the classroom. They have several benefits for students with learning disabilities; it reduces the cognitive load/effort and fatigue, it allows them to complete school- or work-related tasks independently and helps them build confidence (Adebisi, Liman, & Longpoe 2015).

SUMMARY

This chapter discussed the characterization of specific learning disabilities, the cognitive bases for different variations and subtypes (reading, writing, and mathematics), and how SLD manifests in different languages. We present the different models used for SLD diagnosis and the advantages and disadvantages of each model. We describe the relationship between IQ and SLD, issues measuring IQ in individuals with SLD, and why professionals should avoid using IQ scores to identify SLD. This chapter also focuses on comorbid disorders in SLD and why individuals with SLD are at higher risk of these comorbid conditions. SLD manifests in different developmental stages and risk and protective factors affect individual outcomes in different areas (e.g. social-emotional, educational, occupational). The chapter concludes with an overview of the different treatment methods for SLD, including pharmacological and psychological interventions, academic remediation, and use of assistive technology.

Reflective Questions

1. What are the diagnostic criteria of SLD according to the DSM-5?
2. Explain whether or not the measurement of IQ is necessary for the diagnosis of SLD and why?
3. How does SLD manifest in different languages?
4. Explain the association between ADHD and SLD.
5. What are some of the diagnostic models for SLD? What are the advantages and disadvantages of each?
6. What are the risk factors and protective factors for the long-term outcomes of individuals with SLD?
7. Why are individuals with SLD at higher risk of mental health challenges, and what mental health conditions are common in individuals with SLD?
8. What are evidence-based interventions strategies for improving reading disability?
9. What is the importance of mental and social interventions for individuals with SLD?
10. In what ways can individuals with SLD benefit from assistive technology?

Recommended Videos

See this video for more information on gender related bias in diagnosis of SLD

https://youtu.be/psJ48JbYQpY

See this video for a simulation of how individuals with SLD visually perceive printed words

https://youtu.be/nhv-6ReBALA

See this video for an example of an SLD examination session

https://youtu.be/DNu4WiQaVTI

See this video for a lecture by Linda Siegel on the issues of underdiagnosing SLD and using the discrepancy model for diagnosing of SLD

www.youtube.com/watch?v=5Zmj2fsqatc

See this video for more information on mental disorders comorbid with SLD

https://youtu.be/t5T_OsnqAUM

See this video for more information on the emotional impact of having SLD

https://youtu.be/eUV6xHYH3CU

See this video for more information on psychological and emotional challenges of students with SLD and how early diagnosis and intervention can help them

https://youtu.be/oJ7xa6meD2Q

See this video on coexisting conditions with SLD

https://youtu.be/GW8jfXNYDhU

See this video for signs of SLD at different ages
https://youtu.be/lkOd0GFu5k0

See this video for more information on the challenges of students with SLD in college
https://youtu.be/kSz_zjiS3E8

See this video for more information on the students with SLD's perspective on their own challenges
www.youtube.com/watch?v=mpqluwIstjM

See this video for more information on teaching self-advocacy skills to students with SLD
https://youtu.be/Qt8YSxckFNU

See this video on Early intervention, identification and appropriate teaching for SLD
www.youtube.com/watch?v=0nfdeQiT3Oo

See the video for more information on reading intervention
https://youtu.be/J6fyNvtp1r8

See this video for more information on strategies to improve mathematic disorder
https://youtu.be/saJxN8PlFq4

See this video for the advantages of inclusive teaching strategies and impact of special classrooms for students with SLD
https://youtu.be/NdrBpOV67DY

See these videos for more information on the importance of assistive technology in education of SLD
https://youtu.be/kRt-UFa07bY

https://youtu.be/nAeXu20V19w

REFERENCES

Adebisi, R. O., Liman, N. A., & Longpoe, P. K. (2015). Using assistive technology in teaching children with learning disabilities in the 21st century. *Journal of Education and Practice*, 6(24), 14–20.

Agaliotis, I., & Kalyva, E. (2008). Nonverbal social interaction skills of children with learning disabilities. *Research in Developmental Disabilities*, 29(1), 1–10.

Alloway, T. P. (2009). Working memory, but not IQ, predicts subsequent learning in children with learning difficulties. *European Journal of Psychological Assessment*, 25(2), 92–98.

Alloway, T. P., Gathercole, S. E., Adams, A. M., Willis, C., Eaglen, R., & Lamont, E. (2005). Working memory and other cognitive skills as predictors of progress toward early learning goals at school entry. *British Journal of Developmental Psychology*, 23, 417–426.

American Psychiatric Association. (2000). Neurodevelopmental disorders. In *Diagnostic and Statistical Manual of Mental Disorders (4th edn, text rev.)*.

American Psychiatric Association. (2013). Neurodevelopmental disorders. In *Diagnostic and Statistical Manual of Mental Disorders (5th edn)*.

Balikci, O. S., & Melekoglu, M. A. (2020). Early signs of specific learning disabilities in early childhood. *International Journal of Early Childhood Special Education*, *12*(1), 84–95.

Beauchemin, J., Hutchins, T. L., & Patterson, F. (2008). Mindfulness meditation may lessen anxiety, promote social skills, and improve academic performance among adolescents with learning disabilities. *Complementary Health Practice Review*, *13*(1), 34–45.

Bekirogullari, Z. (2018). Cognitive behavioural therapy in treating persons with learning disabilities. *Online Submission*, *8*(2), 31–39.

Bender, W. N., Rosenkrans, C. B., & Crane, M. K. (1999). Stress, depression, and suicide among students with learning disabilities: Assessing the risk. *Learning Disability Quarterly*, *22*(2), 143–156.

Berninger, V. W., Nielsen, K. H., Abbott, R. D., Wijsman, E., & Raskind, W. (2008). Gender differences in severity of writing and reading disabilities. *Journal of School Psychology*, *46*(2), 151–172.

Bhandari, A., & Goyal, G. (2004). Learning disabilities: Nature, causes and interventions. *Counselling: Theory, Research and Practice*, 163–187.

Bonti, E., Giannoglou, S., Georgitsi, M., Sofologi, M., Porfyri, G. N., Mousioni, A., ... & Diakogiannis, I. (2021). Clinical profiles and socio-demographic characteristics of adults with specific learning disorder in Northern Greece. *Brain Sciences*, *11*(5), 602.

Brueggemann, A. E., Kamphaus, R. W., & Dombrowski, S. C. (2008). An impairment model of learning disability diagnosis. *Professional Psychology: Research and Practice*, *39*(4), 424.

Butterworth, B. (2004). Developmental dyscalculia. In J. D. Campbell (ed.), *The Handbook of Mathematical Cognition* (pp. 455–469). New York: Psychology Press.

Capellini, S. A., Coppede, A. C., & Valle, T. R. (2010). Fine motor function of school-aged children with dyslexia, learning disability and learning difficulties. *Pró-Fono Revista de Atualizacao Científica*, *22*, 201–208.

Cooray, S. E., & Bakala, A. (2005). Anxiety disorders in people with learning disabilities. *Advances in Psychiatric Treatment*, *11*(5), 355–361.

DaDeppo, L. M. (2009). Integration factors related to the academic success and intent to persist of college students with learning disabilities. *Learning Disabilities Research & Practice*, *24*(3), 122–131.

De Rodrigues, M. C., Mello, R. R., & Fonseca, S. C. (2006). Learning difficulties in schoolchildren born with very low birth weight. *Jornal de Pediatria*, *82*, 6–14.

Deb, S. (2007). The role of medication in the management of behaviour problems in people with learning disabilities. *Advances in Mental Health and Learning Disabilities*, *1*(2), 26–31.

DuPaul, G. J., Gormley, M. J., & Laracy, S. D. (2013). Comorbidity of LD and ADHD: Implications of DSM-5 for assessment and treatment. *Journal of Learning Disabilities*, *46*(1), 43–51.

Eloranta, A. K., Närhi, V. M., Muotka, J. S., Tolvanen, A. J., Korhonen, E., Ahonen, T. P., & Aro, T. I. (2021). Psychiatric problems in adolescence mediate the association between childhood learning disabilities and later well-being. *Learning Disability Quarterly*, *44*(4), 304–317.

Embleton, P. R. (2021). *Diagnostic Utility of Machine Learning in the Identification of Specific Learning Disabilities* (Doctoral dissertation, University of Colorado at Denver).

Fletcher, J. M., & Miciak, J. (2019). *The Identification of Specific Learning Disabilities: A Summary of Research on Best Practices*. Austin, TX: Meadows Center for Preventing Educational Risk.

Forgrave, K. E. (2002). Assistive technology: Empowering students with learning disabilities. *The Clearing House, 75*(3), 122–126.

Fuller-Thomson, E., Carroll, S. Z., & Yang, W. (2018). Suicide attempts among individuals with specific learning disorders: An underrecognized issue. *Journal of Learning Disabilities, 51*(3), 283–292.

Gilger, J. W. (2001). Current issues in the neurology and genetics of learning-related traits and disorders: Introduction to the special issue. *Journal of Learning Disabilities, 34*(6), 490–491.

Gilger, J. W., & Kaplan, B. J. (2001). Atypical brain development: A conceptual framework for understanding developmental learning disabilities. *Developmental Neuropsychology, 20*(2), 465–481.

Giofrè, D., & Cornoldi, C. (2015). The structure of intelligence in children with specific learning disabilities is different as compared to typically development children. *Intelligence, 52,* 36–43.

Görker, I. (2019). The prevalence and gender differences in specific learning disorder. In *Learning Disabilities-Neurological Bases, Clinical Features and Strategies of Intervention* (p. 13). IntechOpen.

Guttorm, T. K., Leppänen, P. H., Poikkeus, A. M., Eklund, K. M., Lyytinen, P., & Lyytinen, H. (2005). Brain event-related potentials (ERPs) measured at birth predict later language development in children with and without familial risk for dyslexia. *Cortex, 41*(3), 291–303.

Halonen, A., Aunola, K., Ahonen, T., & Nurmi, J.-E. (2006). The role of learning to read in the development of problem behaviour: A cross-lagged longitudinal study. *British Journal of Educational Psychology, 76,* 517–534

Jorgensen, M., Budd, J., Fichten, C. S., Nguyen, M. N., & Havel, A. (2018). Graduation prospects of college students with specific learning disorder and students with mental health related disabilities. *International Journal of Higher Education, 7*(1), 19–31.

Klassen, R., Tze, V., & Hannok, W. (2013). Internalizing Problems of Adults With Learning Disabilities: A Meta-Analysis. *Journal of Learning Disabilities, 46*(4), 317–327. https://doi.org/10.1177/0022219411422260

Kopelman-Rubin, D., Brunstein Klomek, A., Al-Yagon, M., Mufson, L., Apter, A., & Mikulincer, M. (2012). Psychological intervention for adolescents diagnosed with learning disorders-I Can Succeed (ICS) treatment model, feasibility and acceptability. *International Journal for Research in Learning Disabilities, 1*(1), 37–54.

Leichtentritt, J., & Shechtman, Z. (2010). Children with and without learning disabilities: A comparison of processes and outcomes following group counseling. *Journal of Learning Disabilities, 43*(2), 169–179.

Lewis, R. B., & Lewis, R. B. (1998). Assistive technology and learning disabilities: Today's realities and tomorrow's promises. *Journal of Learning Disabilities, 31*(1), 16–26.

Mago, R. (2016). Adverse effects of psychotropic medications: a call to action. *Psychiatric Clinics, 39*(3), 361–373.

McArthur, G. M., Hogben, J. H., Edwards, V. T., Heath, S. M., & Mengler, E. D. (2000). On the 'specifics' of specific reading disability and specific language impairment. *The Journal of Child Psychology and Psychiatry and Allied Disciplines, 41*(7), 869–874.

McNulty, M. A. (2003). Dyslexia and the life course. *Journal of Learning Disabilities*, *36*(4), 363–381.

Moll, K., Göbel, S. M., Gooch, D., Landerl, K., & Snowling, M. J. (2016). Cognitive risk factors for specific learning disorder: Processing speed, temporal processing, and working memory. *Journal of Learning Disabilities*, *49*(3), 272–281.

Moll, K., Kunze, S., Neuhoff, N., Bruder, J., & Schulte-Körne, G. (2014). Specific learning disorder: Prevalence and gender differences. *PLoS One*, *9*(7), e103537.

Morrison, G. M., & Cosden, M. A. (1997). Risk, resilience, and adjustment of individuals with learning disabilities. *Learning Disability Quarterly*, *20*(1), 43–60.

Nayton, M., Hettrich, E. L., Samar, S., & Wilkinson, C. (2017). Evidence-based assessment and interventions for problems with Reading in school psychology. In *Handbook of Australian School Psychology* (pp. 173–195). Springer, Cham.

O'Connor, S. C., & Spreen, O. (1988). The relationship between parents' socioeconomic status and education level, and adult occupational and educational achievement of children with learning disabilities. *Journal of Learning Disabilities*, *21*(3), 148–153.

Partanen, M., & Siegel, L. S. (2014). Long-term outcome of the early identification and intervention of reading disabilities. *Reading and Writing*, *27*(4), 665–684.

Rourke, B. P. (2005). Neuropsychology of learning disabilities: Past and future. *Learning Disability Quarterly*, *28*(2), 111–114.

Sahin, B., Bozkurt, A., & Karabekiroglu, K. (2019). Perinatal and medical risk factors in children with attention deficit hyperactivity disorder, autism spectrum disorder or specific learning disorder: Comparison between diagnostic groups. *Istanbul Medical Journal*, *20*(6).

Serrano, F., & Defior, S. (2008). Dyslexia speed problems in a transparent orthography. *Annals of Dyslexia*, *58*(1), 81–95.

Sexton, C. C., Gelhorn, H. L., Bell, J. A., & Classi, P. M. (2012). The co-occurrence of reading disorder and ADHD: Epidemiology, treatment, psychosocial impact, and economic burden. Journal of learning disabilities, 45(6), 538–564.

Seymour, P. H., Aro, M., Erskine, J. M. (2003). Foundation literacy acquisition in European orthographies. *British Journal of Psychology*, *94*(2), 143–174.

Shaywitz, S. E., Shaywitz, B. A., Fletcher, J. M., & Escobar, M. D. (1990). Prevalence of reading disability in boys and girls: Results of the Connecticut longitudinal study. *Jama*, *264*(8), 998–1002.

Siegel, L. S. (1988). Evidence that IQ scores are irrelevant to the definition and analysis of reading disability. *Canadian Journal of Psychology / Revue canadienne de psychologie*, *42*(2), 201–215. https://doi.org/10.1037/h0084184

Siegel, L. S. (1989). IQ is irrelevant to the definition of learning disabilities. *Journal of Learning Disabilities*, *22*(8), 469–478.

Siegel, L. S. (1999). Issues in the definition and diagnosis of learning disabilities: A perspective on Guckenberger v. Boston University. *Journal of Learning Disabilities*, *32*(4), 304–319.

Silver, L. B. (2008). *Attention-Deficit/Hyperactivity Disorder: A Clinical Guide to Diagnosis and Treatment for Health and Mental Health Professionals*. American Psychiatric Pub.

Snowling, M. J. (1995). Phonological processing and developmental dyslexia. *Journal of Research in Reading*. 18, 132–138.

Sorrenti, L., Spadaro, L., Mafodda, A. V., Scopelliti, G., Orecchio, S., & Filippello, P. (2019). The predicting role of school Learned helplessness in internalizing and externalizing problems. An exploratory study in students with specific learning disorder. *Mediterranean Journal of Clinical Psychology*, 7(2).

Stanovich, K. E. (2005). The future of a mistake: Will discrepancy measurement continue to make the learning disabilities field a pseudoscience? *Learning Disability Quarterly*, 28(2), 103–106.

Steinle, P. K., Stevens, E., & Vaughn, S. (2022). Fluency interventions for struggling readers in grades 6 to 12: A research synthesis. *Journal of Learning Disabilities*, 55(1), 3–21.

Swanson, H.L., & Keogh, B.K. (Eds.). (1990). Learning Disabilities: Theoretical and Research Issues (1st ed.). Routledge. https://doi.org/10.4324/9780203052303

Swanson, H. L. (2015). Cognitive strategy interventions improve word problem solving and working memory in children with math disabilities. *Frontiers in Psychology*, 6, 1099.

Toffalini, E., Giofrè, D., & Cornoldi, C. (2017). Strengths and weaknesses in the intellectual profile of different subtypes of specific learning disorder: a study on 1,049 diagnosed children. *Clinical Psychological Science*, 5(2), 402–409.

Toffalini, E., Pezzuti, L., & Cornoldi, C. (2017). Einstein and dyslexia: Is giftedness more frequent in children with a specific learning disorder than in typically developing children? *Intelligence*, 62, 175–179.

Vaughn, S., Linan-Thompson, S., & Hickman, P. (2003). Response to instruction as a means of identifying students with reading/learning disabilities. *Exceptional children*, 69(4), 391–409.

Wagner, R. K., Francis, D. J., & Morris, R. D. (2005). Identifying English language learners with learning disabilities: Key challenges and possible approaches. *Learning Disabilities Research & Practice*, 20(1), 6–15.

Whittaker, M., & Burns, M. K. (2019). *Evaluation for Specific Learning Disabilities: Allowable Methods of Identification and Their Implications*. Washington, DC: National Center for Learning Disabilities.

Willcutt, E. G., Petrill, S. A., Wu, S., Boada, R., DeFries, J. C., Olson, R. K., & Pennington, B. F. (2013). Comorbidity between reading disability and math disability: Concurrent psychopathology, functional impairment, and neuropsychological functioning. *Journal of Learning Disabilities*, 46(6), 500–516.

Wilson, A. J., Andrewes, S. G., Struthers, H., Rowe, V. M., Bogdanovic, R., & Waldie, K. E. (2015). Dyscalculia and dyslexia in adults: Cognitive bases of comorbidity. *Learning and Individual Differences*, 37, 118–132.

Yule, W. (1973). Differential prognosis of reading backwardness and specific reading retardation. *British Journal of Educational Psychology*, 43(3), 244–248.

Zablotsky, B., & Alford, J. M. (2020). Racial and ethnic differences in the prevalence of attention-deficit/hyperactivity disorder and learning disabilities among US children aged 3-17 years. *NCHS Data Brief. No. 358*. National Center for Health Statistics.

11
ATTENTION DEFICIT/ HYPERACTIVITY DISORDER

> ### Learning Objectives
>
> After reading this chapter, you should be able to:
>
> - Review the main theories of AD/HD
> - Understand risk factors associated with AD/HD
> - Understand the developmental course of AD/HD
> - Review the diagnostic process for AD/HD
> - Review the pharmacological and psychosocial interventions for AD/HD

Attention Deficit Disorder with or without hyperactivity (AD/HD) is a neurodevelopmental disability that is presumed to be present at birth but not detected until later in childhood. This is because the behaviours that define AD/HD are not evident until school age when the child's level of motor activity far exceeds what is typical for their age (in cases with hyperactivity). In addition, the child's abilities to concentrate on tasks, regulate their behaviour and execute actions are not meeting age expectations.

The term 'attention deficit' can be misleading when considering the challenges that individuals with AD/HD face. These individuals often have difficulty with intrinsic motivation for nonpreferred tasks (e.g. homework) yet they may be overly focused on a preferred task (e.g. a video game). Individuals with AD/HD frequently lack the self-control to resist temptation for immediate gratification and find it challenging to sustain attention to a non-preferred task that is effortful. Low self-efficacy and negative beliefs about the self, further impair their motivation.

AD/HD is one of the most prevalent developmental conditions of childhood and, in most cases, persists into adulthood and old age (Rooney & Pfiffner 2018). It is estimated to affect

2.2% of children worldwide (Fayyad et al. 2017). Prevalence rates vary widely across studies depending on the country and culture sampled, however, this is most likely due to differences in diagnostic practices, methodology, and definition, and not ethnic or cultural differences per se. However, environmental and cultural factors do contribute to differential prevalence rates (Polanczyk,, Lima, Horta, Biederman, Rohde 2007). For example, differences in parenting beliefs and practices, as well as societal and cultural norms for behaviour may influence the behavioural expression of AD/HD symptoms and/or lead to differing referral rates for an AD/HD assessment.

Data from 20 twin studies (including United States, European Union, Scandinavia and Australia) estimate the mean heritability of AD/HD to be as high as 76%, suggesting that the diagnosis of AD/HD is inherited and family or extended family members share the diagnosis (Faraone et al. 2005). The broader phenotype, or traits associated with AD/HD, such as impulsivity, hyperactivity, and inattention also appear to be inherited. This suggests that the same genes that are responsible for normal variation in personality traits like impulsivity, hyperactivity, and inattention can aggregate and contribute to the risk for AD/HD. Therefore, the more of the genes associated with AD/HD traits that a child inherits, the more likely it is that they will be diagnosed with the developmental disability. The evidence points to a polygenic (multiple genes) inheritance mechanism, whereby a certain number of specific genes must be present to contribute to a diagnosis of AD/HD. An international large sample study discovered that genetic variants accounted for 22% of the risk for AD/HD (Demontis et al. 2019). Genetic variants refer to variations in DNA structure from what is commonly seen in the Normal population. Although researchers have identified 25+ genes that are suspected to be related to AD/HD, we do not know what number of genes, which combination of genes, or how the genes confer risk for AD/HD. AD/HD is a complex and heterogenous condition involving multiple genes and mechanisms from molecular through to societal level factors. Once we uncover the 'genetic lottery' or more likely 'genetic lotteries' for AD/HD, we still have to uncover the precise role of the identified genes and how they interact with a host of proximal and distal environmental factors to fully understand the cause(s) of AD/HD.

Given the polygenic inheritance and heterogeneity of AD/HD, researchers are rethinking the notion of one underlying cause for AD/HD and, instead, are studying endophenotypes to understand the potential multiple causes that either independently or synergistically contribute to a diagnosis of AD/HD. *Endophenotypes* are conceptualized as intermediaries between the observed behaviour (i.e., phenotype) of the individual such as the symptoms of AD/HD and the genotypes and environment that cause the condition (Gottesman & Gould 2003). These endophenotypes can be studied at many levels; physiological, neurophysiological, and cognitive. As we will see in the next section, different theories of AD/HD emphasize the role of endophenotypes in the development of AD/HD but at different levels. For example, there are theories of AD/HD that underscore the importance of physiological arousal; other theories emphasize the neurophysiological brain reward mechanisms, and still others, cognitive control mechanisms such as executive functioning. There is growing evidence that multiple endophenotypes are implicated in AD/HD.

Endophenotypes

Gottesman and Shield (1972) first proposed the concept of endophenotypes in the field of psychiatry to help narrow the search for genetic susceptibility to mental disorder. Endophenotypes were originally defined as 'internal' biological indices of susceptibility and later broadened to 'simpler clues to the genetics underpinning psychiatric diseases than the disease syndrome itself' (Gottesman & Gould 2003).

Endophenotypes are considered intermediate pathways in the developmental course that leads to a behavioural syndrome. Any fundamental process (e.g., neuroanatomical, neurochemical, neurophysiological, neuropsychological) that is theoretically and/or empirically linked to the phenotype of interest would be a candidate endophenotype.

In psychology we often consider cognitive mechanisms as endophenotypes. For example, rather than look for the genes that cause a complex polygenic condition like AD/HD, behavioural geneticists may have an easier time focusing on the genes that contribute to executive functioning or impulsivity that are common challenges for individuals with AD/HD. This reduces the genetic complexity a little by narrowing in on underlying traits that like impulsivity vary in the normal population but may be at the 'extreme' end of the normal curve in the AD/HD population.

ASSOCIATED RISK FACTORS

In addition to endophenotypes of AD/HD, there are a number of prenatal risk factors that have been found to be associated with, and even predict, AD/HD in children. Prospective studies have consistently found a link between smoking during pregnancy and hyperactivity and inattention in the offspring (Cornelius & Day 2009; Galéra et al. 2011). However, it is less clear whether a link exists between prenatal exposures to alcohol, illicit drugs, and psychotropic medications and the risk for AD/HD. Also, during pregnancy, the mother's well-being may be a factor. Studies have found that maternal stress and psychosocial adversity increases the risk of AD/HD in their offspring (Rodriguez et al. 2009; Galéra et al. 2011).

Being born prematurely as well as with low birth weight each seems to confer an increased risk for inattention and hyperactivity/impulsivity in children (Lindström, Lindblad, & Hjern 2011; Yang et al. 2015).

Children with AD/HD may have food sensitivities that are associated with worse symptoms (Kim et al. 2018), but there is no empirical evidence that certain foods, including sugar, cause ADHD or associated symptoms (Del-Ponte et al. 2019).

Too much television watching or video game playing is not recommended for children, however, these do not cause AD/HD. Symptoms of AD/HD may increase when children do not have the opportunity to release their energy through physical activity.

Poor parenting can exacerbate AD/HD symptoms but does not cause the condition. For example, when parents are overly controlling or punishing they miss opportunities to reward good behaviour. This in turn, may lead to inadvertently reinforcing negative behaviour in children. Parenting styles and behavioural problems in children appear to be bi-directionally related (Latimer et al. 2003; Chronis et al. 2007), meaning that difficulties in parenting are associated with increased behaviour problems in children and increased levels of behaviour problems in children predict harsher parenting practices. This vicious cycle is usually altered by intervening with the parent to train them to use behavioural strategies to set clear expectations for their children and reduce negative parent–child interactions.

Without the benefit of early identification and intervention, people with AD/HD are at greater risk for adverse life events such as dropping out of school, substance addiction, early pregnancy, and trauma (Barkley et al. 2008).

THEORIES OF AD/HD

Theories of AD/HD fall under two main categories; those that focus on 'top-down' cognitive control of behaviour and those that emphasize 'bottom-up' motivational or energetic factors. One of the original top-down theories posited that the attention problems and impulsive behaviour seen in children with AD/HD were the result of underlying difficulties in higher order, cognitive brain mechanisms of executive functioning (Pennigton & Ozonoff 1996). Other top-down theories have since elaborated on the role of executive functioning in AD/HD. A well-studied theory is Barkley's Executive Function (EF) Theory of AD/HD (Barkley, 1997, 2001). EF refers broadly to higher level cognitive control processes that allow one to evaluate a situation and to determine, and successfully carry out, an appropriate course of action toward a goal. This theory proposes that behavioural inhibition, one's ability to inhibit a response when necessary; is the core issue in children with AD/HD, not attention problems. Barkley argues that self-control, which is integrally related to executive functioning, is the primary difficulty in AD/HD. *Behavioural inhibition* consists of three interrelated processes: (1) the ability to inhibit a pre-potent (automatic) response; (2) the ability to delay a response or extinguish a response that has been initiated; and (3) the ability to sustain focus on a response, preventing interference from distracting stimuli.

Executive Function

There is significant debate about whether to conceptualize EF as a unitary, componential, or integrative framework. The unitary view propose a singular underlying ability that controls goal-oriented thoughts and actions (Goldstein, Naglieri, Princiotta, & Otero, 2014). Unitary theories conceptualize EF as a limited capacity system that prioritizes processing of and response to goal-relevant information, in the presence of irrelevant and/or competing information. Over time, children master this ability through increasing complexity and flexibility in mental representations of rules and goals (Zelazo 1998; Munakata 2012). Componential models of EF propose that multiple processes subserve EF (Nigg 2000). For example, different systems of inhibitory control (e.g. motor, cognitive, and behavioural) that work together to help the individual accomplish a goal-relevant action. The integrative theory views EF as both separable and interrelated, that is, there are subcomponents of EF that work together to regulate thoughts and actions to achieve a specific goal.

According to Barkley's theory, deficits in behavioural inhibition interfere with four interconnected executive functions: (1) *Internalization of speech* serves to transfer external events to internal, private rules for behaviour and action. When young, children's behaviour is mostly directed by external stimuli as seen when infants automatically orient their attention to the sound of a rattle. However, as children grow they learn to transfer control of their action and behaviour from external control to self-control. Internalizing their speech is one important step in that process; (2) *Reconstitution* refers to the analysis and synthesis of verbal and non-verbal information for more sophisticated language and actions; (3) *Working memory* allows the manipulation of information in memory when problem solving a task, even if there is no external stimulus. For example, when doing mental math, one must keep certain information in mind while manipulating it and solving the problem; and (4) *Self-regulation of affect-motivation-arousal* is the ability to control one's emotions, motivation and actions in the service of achieving adaptive goals. For example, children need to muster the motivation and positive attitude to study in order to succeed at academic tasks (Barkley 1997).

The disruption of the four interconnected executive functions (*Internalization of speech, reconstitution, working memory,* and *self-regulation of affect-motivation-arousal*) creates many challenges for the child in executing goal-directed behaviours in a variety of settings which compound over time.

Based on a meta-analysis of several research studies, researchers concluded that it is difficult to determine whether EF challenges and AD/HD symptoms are causally related and, if so, how. That is, we do not know if EF challenges are what cause the AD/HD symptoms or if the AD/HD symptoms lead to EF challenges in certain children. There are researchers who suspect that EF challenges are a symptom rather than a cause of AD/HD (Willcutt, Doyle, Nigg, Faraone, & Pennington 2005).

The cognitive-energetic model (CEM) (Sergeant 2000) is a bottom-up theory, because it proposes that lower level arousal and motivational processes are involved in AD/HD. This theory proposes that energetic pools (i.e., arousal, activation, and effort) are the root cause of AD/HD. The failure in inhibition is thought to be a consequence of the individual's faulty energetic system. Proponents of this model argue that Barkley's premise that AD/HD is primarily an inhibition deficit is an oversimplification. Evidence to support this claim comes from a series of studies wherein different tasks were used to measure behavioural inhibition but no inhibition deficit was found in children with AD/HD as compared to typically developing (TD) children. This was the case also when the inhibition performance of children with AD/HD was compared to that of children with conduct disorder (CD), and to children with AD/HD and co-occurring CD. The CEM proposes three levels (Sergeant 2000, 2005): Level 1 consists of encoding, central processing, and response organization; Level 2 consists of the energetic pools: arousal, activation, and effort; Level 3 consists of the management of the executive function system. There is evidence that children with AD/HD show deficiencies of the first two levels but not Level 3. However, a direct measure of the energetic pools (i.e., arousal, activation, and effort) has not been possible and therefore, it is difficult to find support for the CEM and its claims that impaired energetic pools are responsible for behavioural inhibition difficulties in AD/HD.

There have been attempts to integrate the top-down (inhibition) and bottom-up (arousal/motivation) factors into a comprehensive model. One theory (Sonuga-Barke 2005) explains inattention as a result of impairment in EF and response inhibition, and impulsivity as the result of limitations in motivational responding. This theory predicts that the neural processes involved in EF and motivational responding compete, resulting in the inconsistent and impulsive behaviour style commonly observed in individuals with AD/HD.

Another theory (Castellanos & Tannock 2002) proposes that multiple systems acting together lead to AD/HD symptoms: (1) atypical reward-related brain circuitry that leads to difficulty with delay of gratification; (2) deficits in temporal processing, the ability to perceive and organize sequences of actions, resulting in within-individual variability in response and attention, and (3) deficits in working memory.

To explain the difference between the inattentive and the combined inattentive/hyperactivity subtypes of AD/HD, certain theories have proposed that the inattentive subtype is primarily a cognitive impairment of working memory and/or 'cool' EF system whereas the combined inattentive/hyperactivity subtype involves the 'hot' EF system responsible for processing emotional stimuli (Castellanos, Sonuga-Barke, Milham, & Tannock 2006). Other theories predict that both cognitive and affect regulation are impaired in individuals with AD/HD regardless of the subtype (Nigg & Casey 2005; Willcutt, Doyle, Nigg, Faraone, & Pennington 2005). However, they predict that each subtype would have distinct neuropsychological profiles.

Hot and Cool Executive Functions

Hot executive functions refer to self-regulation skills that we use when we are under pressure or we are emotionally aroused.

Cool executive functions refer to the skills we use when we are not emotionally aroused and we are free of pressure.

You may have guessed that most problem solving that we engage in regularly involves both working together to accomplish a goal and learn efficiently. The brain can quickly shift back and forth between them.

As we grow older, and with practice, we are better at balancing emotional and rational decision making but there are also individual differences in this ability. For example, children with ADHD, who can be quite impulsive, may have a harder time delaying gratification compared to children who are less impulsive and more reflective. However, interventions that emphasize stopping and thinking before acting would help this child engage their cool EF to decide whether acting in a particular situation would lead to a desirable outcome or have a negative consequence.

Wilicut et al's (2005) meta-analysis suggests that it is difficult to determine whether EF challenges and AD/HD symptoms can be attributed to common etiologic influences. It is difficult to determine if EF challenges are what lead to the AD/HD or if the AD/HD leads to EF challenges in certain children. The authors believe that EF difficulties are a symptom rather than a cause of AD/HD.

DEVELOPMENTAL COURSE OF AD/HD

Behavioural differences in children with AD/HD are observed as early as the preschool years. Although high activity levels, weak inhibitory control, and short attention span are common in young children, in school age children with AD/HD they are more pronounced and persist over time. In addition, these symptoms are associated with maladaptive functioning such as high rates of physical injury, behaviour problems in the home and school, and lower academic performance. Preschoolers with AD/HD also have co-occurring conditions, such as language and learning challenges, oppositional defiant disorder (ODD), and anxiety disorders. (Posner et al. 2007). Symptoms of hyperactivity decrease with age but symptoms of inattention become more evident with age, trajectories of hyperactivity and inattention in early childhood are significantly associated with each other, and higher measures on one, predict higher measures on the other (Galéra, et al. 2011). Preschool AD/HD persists into school age in approximately 50% of cases, with the combined subtype showing most persistence; however, AD/HD subtypes tend to be unstable over time, with many children shifting between them (Lahey et al. 2005).

Most diagnoses of AD/HD are made during the school-age years when children are identified and referred because of behaviour and/or academic difficulties in the classroom. Children with AD/HD also have difficulties with family and peer relationships. The majority of children with AD/HD have one or more other disorders that further impede the child's adaptive functioning. These typically impact behaviour (Oppositional Defiant Disorder), mental health (anxiety disorders) and learning (learning disorders) (Barkley 2006). Although symptoms of inattention persist, hyperactivity symptoms decrease during the school years (Lahey et al. 2004). However, despite a decline with age in hyperactivity and, to a lesser extent, impulsivity, 2/3 of youth continue to show challenges associated with AD/HD symptoms into adulthood (Cherkasova, Ponde, & Hechtman 2012). The developmental outcomes of adults with AD/HD vary but most show a continuity of risky behaviour, motor vehicle infractions and injuries, lower academic achievement, relationship and marital problems, and mental health concerns (Barkley, Murphy, & Firscher 2008; Molina et al. 2009). Adults with ADHD have higher rates of criminal behaviour, according to the ADHD foundation the rates of prisoners with AD/HD (25%) are far higher than the rates of prisoners in the general population (2.5%). Adults with ADHD are also more likely to be the victims of criminal acts (Fletcher & Wolfe 2009; Young, Moss, Sedgwick, Fridman, & Hodgkins 2015).

It is important to consider that environment plays a role in AD/HD symptoms and their impact on the individual. When the environment is better tailored to the individual's needs, for example, when a school individual education plan (IEP) allows for physical breaks and includes positive behavioural supports, the child's symptoms may subside and many more of their talents and positive behaviours will be apparent. Similarly, with age, the individual is better able to select their environment and choose a career that is a good match with their interests and cognitive style. In this case, their talents and strengths would be highlighted and valued and any challenges would be less noticeable or even overlooked.

DIAGNOSIS OF AD/HD

The diagnosis of AD/HD is made on the basis of observed and reported behavioural symptoms. Two main diagnostic systems are used to diagnose AD/HD; the Diagnostic and Statistical Manual of Mental Disorders 5th edition (DSM-5) and the International Classification of Mental and Behavioural Disorders 11th revision (ICD-11). The DSM-5 diagnostic criteria include an *Inattention* symptom cluster which describes a series of items consisting of difficulties with: sustaining attention, distractibility, listening, following instructions, organizing tasks and activities, losing things, forgetfulness, and distractibility and a *Hyperactivity and Impulsivity* symptom cluster, which describes a series of items consisting of difficulties with: fidgeting, restlessness, talking excessively, blurting out answers, waiting one's turn and interrupting or intruding on others (see 5th edn; DSM-5; American Psychiatric Association, 2013). The DSM-5 requires that the symptoms have been present for at least six months. Both the DSM-5 and ICD-11 require that AD/HD symptoms are present in several settings such as school/work, home life and leisure activities and adversely affect psychological, social and/or educational/occupational functioning. This means that the AD/HD symptoms are not only present but also cause *functional impairment*. Symptoms should be evident in early life, before 12 years but may persist into adulthood.

Functional Impairment

A functional impairment refers to the impact of a condition on an individual's ability to carry out certain functions necessary for everyday life. The diagnosis or symptoms may exist in the individual with AD/HD but they may not necessarily cause a functional impairment. For example, a person who is 'hyperactive' but who has a job or lifestyle wherein being overly active does not interfere with their performance or does not impede their ability to carry out their daily tasks would not be considered functionally impaired by this symptom. However, a child whose hyperactivity is causing him injury and interfering with making friends because they are too rough with other children would be described as having a functional impairment.

There is great variability in the severity of symptoms and extent of functional impact. For a few individuals the impact of AD/HD may cause minimal impairment in only certain areas such as the ability to complete homework, chores, or developing positive peer relationships. In others, the impact is pervasive and involves multiple symptoms of hyperactivity, inattention, and impulsivity that are severe and cause significant impairment across multiple areas of life including behaviour problems, academic failure, social isolation, and mental health problems.

The majority of children with AD/HD are diagnosed with the Hyperactivity subtype. However, there are those who meet the DSM-5 criteria for the Inattention cluster but not the Hyperactivity and Impulsivity cluster. These children would be diagnosed with AD/HD with a Predominantly inattentive presentation. Similarly, those children who do not meet the DSM-5 criteria for the Inattention cluster but do meet the criteria for the Hyperactivity and Impulsivity cluster would be given the diagnosis of AD/HD with a Predominantly hyperactive/impulsive presentation.

Case Study in Attention Deficit Hyperactivity Disorder

Julian is an eight-year-old male, Grade 2 student, who lives in Vancouver, Canada with his parents. He is the youngest of three children. His parents are both employed fulltime as police officers. There is an extended family history of Attention Deficit/Hyperactivity Disorder (AD/HD) and mental health concerns as well as learning challenges. Julian is an intelligent and exuberant young boy who enjoys spending time with his friends, and participating in physical activities such as martial arts and hockey. He also enjoys participating in social events, and is often invited to, and initiates, play dates. Although Julian is popular with peers his own age, his parents reported that he can be easily led and influenced by others. They also noted that Julian can become upset when he does not have his friends' attention. His teacher reported that in the classroom, Julian exhibits attention-seeking behaviour by poking children, distracting them during work time and laughing when the teacher is teaching. Julian recognizes that he has difficulties with focusing and sustaining his attention to his school work, and sitting still in class. However, he does not agree with his parents who say that he 'hyper focuses' on his video games.

Julian's parents reported that he is often restless, and cannot sit down for an extended period of time. For example, during dinner time he is described as standing or running around and fiddling with his utensils. Julian has difficulties listening and following instructions at school and his teacher has noticed that he often blurts out answers and disrupts class activity with irrelevant comments. Julian is able to recognize that his behaviour upsets others at times but he can't seem to stop himself.

When asked if he likes school Julian shrugged his shoulders and said that he liked gym and recess but not much else. Julian finds reading very challenging; his teacher said that it is slow and laborious for him. He notices how his reading is different from that of other children in the class and is embarrassed to read in class. He would rather play with his friends than do classwork.

His parents reported that he often forgets to do what he is instructed and will leave a task midway through. His room is often messy and disorganized and he loses his things. According to his parents doing homework is 'painful' because Julian becomes very frustrated and emotionally dysregulated. He has tantrums regularly after school, screaming 'I've worked all day why do I have to do more now.'

Julian's parents felt that their son needs extra support to succeed in school so they came to the clinic in order to seek a comprehensive assessment. The psychologist first took a developmental history from the parents and then began to consider which tests would be appropriate given the presenting problem. She also determined that a structured classroom observation and an unstructured play time observation would be helpful. After administering an IQ assessment, achievement test, behavioural rating scales, and an adaptive functioning assessment and conducting school observations, the psychologist concluded that Julian met DSM-5 criteria for attention deficit hyperactivity disorder as well as specific learning disorder in the areas of reading and written expression. Julian's parents were referred to a physician to consult about possible psychopharmacological options and the school resource team set up an Individual Educational Plan (IEP) for Julian with a specific focus on reading and writing remediation. His teacher was trained to set up a behavioural plan in the classroom to improve his on task behaviour and his parents participated in a homework skills intervention to improve study and organizational skills and reduce family stress. Julian continued with martial arts and hockey but his coaches were informed of his diagnosis so that they could better understand and support him if he needed it.

Co-morbidities

Symptoms of AD/HD can overlap with those of other disorders and, therefore, it is important to carefully differentiate between AD/HD and other disorders. However, it is also possible to diagnose AD/HD alongside another disorder(s). Since AD/HD co-occurs with other conditions like autism spectrum disorder (ASD) or ODD as well as mental health disorders such as anxiety and depression, it is helpful to tease apart what functional impairments are due to the AD/HD symptoms and what impairments are due to the other condition(s) in order to make appropriate recommendations for interventions. Typically, the most functionally debilitating condition is treated first. In many cases this would be a mental health disorder such as anxiety or depression because it can prevent the individual from benefitting from psychosocial interventions designed to target cognitive and emotional regulation.

Rates of learning disabilities (LD) in children with AD/HD range from 25% to 50% (Barkley 1994) to as high as 70% (Mayes, Calhoun, & Crowell 2000). Coupled with their attentional and executive functioning difficulties, LD can be a major obstacle to school success in children with AD/HD. Despite average or above average intelligence, children with LD show a discrepancy between their potential and their academic performance due primarily to the processing challenges they have with specific academic tasks such as reading. If the LD is not addressed it can have a detrimental effect on the child's motivation and self-esteem, further contributing to the existing academic barriers for students with AD/HD.

In each case, it is important to separate the effects of AD/HD from those of the co-morbid condition. This is because each condition must be addressed with specific interventions. Helping a child with learning and other challenges separately from behavioural and attention concerns will mean that priorities will need to be set to effectively target the most pressing needs and those that interfere with the child's ability to benefit from other interventions.

Gender Differences

Boys are 4–5 times more likely to be diagnosed with AD/HD than girls. Girls and women are less likely to be referred for an AD/HD assessment, and are more likely to have AD/HD that is undiagnosed (Young et al. 2020). Girls and women are more likely to receive another diagnosis of a mental health or neurodevelopmental condition which may be incorrect, and even mask the AD/HD. This means that professionals are less likely to see AD/HD if the girl or woman already has another diagnosis because they may attribute the symptoms to the other disorder (e.g. anxiety disorder) rather than AD/HD. Girls with AD/HD tend to show lower levels of hyperactivity and externalizing behaviours than boys with AD/HD but may have greater cognitive difficulties. It has also been found that girls with AD/HD as compared to those without AD/HD have higher rates of eating disorders, self-injury, and suicide attempts (Hinshaw et al. 2012), making it even more important to identify these girls as early as possible to help prevent mental health problems.

INTERVENTION AND MANAGEMENT OF AD/HD
Pharmacological Interventions

Medications, particularly stimulants such as Methylphenidate (Ritalin), Dextroamphetamine (Dexedrine) and Dexmethylphenidate (Focalin) are one of the first line treatments recommended by the American Academy of Pediatrics (AAP) for children over six years of age diagnosed with AD/HD. This is because the benefits have been shown to outweigh the side effects of the medications. That is, many school age children and adults with AD/HD show relief of hyperactivity and distractibility symptoms and are able to manage side effects such as a decrease in appetite and delayed growth. However, beyond the immediate relief of the core symptoms of AD/HD there is the need to prevent adverse long-term functional outcomes in children with AD/HD including comorbid psychiatric disorders, academic difficulties and drop out, accidents and injuries and motor vehicle accidents among others. A recent literature review and meta-analysis on the effects of AD/HD medications and functional outcomes found significant benefits of AD/HD medication, particularly stimulants, in the treatment of associated functional impairments of AD/HD (Boland et al. 2020). For example, there was less risk of mood disorders, suicidality, criminality, substance use disorders, accidents and injuries, traumatic brain injury, automobile crashes, and academic difficulties in individuals who were using AD/HD medications. The protective effects of the AD/HD medications were found mostly during periods when the study participants were adhering to their medication regimen as compared to periods of non-adherence, providing strong evidence that the medication was helping to reduce the adverse functional impact of AD/HD on the individual's life. These findings highlight the importance of considering medication in the treatment of AD/HD, but also the need to work with the child and family to improve compliance to the medication regimen. However, it is important to keep in mind that AD/HD medications have several side effects that need to be weighed against the benefits that they provide and this should be done on a case by case basis. It is also the case that, for approximately 20–30% of individuals with AD/HD, medications may not be effective and, for others, they may not be a desirable option (Storebo et al. 2015). For example, a critical consideration in the use of medication in teens and adults with AD/HD is the co-occurrence of substance misuse in this population. Professionals must carefully monitor interactions with other drugs and their potentially harmful side effects.

Proper assessment and diagnosis should be conducted prior to prescribing medication for AD/HD as recommended by the Clinical Practice Guidelines of the American Academy of Pediatrics (Wolraich et al. 2019). Once prescribed, monitoring of the effects of the medication is also essential, preferably with teachers who are unaware of the medication status of the child so they can provide an unbiased rating of the child's behaviour in the school context. This, along with parent ratings and physician exams, should be considered to chart whether the benefits of the medication outweigh the risks with regard to the effects on the child's overall functioning. Though, even when the benefits outweigh the risks, medications alone will not address skill deficits that contribute to functional outcomes for children with AD/HD. Often the greatest benefits will be derived with a combination of medication and psychosocial interventions (Carey 2000). Combining medication and behavioural interventions may result in marked improvements in adaptive functioning than medication alone. In turn, better functioning in the individual would permit lower doses (or intensity) of the medications (Pelham et al. 2005).

Psychosocial Interventions

Co-occurring mental health conditions, learning difficulties, social skill deficits, academic achievement gaps, and poor peer relations in children with AD/HD are not addressed with medication alone. Psychosocial interventions are needed to address these associated features of AD/HD. In the next section, we briefly review the main psychosocial interventions that have been shown to be effective in addressing the common challenges faced by individuals with AD/HD.

Parent Training

Having a child with AD/HD increases the likelihood that parents will experience stress in parenting and strained family relationships. Thus, parent training is a key component of an overall intervention plan for children with AD/HD. In addition, for children under six years of age, parent training is the recommended treatment, before medications are considered. Parent training usually involves teaching parents the basic principles of behaviour therapy, learning how to identify and reward positive behaviours, ignore undesirable behaviour, and extinguish harmful behaviour. Parents also learn skills and strategies to help their child with AD/HD succeed at school, and relate better with siblings and peers. Learning and practising behaviour management techniques require time, effort and patience but once parents master these skills they can empower parents to be more confident about parenting. They are effective tools in improving their child's behaviour and reducing family stress, creating lasting benefits for the child and the family. When parents are equipped with the necessary tools to parent children with AD/HD the child and family long-term outcomes improve. Several studies have found parent training programmes effective for both preschoolers and school-aged children (Young & Myanthi Amarasinghe 2010).

Cognitive Behaviour Therapy

Cognitive Behaviour Therapy (CBT) is based on the idea that thoughts, feelings, and behaviour are connected and, therefore, having control of how we think about problems that we encounter can help children manage their feelings and behaviour. Children develop goals for adaptive behaviour and are taught strategies that they can use to achieve their goals. For example, children may be taught to stop and evaluate the possible consequences of their behaviour before they act. Once a strategy is mastered, it can be useful in many different situations such as when children are relating to peers, parents and teachers. CBT can be conducted in a group format or individually and has been found to help children and adults to learn to take a more reflective, and goal-oriented approach to everyday problem solving. The benefits are also seen in the domain of academic functioning. CBT is a versatile treatment method that can be conducted online and, in adults, has been shown to be effective in reducing AD/HD symptoms, including at six months follow-up with participants of an online program (Pettersson et al. 2017). Due to the high rates of co-morbidity of mood and anxiety disorders in AD/HD (Spencer, Biederman, & Wilens 1999) it is often the case that CBT is used to treat the most disabling comorbid mental health conditions before AD/HD symptoms are addressed.

Cognitive Training

Cognitive training is a process of training specific abilities like attentional focus, working memory and executive functioning. Usually attention training targets subcomponents of attentional control such as task switching, inhibition, focused attention, and working memory. Working Memory (WM) training targets visuo-spatial and verbal working memory meant to increase the threshold of objects that can be remembered and manipulated in memory during problem solving. WM training is thought to improve fluid intelligence and sustained attention, and yields improvements of AD/HD symptoms.

Attentional control skills are thought to be the foundation of many cognitive functions such as working memory, sustained attention, behaviour inhibition, and orienting attention and therefore, improvements in these skills should impact many areas of functioning. In a meta-analysis including studies of children with AD/HD as young as 4.25 years and adults as old as 84.50 years who were given attention training targeting 'alerting' attention (sustained attention, vigilance), orienting attention (shifting resources amongst stimuli), and executive attention (decision making, executive function control) as compared to a *passive* control groups who received no training at all, and an *active* control group who received training unrelated to attention or executive functions, found that attention training significantly improved attention with a *medium effect size*. In addition the meta-analysis found that training the 'orienting' attention network showed significantly stronger effects on attention performance than training the alerting network although no differences were observed between executive and orienting, or executive and alerting. As compared to the control groups, attention training improved performance on the related attention measures, especially among the younger people with ADHD (Peng & Miller 2016).

Effect Size

Effect size is a way of quantifying the magnitude of the difference between two groups. Typically, research studies will comprise a target group such as those who receive the intervention and a control group of those who do not. The target group may receive an intervention which is expected to have a specific outcome.

Psychologists want to know if an intervention works but also how much the intervention affected the predicted outcome of the target group. The effect size value corresponds to descriptors such as a small, medium, or large effect.

0.0	50%
Small effect size .2 is	58% of the control group below the mean of the target group
Medium effect size .5 is	69%
Large effect size .8 is	79%
1.4	92%

The larger the effect size the greater the the impact of the intervention. For example, in this case the attention training intervention had a *medium effect size* on improving attention in the target group of children with AD/HD.

The effects of the cognitive training programmes that target orienting, selective/focused, divided, and sustained attention processes seem to be most effective at improving the cognitive functions they target (near-transfer effects) but less likely to generalize and lead to improvements in behavioural and functional outcomes that were not directly trained such as academic performance and peer relations (far-transfer effects) (Rapport, Orban, Kofler, & Friedman 2013).

Social Skills Training

Social skill deficits and poor peer relations are common in children with AD/HD and may be related to social cognitive deficits and/or behavioural difficulties. Social cognitive deficits in Theory of Mind (TOM), the ability to understand that other people have independent thoughts and a different perspective than one's own, have been studied in children with AD/HD. Researchers reasoned that since TOM helps children predict how others might think and feel in situations, if children with AD/HD are not proficient at predicting others' behaviour this may adversely affect their interactions with their peers. Moreover, TOM is associated with executive functioning which we know is impaired in children with AD/HD. However, the evidence is mixed on whether children with AD/HD have theory of mind deficits. It may be that executive functioning and attentional difficulties in AD/HD contribute to TOM and, possibly other social cognitive difficulties, yet the available research is sparse and not conclusive (Pineda-Alhucema et al. 2018).

Another factor that may be contributing to the social challenges of children with AD/HD are behavioural difficulties. Frequent impulsivity, and higher than typical levels of aggressiveness and hyperactivity reduce the likelihood that peers will initiate and sustain friendships with children with AD/HD (Hoza et al. 2005; Normand et al. 2013). These externalizing behaviours are easily noticeable to parents and teachers, but also, to peers. Teachers may play a critical role in either highlighting the child's challenges (e.g. 'You're always blurting out the answer and disrupting the class!') to their classmates or reframing it to model an empathic response (e.g. 'It seems that you're excited to share your ideas, maybe you could write them down and raise your hand when you have chosen one to share with the group'). However, once a child with AD/HD has developed a bad reputation in the classroom and school, it can be difficult for others to change their perceptions of that child (Mikami, Smit, & Johnston 2019). Research shows that children with AD/HD as compared to their typically developing peers are less likely to be accepted by their peers, have fewer friends, and are more likely to lose friendships and to experience social rejection. Children with AD/HD who have social difficulties are also at risk for school dropout, substance abuse, criminality and adverse health events in adulthood (Mikami & Hinshaw 2006; Dalsgaard et al. 2015, Maibing et al. 2015). Social interventions are needed to prevent many of the negative psychosocial outcomes in children and adults with AD/HD. However, implementing Social Skills Training (SST) programmes exclusively for the purposes of changing the child's behaviour may not have the expected desired effect (deBoo & Prins 2007; Willis, Siceloff, Morse, Neger, & Flory 2019). The reason for this is that there are other factors to consider when the goal is to improve social competency and functioning. Cultivating the social context may be equally if not more important to improving the social experience of children with AD/HD. Evidence for this comes from a study on Friendship Coaching Intervention (PFC) wherein researchers trained parents of children with ADHD to coach their children on how to get along by teaching social skills, but also by providing support with organizing playdates to increase opportunities for children with AD/HD to initiate and sustain friendships. The results of this intervention showed improved social skills and friendships, as well as greater teacher-rated peer acceptance (Mikami, Lerner, Griggs, Mcgrath, & Calhoun 2010). Social skills interventions are also helpful in the classroom setting to support children with AD/HD to develop positive connections with their peers and to be included by their peers (Mikami et al. 2013). This may have the added benefit of improving children's motivation to go to school and stay in school.

A recent review of the literature found that effective SST interventions include a parent training component that focuses on social skills coaching paired with positive parenting and behavioural management strategies. The expectation is that parents will acquire skills on social coaching that they can continue to use with their child after the SST programme ends. The SST interventions seem to be equally effective for children with and without prescription medication for AD/HD. However, children with AD/HD who have co-morbidities such as oppositional defiant disorder (ODD) may present challenges that are not addressed by the SST interventions and therefore, these must be addressed before they can benefit from the SST (Willis, Siceloff, Morse, Neger, & Flory 2019).

Organizational Skills Training

In addition to symptoms of attention and/or hyperactivity and impulsivity, children with AD/HD have marked difficulties in executive functioning. Executive functioning difficulties interfere with planning and executing goals, organization, and time management. Although these issues may seem secondary to the core symptoms of AD/HD, they may be more likely to impede progress in academic and adaptive domains and, in adulthood, affect employment and overall quality of life, than the core symptoms. There is research evidence that the connection between AD/HD symptoms and negative long-term outcomes such as delinquency is largely mediated by low academic achievement (Defoe, Farrington, & Loeber 2013), stressing the importance of addressing academic challenges in this population.

Organizational skills training (OST) attempts to minimize impairment in daily life by maximizing adaptive skills (Pelham et al. 2008; Gallagher, Abikoff, Spira 2014). The main goal of OST programmes is to teach children and their parents how to be organized and to plan ahead within the context of age specific academic and daily living tasks. Behavioural techniques including modeling, rehearsal, and contingency management are used to teach organizational skills needed to complete homework and projects. Parents are taught to use prompts when needed and to praise and reward their child in learning organizational skills. OST interventions target skill deficits in study skills, time management and organizing materials, but are also thought to concurrently address performance deficits (the lack of motivation to perform the skill) and the neurocognitive functions such as sustained attention and cognitive control that may underlie specific organizational skills (Abikoff et al. 2013). When children with AD/HD sufficiently practise, they master practical everyday organizational skills needed to succeed in school and daily tasks. Children are also indirectly improving their motivation, focus, and executive function abilities. A meta-analysis based on 12 studies and 1,054 children found that OST interventions showed moderate improvements in organizational skills of children with AD/HD as rated by teachers and large improvements as rated by parents. Modest improvements were reported on the ratings of symptoms of inattention and academic performance (Bikic et al. 2017).

Supporting Teens' Academic Needs Daily (**STAND**) is a parent-adolescent collaborative behavioural intervention for adolescents with **AD/HD** that is delivered in clinic, school, and community settings. Researchers randomly assigned families to receive STAND or the usual services available in their communities. Adolescents who participated in STAND showed greater improvements than the control group in attention, organization and time management skills. They were also better able to stay on task during homework time. Parents who participated in STAND reported that they experienced less stress, a more collaborative relationship with their child, and increased use of behavioural strategies to support their child (Sibley et al. 2013, 2016). STAND uses motivational interviewing (MI), a nonconfrontational collaborative technique between the therapist and client to discover the personal motivation for adaptive behaviour change, to engage adolescents and their parents in developing important skills in organization, time management, and planning. The parent component of training teaches parents how to support their children, all the while encouraging their autonomy. The collaborative approach helps to diminish family conflict and strengthens the parent–child relationship.

The Homework, Organization, and Planning Skills (HOPS) and the Completing Homework by Improving Efficiency and Focus (CHIEF) interventions are other examples of OST that have shown positive results with regard to improving the organizational skills and homework management of adolescents. These interventions were designed to be implemented in schools by professionals (mental health workers) or paraprofessionals (undergraduates) either during or after school. HOPS was designed to address the organization and planning aspects of the homework completion including recording assignment, organizing materials needed and planning for studying and completing homework whereas the CHIEF intervention focuses on providing the adolescent with a behaviour management and points system, setting goals for completing work and providing the space and time for the student to complete their homework and study for tests. Both interventions were brief' the adolescent and school mental health worker met for a total of 16 sessions of approximately 20 minutes each for one school term. There were two meetings with the parents to teach them how to set clear work completion goals and to implement the behavioural point system at home, to encourage focus and efficiency with work completion.

Researchers found that both the HOPS and CHIEF interventions demonstrated significantly greater improvements in Grade 6, 7, and 8 students when compared with a waitlist group on parent ratings of homework problems and organizational skills. HOPS participants also demonstrated moderate improvements on managing their materials and organized action behaviours according to teachers. Participants with more severe psychopathology and executive function difficulties benefitted more from the HOPS intervention as compared to the CHIEF intervention. Because the intervention took place in the school, attrition was low; over 90% of the adolescents participated in all 16 sessions. The improvements were maintained when researchers re-assessed the youth at the six-month follow-up. Researchers concluded that brief school-based interventions implemented by school staff can be effective in addressing organizational skills and academic performance in youth with AD/HD (Langberg et al. 2016).

Adults with AD/HD also struggle in many functional domains, including education, employment, relationships, and domestic responsibilities. Thus, they may benefit from acquiring adaptive skills that are necessary to function effectively in these domains. In particular adults with AD/HD may benefit from job coaching to improve working relationships and job performance, and behavioural therapy to teach organizational skills for school, home, and work settings.

Exercise Intervention

Exercise is not only beneficial to physical health and well-being but researchers have suggested that it may be particularly helpful in alleviating symptoms in children with AD/HD. Exercise may be especially well suited for children with the hyperactivity subtype of AD/HD who seem to naturally gravitate towards physical movement. However, there is evidence that, beyond the physical benefits of exercise, it improves executive functions such as inhibition, working memory, and cognitive flexibility (switching between tasks) in children with AD/HD. A few systematic reviews of studies in the area found that a variety of exercise programmes, ranging from 8 to 12 weeks' duration of moderate exercise, reported improvements in executive functioning (Hoza et al., 2015). Studies have also reported benefits in motor skills, physical fitness, attention, and social behaviour in children with ADHD (Jeyanthi, Arumugam, & Parasher 2019). However, there was a dearth of information on school-based exercise programmes, the effects of structured exercise programmes independently or in combination with cognitive-based therapies, and the long-term benefits of exercises in children with AD/HD.

Despite the promising findings associated with physical activity other research points to reduced physical activity levels in children with an AD/HD. For example, one study found that children with an AD/HD diagnosis had 20% lower odds of engaging in daily exercise than their peers without AD/HD (Mercurio et al. 2019). This means that more research is needed to understand factors related to sedentary behaviour and challenges with engaging in physical activity among children with AD/HD. It may be wise to take a preventative, health promotion approach to improve physical activity in children with AD/HD to improve their physical health, in addition to using exercise as a specific means of intervention to improve executive functioning in children with AD/HD.

Although there is some support for all of the intervention approaches reviewed, a multi-modal approach to intervention is likely to be needed to address the many areas of the child's life that are affected by AD/HD. In most cases this means combining interventions, including pharmacological aids to help with focus and hyperactivity, teaching parents how to effectively parent their child with AD/HD, helping teachers implement behavioural techniques in the classroom to improve the child's behaviour and collaborating with the child to take responsibility for monitoring and managing their own behaviour. A support plan that includes clear rules and expectations for behaviour, providing the child with choices and interspersing difficult tasks with physical breaks, reinforcing positive behaviour, and offering help with homework, will increase the likelihood that the child will succeed and reduces the risk of school dropout.

SUMMARY

AD/HD is a complex multifaceted developmental disability that affects many aspects of a child's development. Beyond genetics that confer high heritability for AD/HD traits, there are early developmental factors that increase risk for AD/HD. The main symptoms of AD/HD persist, but also, manifest differently over time. Although physical hyperactivity decreases with age, restlessness in older youth and adults may be expressed as incessant talking or racing thoughts. AD/HD symptoms are important intervention targets because they often produce functional impairments in the short term and confer risk for negative outcomes in the long term. Although AD/HD symptoms can be treated effectively with stimulant medications, psychosocial interventions are also needed to address specific functional impairments and skill deficits. Interventions need to be developmentally informed and delivered at the optimal time. During the preschool years when symptoms become evident, symptom severity, cognitive functioning, and parent support is critical because they predict school age outcomes. Later, during the school age and teen years, academic functioning and peer relations take priority but family functioning is still important. During the adult years, postsecondary education, employment, and relationship coaching are needed. A combination of pharmacological and psychosocial interventions from early in development through to adulthood may be required. Parent training as well as behavioural and organizational training help children structure their environment and learn how to monitor and regulate their own behaviour so that benefits persist over the long term. Many children with AD/HD have comorbidities such as academic and learning problems, social and emotional difficulties; these must also be addressed as comorbidity is a significant predictor of long-term outcomes and, in some cases, is more debilitating than the AD/HD symptoms. Executive functioning is important throughout the lifespan and interventions that target working memory, inhibition and attentional focus have shown promise. However, these must be accompanied by changes in practical organizational and adaptive skills as they are crucial in sustaining positive outcomes in adulthood.

Reflective Questions

1 What evidence is there that AD/HD is highly heritable?
2 Name a few of the common associated risk factors for AD/HD?
3 Describe the developmental course of AD/HD through to adulthood
4 What are the diagnostic criteria for AD/HD according to the DSM 5?
5 What are some ways that women with AD/HD may differ from men with AD/HD?
6 Describe the main components of a multi-modal intervention for AD/HD?
7 Why is it important to tackle individual, parent/family and school goals for intervention for long-term outcomes?

Recommended Videos

See these videos for an example of AD/HD in children

https://www.youtube.com/watch?v=ouZrZa5pLXk
https://www.youtube.com/watch?v=vatJ46t1WNI

See this video for parenting strategies for children with AD/HD

https://www.youtube.com/watch?v=ktb520seHYk

See this video for an example of AD/HD in adulthood

https://www.youtube.com/watch?v=-8J4wl9eUe4

REFERENCES

Abikoff, H., Gallagher, R., Wells, K. C., Murray, D. W., Huang, L., Lu, F., & Petkova, E. (2013). Remediating organizational functioning in children with ADHD: immediate and long-term effects from a randomized controlled trial. *Journal of Consulting and Clinical Psychology, 81*(1), 113–128. https://doi.org/10.1037/a0029648.

American Psychiatric Association. (2013). *Diagnostic and Statistical Manual of Mental Disorders (5th edn)*. https://doi.org/10.1176/appi.books.9780890425596.

Barkley, R. A. (1994). What to look for in a school for a child with ADHD. ADHD report, 2(3), 1–2.

Barkley, R. A. (1997). *AD/HD and the Nature of Self-control*. New York, NY: Guilford Press.

Barkley, R. A. (2001). The executive functions and self-regulation: An evolutionary neuropsychological perspective. *Neuropsychology Review, 11*(1), 1–29. https://doi.org/10.1023/A:1009085417776.

Barkley, R. A. (2006). *Attention Deficit Hyperactivity Disorder: A Handbook for Diagnosis and Treatment, Third Edition*. Guilford Press

Barkley, R. A., Murphy, K. R., & Fischer, M. (2008). *ADHD in Adults: What the Science Says*. Guilford Press.

Bikic, A., Reichow, B., McCauley, S. A., Ibrahim, K., & Sukhodolsky, D. G. (2017). Meta-analysis of organizational skills interventions for children and adolescents with Attention-Deficit/Hyperactivity Disorder. *Clinical Psychology Review*, *52*, 108–123. https://doi.org/10.1016/j.cpr.2016.12.004.

Boland, H., DiSalvo, M., Fried, R., Woodworth, K. Y., Wilens, T., Faraone, S. V., & Biederman, J. (2020). A literature review and meta-analysis on the effects of ADHD medications on functional outcomes. *Journal of Psychiatric Research*, *123*, 21–30. https://doi.org/10.1016/j.jpsychires.2020.01.006.

Carey, W. B. (2000). What the multimodal treatment study of children with attention-deficit/hyperactivity disorder did and did not say about the use of methylphenidate for attention deficits. *Pediatrics*, *105*(4), 863–864. https://doi.org/10.1542/peds.105.4.863.

Castellanos, F. X., Sonuga-Barke, E. J., Milham, M. P., & Tannock, R. (2006). Characterizing cognition in ADHD: Beyond executive dysfunction. *Trends in Cognitive Sciences*, *10*(3), 117–123. https://doi.org/10.1016/j.tics.2006.01.011.

Castellanos, F. X., & Tannock, R. (2002). Neuroscience of attention-deficit/hyperactivity disorder: The search for endophenotypes. *Nature Reviews Neuroscience*, *3*, 617–628. http://dx.doi.org/10.1038/nrn896.

Cherkasova, M. V., Ponde, M. P., & Hechtman, L. (2012). Adolescent and adult outcome of attention deficit hyperactivity disorder: Presentation and predictors. *Minerva Psichiatrica*, *53*(1), 11–27.

Chronis, A. M., Lahey, B. B., Pelham Jr, W. E., Williams, S. H., Baumann, B. L., Kipp, H., Jones, H., & Rathouz, P. J. (2007). Maternal depression and early positive parenting predict future conduct problems in young children with attention-deficit/hyperactivity disorder. *Developmental Psychology*, *43*(1), 70. https://doi.org/10.1037/0012-1649.43.1.70.

Cornelius, M. D., & Day, N. L. (2009). Developmental consequences of prenatal tobacco exposure. *Current Opinion in Neurology*, *22*(2), 121. https://dx.doi.org/10.1097%2FWCO.0b013e328326f6dc.

Dalsgaard, S., Østergaard, S. D., Leckman, J. F., Mortensen, P. B., & Pedersen, M. G. (2015). Mortality in children, adolescents, and adults with attention deficit hyperactivity disorder: a nationwide cohort study. *The Lancet*, *385*, 2190–2196. https://doi.org/10.1016/S0140-6736(14)61684-6.

deBoo, G. M., & Prins, P. J. (2007). Social incompetence in children with ADHD: Possible moderators and mediators in social-skills training. *Clinical Psychology Review*, *27*(1), 78–97. https://doi.org/10.1016/j.cpr.2006.03.006.

Defoe, I. N., Farrington, D. P., & Loeber, R. (2013). Disentangling the relationship between delinquency and hyperactivity, low achievement, depression, and low socioeconomic status: Analysis of repeated longitudinal data. *Journal of Criminal Justice*, *41*(2), 100-107. https://doi.org/10.1016/j.jcrimjus.2012.12.002.

Del-Ponte, B., Anselmi, L., Assunção, M. C. F., Tovo-Rodrigues, L., Munhoz, T. N., Matijasevich, A., Rohde, L. A., Santos, I. S. (2019). Sugar consumption and attention-deficit/hyperactivity disorder (ADHD): A birth cohort study, *Journal of Affective Disorders*, *243*, 290–296. https://doi.org/10.1016/j.jad.2018.09.051.

Demontis, D., Walters, R. K., Martin, J., Mattheisen, M., Als, T. D., Agerbo, E., Baldursson, G., Belliveau, R., Bybjerg-Grauholm, J., Bækvad-Hansen, M., Cerrato, F., Chambert, K.,

Churchhouse, C., Dumont, A., Eriksson, N., Gandal, M., Goldstein, J. I., Grasby, K. L., Grove, J, ... & Neale, B. M. (2019). Discovery of the first genome-wide significant risk loci for attention deficit/hyperactivity disorder. *Nature Genetics*, *51*(1), 63–75. https://doi.org/10.1038/s41588-018-0269-7.

Faraone, S. V., Perlis, R. H., Doyle, A. E., Smoller, J. W., Goralnick, J. J., Holmgren, M. A., & Sklar, P. (2005). Molecular genetics of attention-deficit/hyperactivity disorder. *Biological Psychiatry*, *57*(11), 1313–1323. https://doi.org/10.1016/j.biopsych.2004.11.024.

Fayyad, J., Sampson, N. A., Hwang, I., Adamowski, T., Aguilar-Gaxiola, S., Al-Hamzawi, A., Andrade, L. H., Borges, G., de Girolamo, G., Florescu, S., Gureje, O., Haro, J. M., Hu, C., Karam, E. G., Lee, S., Navarro-Mateu, F., O'Neill, S., Oennell, B., Piazza, M., ... & WHO World Mental Health Survey Collaborators. (2017). The descriptive epidemiology of DSM-IV Adult ADHD in the world health organization world mental health surveys. *ADHD Attention Deficit and Hyperactivity Disorders*, *9*(1), 47–65. https://doi.org/10.1007/s12402-016-0208-3.

Fletcher, J., & Wolfe, B. (2009). Long-term consequences of childhood ADHD on criminal activities. *The Journal of Mental Health Policy and Economics*, *12*(3), 119–138.

Galéra, C., Côté, S. M., Bouvard, M. P., Pingault, J. B., Melchior, M., Michel, G., Bolvin, M., & Tremblay, R. E. (2011). Early risk factors for hyperactivity-impulsivity and inattention trajectories from age 17 months to 8 years. *Archives of General Psychiatry*, *68*(12), 1267–1275. https://doi.org/10.1001/archgenpsychiatry.2011.138

Gallagher, R., Abikoff, H. B., & Spira, E. G. (2014). *Organizational Skills Training for Children with ADHD: An Empirically Supported Treatment*. Guilford Publications.

Goldstein, S., Naglieri, J. A., Princiotta, D., & Otero, T. M. (2014). Introduction: A history of executive functioning as a theoretical and clinical construct. In S. Goldstein & J. A. Naglieri (eds), *Handbook of Executive Functioning* (pp. 3–12). Springer.

Gottesman, I. I., & Shields, J. (1972). *Schizophrenia and Genetics*. A Twin Study Vantage Point. Academic Press.

Gottesman, I. I., & Gould, T. D. (2003). The endophenotype concept in psychiatry: Etymology and strategic intentions. *American Journal of Psychiatry*, *160*(4), 636–645. https://doi.org/10.1176/appi.ajp.160.4.636.

Hinshaw, S. P., Owens, E. B., Zalecki, C., Huggins, S. P., Montenegro-Nevado, A. J., Schrodek, E., & Swanson, E. N. (2012). Prospective follow-up of girls with attention-deficit/hyperactivity disorder into early adulthood: Continuing impairment includes elevated risk for suicide attempts and self-injury. *Journal of Consulting and Clinical Psychology*, *80*(6), 1041. https://doi.org/10.1037/a0029451.

Hoza, B., Mrug, S., Gerdes, A. C., Hinshaw, S. P., Bukowski, W. M., Gold, J. A., Kraemer, H. C., Pelham, W. E., Wigal, T., & Arnold, L. E. (2005). What aspects of peer relationships are impaired in children with attention-deficit/hyperactivity disorder? *Journal of Consulting and Clinical Psychology*, *73*(3), 411–423. https://doi.org/10.1037/0022-006X.73.3.411.

Hoza, B., Smith, A. L., Shoulberg, E. K., Linnea, K. S., Dorsch, T. E., Blazo, J. A., Aldering, C. M., & McCabe, G. P. (2015). A randomized trial examining the effects of aerobic physical activity on attention-deficit/hyperactivity disorder symptoms in young children. *Journal of Abnormal Child Psychology*, *43*(4), 655–667. https://doi.org/10.1007/s10802-014-9929-y.

Jeyanthi, S., Arumugam, N., & Parasher, R. K. (2019). Effect of physical exercises on attention, motor skill and physical fitness in children with attention deficit hyperactivity disorder: A systematic review. *ADHD Attention Deficit and Hyperactivity Disorders, 11*(2), 125–137. https://doi.org/10.1007/s12402-018-0270-0.

Kim, K. M., Lim, M. H., Kwon, H.-J., Yoo, S.-J., Kim, E.-J., Kim, J. W., Ha, M., Paik, K. C. (2018). Associations between attention-deficit/hyperactivity disorder symptoms and dietary habits in elementary school children. *Appetite, 127*, 274–279. https://doi.org /10.1016/j.appet.2018.05.004.

Lahey, B. B., Pelham, W. E., Loney, J., Kipp, H., Ehrhardt, A., Lee, S. S., Willcutt, E. G., Hartung, C. M., Chronis, A., & Massetti, G. (2004). Three-year predictive validity of DSM-IV attention deficit hyperactivity disorder in children diagnosed at 4–6 years of age. *American Journal of Psychiatry, 161*(11), 2014–2020. https://doi.org/10.1176/appi.ajp.161.11.2014.

Lahey, B. B., Pelham, W. E., Loney, J., Lee, S. S., & Willcutt, E. (2005). Instability of the DSM-IV subtypes of ADHD from preschool through elementary school. *Archives of General Psychiatry, 62*(8), 896–902. https://doi.org/10.1001/archpsyc.62.8.896.

Langberg, J. M., Dvorsky, M. R., Molitor, S. J., Bourchtein, E., Eddy, L. D., Smith, Z. R., Oddo, L. E., & Eadeh, H. M. (2018). Overcoming the research-to-practice gap: A randomized trial with two brief homework and organization interventions for students with ADHD as implemented by school mental health providers. *Journal of Consulting and Clinical Psychology, 86*(1), 39–55. https://psycnet.apa.org/doi/10.1037/ccp0000265.

Langberg, J. M., Evans, S. W., Schultz, B. K., Becker, S. P., Altaye, M., & Girio-Herrera, E. (2016). Trajectories and predictors of response to the challenging horizons program for adolescents with ADHD. *Behavior Therapy, 47*(3), 339–354.

Latimer, W. W., August, G. J., Newcomb, M. D., Realmuto, G. M., Hektner, J. M., & Mathy, R. M. (2003). Child and familial pathways to academic achievement and behavioral adjustment: A prospective six-year study of children with and without ADHD. *Journal of Attention Disorders, 7*(2), 101–116. https://doi.org/10.1177%2F108705470300700204.

Lindström, K., Lindblad, F., & Hjern, A. (2011). Preterm birth and attention-deficit/hyperactivity disorder in schoolchildren. *Pediatrics, 127*, 858–865. doi:10.1542/peds.2010-1279.

Maibing, C. F., Pedersen, C. B., Benros, M. E., Mortensen, P. B., Dalsgaard, S., & Nordentoft, M. (2015). Risk of schizophrenia increases after all child and adolescent psychiatric disorders: A nationwide study. *Schizophrenia Bulletin, 41*(4), 963–970. https://doi.org/10.1093/schbul/sbu119.

Mercurio, L. Y., Amanullah, S., Gjelsvik, A., & Gill, N. (2019). Children with Attention Deficit Hyperactivity Disorder less likely to meet daily physical activity recommendations. *Pediatrics, 144*, 179. https://doi.org/10.1542/peds.144.2_MeetingAbstract.179.

Mikami, A. Y., Griggs, M. S., Lerner, M. D., Emeh, C. C., Reuland, M. M., Jack, A., & Anthony, M. R. (2013). A randomized trial of a classroom intervention to increase peers' social inclusion of children with attention-deficit/hyperactivity disorder. *Journal of Consulting and Clinical Psychology, 81*(1), 100–112. https://doi.org/10.1037/a0029654.

Mikami A. Y., & Hinshaw S.P. (2006). Attention-Deficit/Hyperactivity Disorder in girls. In: K. McBurnett & L. J. Pfiffner (eds), *Attention Deficit/Hyperactivity Disorder: Concepts, Controversies, New Directions* (pp. 259–272). Informa Healthcare.

Mikami, A. Y., Smit, S., & Johnston, C. (2019). Teacher attributions for children's attention-deficit/hyperactivity disorder behaviors predict experiences with children and with classroom behavioral management in a summer program practicum. *Psychology in the Schools, 56*(6), 928–944. https://doi.org/10.1002/pits.22250.

Mikami, A. Y., Lerner, M. D., Griggs, M. S., McGrath, A., & Calhoun, C. D. (2010). Parental influence on children with attention-deficit/hyperactivity disorder: II. Results of a pilot intervention training parents as friendship coaches for children. *Journal of Abnormal Child Psychology, 38*(6), 737–749. https://doi.org/10.1007/s10802-010-9403-4.

Molina, B. S., Hinshaw, S. P., Swanson, J. M., Arnold, L. E., Vitiello, B., Jensen, P. S., Epstein, J., Hoza, B., Hechtmen, L., Abikoff, H. B., Elliott, G. R., Greenhill, L. L., Newcorn, J. H., Wells, K. C., Wigal, T., Gibbons, R., Hur, K., Houck, P., & The MTA Cooperative Group. (2009). The MTA at 8 years: Prospective follow-up of children treated for combined-type ADHD in a multisite study. *Journal of the American Academy of Child & Adolescent Psychiatry, 48*(5), 484–500. https://doi.org/10.1097/CHI.0b013e31819c23d0.

Munakata, Y., Snyder, H. R., & Chatham, C. H. (2012). Developing cognitive control: Three key transitions. *Current Directions in Psychological Science, 21*(2), 71–77. https://dx.doi.org/10.1177%2F0963721412436807.

Nigg, J. T. (2000). On inhibition/disinhibition in developmental psychopathology: Views from cognitive and personality psychology and a working inhibition taxonomy. *Psychological Bulletin, 126*(2), 220–246. https://doi.org/10.1037/0033-2909.126.2.220.

Nigg, J. T., & Casey, B. J. (2005). An integrative theory of attention-deficit/hyperactivity disorder based on the cognitive and affective neurosciences. *Development and Psychopathology, 17*(3), 785–806. https://doi.org/10.1017/S0954579405050376.

Normand, S., Schneider, B. H., Lee, M. D., Maisonneuve, M. F., Chupetlovska-Anastasova, A., Kuehn, S. M., & Robaey, P. (2013). Continuities and changes in the friendships of children with and without ADHD: A longitudinal, observational study. *Journal of Abnormal Child Psychology, 41*(7), 1161–1175. https://doi.org/10.1007/s10802-013-9753-9.

Pelham, W. E., Burrows-MacLean, L., Gnagy, E. M., Fabiano, G. A., Coles, E. K., Tresco, K. E., Chacko, A., Wymbs, B. T., Wienke, A. L., Walker K. S., & Hoffman, M. T. (2005). Transdermal methylphenidate, behavioral, and combined treatment for children with ADHD. *Experimental and Clinical Psychopharmacology, 13*(2), 111–126. https://psycnet.apa.org/doi/10.1037/1064-1297.13.2.111.

Pelham Jr, W. E., & Fabiano, G. A. (2008). Evidence-based psychosocial treatments for attention-deficit/hyperactivity disorder. *Journal of Clinical Child & Adolescent Psychology, 37*(1), 184–214. https://doi.org/10.1080/15374410701818681.

Peng, P., & Miller, A. C. (2016). Does attention training work? A selective meta-analysis to explore the effects of attention training and moderators. *Learning and Individual Differences, 45*, 77–87. https://doi.org/10.1016/j.lindif.2015.11.012.

Pennington, B. F., & Ozonoff, S. (1996). Executive functions and developmental psychopathology. *Journal of Child Psychology and Psychiatry, 37*(1), 51–87. https://doi.org/10.1111/j.1469-7610.1996.tb01380.x.

Pettersson, R., Söderström, S., Edlund-Söderström, K., & Nilsson, K. W. (2017). Internet-based cognitive behavioral therapy for adults with ADHD in outpatient psychiatric care: A randomized trial. *Journal of Attention Disorders, 21*(6), 508–521. https://doi.org/10.1177%2F1087054714539998.

Pineda-Alhucema, W., Aristizabal, E., Escudero-Cabarcas, J., Acosta-López, J. E., & Vélez, J. I. (2018). Executive function and theory of mind in children with ADHD: A systematic review. *Neuropsychology Review, 28*(3), 341–358. https://doi.org/10.1007/s11065-018-9381-9.

Polanczyk, G., De Lima, M. S., Horta, B. L., Biederman, J., & Rohde, L. A. (2007). The worldwide prevalence of ADHD: a systematic review and metaregression analysis. *American Journal of Psychiatry, 164*(6), 942–948. https://doi.org/10.1176/ajp.2007.164.6.942.

Posner, K., Melvin, G. A., Murray, D. W., Gugga, S. S., Fisher, P., Skrobala, A., Cunningham, C., Vitiello, B., Abikoff, H. B., Ghuman, J. K., Kollins, S., Wigal, S. B., Wigal, T., McCracken, J. T., McGough, J. J., Kastelic, E., Boorady, R., Davies, M., Chaung, S. Z., … Greenhill, L. L. (2007). Clinical presentation of attention-deficit/hyperactivity disorder in preschool children: The preschoolers with attention-deficit/hyperactivity treatment study (PATS). *Journal of Child and Adolescent Psychopharmacology, 17*(5), 547–562. https://doi.org/10.1089/cap.2007.0075.

Rapport, M. D., Orban, S. A., Kofler, M. J., & Friedman, L. M. (2013). Do programs designed to train working memory, other executive functions, and attention benefit children with ADHD? A meta-analytic review of cognitive, academic, and behavioral outcomes. *Clinical Psychology Review, 33*(8), 1237–1252. https://doi.org/10.1016/j.cpr.2013.08.005.

Rodriguez, A., Olsen, J., Kotimaa, A. J., Kaakinen, M., Moilanen, I., Henriksen, T. B., Linnet, K. M., Miettunen, J., Obel, C., Taanila, A., Ebeling, H., & Järvelin, M. R. (2009). Is prenatal alcohol exposure related to inattention and hyperactivity symptoms in children? Disentangling the effects of social adversity. *Journal of Child Psychology and Psychiatry, 50*(9), 1073–1083. https://doi.org/10.1111/j.1469-7610.2009.02071.x

Rooney, M., & Pfiffner, L. J. (2018). Attention-Deficit/Hyperactivity Disorder. In J. N. Butcher & P. C. Kendall (eds), *APA Handbook of Psychopathology: Child and Adolescent Psychopathology* (pp. 417–445). American Psychological Association. https://doi.org/10.1037/0000065-019.

Sergeant, J. (2000). The cognitive-energetic model: An empirical approach to attention-deficit hyperactivity disorder. *Neuroscience & Biobehavioral Reviews, 24*(1), 7–12. https://doi.org/10.1016/S0149-7634(99)00060-3.

Sergeant, J. A. (2005). Modeling attention-deficit/hyperactivity disorder: A critical appraisal of the cognitive-energetic model. *Biological Psychiatry, 57*(11), 1248–1255. https://doi.org/10.1016/j.biopsych.2004.09.010.

Sibley, M. H., Graziano, P. A., Kuriyan, A. B., Coxe, S., Pelham, W. E., Rodriguez, L., Sanchez, F., Derefinko, K., Helseth, S., & Ward, A. (2016). Parent–teen behavior therapy+ motivational interviewing for adolescents with ADHD. *Journal of Consulting and Clinical Psychology, 84*(8), 699–712. https://doi.org/10.1037/ccp0000106.

Sibley, M. H., Pelham, W. E., Derefinko, K. J., Kuriyan, A. B., Sanchez, F., & Graziano, P. A. (2013). A pilot trial of Supporting Teens' Academic Needs Daily (STAND): A parent-adolescent collaborative intervention for ADHD. *Journal of Psychopathology and Behavioral Assessment, 35*(4), 436–449. https://doi.org/10.1007/s10862-013-9353-6.

Sibley, M. H. (2016). *Parent-Teen Therapy for Executive Function Deficits and ADHD: Building Skills and Motivation.* Guilford Publications.

Sonuga-Barke, E. J. (2005). Causal models of attention-deficit/hyperactivity disorder: From common simple deficits to multiple developmental pathways. *Biological Psychiatry, 57*(11), 1231–1238. https://doi.org/10.1016/j.biopsych.2004.09.008.

Spencer, T., Biederman, J., & Wilens, T. (1999). Attention-deficit/hyperactivity disorder and comorbidity. *Pediatric Clinics of North America, 46*(5), 915–927. https://doi.org/10.1016/S0031-3955(05)70163-2.

Storebø, O. J., Ramstad, E., Krogh, H. B., Nilausen, T. D., Skoog, M., Holmskov, M., Rosendal, S., Groth, C., Magnusson, F. L., Moreira-Maia, C. R., Gillies, D., Rasmussen, K. B., Gauci, D., Zwi, M., Kirubakaran, R., Forsbøl, B., Simonsen, E., & Gluud, C. (2015). Methylphenidate for children and adolescents with attention deficit hyperactivity disorder (ADHD). *Cochrane Database of Systematic Reviews, 11*, CD009885. https://doi.org/10.1002/14651858.CD009885.pub2.

Wass, S. V., Scerif, G., & Johnson, M. H. (2012). Training attentional control and working memory–Is younger, better?. *Developmental Review, 32*(4), 360–387. https://doi.org/10.1016/j.dr.2012.07.001.

Willcutt, E. G., Doyle, A. E., Nigg, J. T., Faraone, S. V., & Pennington, B. F. (2005) Validity of the executive function theory of attention-deficit/hyperactivity disorder: a meta-analytic review. *Biological Psychiatry, 57*(11), 1336–1346. https://doi.org/10.1016/j.biopsych.2005.02.006.

Willis, D., Siceloff, E. R., Morse, M., Neger, E., & Flory, K. (2019). Stand-alone social skills training for youth with ADHD: A systematic review. *Clinical Child and Family Psychology Review, 22*(3), 348–366. https://doi.org/10.1007/s10567-019-00291-3.

Wolraich, M. L., Hagan, J. F., Allan, C., Chan, E., Davison, D., Earls, M., Evans, S. W., Flinn, S. K., Froehlich, T., Frost, J., Holbrook, J. R., Lehmann, C. U., Lessin, H. R., Okechukwu, K., Pierce, K. L., Winner, J. D., Zurhellen, W., & Subcommittee on Children and Adolescents with Attention-Deficit/Hyperactive Disorder. (2019). Clinical practice guideline for the diagnosis, evaluation, and treatment of attention-deficit/hyperactivity disorder in children and adolescents. *Pediatrics, 144*(4), e20192528. https://doi.org/10.1542/peds.2019-2528.

World Health Organization. (1993). *The ICD-10 Classification of Mental and Behavioural Disorders: Diagnostic Criteria for Research* (Vol. 2). World Health Organization.

Yang, P., Chen, Y.-H., Yen, C.-F., Chen, H.-L. (2015). Psychiatric diagnoses, emotional-behavioral symptoms and functional outcomes in adolescents born preterm with very low birth weights. *Child Psychiatry & Human Development, 46*, 358–366. doi:10.1007/s10578-014-0475-1.

Young, S, Moss, D., Sedgwick, O., Fridman, M., & Hodgkins, P. (2015). A meta-analysis of the prevalence of attention deficit hyperactivity disorder in incarcerated populations. *Psychol Med., 45*(2), 247–258.

Young, S., & Myanthi Amarasinghe, J. (2010). Practitioner Review: Non-pharmacological treatments for ADHD: A lifespan approach. *Journal of Child Psychology and Psychiatry, 51*(2), 116–133. https://doi.org/10.1111/j.1469-7610.2009.02191.x.

Young, S., Adamo, N., Ásgeirsdóttir, B. B., et al. (2020). Females with ADHD: An expert consensus statement taking a lifespan approach providing guidance for the identification and treatment of attention-deficit/ hyperactivity disorder in girls and women. *BMC Psychiatry, 20*, 404. https://doi.org/10.1186/s12888-020-02707-9.

Zelazo, P. D., Carter, A., Reznick, J. S., & Frye, D. (1997). Early development of executive function: A problem-solving framework. *Review of General Psychology, 1*(2), 198–226. https://doi-org.proxy.lib.sfu.ca/10.1037/1089-2680.1.2.198.

PART IV
DEVELOPMENTAL DISABILITY IN CONTEXT

12
INTELLECTUAL DISABILITY IN THE FAMILY CONTEXT

Learning Objectives

After reading this chapter, you should be able to:

- Learn about the ways that family experiences impact development of individuals with intellectual disability (ID)
- Learn about the impact of a family member with intellectual disability on parents and siblings
- Learn about interventions and supports for families of individuals with ID
- Learn about sociological factors that impact the lives of families of individuals with ID

In this chapter, we broaden the focus of our study of ID beyond the individual to examine the relationships between people with ID and their families. Throughout their lives, people with ID are influenced not only by genetic and biological factors, they are also impacted by ongoing interactions and experiences with their parents, siblings, and other family members. A great deal of research over the past 50 years has focused on the nature of relationships within families of people with ID. Much of this work has explored how specific family characteristics and parenting behaviours influence the development of children with ID. This work has uncovered important insights about how some parenting behaviours can help children with ID learn and grow, and others are related to challenging behaviours in a child with ID. Our examination of the impact of family relationships will help us better understand individual growth and development in ID and can help explain how and why many children with similar conditions demonstrate different outcomes.

But there is more to the story than studying the influence of parents on children with ID. Another important set of questions focuses on how the presence of a person with ID impacts the family unit. Parenting a child with ID is, in many ways, like parenting any child. But it also involves a unique set of experiences that impact the way parents may feel, cope, and live their lives. Parents of children with ID may experience the rewards of helping their child learn and grow, but they may also spend more time advocating for additional supports and services for their child in school and community settings. They may celebrate more profoundly the learning of a new skill that was difficult for their child to master. But they may also experience moments of realization when their child's peers achieve in ways that their own child has not yet achieved.

Growing up as the sibling of a person with ID may be filled with many experiences common to siblings in general, but they, too, may involve unique dimensions as well. In addition to the companionship often observed among brothers and sisters within a family unit, a sibling of a child with ID may experience the achievement of milestones at a faster pace than their sibling who may be near in age, leading to more advanced skills and greater independence than their brother or sister. Siblings may take on the responsibility of helping their sibling with ID communicate effectively and be understood by the broader community around them. They may also learn early on how to model play activities for their sibling, or how to help their sibling engage in activities of daily living.

Throughout this chapter, we will examine the many ways that an individual with ID and their family members impact one another. We will also examine a range of additional factors, like parental mental health, family financial well-being, parental employment, and how different conditions associated with ID may impact families differently. Each of these issues will help us place our study of ID into context, and gain a richer understanding of the lived experiences of this population and their immediate families.

PARENTING CHILDREN WITH ID

Parenting Behaviours

Parents are often a day-to-day presence in the life of a child with ID. Because of this, parenting behaviours can have a pronounced impact on a child's development. From an educational perspective, if researchers can identify specific parenting approaches that facilitate growth and development in a child with ID, this knowledge can be used to inform supports, interventions, and recommendations for families seeking help and guidance.

Responsivity

A great deal of research has shown that the way that parents respond to their child with ID may play a key role in supporting their child's development (Warren & Brady 2007). When parents show a high degree of 'responsivity', or attuned reactions to their child, research has shown that children with ID show more positive outcomes. Several categories of parenting behaviour are considered to be part of a responsive style. Perhaps most straightforwardly, parents who react to their child in contingent ways are considered responsive. If a child points to a toy on a shelf and appears excited to play with it, a contingent response would be for a parent to reach for the toy and hand it to the child. The behaviour of the parent is shaped by the communicative intent of the child, and the parent recognizes the importance of cues produced by the child to inform their behaviour.

In addition to contingency, emotional support is a key component of a responsive parenting style (Warren & Brady 2007). Emotional support involves accurately interpreting a child's emotional state and allowing that information to guide parenting behaviours. This involves taking into account a child's perspective, gaining an understanding of what their skills and capabilities are at a given time, and then selecting responses that are appropriate for those factors. Responsivity can also be observed in the language used by a parent. In responsive parenting interactions, parents use language that is appropriate for the overall developmental level of the child, which makes communication effective and addresses their child's needs (Warren & Brady 2007).

The accumulated impact of responsive parenting may facilitate important outcomes for children with ID. In one study, children with fragile X syndrome, a neurogenetic condition associated with ID, were observed at multiple timepoints as they interacted with their mothers (Brady, Warren, Fleming, Keller, & Sterling 2014). When parent responsivity was calculated over time, children with more responsive mothers demonstrated better language understanding and more advanced language production than children with less responsive mothers (Brady et al. 2014). Responsive parenting at home may also facilitate learning in other contexts. In one study, young children with ID who enrolled in an intervention study made significantly greater gains if they had experienced responsive parenting than if they did not (Yoder & Warren 2002). Responsivity may also help children with ID maintain skills during different phases of the lifespan. In a longitudinal study of children with fragile X syndrome, higher degrees of maternal responsivity were associated with fewer declines in adaptive behaviour (Warren, Brady, Fleming, & Hahn 2017). Research on the topic of parental responsivity continues to demonstrate the cumulative impact of an attuned parenting style, and suggests that the contingent, warm, and positive day-to-day interactions that parents have with their children make a big difference over time.

Directiveness

Though evidence is mounting for the importance of parental responsivity, there is also evidence that parents of children with ID may be more likely than other parents to use a 'directive' parenting style. When parents structure and organize their child's interactions, and tell them what behaviours they would like for their child to produce, this type of parenting behaviour is considered to be directive. Directive parenting behaviours often involve the use of verbal commands and they tend to limit the choices available for a child to select (Wieland, Green, Ellingsen, & Baker 2014). Though parents of children with and without ID may show comparable levels of engagement and warmth, the greater frequency of directives may have a cumulative effect on child development. In one study, increased use of directive behaviours by parents of children with Down syndrome was associated with greater difficulties in aspects of child executive function (Schworer, Fidler, Lunkenheimer, & Daunhauer 2019). This finding suggests that frequent demands or requests made that guide child behaviour may indirectly impact the development of a child's ability to organize and control their own thinking, perhaps because of fewer opportunities to generate well-organized plans autonomously.

However, there is an alternative interpretation of parental directiveness research, which holds that directiveness in parents of children with ID may support developmental skill acquisition and may be a necessary feature of parenting for a child who may have difficulty with sustained engagement in interactions or tasks. In one study, parents of children with fragile X syndrome were found to be more directive than parents of children without this condition. However, this behaviour style was seen as a beneficial adaptation, as it appeared to support and guide the development of language skills (Abbeduto et al. 1999). It may be the case that directive behaviours from parents help children complete tasks successfully, but over time this approach may indirectly impact a child's ability to organize their own strategies and actions independently.

Harsh Parenting

Not all families have the capacity for resilience in response to the demands of caregiving for an individual with ID. Several studies have demonstrated that children with developmental delays are at greater risk for experiencing negative parenting behaviours, including intrusive and harsh parenting styles that involve a greater degree of negative emotion (Brown, McIntyre, Crnic, Baker, & Blacher 2011). In one large study of families of children with cognitive delays, the strongest factors that were associated with child problem behaviours were parenting dimensions. In particular, when 4–5-year-old children were exposed to either angry/harsh parenting or inconsistent parenting, they were three times more likely to demonstrate problem behaviours than their counterparts who had not been exposed to this type of parenting (Emerson, Einfeld, & Stancliffe 2011). Follow up with the same cohort throughout childhood through to age nine found that angry/harsh parenting continued to be among the strongest predictors of conduct problems (Emerson et al. 2011).

These findings extend to the overall emotional climate that is set by parents. In a study where parenting behaviours were observed by researchers in the home environment, parents of children with ID who demonstrated high levels of negative emotion, including a harsh tone of voice or looks of disgust, tended to have children with poorer social skills outcomes (Green & Baker 2011). Because of these links between negative parenting and child outcomes, the development of interventions that support positive parent–child relationships and reduce the use of harsh parenting behaviours may be particularly impactful for children with ID (Totsika, Hastings, Emerson, & Hatton 2020).

IMPACT OF AN INDIVIDUAL WITH ID ON FAMILY MEMBERS

Just as there is a great deal of heterogeneity in outcomes among individuals with ID, there is also a range of outcomes that are experienced by families of individuals with ID. Several decades of research in the latter part of the twentieth century focused on the added stresses, strains, and burdens that parents face in raising a child with unique needs. This work carefully examined the various child factors that elicit greater or lesser degrees of stress, and will be reviewed below. However, it is important to identify at the outset that the story of increased stress and strain on families is an incomplete picture for many families. Since the 2000s, there has been a growing interest in understanding how the presence of a child with ID may also impact families in positive ways, in terms of rewarding experiences, resilience, and unique insights on their understanding of purpose and meaning in life. We will explore these issues and synthesize these findings, but always with a recognition of each family's unique path through the journey of raising a child with ID.

Parenting Stress and Mental Health

The cumulative effect of child rearing in families of children with ID has a notable impact on some parents. Recent estimates from the United States Panel Study of Income Dynamics suggests that parents of adults with a developmental disability, including ID, were three times more likely to have mental health challenges than parents of adults without disabilities (Hoyle, Laditka, & Laditka 2021). Elevated risk is even greater in minoritized groups, as Hispanic mothers report higher rates of mental health challenges than other groups (Hoyle et al. 2021). To understand this risk more deeply, and to address it most effectively, it is important to examine specific constructs that impact the overall well-being of parents, like stress.

Stress

Though it can be defined in variety of ways, many researchers who study individuals with ID think of family stress as involving negative reactions to the various experiences associated with being a family member of someone with ID. Parenting stress, in particular, is thought to include child-related or parenting events that are coupled with negative evaluations of those events by the parent (Deater-Deckard 1998). Understanding stress in parents and families of individuals with ID is important because its ongoing presence can impact the quality of relationships, and over time, may accumulate and lead to decreased mental health and well-being for family members.

The birth of a child with ID constitutes a major life event for any parent, and as such, likely elicits a range of emotions and responses, and likely, some degree of stress. However, stress in families of children with ID is often rooted in smaller-scale, ongoing experiences that unfold over years of parenting. The day-to-day experiences associated with parenting any child often include enjoyable, rewarding interactions, but they also inevitably include some degree of inconvenience and challenge, often referred to as 'daily hassles' (Crnic & Greenberg 1990).

These daily hassles are thought to be important for understanding family functioning, both because they are found almost universally among families, and because they may contribute to the nature and quality of parent–child relationships (Crnic & Low 2002). As they accumulate over time, daily hassles can interact with parent personality dimensions, expectations, and ideas regarding parenting and child behaviour, and the overall social context in which the family exists (Crnic & Low 2002). For families of children with ID, daily hassles may be increased, and they may take unique forms. Consider the inconvenience of delay in access to much-needed therapies for a child because of physician or insurance-related approvals. Though a situation like this might be remedied by phone calls and additional parental follow up, over time, these additional responsibilities may interact with a parent's appraisal of their child's development in other unrelated domains, and the overall sense of how much perceived support a parent experiences. In these contexts, the hassle of additional phone calls may be emotionally charged with additional feelings of isolation, lack of support, or pessimism about their child's growth and development.

With the potential for increased frequency of daily hassles, the subjective interpretation and understanding that parents assign to their experiences plays an important role in parental well-being (Lazarus 1984; Crnic & Low 2002). This is why some researchers and clinicians believe that the family is an important unit to target for intervention. Supporting parents and their well-being, and helping them appraise their situation in adaptive ways, may lead to more positive trajectories for themselves and their children with ID.

Child Eliciting Factors

Because of the range of outcomes among parents of children with ID, researchers in the 1980s and 1990s conducted numerous studies to examine whether specific child characteristics may contribute to differences in family stress and rewardingness outcomes. An obvious factor that was examined initially was child degree of ID, with the idea that a child who demonstrates greater degrees of intellectual challenge would place a greater degree of stress on families. This hypothesis was generally not supported in the research conducted at the time (Beckman 1983; Walker, Van Slyke, & Newbrough 1992). More conclusive findings were observed, however, when factors such as challenging behaviours were examined. Across many studies, when a child with ID demonstrates higher levels of challenging behaviours, like aggression, families report higher levels of overall stress (McIntyre, Blacher, & Baker 2002; Blacher & McIntyre 2006; Baker, Seltzer, & Greenberg 2012).

Aetiology Specific Findings

The impact of child behaviour on families can also be informed by the study of phenotypic profiles, or patterns of strength and challenge associated with various genetic aetiologies (causes) of intellectual disability. Different conditions associated with ID predispose children to varying levels of challenging behaviour and other areas of developmental relative strength and challenge. This insight launched a line of research that examined how phenotypic features associated with specific neurogenetic syndromes may elicit certain types of outcomes in families in systematic ways.

Robert Hodapp (1997) identified this phenomenon, which he termed the 'indirect effects' of a child's neurogenetic condition on family members. Within this model, when a child is born with a neurogenetic condition associated with ID, they are predisposed to a range of outcomes across many different developmental domains. In addition, the condition increases the likelihood that families will experience certain outcomes in response to their child's profile as well (Hodapp 1997). Hodapp's indirect effects framework has been applied across a variety of neurogenetic conditions, and the impact of aetiology-related phenotypes on family outcomes has been well-characterized for a range of neurogenetic conditions. For example, when compared to families of children with other types of ID, families of children with Prader-Willi syndrome (PWS) report higher levels of stress (Hodapp, Dykens, & Masino 1997). PWS is associated with borderline/mild ID in many cases, but it is also associated with a range of challenging behavioural outcomes, including food preoccupations and obsessive-compulsive behaviour (Dykens, Leckman, & Cassidy 1996). When family outcomes were examined more closely, factors such as child age and IQ were found not to be associated with stress (Hodapp, Dykens, & Masino 1997). However, child aggressive behaviours and thought problems (including obsessive thoughts) were strongly associated with reported stress by parents (Hodapp, Dykens, & Masino 1997).

Cross-syndrome comparisons of the indirect effects of neurogenetic conditions on families have revealed the complex interplay between syndrome profiles and family outcomes. In one study that compared outcomes among families of young children with Down syndrome, Smith-Magenis syndrome, and Williams syndrome, it was found that families of children with Smith-Magenis syndrome reported substantially higher levels of parent and family problems and pessimism than families of children with Down syndrome (Fidler et al. 2000). Families of children with Williams syndrome showed somewhat lower levels of these challenging dimensions than families of children with Smith-Magenis syndrome, but higher than families of children with Down syndrome. These findings are notable in that Smith-Magenis syndrome and Williams syndrome are both associated with elevated risk for different types of behaviour challenges, including self-injury (Smith-Magenis syndrome) and anxiety (Williams syndrome). Interestingly, across several studies, families of children with Down syndrome have reported lower levels of overall stress when compared to families of children with other ID-related diagnoses (Hodapp et al. 2001). This may be attributable to lower levels of challenging behaviours and adaptive behaviour strengths among some children with Down syndrome, but other factors may be at play as well, such as advanced maternal age (Corrice & Glidden 2009). While family outcomes are likely influenced by a wide range of factors, it is clear that syndrome-related patterns can be observed when considering the indirect effects of neurogenetic conditions on families. Regardless of aetiology, identifying ways to address challenging behaviours within a child's profile may be an important strategy for supporting effective caregiving and more positive outcomes for all family members.

Siblings

Though parents are often the focus of family research in ID, understanding the nature of sibling relationships is also of great significance. Siblings are connected to one another across different phases of the lifespan, and their relationships are unique in that they are often in a similar phase of the lifespan at the same time (childhood; adolescence). Sibling relationships are also important for the simple fact that they can serve as the longest relationships that an individual has throughout their lives. Being the sibling of someone with ID often leads to some unique experiences, such as distinctive caretaking roles, and the facilitation of interactions between a sibling with ID and members of the community. The longevity of sibling relationships also takes on additional importance when a sibling has ID: siblings of someone with ID may be asked to contribute to caregiving or oversight of care later in life, as parents age or pass away.

Research on siblings of children with ID has generated a wide range of findings that are often contradictory. Some studies report a positive impact on siblings, while other studies report a negative impact, and others report no impact (see Marquis et al. 2019 for a review). In a few studies, siblings report lower levels of conflict and more positive relationship features when one sibling has ID than when neither sibling has ID (Eisenberg, Baker, & Blacher 1998; Floyd, Purcell, Richardson, & Kupersmidt 2009). Certain factors impact siblings and their experiences, like the presence of maladaptive behaviour in their sibling with ID. Some of the same factors that are implicated in overall family well-being are also found to specifically impact siblings, including income, and perhaps also neighborhood dimensions and parent education (Marquis, Hayes, & McGrail 2019).

But perhaps the best way to understand outcomes in siblings of individuals with ID is to ask them to talk about their experiences in open-ended ways. In one such study, a range of thoughts and reactions were described regarding the experience of having a brother or sister with ID (Moyson & Roeyers 2012). A few siblings expressed a sense of acceptance of their sibling's abilities, and others also expressed that their sibling's disability made it difficult to fully engage in activities together (Moyson & Roeyers 2012). A few siblings expressed a desire for time away from their role as sibling of someone with ID, and a desire for time that they could spend with their parents individually (Moyson & Roeyers 2012). There were those who described that they longed to understand their brother or sister with ID better, to know what their internal thoughts and feelings are, and to be similarly understood by their sibling as well (Moyson & Roeyers 2012). Taking a larger view, a few siblings described that the reactions of the community toward their sibling with ID greatly influenced their experience – when community members accept their sibling with ID, siblings described more positive experiences for themselves as well (Moyson & Roeyers 2012). These varied perspectives remind us that from the outside looking in, we may catch a glimpse of sibling and family functioning, however, the day-to-day experiences of family members of an individual with ID are complex and varied, and even amidst some common themes, many nuances and differences are present as well.

Family Intervention and Parent Training

Because of the range of influences that family members have on an individual with ID, and the unique ways that a child with ID influences families, researchers and clinicians have sought effective ways to support child well-being by working with family members. Parent intervention approaches have been developed that are rooted in the notion that ongoing positive parenting experiences are beneficial to children with ID. These approaches are generally built around following the interests of the child with the idea of adhering to certain stylistic guidances in an ongoing way throughout daily life (Brady et al. 2009).

Training For Responsivity

As described earlier in this chapter, certain parenting styles, such as responsive parenting, are associated with more adaptive outcomes for children with ID. To support the development of a more responsive parenting style, parents are taught to use behaviours such as modelling and asking their child questions (Brady et al. 2009). They can be taught to respond to their child in ways that follow their child's interest in an activity, when it would be natural to do so (Brady et al. 2009). Some of the more commonly used approaches include Playing and Learning Strategies (PALS) and the Hanen Approach (It Takes Two to Talk; (Girolametto & Weitzman 2006), each of which have a growing empirical base that demonstrates an impact on parenting behaviour, and in some cases, child outcomes as well. Although existing interventions may take different approaches to enhancing responsivity, they generally are effective when they are informed by developmental timing (Brady et al. 2009), and when they aim to teach responsivity in a variety of manifestations, such as enhancing parental contingency in their responses, encouraging parents to notice and wait for their child's initiations, and the guided use of parent input language (Brady et al. 2009).

Training For Behaviour Management

Another focus of family intervention in ID has aimed to support parents in their management of challenging child behaviours (McIntyre 2008). Though specific behaviour challenges are often linked to underlying neurogenetic aetiologies (e.g. Smith-Magenis syndrome, Prader-Willi syndrome; (Dykens & Shah 2003; Shelley & Robertson 2005), these outcomes may still be influenced by parenting behaviour. Providing resources to parents through education and support networks may be an effective means to reduce child problem behaviours (McIntyre 2008). McIntyre and Brown (2013) describe the importance of promoting positive parenting behaviours as a pathway towards the reduction of behavioural disorders in children with ID. They discuss the utility of a three-tiered model approach to family intervention in ID, wherein universal prevention approaches are accompanied by a second tier of targeted prevention strategies 'selected' for those at elevated risk, as well as approaches for those individuals for whom treatment is already 'indicated' (McIntyre & Brown, 2013). The specific interventions employed may focus on increasing social support for families, improving stress management, and parent education regarding behavioural approaches.

Contemplative Approaches

In recent years, researchers have begun to demonstrate the positive effects of mindfulness training for parents of children with developmental disabilities. Mindfulness approaches generally include strategies for increasing awareness from moment to moment, promoting acceptance, and nonjudgmental interpretation of events (Bazzano et al., 2015). Recent studies that used a Mindfulness Based Stress Reduction (MBSR) framework involved learning basic information about the construct of mindfulnesss, engaging in training exercises with other parents and in between sessions, and shared reflection with other parents (Bazzano et al., 2015; Neece et al., 2019). Results of this work have demonstrated that MBSR improves mental health outcomes for parents and reduced behaviour challenges for children with developmental disabilities, and the effects seem to generalize across ethnic and cultural groups (Bazzano et al., 2015; Neece, Chan, Klein, Roberts, & Fenning, 2019).

Summary

In recent years, researchers have begun to integrate varying approaches toward family intervention in ID (Crnic, Neece, McIntyre, Blacher, & Baker, 2017). This work acknowledges the interconnection between the presence of family stress and the successful implementation of behavioural intervention strategies. When parents experience stress, it may be difficult for them to use the techniques and strategies that are included in such parenting intervention models. Researchers who argue for a more integrated model describe that targeting stress levels in families can have important downstream effects for families in many ways (Crnic et al., 2017). Though intervention to support families of children with ID is an area with great potential for continued growth, the gains that have been made to date are nonetheless meaningful, and are an integral part of promoting well-being for individuals with ID.

THE OTHER SIDE OF THE COIN: POSITIVE PERSPECTIVES ON PARENTING CHILDREN WITH ID

Research on stress in families of children with ID clearly demonstrates that certain behaviour profiles elicit higher degrees of stress and strain for family members. However, makes the case that the link between the presence of ID (or other developmental disabilities) and negative outcomes is not necessarily straightforward. He describes that, in work conducted in the United

Kingdom, higher levels of anxiety and depression were observed in mothers and fathers of children with ID and other developmental disabilities. However, he also notes that the actual rates of depression in mothers of school age children with ID were approximately 8%, which is only slightly higher than the 5% rate observed in the general population of adult females in the UK population. Anxiety rates were higher (approximately 30%). However, Hastings (2016) points out that the majority of mothers of school-age children with ID do not have clinical levels of anxiety or depression. In other words, there may be elevated likelihood for mental health challenges in parents of children with ID, but the vast majority of parents do not demonstrate these outcomes. Similar patterns of slightly elevated difficulty scores reported by siblings of children with ID, but once again, Hastings (2016) noted that most siblings did not report emotional and behavioural problems. All of these findings converge on the idea that there is a somewhat elevated risk for mental health challenges in families of children with ID, but the majority of family members do not experience these outcomes.

Resilience

Though families of children with ID may face some shared experiences, families also demonstrate a wide range of responses, with some demonstrating a great deal of resilience. Resilience is the ability to respond to and recover from difficulties – in colloquial terms, it is the ability to 'bounce back'. Research into the qualities of families that are able to be resilient in the face of the challenges associated with having a family member with ID include the use of cognitive strategies, such as the ability reframe or 'put a positive spin' on a given set of circumstances (Piazza, Floyd, Mailick, & Greenberg 2014). Hastings et al. (2002) found that when mothers were better able to use reframing as a coping strategy, they also tended to see their child as a source of personal fulfillment, growth, maturity, and happiness. Hastings et al. (2002) argued that the ability to perceive their lives positively may help parents cope with the additional stresses that they may experience with their child with ID.

Another way that parents of children with ID may cope is through more active problem solving, or through 'problem-focused' approaches (Piazza et al., 2014). This category of coping styles involves generating strategies to actively change stressful circumstances, rather than to change or reframe how they are understood. Parents of children with ID may benefit from taking control over modifiable circumstances, like advocating for a different school placement for their child, or seeking out additional caregiving support when feeling taxed. In one study, parents who used such problem-focused approaches demonstrated lower levels of stress and they reported having better relationships with their child with ID during adulthood (Kim, Greenberg, Seltzer, & Krauss 2003). However, parents may also inevitably encounter circumstances that are more difficult to modify, like some aspects of their child's skillset. Under these circumstances, additional reframing strategies may be a more effective coping mechanisms.

Rewardingness

Over the past few decades, families of children with ID have also been examined in a different light. Rather than focusing unidimensionally on family stress, research studies included more questions regarding the potentially positive impact of a child with ID on the family unit. Researchers have begun to examine family outcomes like fulfilment, personal growth, and maturity that may result from the experience of raising a child with ID (Hastings, Allen, McDermott, & Still 2002). Additional studies examined the empathic and the potential contributions to society that these families may have (Scorgie & Sobsey 2000; Scorgie, Wilgosh, & Sobsey 2004).

Beyond these reported positive outcomes, having a child with ID may also modify how parents interface with their communities in ways that enhance their feeling of community and connection. Interacting with educators, therapists, and job coaches who are working towards supporting their child's well-being may provide a support system to parents, as well as additional meaningful collaborations in the community that they would otherwise not have. Witnessing inclusive activities and spontaneous kindness among classmates in integrated settings may serve as more of a frequent reminder of the good in others, and the compassion that humans can show one another. Recreational activities that bring together children with ID and their peers, such as unified sports or theatre, can serve as a model for how to welcome everyone into a community. In this way, families of children with ID may experience a uniquely meaningful and inspiring set of interactions with those around them, enriched by the increased opportunities to witness the kindness of others.

ADDITIONAL FACTORS AND RECENT FINDINGS

Supporting Families of Children with ID

Just as a child with ID exists within a family context, families of children with ID exist within a larger social network as well. These networks can be important sources of social support for families, and can make a large difference in terms of the overall well-being of a family. Support from a community may come from several sources. There are informal supports from extended family members, like grandparents, aunts, and uncles, who provide various types of help without being formally hired or paid to do so. There are also formal social supports, such as care providers, advocates, and other professionals who work for agencies or support-related organizations.

There are many different categories of support that families can benefit from. In a review of the literature on social support in families of children with disabilities, categorized the broad range of services and help that can be made available to families of children with ID. One important type of support is *informational support*, which involves providing families with more comprehensive knowledge and insight regarding their child's development, the types of services available to them, the types of services that their child could benefit from, and other parenting resources related to their child's diagnosis. Advocacy groups can play an important role in providing informational support, especially when they have specialized knowledge regarding a particular diagnosis. Therapists, educators, and service coordinators can provide informational support in academic and clinical settings. Perhaps most importantly, informational support can come from parents supporting other parents with their own insights and experiences. Parents of children with disabilities often have many systems to navigate and decisions to make regarding their child's educational, therapeutic, and vocational services. Receiving informational support to guide decision making from these members of a social network can make a big difference for families and their outcomes.

Legal and financial support are also important sources of assistance for families of children with ID (Tétreault et al. 2014). Parenting a child with ID can sometimes require knowledge regarding a child's rights and legal access to education and services. Most parents of children with ID do not have training and expertise in these areas prior to becoming parents, and often need to equip themselves with legal knowledge regarding the resources to which their child and family are entitled within a given local and national context. Organizations that provide access for this knowledge can play a key role in improving and enhancing the well-being for a child with ID and their family.

Help for families of children with ID also comes in the form of *psychological support* from parent organizations, therapy, and other recreational means for families to connect with one another (Tétreault et al. 2014). The isolation associated with increased caregiving demands and the isolation associated with parenting a child with unique needs that differ from chronological age-peers can leave parents at risk for loneliness and separation from community. Participating in activities where parents can share their experiences, offer emotional support, and provide ways for engaging with other members of the community can make an important difference for the overall well-being and mental health of a family unit.

Respite care is often a foundational support for families of children with ID (Tétreault et al. 2014). Whereas all children require moment-to-moment caregiving during early childhood, middle childhood and adolescence is generally marked by increasing independence. This increased independence translates to less moment-to-moment caregiving demands for parents, though other types of monitoring and psychological relating may become increasingly important. For parents of children with ID, however, an increase in independence may come more slowly, or not at all. Maintaining a high degree of moment-to-moment parent-child interaction may have a cumulative effect on parent mental health and well-being, and finding ways to alleviate some of this burden can be important for maintaining a positive, warm parent-child relationship over time. Respite care, or care provided by non-parents for a child with ID, can allow parents to shift their attention to other aspects of their daily lives for a set period of time. Whether it is uninterrupted parenting time for siblings, leisure time activities with a spouse, significant other, or friends, or even a chance to tend to house-related chores, respite care can have a far-reaching impact on parent emotional well-being, and may make it possible for parents to return to caregiving refreshed and with renewed emotional resources.

Sociological Dimensions

Families exist within a social context, as described in the previous section, but it is also important to recognize the larger societal context as well. When compared to others, families of children with ID often face greater risks that are related to sociological factors. Children with ID (and other disabilities) are twice as likely to come from lower socioeconomic status backgrounds than children without disabilities (Spencer, Blackburn, & Read 2015), and are more likely to experience exposure to environmental risk factors, like poverty, before the age of three years (Emerson et al. 2014). Young children who demonstrate cognitive delays in the UK are less likely than their counterparts without ID to live with two biological parents, and they are also less likely to live with mothers who are married (Hatton, Emerson, Graham, Blacher, & Llewellyn 2010). Emerson et al. (2014) suggest that some of the challenging behaviours that are elevated in some children with ID may be attributed to these early risks, rather than cognitive and intellectual factors.

Family Resources

Though poverty and environmental risk are linked to ID, there may also be an impact of the presence of ID on family financial well-being over time. For parents of children with ID, the ability to gain and maintain employment is contingent on factors like childcare, transportation, and job availability. Each of these factors may be uniquely impacted in families of children with ID (Parish & Cloud 2006). Childcare can be harder to find and more expensive for children with disabilities and other special health care needs (Parish & Cloud 2006), and the scope of supports needed is far greater, including therapies, adaptive equipment, medication, and accommodations to the home physical environment. The increased time demands associated with caregiving for a child with ID may necessitate flexibility regarding working hours and requests for time away from work for child-related needs (Parish & Cloud 2006).

Maternal employment has also been linked to the degree of the child's disability, and the number of children with disabilities in the family (Lukemeyer, Meyers, & Smeeding 2000). Furthermore, certain diagnoses associated with ID may impact family finances in different ways. In one study of families of children with fragile X syndrome, a neurogenetic condition associated with ID and autism features, parents were almost twice as likely to report reducing their employment than families of children with other ID-related conditions (Ouyang et al. 2014). They also reported a much greater financial burden than other families. In families of children with Down syndrome, another common neurogenetic condition associated with ID, 38% of families reported that they experienced financial challenges because of their child's ID-related condition, and 42% reported that a family member stopped working because of their child with DS (Schieve, Boulet, Kogan, Van Naarden-Braun, & Boyle 2011). Nearly 30% reported that they needed additional income to cover their child's health-care related needs (Schieve et al. 2011). These financial and resource-related outcomes for families of children with ID are important because they provide more information regarding the risks and lived experiences of individuals with ID and their families.

Families and Biological Factors

Though parents of children with ID and other disabilities may report a range of subjective experiences, including stress and rewardingness, recent research suggests that lifelong caregiving may take a physical toll (Seltzer et al. 2009a). Differences in stress hormone levels have been reported when comparing parents of adults who had a range of psychiatric and intellectual disabilities to parents of adults without these conditions (Seltzer et al. 2009b). Levels of stress hormones may be an indicator of the physical stress experienced by caregivers of children with extensive needs.

There is also evidence that certain biological factors may increase vulnerability to stress in parents of children with certain ID-related conditions. In conditions that are passed on from one generation to another, parents may 'carry' risk for the condition. In fragile X syndrome, for example, mothers carry a genetic risk that not only leads to the ID-related condition in their child, but also places them at elevated likelihood for milder cognitive and behavioural features in themselves (Wheeler et al. 2014). However, while mothers of children with fragile X syndrome demonstrate elevated risk for anxiety and depression (Head & Abbeduto 2007), child problem behaviour and not carrier status plays the most significant role in influencing parent outcomes (Bailey et al. 2008).

These findings remind us that the psychological and sociological outcomes described for families of children with ID in this chapter impact well-being in a multitude of ways. Detecting elevated physiological responses to stress, and identifying increased risk for mood disorders associated with a particular neurogenetic syndrome remind us that no phenomenon can be viewed in isolation. Understanding families of children with ID requires a multi-level, wholistic approach that encompasses the gamut from genes to society.

Family Related Quality of Life

When tying together the various themes of this chapter – the bidirectional impact of parents and children with ID on one another, family stress, intervention, supports, access to resources – what emerges is the larger notion of 'family quality-of-life' (Gardiner & Iarocci 2012). In the past two decades, researchers have become increasingly interested in measuring the degree to which families have their needs met, are empowered to reach their goals, and have an overall sense of well-being (Park et al. 2003; Brown & Brown 2005; Gardiner & Iarocci 2012). Identifying that quality of life is a critical, measurable outcome for families of children with ID helps us remember the underlying motivation for this line of scientific and clinical research. Family quality-of-life models integrate family members' emotional and physical well-being, and consider whether families have access to adequate resources to meet their needs (Gardiner & Iarocci 2012). Placing this construct at the center of research on families of individuals with ID is a reminder that our goals should not be limited to reducing stress or risk for mental health challenges; our goals should involve identifying ways for families of individuals with ID to live fulfilled lives. By keeping the overall family quality of life at the centre of our vision, the goal for researchers and practitioners is to find new ways to improve the structures and systems in place that are designed to serve people with ID and their families, and to promote enhanced well-being for them throughout the lifespan.

Reflective Questions

1. Imagine learning that your child has a diagnosis associated with ID. What types of support might you find most helpful? What questions would you have?
2. What are some of the challenges that families of an individual with ID might experience during different phases of the lifespan? During early childhood? Middle childhood? Adolescence? Adulthood?
3. What are some of the positive outcomes that families of an individual with ID might experience during different phases of the lifespan? During early childhood? Middle childhood? Adolescence? Adulthood?
4. How do you think the experience of providing care for a family member with ID might change over time?
5. What societal supports do you think could be helpful to promote the well-being and quality of life for families of children with ID?

REFERENCES

Abbeduto, L., Seltzer, M. M., Shattuck, P., Krauss, M. W., Orsmond, G., & Murphy, M. M. (2004). Psychological well-being and coping in mothers of youths with autism, down syndrome, orfragile X syndrome. *American Journal on Mental Retardation, 109*(3), 237–254.

Bailey Jr, D. B., Sideris, J., Roberts, J., & Hatton, D. (2008). Child and genetic variables associated with maternal adaptation to fragile X syndrome: A multidimensional analysis. *American Journal of Medical Genetics Part A, 146*(6), 720–729.

Baker, J. K., Seltzer, M. M., & Greenberg, J. S. (2012). Behaviour problems, maternal internalising symptoms and family relations in families of adolescents and adults with fragile X syndrome. *Journal of Intellectual Disability Research, 56*(10), 984–995.

Bazzano, A., Wolfe, C., Zylowska, L., Wang, S., Schuster, E., Barrett, C., & Lehrer, D. (2015). Mindfulness based stress reduction (MBSR) for parents and caregivers of individuals with developmental disabilities: a community-based approach. *Journal of Child and Family Studies, 24*(2), 298–308.

Beckman, P. J. (1983). Influence of selected child characteristics on stress in families of handicapped infants. *American Journal of Mental Deficiency*.

Blacher, J., & McIntyre, L. L. (2006). Syndrome specificity and behavioural disorders in young adults with intellectual disability: Cultural differences in family impact. *Journal of Intellectual Disability Research, 50*(3), 184–198.

Brady, N., Warren, S. F., & Sterling, A. (2009). Interventions aimed at improving child language by improving maternal responsivity. *International review of research in mental retardation, 37*, 333–357.

Brady, N., Warren, S. F., Fleming, K., Keller, J., & Sterling, A. (2014). Effect of sustained maternal responsivity on later vocabulary development in children with fragile X syndrome.

Brown, M. A., McIntyre, L. L., Crnic, K. A., Baker, B. L., & Blacher, J. (2011). Preschool children with and without developmental delay: Risk, parenting, and child demandingness. *Journal of Mental Health Research in Intellectual Disabilities, 4*(3), 206–226.

Brown, R., & Brown, I. (2005). The application of quality of life. *Journal of Intellectual Disability Research, 49*(10), 718–727.

Corrice, A. M., & Glidden, L. M. (2009). The Down syndrome advantage: fact or fiction?. *American Journal on Intellectual and Developmental Disabilities, 114*(4), 254–268.

Crnic, K., & Low, C. (2002). Everyday stresses and parenting.

Crnic, K. A., & Greenberg, M. T. (1990). Minor parenting stresses with young children. *Child Development, 61*(5), 1628–1637.

Crnic, K. A., Neece, C. L., McIntyre, L. L., Blacher, J., & Baker, B. L. (2017). Intellectual disability and developmental risk: Promoting intervention to improve child and family well-being. *Child Development, 88*(2), 436–445.

Deater-Deckard, K. (1998). Parenting stress and child adjustment: Some old hypotheses and new questions. *Clinical psychology: Science and practice, 5*(3), 314–332.

Dykens, E., & Shah, B. (2003). Psychiatric disorders in Prader-Willi syndrome. *CNS drugs, 17*(3), 167–178.

Dykens, E. M., Leckman, J. F., & Cassidy, S. B. (1996). Obsessions and compulsions in Prader-Willi syndrome. *Journal of Child Psychology and Psychiatry, 37*(8), 995–1002.

Eisenberg, L., Baker, B. L., & Blacher, J. (1998). Siblings of children with mental retardation living at home or in residential placement. *Journal of Child Psychology and Psychiatry, 39*(3), 355–363.

Emerson, E., Blacher, J., Einfeld, S., Hatton, C., Robertson, J., & Stancliffe, R. J. (2014). Environmental risk factors associated with the persistence of conduct difficulties in children with intellectual disabilities and autistic spectrum disorders. *Research in Developmental Disabilities, 35*(12), 3508–3517.

Emerson, E., Einfeld, S., & Stancliffe, R. J. (2011). Predictors of the persistence of conduct difficulties in children with cognitive delay. *Journal of Child Psychology and Psychiatry, 52*(11), 1184–1194.

Floyd, F. J., Purcell, S. E., Richardson, S. S., & Kupersmidt, J. B. (2009). Sibling relationship quality and social functioning of children and adolescents with intellectual disability. *American Journal on Intellectual and Developmental Disabilities, 114*(2), 110–127.

Gardiner, E., & Iarocci, G. (2012). Unhappy (and happy) in their own way: A developmental psychopathology perspective on quality of life for families living with developmental disability with and without autism. *Research in Developmental Disabilities*, *33*(6), 2177–2192.

Girolametto, L., & Weitzman, E. (2006). It takes two to talk—The Hanen program for parents: Early language intervention through caregiver training. *Treatment of Language Disorders in Children*, 77–103.

Green, S., & Baker, B. (2011). Parents' emotion expression as a predictor of child's social competence: children with or without intellectual disability. *Journal of Intellectual Disability Research*, *55*(3), 324–338.

Hastings, R. P., Allen, R., McDermott, K., & Still, D. (2002). Factors related to positive perceptions in mothers of children with intellectual disabilities. *Journal of Applied Research in Intellectual Disabilities*, *15*(3), 269–275.

Hatton, C., Emerson, E., Graham, H., Blacher, J., & Llewellyn, G. (2010). Changes in family composition and marital status in families with a young child with cognitive delay. *Journal of Applied Research in Intellectual Disabilities*, *23*(1), 14–26.

Head, L. S., & Abbeduto, L. (2007). Recognizing the role of parents in developmental outcomes: A systems approach to evaluating the child with developmental disabilities. *Mental Retardation and Developmental Disabilities Research Reviews*, *13*(4), 293–301.

Hodapp, R. M. (1997). Direct and indirect behavioral effects of different genetic disorders of mental retardation. *American Journal on Mental Retardation*, *102*(1), 67–79.

Hodapp, R. M., Ly, T. M., Fidler, D. J., & Ricci, L. A. (2001). Less stress, more rewarding: Parenting children with Down syndrome. *Parenting: Science and practice*, *1*(4), 317–337.

Hodapp, R. M., Dykens, E. M., & Masino, L. L. (1997). Families of children with Prader-Willi syndrome: Stress-support and relations to child characteristics. *Journal of Autism and Developmental Disorders*, *27*(1), 11–24.

Hoyle, J. N., Laditka, J. N., & Laditka, S. B. (2021). Mental health risks of parents of children with developmental disabilities: A nationally representative study in the United States. *Disability and Health Journal*, 101020.

Kim, H.-W., Greenberg, J., Seltzer, M., & Krauss, M. (2003). The role of coping in maintaining the psychological well-being of mothers of adults with intellectual disability and mental illness. *Journal of Intellectual Disability Research*, *47*(4-5), 313–327.

Lazarus, R. S. (1984). On the primacy of cognition.

Lukemeyer, A., Meyers, M. K., & Smeeding, T. (2000). Expensive children in poor families: out-of-pocket expenditures for the care of disabled and chronically ill children in welfare families. *Journal of Marriage and Family*, *62*(2), 399–415.

Marquis, S., Hayes, M. V., & McGrail, K. (2019). Factors that may affect the health of siblings of children who have an intellectual/developmental disability. *Journal of Policy and Practice in Intellectual Disabilities*, *16*(4), 273–286.

McIntyre, L. L. (2008). Parent training for young children with developmental disabilities: Randomized controlled trial. *American Journal on Mental Retardation*, *113*(5), 356–368.

McIntyre, L. L., Blacher, J., & Baker, B. L. (2002). Behaviour/mental health problems in young adults with intellectual disability: The impact on families. *Journal of Intellectual Disability Research*, *46*(3), 239–249.

McIntyre, L. L., & Brown, M. (2013). Involving family in the prevention and intervention of behavior problems in individuals with intellectual and developmental disabilities. In *Handbook of Crisis Intervention and Developmental Disabilities* (pp. 245–258): Springer.

Moyson, T., & Roeyers, H. (2012). 'The overall quality of my life as a sibling is all right, but of course, it could always be better'. Quality of life of siblings of children with intellectual disability: the siblings' perspectives. *Journal of Intellectual Disability Research, 56*(1), 87–101.

Neece, C. L., Chan, N., Klein, K., Roberts, L., & Fenning, R. M. (2019). Mindfulness-based stress reduction for parents of children with developmental delays: understanding the experiences of Latino families. *Mindfulness, 10*(6), 1017–1030.

Ouyang, L., Grosse, S. D., Riley, C., Bolen, J., Bishop, E., Raspa, M., & Bailey Jr, D. B. (2014). A comparison of family financial and employment impacts of fragile X syndrome, autism spectrum disorders, and intellectual disability. *Research in Developmental Disabilities, 35*(7), 1518–1527.

Parish, S. L., & Cloud, J. M. (2006). Financial well-being of young children with disabilities and their families. *Social Work, 51*(3), 223–232.

Park, J., Hoffman, L., Marquis, J., Turnbull, A. P., Poston, D., Mannan, H., … Nelson, L. (2003). Toward assessing family outcomes of service delivery: Validation of a family quality of life survey. *Journal of Intellectual Disability Research, 47*(4-5), 367–384.

Piazza, V. E., Floyd, F. J., Mailick, M. R., & Greenberg, J. S. (2014). Coping and psychological health of aging parents of adult children with developmental disabilities. *American Journal on Intellectual and Developmental Disabilities, 119*(2), 186–198.

Schieve, L. A., Boulet, S. L., Kogan, M. D., Van Naarden-Braun, K., & Boyle, C. A. (2011). A population-based assessment of the health, functional status, and consequent family impact among children with Down syndrome. *Disability and Health Journal, 4*(2), 68–77.

Schworer, E., Fidler, D. J., Lunkenheimer, E., & Daunhauer, L. A. (2019). Parenting behaviour and executive function in children with Down syndrome. *Journal of Intellectual Disability Research, 63*(4), 298–312. doi:https://doi.org/10.1111/jir.12575

Scorgie, K., & Sobsey, D. (2000). Transformational outcomes associated with parenting children who have disabilities. *Mental retardation, 38*(3), 195–206.

Scorgie, K., Wilgosh, L., & Sobsey, D. (2004). The experience of transformation in parents of children with disabilities: theoretical considerations. *Developmental Disabilities Bulletin, 32*(1), 84–110.

Seltzer, M. M., Abbeduto, L., Greenberg, J. S., Almeida, D., Hong, J., & Witt, W. (2009a). Biomarkers in the study of families of children with developmental disabilities. *International review of research in mental retardation, 37*, 213–249.

Seltzer, M. M., Almeida, D. M., Greenberg, J. S., Savla, J., Stawski, R. S., Hong, J., & Taylor, J. L. (2009b). Psychosocial and biological markers of daily lives of midlife parents of children with disabilities. *Journal of Health and Social Behavior, 50*(1), 1–15.

Shelley, B. P., & Robertson, M. M. (2005). The neuropsychiatry and multisystem features of the Smith-Magenis syndrome: a review. *The Journal of Neuropsychiatry and Clinical Neurosciences, 17*(1), 91–97.

Spencer, N. J., Blackburn, C. M., & Read, J. M. (2015). Disabling chronic conditions in childhood and socioeconomic disadvantage: a systematic review and meta-analyses of observational studies. *BMJ Open, 5*(9).

Tétreault, S., Blais-Michaud, S., Marier Deschênes, P., Beaupré, P., Gascon, H., Boucher, N., & Carrière, M. (2014). How to support families of children with disabilities? An exploratory study of social support services. *Child & Family Social Work, 19*(3), 272–281.

Totsika, V., Hastings, R. P., Emerson, E., & Hatton, C. (2020). Early years parenting mediates early adversity effects on problem behaviors in intellectual disability. *Child Development, 91*(3), e649–e664.

Walker, L. S., Van Slyke, D. A., & Newbrough, J. R. (1992). Family resources and stress: A comparison of families of children with cystic fibrosis, diabetes, and mental retardation. *Journal of Pediatric Psychology, 17*(3), 327–343.

Warren, S. F., Brady, N., Fleming, K. K., & Hahn, L. J. (2017). The longitudinal effects of parenting on adaptive behavior in children with fragile X syndrome. *Journal of Autism and Developmental Disorders, 47*(3), 768–784.

Warren, S. F., & Brady, N. C. (2007). The role of maternal responsivity in the development of children with intellectual disabilities. *Mental Retardation and Developmental Disabilities Research Reviews, 13*(4), 330–338.

Wheeler, A.C., Bailey Jr, D.B., Berry-Kravis, E., Greenberg, J., Losh, M., Mailick, M., Milà, M., Olichney, J.M., Rodriguez-Revenga, L., Sherman, S. and Smith, L. (2014). Associated features in females with an FMR1 premutation. *Journal of neurodevelopmental disorders, 6*(1), 1–14.

Wieland, N., Green, S., Ellingsen, R., & Baker, B. (2014). Parent–child problem solving in families of children with or without intellectual disability. *Journal of Intellectual Disability Research, 58*(1), 17–30.

Yoder, P. J., & Warren, S. F. (2002). Effects of prelinguistic milieu teaching and parent responsivity education on dyads involving children with intellectual disabilities. *Journal of Speech, Language, and Hearing Research.*

13
BROADENING PERSPECTIVES ON DEVELOPMENTAL DISABILITY

In this textbook we have learned about a variety of developmental disabilities, how they are different and the commonalities they share. We have seen that people with developmental disabilities develop differently than those without developmental disabilities and that their cognitive, social, communication and emotional profiles are unique yet similar to others who share the same disability. It is important to note that although persons with developmental disabilities have personal challenges with cognitive, social, communication, and/or emotional aspects of their daily lives, these challenges are best understood from a relational context. By this we mean that how others interact with, react to, and support, people with disabilities will affect the extent to which people with developmental disabilities are impacted by their disability. For example, a person with intellectual disability may take more time to process information and not respond as quickly to a greeting from a friend. If the friend is patient and allows more time for a response to their greeting, the social interaction can proceed more effectively and in a mutually beneficial way instead of falling flat or ending in a missed opportunity for social connection. This is just one example of the numerous, and often, subtle ways that people with and without disabilities influence each other's behaviour for better or worse.

Historically in the field of developmental disabilities we have focused almost exclusively on the child with developmental disabilities, understanding their genetics, cognitive profile, and development. It was only later, around the 1960–1970s, that researchers began to shift their focus to the parent-child interaction, as well as family context of the child's development. This was largely due to the parents' movement which worked on improving conditions in state institutions that housed people with developmental disabilities. Parents called for better living conditions, community services, educational and employment opportunities for their children.

A great deal of essential knowledge about developmental disabilities and how they impact the individual and their families has been accumulated over the years (some of which is presented in this textbook), however, without a balanced perspective, the knowledge may be interpreted as evidence that what is needed is remediation of the child, their parents or family situation. Instead, what is becoming increasingly clear is that individuals with developmental disabilities need to be accepted as they are and not 'remediated/fixed'. This is not to say that they do not need support or in some cases interventions, but the focus is on addressing the obstacles that interfere with their ability to express their full potential thereby 'levelling the playing field' rather than shaping their behaviour to meet societal norms in ways that go beyond what would be expected of a non-disabled individual. We all have to shape our behaviour to meet societal norms, to some extent, but non-disabled people have more of a choice of when and where to push the boundaries (and where not to!). People with disabilities should be enabled to do the same.

Moving forward, the research on developmental disabilities would benefit from a more dynamic and holistic approach to understanding not only the individual with developmental disability but also how others' perceptions, attitudes and behaviour affect the day to day functioning, mental health, quality of life and development of people with developmental disabilities. Within Bronfenbrenner's ecological systems theory, child development is understood as a complex and dynamic system of relationships affected by multiple facets of the environment, from proximal settings of family and school to more distal cultural values, laws, and policies. Bronfenbrenner's work looked beyond individual development, and took into account the context (or ecology) of development.

A few examples of the way Bronfenbrenner's ecological systems theory can help us broaden our conceptual and research focus is by highlighting how influences flow from the child but also towards the child, showing that proximal systems surrounding the child have a prominent and large influence but also, that these systems are embedded within other distal systems which have gradual and more subtle influences on the child but not necessarily less impactful. For example, policies on screening for Down syndrome are operating at what Bronfrenbrenner calls the Exosystem and Macrosystem levels and are quite distal to the child. As prenatal screening technologies were developed and became readily available, several countries began adopting prenatal screening as a qualification for prenatal diagnosis. As of 2021, 76.9% of countries have government funded diagnostic testing for Down syndrome (Wilmot et al. 2023). Since universal screening was introduced in Denmark, the number of children born with Down syndrome has markedly decreased. In 2019, only 18 children with Down syndrome were born in the entire country as compared to the United States where 6,000 children with Down syndrome are born each year (Zhang 2020). Denmark has a population of 5.86 million, and therefore, DS births are .0000031%; the US has 332 million and DS births are .00002%. Thus, social policies and healthcare practices which are distal influences have, nonetheless, had a major impact on the birth of children with Down syndrome. Clearly, there is an urgent need to investigate these trends in healthcare practices. Disability advocates have argued for a

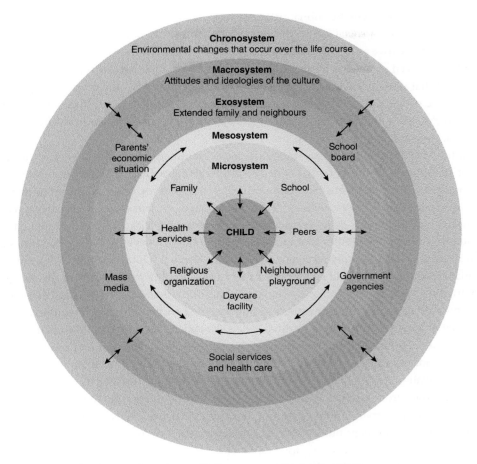

Figure 13.1 Bronfrenbrenner's systems of influence on child development

Source: Rhodes, *Theories of Child Development*, 2013.

wider discussion on genetic screening and diagnosis which includes available options, interventions, and presenting the family with a range of options that are not focused solely on avoidance of the developmental disability.

Another example of distal influences on child well-being that may benefit from more research is societal or cultural stigma and its influence on the social acceptance and inclusion of people with developmental disabilities. For example, several studies have found that autistic individuals' social abilities may not be the only factor influencing their social success. Nonautistic individuals' social perceptions and behaviour contributes to autistic individuals' social difficulties. In a recent study, researchers attempted to improve nonautistic teenagers' views of autistic people by teaching them about autism in a way that they can more easily relate to. They also explored whether quality and quantity of contact with autistic people predicted these perceptions and whether nonautistic people's views of autistic people depend on how they viewed their own social skills. The researchers found that nonautistic high school students showed negative attitudes toward autistic people. However, they found that these views could be improved somewhat by the informative presentation about autism. The researchers also found that nonautistic adolescents who reported themselves as the most socially skilled rated autistic people the most negatively. This may be because they are the most likely to value 'normative' social skills and be more judgemental about those who socialize in a different way. (Scheerer, Sasson, Boucher, & Iarocci, 2022)

Another Macrosystem level issue that needs more examination is our field/society/culture's lack of recognition of the potential benefits of interacting with and accepting people with developmental disabilities into our communities. Researchers are often examining the negative impact children with developmental disabilities have on others (e.g., their parents, families, peers, society) but we rarely consider the positive impact they have. For example, there is evidence from family studies that families of children with developmental disabilities are often resilient. When a family receives a diagnosis of developmental disability, they must re-negotiate established roles and adjust their expectations for child rearing within this new and uncharted context, however, they also have opportunities to develop resilience. Their family belief systems allow individual members to find meaning within adversity, maintain an optimistic outlook, and to have strong spiritual beliefs. These families have organizational patterns that are flexible, connected, and include access to necessary social and economic resources; and they have communication processes that are characterized by clarity, open emotional expression, and collaborative problem solving. Qualitative studies have revealed diverse experiences and perspectives from families raising children with developmental disabilities with certain families reporting: certain families reporting positive experiences suggesting that families are not only able to be resilient but also thrive, not despite their child's developmental disability, but because of it. Families who care for a child with a developmental disability may not have the benefit of their extended family's wisdom to address their unique parenting challenges, yet they are less bound by social and cultural norms on parenting, and this very deliberate engagement in the parenting process may lead to more mindful awareness and deliberate engagement in child rearing (Gardiner & Iarocci 2012).

Similarly, the benefits for peers of children with developmental disabilities are often neglected. Peer-mediated interventions are an evidence-based practice designed specifically to promote the social and learning outcomes of students with autism and other developmental disabilities. However, only a few studies have examined the impact on peers who participate in these interventions. One study found that a semester-long peer-to-peer partners programme at eight public high schools in the United States had a positive effect on academic performance, absences and behavioural referrals, as well as suspensions on participating peer volunteers (Owen-DeSchryver, Ziegler, Matthews, Mayberry, & Carter 2022). The researchers concluded that school personnel should actively recruit diverse peer partners in their peer-to-peer programmes by including students with academic or behavioural challenges, rather than only high-achieving students. Peer-mediated interventions are one example of mutually beneficial opportunities that create natural supports for students with developmental disabilities, and also have a positive impact for at-risk peers.

Similar benefits were seen in a peer mentoring programme in a university setting. Autistic students in a Canadian university who participated in the Autism Mentorship Initiative (AMI), a peer mentoring programme for autistic undergraduates (mentees), who received one-on-one support from upper-level undergraduate or graduate students (mentors) while in the first few years of university were surveyed (Trevisan, Leach, Iarocci, & Birmingham 2021). Researchers found that both mentors and mentees reported personal, academic, and professional benefits from participating in AMI. The study provided preliminary evidence for the benefits of a relatively easily implemented and cost-effective peer mentorship program that has reciprocal benefits for autistic and nonautistic students in a postsecondary setting.

Beyond individual and systems level influences we must consider the research process itself. Currently, much of the research conducted in the field of developmental disabilities is done without the involvement of the very people who have most to gain (or lose) from research findings, people with developmental disabilities. The neurodiversity movement has alerted us to the problem of subscribing to a deficit model of disability that threatens the very existence of people with developmental disabilities. Instead, they propose a social model of disability that acknowledges that developmental disabilities are a form of nonpathological variation in the human brain that influences movement, sociability, learning, and/or attention, among other mental functions. The neurodiversity perspective emphasizes the need for accommodation, support, and amelioration of issues that threaten the individual's quality of life but reject the idea that people with developmental disabilities should be cured or aspire to be 'normal' (Kapp et al. 2013). Aligned with this view is the notion that people with developmental disabilities should have agency over their lives and that includes research that pertains to them. In order for research to be meaningful and helpful to people with developmental disabilities, they must be active participants in the research process. The 'community engaged' or 'community based participatory' research framework is defined as a set of practices, values, and objectives that enable the active participation of the individuals and communities directly affected by research activities. Within this framework, academic researchers meaningfully partner with individuals and communities for the design, methods, analysis and translation of research.

There are many mutual benefits for both partners with developmental disabilities and researchers. Involvement in research gives partners with developmental disabilities a voice and empowers them in their plight to attain a better quality of life while the researcher gains a better understanding of the issues faced by people with lived experience. Partners with developmental disabilities gain some ownership of the research while researchers earn access to new research opportunities. Partners with developmental disabilities secure help in advocating for their needs and researchers achieve greater impact of the work. As we move forward together as partners in this important research work, we will encounter many challenges along the way. However, it is those very challenges that create the needed growth and development of our field.

REFERENCES

Bronfenbrenner, U. (1977). Toward an experimental ecology of human development. *American Psychologist, 32* (7), 513–531.

Gardiner, E., & Iarocci, G. (2012). Unhappy (and happy) in their own way: A developmental psychopathology perspective on quality of life for families living with developmental disability with and without autism, *Research in Developmental Disabilities, 33*, 2177–2192.

Kapp S.K., Gillespie-Lynch K., Sherman L.E., Hutman T. (2013). Deficit, difference, or both? Autism and neurodiversity. *Dev Psychol., 49*(1), 59–71. doi: 10.1037/a0028353.

Owen-DeSchryver, J., Ziegler, M., Matthews, A., Mayberry, M., & Carter, E (2022). The reciprocity of peer-mediated interventions: examining outcomes for peers, *School Psychology Review*, DOI: 10.1080/2372966X.2022.2039959.

Scheerer, N. E., Boucher, T. Q., Sasson, N. J., & Iarocci, G. (2022). Effects of an Educational Presentation About Autism on High School Students' Perceptions of Autistic Adults. *Autism in adulthood : challenges and management, 4*(3), 203–213. https://doi.org/10.1089/aut.2021.0046

Trevisan, D. A., Leach, S., Iarocci, G., & Birmingham, E. (2021). Evaluation of a peer mentorship program for autistic college students. *Autism in Adulthood, 3*(2), 187–194. https://doi-org.proxy.lib.sfu.ca/10.1089/aut.2019.0087.

Wilmot, H.C., de Graaf, G., van Casteren, P. et al. (2023). Down syndrome screening and diagnosis practices in Europe, United States, Australia, and New Zealand from 1990–2021. *Eur J Hum Genet*. https://doi.org/10.1038/s41431-023-01330-y.

Zhang, S. (2020). The last children of Down syndrome: Prenatal testing is changing who gets born and who doesn't. This is just the beginning. *The Atlantic*. December Issue.

INDEX

Note: Page numbers followed by "*f*" indicate figure, "*t*" indicate table and "*n*" indicate footnote in the text.

acetylation, 38*f*
adaptive behaviours, 65, 70
adolescence period, 8, 95
adulthood, 9, 95–96
Adult-Theory-of-Mind (A-ToM), 190
aetiology, 39, 105, 127, 292–293
Albertowski, K., 157
alcohol, 106, 107
Alcohol-Related Birth Defects (ARBD), 111
Alcohol-Related Neurodevelopmental Disorders (ARNDs), 110
alerting attention, 272
alexithymia, 182, 184
algorithmic level, 177
allele, 28–29
Allen, 153
alpha-fetoprotein(AFP), 43
Alzheimer's Disease, 91, 96
American Academy of Pediatrics (AAP), 132, 138, 269
American Association on Intellectual and Developmental Disabilities (AAIDD), 64–65, 72
American Psychiatric Association, 146
amniocentesis, 44
Amyloid Precursor Protein (APP), 96
anal stage, 8
Angelman syndrome (AS), 38–39, 137–138
anxiety, 265, 296
articulatory suppression, 192
Asperger, Hans, 147, 148
Asperger Disorder/Asperger's syndrome, 153, 153
assessment
    adaptive behaviour, 72–73
    behavioural observations, 72
    cognitive ability, 71–72
    comprehensive, 74, 76
    ecologically valid methods of, 196
    IQ, 72, 73
    neurobehavioural, 108–109
    one-to-one contact, 72
    testing the limits, 72

assistive technology, 251
Attention Deficit and Hyperactivity Disorder (ADHD), 88, 111–112
attention deficit/hyperactivity disorder (AD/HD), 259
    behavioural differences in, 265
    behavioural techniques, 274
    case study, 267–268
    cognitive behaviour therapy (CBT), 271
    cognitive training, 261–273
    combined inattentive, 264
    co-morbidities, 268–269
    developmental course of, 265–266
    diagnosis of, 266–269
    effect size, 272
    exercise intervention, 276
    functional impairment, 266–267
    gender differences, 269
    inattention, 264, 266, 267
    medications, 269, 269
    organizational skills training (OST), 274–276
    parent training, 295–296
    pharmacological interventions, 269–270, 277
    polygenic inheritance, 260
    psychological interventions, 249
    reconstitution, 263
    risk factors, 261–262
    social skills training, 273–274
    symptoms of, 260, 262, 264, 266
    theories of, 262–263
autism, 39, 60, 61, 66, 74, 88, 93, 145–147, 160, 310
    Bayesian accounts, 204
    behavioural features, 159*t*
    Broad Autism Phenotype (BAP), 161–162
    concept of, 163, 207
    context of, 179n2, 186
    DSM-5, 149–151, 149*t*
    DSM-5 *vs*. DSM, 151–152
    emotional account, 181–182, 181n3

epidemic of, 163
  executive function (EF) accounts, 191–197, 205
  explanations of, 176–177, 177f
  features, 146
  frameworks, 175–180, 190
  historical background, 146–148
  identification, 145–146, 148–154
  incidence, 162
  instruments, 155–160
  interpersonal account, 181
  medical/disease-oriented model, 146
  mentalizing, 190
  men than in women, 163–166
  meta-analysis, 152
  multidimensional analytical space, 180
  multidimensional space, 179
  non-clinical autism, 161–162
  paradigms, 190–207
  phenocopy, 162
  prevalence, 162
  psychological accounts, 180–184
  psychological processes, 204–207
  psychological theories and explanations, 175–208
  Sally-Anne task, 185f, 186, 187
  screening, 158–160
  sensory, 198
  sex ratio, 164
  social account, 180
  systematic approaches, 148–154
  working memory, 191n4
Autism Diagnostic Interview (ADI), 155–157
Autism Diagnostic Interview – Revised (ADI-R), 70, 155, 157
Autism Diagnostic Observation Schedule (ADOS), 155–157, 156t
Autism Mentorship Initiative (AMI), 311
autism spectrum disorder (ASD). *see* autism
Autism Spectrum Quotient (AQ), 161, 161t
autistic individuals, 309, 310

Bailey, A., 161
Bankart, J., 153
Barkley, R.A., 262
Barnett, E., 190
Baron-Cohen, S., 161, 161n2, 186, 189
Barton, M. L., 159
Bayesian decision theory, 203
Bechtel, W., 180
Becker, J., 157
Behavioral Assessment of the Dysexecutive Syndrome (BADS), 196
Behavior Rating Inventory of Executive Functioning (BRIEF), 197

behavioural geneticists, 28, 29
behavioural inhibition, 264–264
behavioural phenotypes, 127–128
behavioural problems, 247, 262
behaviourist, 10–11, 176
behaviour management training, 295
Berggren, S., 155
Bernadin, C. J., 205
biological parents, 23, 41
Bird, G., 189
block design task, 199f
Bolton, P., 161
Bowler, D. M., 153, 181, 187–189, 206
brain injury, 64
Brewaeys, K., 201
Brewer, N., 190
Brewer, R., 189
Broad Autism Phenotype (BAP), 161–162
Brock, J., 203
Bronfenbrenner, Urie, 17–18, 31–32, 308
Brugha, T. S., 153
Burack, J. A., 127
Burr, D., 203

Cambridge Automated Neuropsychological Test Battery (CANTAB), 194
Canadian Community Health Survey, 247
Canadian FASD Research Network, 116
Carpenter, M., 188
Catmur, C., 189
challenging behaviours, 292, 293
Charman, T., 160, 206
Cheblowski, C., 160
Checklist for Autism in Toddlers (CHAT), 159
child eliciting factors, 292
Childhood Autism Rating Scale (CARS), 159
Children's Embedded Figures Test, 198, 199f
Cholemkery, H., 157
Chouinard, P. A., 162
chromosome, 30–31
chronological age (CA), 63, 71
Clubley, E., 161
co-action, 34, 35f
cognition, 89
cognitive ability, 28
cognitive behaviour therapy (CBT), 271
cognitive development, 6–7, 15, 27
cognitive-energetic model (CEM), 263, 264
cognitive impairment, 64
cognitive level of analysis, 178
Cognitive Processing Index (CPI), 243
cognitive training, 271–273
communication, 221, 222
    crying, 14, 14f

development, 223–226
dyadic signalling, 224
human, 222
interventions, 233–235
joint attention, 225, 225
language vs., 223
nonverbal, 222, 224
primary intersubjectivity, 223–224
secondary intersubjectivity, 224–225
skills, 221
social, 151, 184, 223–225
sophistication, 14, 15f
triadic, 224, 225
community engaged/community based participatory, 311
comorbidity, 246–247
Completing Homework by Improving Efficiency and Focus (CHIEF), 275
comprehensive assessment, 74, 76
computational level, 177
conceptual skills, 72
conduct disorder (CD), 263
conductive hearing loss, 87
congenital heart defects, 87
Coniston, D., 188
conjunctive visual search task, 201
Connor, P. D., 113
constructivist approach, 5
contemplative approaches, 296
Continuous Performance Task, 194
co-occurring, 34, 183
copy number variations (CNVs), 129, 134
Cornoldi, C., 240, 243
critics, 17
cytosine-guanine-guanine (CGG), 39

DaDeppo, L. M., 248
daily hassles, 291–292
Damasio, A. R., 191
deconstructionist, 4
democratic society, 41–42
depression, 297
detection rate, 43
Developmental, Dimensional and Diagnostic Interview (3Di), 158
developmental approach, 4
    adolescence period, 8
    adulthood, 9
    age of 18 months, 13f
    anal stage, 8
    crying, 14, 14f
    developing infant, 13f
    early childhood period, 8
    environment on, 17–18
    formal, 18
    fundamentals of, 18–21
    genital stage, 8
    latency stage, 8
    newly born infant, 12f
    old-age period, 9
    operational stage, 7
    oral stage, 8
    orthogenetic principle, 11–17
    to persons with developmental conditions, 5
    phallic stage, 8
    play age period, 8
    putative stage, 8
    school age period, 8
    sensorimotor stage, 6, 15
    young adult period, 8–9
developmental history, 70–71
developmental period, 63
developmental progression, 11–17
developmental screening, 65–68, 75
developmental theory, 7–8, 16
diagnosis, 61–64
    application of, 64
    of DS, 85
    of foetal alcohol spectrum disorder, 108–111
    IDD, 64
    neurogenetic syndromes, 130–133
    psychiatric, 135
Diagnostic and Statistical Manual of Mental Disorders (DSM), 61, 63, 74
Diagnostic and Statistical Manual of Mental Disorders 5th edition (DSM-5), 63, 65, 108, 149, 150, 153–154, 207, 240, 243, 245, 246, 266, 267
diagnostic assessment, 65, 68–69
Diagnostic Interview for Social and Communication Disorders (DISCO), 157–158
directiveness parenting, 289–290
discrepancy theory, 245–246
disjunction, 30
DNA
    chip technology, 131
    methylation, 36
down syndrome, 30–33
    adolescence, 95
    adulthood, 95–96
    auto-immune conditions, 87
    behavioural and developmental outcomes, 89–90
    biomedical intervention, 97
    causes of, 84
    cognition, 89
    conductive hearing loss, 87

congenital heart defects, 87
co-occurring neurodevelopmental
  conditions, 88
definition of, 83–86
diagnosis, 85
executive function, 89
explicit memory, 91
genetic influences, 86
implicit memory, 91
inclusion, 97
infants with, 90
language, 92–93
lifespan, 85, 94
maladaptive behaviour, 88
maternal age, 84
memory, 90–82
middle childhood, 95
motor development, 93
phenotypic outcomes, 84
rates of, 84
sensorineural hearing loss, 87
sensory impairments, 87
social-emotional development, 93
in time and place, 85–86
treatment for, 96–97
well-being, 97
working memory, 91–93
Down Syndrome Disintegrative Disorder, 95
Dykens, Elisabeth, 127
dyscalculia, 244
dyslexia, 244, 246

early childhood period, 8
Early Start Denver Model (ESDM), 67, 233–234
ecological systems theory, 17–18, 32f, 308, 309f
electroencephalogram (EEG), 70
Elliott, M. V., 194
Emerson, E., 300
endophenotypes, 260, 261
Enhanced Perceptual Functioning Theory (EPF), 202
environments, 17–18, 23, 25
  non-shared, 40
  positive, 73
  primacy, 176
epigenetics, 36–39, 37f
Erikson, Erik, 7, 8, 14, 16
essentialist, 164
event-related potential (ERP), 242
Evers, K., 201
evocative interaction, 24
executive function (EF), 262–264
  accounts, 191–197, 205
  cool, 264–265
  hot, 264

exosystem, 18
explicit memory, 91
extradimensional shift stage, 195
Eyal, G., 166

false positive, 43
familial intellectual disability, 29
family context
  aetiology-related phenotypes on, 293
  and biological factors, 301
  child eliciting factors, 292
  contemplative approach, 296
  contingency, 289
  emotional support, 289
  harsh parenting, 290
  ID impact, 291–298
  informational support, 298
  intervention, 295–296
  legal and financial support, 298
  mindfulness approaches, 296
  neurogenetic conditions, 293
  parent-child interaction, 307
  parenting behaviours, 288–290
  parenting stress, 291–282
  problem-focused approaches, 297
  psychological support, 299–300
  quality of life, 301
  resilience, 297, 310
  resources, 300–301
  respite care, 293
  rewardingness, 299
  siblings, 288, 295
  social context, 300–301
Fein, D., 159
fixed genetic factors, 86
Flannigan, K., 119
Fletcher, J. M., 246
fluorescence in situ hybridization (FISH), 131
Fodor, G., 178
foetal alcohol spectrum disorders (FASD), 105
  attention problems, 112–113
  challenges, 117t
  cognitive signs, 106, 118
  consequences of, 118
  course of, 107
  definition of, 106
  diagnosis of, 108–111
  diagnostic criterion by disorder, 109–111
  differential diagnosis, 108
  drink, 105–106
  educational considerations, 116
  executive functions, 113
  family, 115
  intellectual functioning, 111

intervention, 116–117
language, 113
learning, 113
maternal alcohol use, 109
memory, 113
motor skills, 113
neurobehavioural assessment, 108–109
physical examination, 108
protective factors, 115
relationship-focused interventions, 117
risk factor, 115
screening, 108
social, 114–115
strengths-based approach, 119
treatment, 105
Foetal Alcohol Syndrome (FAS), 110
Folstein, S., 161
Fragile X Mental Retardation Protein (FMRP), 39, 133
Fragile X syndrome (FXS), 37, 39, 131 133–134, 228, 232
Franzen, M. D., 196
Freitag, C. M., 157
Freud, Sigmund, 7–8, 14, 16
Freudian theory, 10
Friendship Coaching Intervention (PFC), 274
Frith, U., 176–178, 186, 186, 200
Frith-Happé Animations Test, 188, 188

Gahremann, M., 157
Galton, Francis, 24–25
gamete, 38
gene-dosage effects, 86
gene-environment interactions, 23–45
bidirectional, 24, 44
co-action, 34, 35f
detection rate, 43
diagnosis, 43–44
evocative interaction, 24
false positive, 43
policy implications of, 40
positive predictive value (PPV), 43–44
proactive interaction, 24
reaction range, 33, 33f, 34
reactive interaction, 24
screening, 43–44
General Ability Index (GAI), 240, 243
genetics, 24–27
aetiology, 27
counselors, 44
diagnosis, 131–132
factors, 40, 128–130
influences, 86
mutation, 30, 36

screening, 41, 44, 45
testing technology, 131
genital stage, 8
genomic, 37
Genotye A, 34
genotype, 23, 33, 35, 44
Geurts, H. M., 153, 194, 196
Ghods, S. S., 164
Gotesman, Iriving, 33
Gotham, K., 160
Gottesman, I. I., 28, 29f, 34, 161, 261
Gottlieb, G., 34
Gould, Glenn, 146
Gould, J., 147
grammatical morphemes, 229
Green, J. A., 160

Hacking, I., 166
Halford, G. S., 206
Hamilton, A., 181
Happé, F. G. E., 181, 182, 187, 205
Harms, M. B., 181
Hastings, R. P, 297
health/medical evaluation, 69–70
Heider, F., 188
heritability, 28
Hermelin, B., 198, 203
Hettrich, E. L., 250
hierarchization, 201
histone, 36, 38f
Hobson, R. P., 181, 181n34, 182
Hodapp, Robert, 127, 293
Hoffman, Dustin, 198n5
Hogeveen, J., 194, 196
Homework, Organization, and Planning Skills (HOPS), 275
Homograph Reading test, 199
Howlin, P. A., 153
Huerta, M., 155
human chorionic gonadotropin (HCG), 43
human foetus, 5
development of, 6f
operational stage, 7
preoperational stage, 6–7
sensorimotor stage, 6
Hwang, J. S., 160

imbecile, 25n1
imitation, 67
implementational/physical level, 177
implicit memory, 91
imprinted genes, 38
Improving Parents as Communication Teachers (ImPACT), 67

impulsivity, 266, 267
individual education plan (IEP), 266, 268
infancy period. *see* putative stage
infantile autism, 154
input-integration-memory-output model, 244
integration disability, 244
intellectual disability (ID), 19–21, 23–45
    biological factors, 125
    children, 40
    definition of, 59–61
    diagnostic category, 61–64
    environmental influences on, 30–32
    familial, 27, 29
    genetic screening, 41
    organic factors, 27
    polygenic inheritance, 28–30
    social factor, 125
intellectual disability/disorder (IDD), 61, 63, 74–75
Intellectual Quotient (IQ), 25, 27–29
    assessments, 72, 73
    normal curve, 62f
    normal distribution, 29f
    score, 61–63
    variation, 30
intelligence, 31–32, 60, 75
internalization of speech, 263
International Classification of Diseases (ICD-11), 60, 62, 65, 148, 149, 154
International Classification of Mental and Behavioural Disorders 11th revision (ICD-11), 154, 266
interoceptive cortex, 183
intersubjectivity, 223
intradimensional-extradimensional shift (IEDS) task, 193f, 195
intradimensional shift stage, 195
IQ scores, 240, 245
islets of ability, 198, 198n5
Itard, J-M. G., 146

Jankowski, K. F., 182
JASPER, 233
Johnson, Lyndon, 17
Johnson, M. H., 206, 207
Johnson, Shaun, 4
Jones, 153
Jones, E. H., 206

Kaat, A. J., 164
Kamp-Becker, I., 157
Kanne, S., 205
Kanner, Leo, 147–150, 161, 163, 179, 180, 198

Kant, Immanuel, 146
karyotyping approach, 131
Kenworthy, L., 196, 197
Klein, Melanie, 146
Krug, M. K., 194

Landry, O., 162
Lane, K. A., 112
language, 92–93, 223, 226
    comprehensive interventions, 234
    development, 226–232
    down syndrome, 92–93
    FASD, 113
    interventions, 234
    modelling behaviours, 234
    morphology, 228–229
    parenting behaviours, 234
    phonemes, 227
    phonology, 226–227
    pragmatics, 231–232
    reading in ID, 228
    responsivity behaviours, 234
    semantics, 230–231
    sign, 227
    syntax, 229
    targeted intervention, 234
    vs. communication, 223
latency stage, 8
learning
    abilities, 241
    difficulties, 239
    disorder, 69
    disorders, 247, 265
learning disabilities (LD), 244, 268
LeCouteur, A., 161
Leslie, A., 186
Lewis, T., 205
literacy learning, 241
Livingston, L. A., 205
Loomes, R., 163

MacDonald, H., 161
macrosystem, 18, 32
Marr, David, 176–178
Marr's scheme, 177
Martin, J., 161
Mason, E., 205
Massand, E., 205
maternal non-disjunction, 84
maternal responsivity, 289
maternal stress, 261
Maurer, R. G., 191
Medda, J. E., 157

meiosis, 30
memory, 91–92
    disability, 244
    down syndrome, 90–92
    FASD, 113
mental activity, 60
mental age (MA), 63, 71
mental health, 291–292
mental retardation, 26t
mental state understanding (MSU), 184, 187, 189
mesosystem, 18
metabolic tests, 70
methylation, 38f
Miciak, J., 246
microarray analysis technology, 131
microsystem, 18
Mindfulness Based Stress Reduction (MBSR), 296
Mitchell, P., 203
modelling behaviours, 234
monogenic disorders, 129
monosomy, 128
monotropism, 204
Moon, S. J., 160
Morbidity and Mortality Weekly Report, 163
Morgan, R., 188
morphemes, 229
morphology, 228–229
Morton, J., 176–178
mosaicism, 89, 128
motivational interviewing (MI), 275
Mottron, L., 202
multi-system disorder, 87

Naturalistic Developmental Behavioural Interventions (NBDIs), 67, 233–234
Navon, D., 166, 201
Navon task, 202f
Nayton, M., 250
neurobehavioural assessment, 108–109
neurocognitive disorders, 64
neurodevelopmental disabilities, 37
Neurodevelopmental Disorder Associated with Prenatal Alcohol Exposure (ND-PAE), 111
neurodiversity, 148, 311
neurogenetic syndromes, 83, 126–128
    behavioural phenotypes, 127–128
    chromosomal, 128–130
    copy number variations (CNVs), 129
    diagnosis, 130–133
    elements, 127
    genetic factors, 128–130
    inherited *vs.* non-inherited, 129
    monogenic disorders, 129

neuroimaging techniques, 70
neuroplasticity, 94
next generation sequencing (NGS), 132
Nicholson, T. M., 183
non-clinical autism, 161–162
non-shared environments, 40
normal distribution, 25, 29f

Oakley, B. F. M., 189
O'Connor, N., 198, 203
old-age period, 9
'Online Mendelian Inheritance in Man' (OMIM), 130
operational stage, 7
oppositional defiant disorder (ODD), 265, 268, 274
oral stage, 8
organization, 178
organizational skills training (OST), 274–276
orienting attention, 271
orthogenetic principle, 11–17

parenting behaviours, 234
parenting stress, 291–292
parent training, 270–271, 277, 295–296
Partanen, M., 249
Partial Foetal Alcohol Syndrome (pFAS), 110
partners, 311
Pellicano, E., 203
Perner, J., 186
Pervasive Developmental Disorder Not Otherwise Specified (PDD-NOS), 153
Pezzuti, L., 240, 243
Pfeifer, J. H., 182
phallic stage, 8
pharmacological interventions, 269–270, 277
phenotype, 23, 28, 35, 97
phenylalanine, 36
phenylketonuria (PKU), 36, 70
phonemes, 227
phonemic awareness skills, 228
phonological awareness, 241, 249, 250
phonological skills, 228
phonology, 226–227
Piaget, Jean, 5, 7–9, 14, 15, 19
Piagetian theory, 9–10
Pickles, A., 161, 206
Plaisted, K., 201
Plato's theory, 16
play age period, 8
Plomin, R., 28, 40
polygenes, 30
polygenic inheritance, 28–30

Popper, Karl, 200n6
positive predictive value (PPV), 43–44, 159
positive screening test, 44
Potter, D., 163
practical skills, 72
Prader-Willi syndrome (PWS), 38, 136–138, 293
pragmatics, 231–232
prediction errors, 204
predictive coding, 204
premutation, 134
prenatal exposure to alcohol (PAE), 109, 112, 114, 118
prenatal screening, 42, 308
preoperational stage, 6–7
primary intersubjectivity, 223–224
proactive interaction, 24
processing speed (PS), 240, 243
psycho-educational interventions, 249
psychological interventions, 249
psychological process, 176–177
psychometric properties, 68t
psychosocial adversity, 261
psychosocial interventions, 270
Pullman, M. Y., 205
putative stage, 8

Qualitative Impairment in Social Interaction, 151
quality of life, 301

Rain Man, 198n5
Rapin, 153
rare disorders, 126, 138
Ratto, A. B., 164–165
reaction range, 33, 33f, 34
reactive interaction, 24
reading disability (RD), 250
reading disorder, 242
Reading the Mind in the Eyes (RMET) test, 189
reality principle, 10
Reciprocal Imitation Training (RIT), 67
Rees, L., 201
relationship-focused interventions, 117–118
representational level. *see* algorithmic level
resilience, 297–298, 310
respite care, 299
Response to Intervention (RtI), 245
responsive parenting, 288–289
responsivity, 288–289
    behaviours, 234
retrospective memory, 91
Rett syndrome, 69
rewardingness, 298–299
Rimland, B., 203

RNA, 37
Roch, M., 200
Rochat, P., 188
Rødgaard, E-M., 165
Rogers, R., 188
Ropar, D., 203
Rutter, M., 161, 163

Samar, S., 250
scepticism, 118
school age period, 8
Scott, F., 153
screening
    autism, 64
    for developmental delay, 65–68
    of foetal alcohol spectrum disorder, 108
    psychometric properties, 68t
    strategy, 66
    tool, 66–67, 75
Screening Tool for Autism in Toddlers & Young Children (STAT), 66, 75
secondary intersubjectivity, 224–225
self-conscious emotions, 182
semantic-pragmatic disorder, 153
semantics, 230–231
sensitivity, 159
sensorimotor stage, 6, 15
sensorineural hearing loss, 87
sensory impairments, 87
sensory processing disorders, 115
Shields, J., 260
Shin, A. L., 159
Shui, A. M., 164
siblings, 294
Siegel, L. S., 245, 249
sign languages, 227
Silver, L. B., 244
Simmel, M., 188
Skinner, R., 161
sleep disorders, 87
Smith, 153
Smith-Magenis syndrome (SMS), 136, 293
social cognition, 231–232
social communication, 151, 184
Social Communication Disorder (SCD), 153
Social Communication Questionnaire (SCQ), 160
social-emotional development, 93
social impairment, 147
Social Responsiveness Scale (SRS), 160
social skills, 72
social skills training (SST), 273–274

socioeconomic status (SES), 27, 242
sophistication, 15f
specificity, 159
specific learning disorder (SLD), 239
    assistive technology, 251
    cognitive basis of, 243–244
    comorbidity, 246–247
    developmental course, 247–248
    diagnosis of, 244–246
    false-negative error, 246
    false-positive errors, 246
    gender differences in, 243
    input disability, 244
    integration disability, 244
    IQ vs., 240
    languages, 241, 242
    learning academic skills, 249–250
    low achievement model, 245
    medical interventions, 248–249
    memory disability, 244
    output disability, 244
    prevalence of, 242–243
    psychological interventions, 249
    risk factors, 241–242, 248
standard deviation (SD), 243
standardized intelligence tests, 75
Strange Stories Test, 187, 190
Strauss, 25
Supporting Teens' Academic Needs Daily (STAND), 275
Swettenham, J., 202
syntax, 229

teratogens, 39, 106
Tétreault, S., 299
Theory of Mind (TOM), 178–179, 184, 186–188, 200, 273
Theory of Psychological Development, 8
Thommen, E., 188, 189
thyroid, 70
Toddler Module, 156, 156t
Toffalini, E., 240, 243
Tower tasks, 191–192, 191f
traditional approaches, 4
triadic communication, 224, 225
triad of impairments, 147
triple screen, 43
trisomy, 128
twin studies, 28
typically developing (TD), 263

Uljarevic, M., 181
Ullman, M. T., 205
uniparental disomy, 129–130
United States, the Center for Disease Control and Prevention (CDC), 107
United States Panel Study of Income Dynamics, 291

valproate, 39
Van der Hallen, R., 201
verbal mental age (VMA), 182
veridicality, 196
verisimilitude, 196
Vygotsky, Lev, 31

Weak Central Coherence (WCC), 200–203
Wechsler Intelligence Scale for Children-IV (WISC-IV), 243
well-being, 97
Werner, Heinz, 5, 11–12, 14, 15, 19, 25
Wertz, 44
Wheelwright, S., 161, 162
White, S., 188
Wild Boy of Aveyron (Itard), 146
Wilhelm, K. L., 196
Wilkinson, C., 250
Willcutt, E. G., 265
Willfors, C., 155
Williams, D., 181, 182
Williams Beuren syndrome. see Williams syndrome (WS)
Williams syndrome (WS), 134–136, 226, 230, 232, 293
Wimmer, H., 186
Wing, L., 147, 148, 151, 157, 162
Wisconsin Card Sorting Test (WCST), 191, 192, 195f, 193
working memory (WM), 91–92, 191n4, 240, 243, 263, 271
World Health Organization (WHO), 118
Wright, C. D., 180

Yao Ming, 4
Yearsley, J. M., 195–196
Yeats, W. B., 146
Young, R. L., 190
young adult period, 8–9

Zander, E., 151, 153
Zigler, Edward, 18–21, 25, 27, 126–127
Zone of Proximal Development, 31